The Biopolitical Turn
in World Cinema

RECENT TITLES

Paul Deb, *Happiness and Tears, After Cavell*

Ori Levin, *Celluloid Babel*

Roy Grundmann, *On Shoreless Sea*

Dominic Lash, *Haunting the World*

Gohar Siddiqui, *Déjà-Viewed*

Stanley Cavell, *Cavell on Film*

Saverio Giovacchini, *The Celluloid Atlantic*

John Caps, *Overhearing Film Music*

Hannah Holtzman, *Through a Nuclear Lens*

Benedict Morrison, *Eccentric Laughter*

Matthew Cipa, *Is Harpo Free?*

Daniel Varndell, *Torturous Etiquettes*

Seth Barry Watter, *The Human Figure on Film*

Jonah Corne and Monika Vrečar, *Yiddish Cinema*

Jason Jacobs, *Reluctant Sleuths, True Detectives*

Lucy J. Miller, *Distancing Representations in Transgender Film*

Tomoyuki Sasaki, *Cinema of Discontent*

Mary Ann McDonald Carolan, *Orienting Italy*

Matthew Rukgaber, *Nietzsche in Hollywood*

Jason Sperb, *The Hard Sell of Paradise*

A complete listing of books in this series can be found online at www.sunypress.edu.

The Biopolitical Turn in World Cinema

Visual Landscapes of Social Power

Luca Barattoni

SUNY PRESS

Cover: *About Elly* (2009, dir. Asghar Farhadi). Courtesy of Cinema Guild.

Published by State University of New York Press, Albany

EU GPSR Authorised Representative:
Logos Europe, 9 rue Nicolas Poussin, 17000, La Rochelle, France
contact@logoseurope.eu

For information, contact State University of New York Press, Albany, NY
www.sunypress.edu

Library of Congress Cataloging-in-Publication Data

Name: Barattoni, Luca, author.
Title: The biopolitical turn in world cinema : visual landscapes of social
   power / Luca Barattoni.
Description: Albany : State University of New York Press, [2026]. | Series:
   SUNY series, horizons of cinema | Includes bibliographical references
   and index.
Identifiers: LCCN 2025034945 | ISBN 9798855805833 (hardcover : alk.
   paper) | ISBN 9798855807141 (epub) | ISBN 9798855805857 (PDF)
Subjects: LCSH: Motion pictures—Social aspects. | Biopolitics—Social
   aspects. | Ethics in motion pictures. | LCGFT: Film criticism.
Classification: LCC PN1995.9.S6 B36 2025
LC record available at https://lccn.loc.gov/2025034945

Manifest therefore it is, that all men, because they are born in
Infancy, are born unapt for Society. Many also (perhaps most men)
either through defect of minde, or want of education remain unfit
during the whole course of their lives; yet have Infants, as well as
those of riper years, an humane nature; wherefore Man is made
fit for Society not by Nature, but by Education.

— Thomas Hobbes, *De Cive*

Contents

Illustrations

Acknowledgments

Deep gratitude to the community that at different stages has helped me finish this project—my family, Andrea Mirabile, Federico Luisetti, Todd May, Alex Jensen, the Humanities Hub at Clemson University, Sandro Brusco, Luigi Castaldi, Pagan Min, Igor Begio, Mariangela Vaglio, the SUCCEED program at Clemson University, Maziyar Farhidi, Yanhua Zhang, Andrea Righi, Roy Menarini, Su-I Chen, Marco Arnaudo, Paxton Fettel, Jaimie Johansson, Elettra Sara and all the other reviewers, John Robert Smith, all the friends at Worldcinema, Rutracker, rargb and 1lib, Aga Skrodzka, Patricial Nuriel, Zhuoyi Wang, Roberto Chiesi, Lorenzo Fabbri, Mazyar Mahan, Robert Rushing, Lisa Melonçon, Lilya Kaganovsky, the Department of Languages and the Interdisciplinary Studies Department at Clemson University, Elena Oxman, Andrea Maggioli, Olga Volkova, Richard Letteri, Élisa Delaigue at Shellac, Giovanni Cioni, Melis Behlil.

Introduction

The Biopolitical Turn in World Cinema

The body that experiences ever more intensely the indistinction between power and life is no longer that of the individual, nor is it that sovereign body of nations, but that body of the world that is both torn and unified.

—Roberto Esposito, *Bíos: Biopolitics and Philosophy*

The aim of this medium, if any, is to fuse with the world.

—Francesco Casetti, *Theories of Cinema*

A MIDDLE-AGED UKRAINIAN SOLDIER is escorted to a bus stop and handcuffed to a lamp post. A Ukrainian flag is tied around his neck and a sign with the words "EXTERMINATION SQUAD VOLUNTEER" is taped to his chest. He is guarded by two Russian separatists. Passersby begin to gather around him, first a group of young men who stop their sports car to check out the scene. They borrow a cigarette from one of the guards and taunt the soldier, blowing smoke in his face; they bump into a few more friends, whom they greet warmly, grasping each other's arms in delight. Together, they crowd around the post for a group selfie with the captured man. Two young girls pass by; they are invited to join in another photo. Just beyond, bored commuters wait for the bus while further bystanders are drawn to the spectacle. An elderly lady jabs the captive in the stomach with her cane, then pushes a tomato into his face. A mother interrogates him, throwing off her daughter, who attempts to pull her back into the flow of pedestrians in the background. The captive is insulted, kicked, shoved, slapped, and punched, nearly disappearing into the devouring crowd. All the while, cell phones are raised to record the beating. Eventually, the two Russian soldiers intervene and drag him away, followed by throng of pedestrians laughing and shouting, "Why did you tell us to stop? Let's kill him, guys!" Here, the distinction between spectacular violence and the kind of everyday life one finds in cities all around the world is completely absent. People stroll by, doing errands; they laugh, flirt, and joke. Were it not for the man cuffed to the pole, this would be an ordinary sight.

Filmed in one witheringly long take, this is one of the most unpleasant scenes in Ukrainian director Sergei Loznitsa's grim 2018 film *Donbass*, an episodic, documentary-style narrative of the 2014 Russian seizure of Crimea. Here we see a man, a soldier whose citizenship would under other circumstances be unquestioned, his uniform a sign of unequivocal national belonging, who is transformed into a figure cast out from the political community, his life congealed into a species and multiplied as a spectacle, stripped of legal rights, and "at every instant exposed to an unconditional capacity to be killed."[1] In the next sequence, one of the occupying soldiers attends a friend's wedding, where he passes around a recording of the mob violence on his smartphone. Loznitsa's film (which was not released in the United States until 2022) may be regarded as an anatomy of both biopolitical production and extraction in its most intensely mediatized forms. The matryoshka-like explosion of life forms—created, sanctioned, broken down, abandoned, repurposed—transforms the film into an experience that cannot be mistaken for a generic, nondescript chapter in the cinema of civic engagement. In *Donbass* life is qualified, regulated, excluded, and also regarded as a resource from which to experiment, to profit and to exert (bio)power. Lending a double significance to this "production" is its hyper-mediated nature, which is not simply a result of Loznitsa's handheld style and its reality effect: Cameras of all kinds abound in this film; characters are often performers, con artists, or spectators, each passing through biopolitical loci, from maternity wards and military checkpoints to bomb shelters and a school repurposed as a police headquarters, calling explicit attention to the alarming ease with which the rehearsal of new political narratives can refashion subjectivities, imposing a new "script" on life, one in which images and signs no longer coincide with their referent but forcibly append deadly meaning to space, language, and the body, wherein only a white placard is necessary to reinscribe a man as a willing "volunteer" for humiliation and death, while revealing an essential truth about the figure of a soldier, any soldier, whose life is immanently sacrificeable and, in the final analysis, that any life may be sacrificed under the right conditions.

In a 2018 interview, Loznitsa recalled, "one journalist from Australia told me the film was like a dark hallucination, and could not believe something in real life could be like that."[2] Four years later, Russia launched its "special military operation" in Ukraine, a conflict marked by gruesome smartphone footage of what has since been called "the world's first TikTok war," blurring the line between evidence of human suffering and "content," that globally circulating commodity that enriches the tech platforms that host it.[3] Loznitsa's film has been characterized as "satire that's too real," "true lies," even "war in Ukraine, the prequel," emphasizing the "becoming-cinema" or cinematization of contemporary life as it becomes more and more hyperreal, such that real life sometimes feels like cinema while cinema appears "too real."[4] Taken together, *Donbass* and its reception draw a distinct constellation between several points of reference: the nature of representation, the production of bare life, and, not least of all, the capacity for biopolitics to frame the experience of reality itself—a capacity it shares with cinema as such, and which carries with it both danger and promise. Thomas Hobbes, whose words form this book's epigraph, hardly had cinema in mind when he wrote *De Cive*, yet his triangulation of "Man," society, and education strongly resonates with the relationship between life, cinema, and power. Far more agile and (deceivingly?) adaptable than any other medium, film is uniquely poised to capture the dynamic way in which sovereignty, discipline, and control intersect and productively interact.

The relationship between cinema and biopolitics that this book mediates is grounded in the overlap between their respective debates, which thinkers as various as Michel Foucault, Giorgio Agamben, Roberto Esposito, André Bazin, Alain Badiou, and Jacques Rancière (among others) extend as far back as Aristotle and Plato. Until recently, however, there has been relatively little engagement between film studies and biopolitical philosophy, although Agamben and Esposito, two of the most important biopolitical thinkers, have engaged with cinema's biopolitical dimensions to a certain degree. Agamben has published two important essays on cinema, which have occasioned an edited collection exploring the ethics of the image, while Esposito has spoken at some length on the relationship between cinema and biopolitics in a stimulating conversation with Roberto de Gaetano, the editor of Italian film journal *Fata Morgana*, in a special issue called *Bíos*.[5] This present study aims to engage the small but significant body of work on the subject, most notably *Cinema and Agamben: Ethics, Biopolitics and the Moving Image* (2015), edited by Henrik Gustafsson and Asbjørn Grønstadt; Dimitris Papanikolaou's *Greek Weird Wave: A Cinema of Biopolitics* (2021); and Seung-hoon Jeong's *Biopolitical Ethics in Global Cinema* (2023). There are also a few superb articles on the subject whose authors include, among others, Maria Muhle, Nitzan Lebovic, and Elena del Río.[6] That these works, which I engage with in more detail later, were published so recently suggests that the cinematic engagement with biopolitics, especially that of world cinema, is a relatively new and relevant line of inquiry across film studies, political philosophy and critical theory.

The Biopolitical Turn in World Cinema seeks to contribute to these conversations, engaging with and generating new lines of inquiry across the disciplines of film studies, political philosophy, and critical theory. It is informed by my work on Italian cinema (*Italian Post-Neorealist Cinema*, 2012) and the Italian intellectual tradition more broadly, which has cultivated Foucault's concept of biopolitics with remarkable enthusiasm, but is not limited to these.[7] Throughout this book, I also make reference to lesser-known or as-yet-untranslated Italian film scholars such as Daniele Dottorini or Roberto de Gaetano, who provide unique perspectives and points of reference regarding cinema and biopolitics; it is a lesser ambition of this book to make their work somewhat more visible and accessible to an English-language audience. However, while my previous work centered on a single national cinema, this current work is more expansive, concerning "world cinema"—a somewhat vexed and problematic term that has been the subject of many reappraisals and debates, which I will summarize later—and its biopolitical "turn."

As a form, cinema transverses modernity, neoliberalism, and the Anthropocene, carrying with it the capacity to critique and to gesture beyond the forms of life permitted by these periods. The book explores these differences, as well as the commonalities, across a range of films drawn from the corpus of world cinema, each of which is its own biopolitical inquiry and intervention. Together, they offer a multitude of frames for understanding and representing contemporary biopolitical experience. The chapters that follow ask: How does cinema depict the production of truth, identity, and power? How are political technologies of disempowerment translated visually? How are life-shaping protocols of inclusion and exclusion implemented, internalized, resisted? To address these questions, I place a range of thinkers, debates, and films into dialogue with the broad aim of examining two aspects of biopolitics: as a technology of (bio)power and as a mode of contemporary experience. In terms of theory, it is situated between Agamben's bare life and the more affirmative accounts of biopolitics by Esposito, as well as Michael Hardt and Antonio Negri, each of whom is crucial in considering how, and in what ways, world cinema might be a unique medium to convey and, importantly, critique, biopower and biopolitical experience; it is also informed by and critically engages with recent conversations in film studies regarding realism, ethics, and biopolitics, from Lucía Nagib's systematic *Realist Cinema as World Cinema* to Robert Sinnerbrink's *Cinematic Ethics: Exploring Ethical Experiences through Film*, among many other scholars discussed in this book. In what follows of this introduction, I place biopolitics and cinema in dialogue, examining their conceptual affinities and overlapping histories to suggest that cinema is not only a disciplinary apparatus, but can operate as an affirmatively biopolitical medium. I then explore film scholarship that takes a biopolitical approach toward world cinema before attending to the concept of world cinema itself, arguing that as a site where questions about nationality, identity, history, rights, and political belonging are constantly being negotiated, world cinema is especially suited to this task in its ability to register and engage the imposition of biopolitical rationalities in ways that may elude other modes of discourse.

Biopolitics: Key Issues

Since Foucault introduced the concept to philosophy in the late 1970s, biopolitics has been incorporated into numerous disciplines and fields of study by a range of scholars who have found it particularly compelling for understanding the ways power intervenes in, coerces, and qualifies life.[8] Though Foucault's account of biopolitics was by no means systematic, he introduces the term to designate the political rationale of modern governmentality, beginning in the eighteenth century and intensifying in the nineteenth and twentieth centuries.[9] That biopolitics develops alongside liberalism, capitalism, and colonialism is of crucial significance; indeed, the biopolitical emerges, according to Foucault, in response to the unique "problems posed to governmental practice by . . . living beings forming a population."[10] In this formulation, the individual body is subsumed into a mass that must be managed, and consequently life itself becomes the object of governance with the concurrent, expressive creation of segments of the population that fit the biopolitical prescriptions. While many scholars concentrate on the application of biopolitical philosophy to cinema (and vice versa), few, if any, have explicitly remarked on the fact that, if we take Foucault's periodization to be true, the birth of biopolitics—or, more accurately, its culmination in the nineteenth century—is also the birth of photography and cinema. Even the *longue durée* of biopolitics coincides with the seventeenth- and eighteenth-century experiments with innovations and experiments in optics. While anatomists were dissecting cadavers in the seventeenth century, for example, Newton was grinding mirrors for his telescope. Jeremy Bentham's prison panopticon is perhaps the most explicit example of the coincidence between the biopolitical and the optical, whereby systems of control and new ways of seeing perfectly align; indeed, one might observe a similar conjunction in the development of the photography and images of criminals, beginning in the 1850s, or of the "hysterical" women photographed at Salpêtrière in 1885.[11] Another particularly relevant example is the 1914–1918 film, shot at one of Britain's military hospitals, that shows a shell-shock victim unable to walk, his body contorting into disturbing shapes. By the end of the film, presumably cured by the nascent discipline of psychoanalysis, the soldier is shown walking normally (although viewers will notice the nervous, compulsive movement of his hands).[12]

For Foucault, this all marks a transformation in politics whereby the "population" becomes a new political subject on whom and in whose name technologies of classification, measurement, and quantification are deployed. This development, which begins with the political philosophy of right and the concept of natural man, also marks an epistemic transformation from the classical understanding of humans as citizens to humans as species—mass life that must be managed. It is such transformations that lend further weight to Foucault's famous claim, written two years prior to his lectures on biopolitics, that "for millennia, man remained what he was for Aristotle: a living animal with the additional capacity for a political existence; modern man is an animal whose politics place his existence as a living being into question."[13]

Following Foucault, philosophers faced the task of continuing to develop some of his unfinished research. Italian thought in particular has shaped the trajectory of biopolitical thinking, with three major strands of thought, whose approaches have addressed lines of inquiry Foucault did not address or complete before his death: Agamben, the most celebrated of the three, takes up an analysis of the concentration camp as the paradigm of modernity, formulating key biopolitical concepts of bare life and the state of exception, which, he contends, are installed as cornerstones of Western juridical-political systems; Esposito uses the paradigm of immunity to conceive of an affirmative biopolitics, emphasizing the power *of* life (rather than *over* life, as Agamben's paradigm does); Hardt and Negri articulate their own affirmative biopolitics from a Marxist perspective, in terms of production and reproduction. Each of these writers also formulates different critiques of Foucault: Agamben aims to correct Foucault's failure to meaningfully examine the concentration camp as the locus of biopolitics, while Hardt and Negri attend to the loci of an affirmative biopolitics in which the power *of* life resists its exploitation and extraction by biopower. Esposito, meanwhile, takes up Foucault's closing question in *"Society Must Be Defended"* by drawing on the discourses of bodies and the human person in order to articulate a lineage of biopolitics that does not necessarily always terminate in a politics of death, or, as Campbell writes, "[resists] the *dispositifs* of the thanatopolitical" by drawing on the discourses of bodies and the human.[14]

Influenced by both Foucault and Hannah Arendt, Agamben suggests that biopolitics is inherent to sovereignty itself. His *Homo Sacer* project is a reappraisal and extension of their work, beginning with the observation that Arendt failed to link her writing on Greek concepts of life and her incisive understanding of totalitarianism. Agamben then observes that "Foucault, in just as striking a fashion, never dwelled on the exemplary places of biopolitics: the concentration camp and the great totalitarian states of the twentieth century."[15] Following this insight, Agamben departs from Foucault's specific account of modernity by locating a version of biopolitics inherent in and constitutive of Western civilization itself. It is on this basis that Agamben is often criticized: By establishing a single, totalizing political destiny, he risks flattening the specificity and historical contingency of distinctly modern catastrophes.[16] However, his work, which is among the most important contributions to biopolitical thinking, is sincerely interested in understanding the passage from the ancient to the modern world, continuing and extending Foucault's line of inquiry, this time to diagnose the logic of encroaching totalitarian power.

Agamben's crucial intervention into Foucault's account proceeds from the observation that what we simply call "life" was divided into two categories by the ancient Greeks: *bíos* and *zoē*. *Bíos* indicated "the form or way of living proper to an individual or a group," or qualified life, life with secondary characteristics, used by Aristotle to describe "the life of pleasure," the "political life," and the "contemplative life." In concrete terms, and within the context of ancient Athens, *bíos* was the life of a citizen, capable of living a free, positively defined, public form of life precisely because he was invested with political rights. *Zoē* meant "the simple fact of living common to all living beings (animal, men, or gods)"—a word that, Agamben notes, "lacks a plural," indicating an undifferentiated state that not only cannot constitute a community but is by definition excluded from it. It designates life *in general*, "merely reproductive life" as excluded from the *polis*.[17] This circular biopolitical economy of exception through which *bíos* and *zoē* are both separated and co-constituted provokes the question as to what, exactly, divides them. Agamben's answer is the caesura of "bare life" (*nuda vita*). *Zoē* was anything excluded from *bíos*; it defines and is defined against it: *zoē* takes place in private, in the home (*oikos*), and is associated with non-citizens whose function is merely reproductive—women giving birth, slaves (foreigners) and workers performing labor (under duress, in order to survive), and so on.[18] In this sense life has always been politicized and power has always been, at least to some extent, biopower. As Agamben writes, "it can even be said that the production of a biopolitical body is the original activity of sovereign power."[19] Following this, it would be quite simple to conclude that *zoē* is identical with bare life, and indeed many scholars make this claim. However, upon closer inspection it is clear that this is not the case. In fact, Agamben writes, "the entry of *zoē* into the sphere of the *polis*—the politicization of bare life as such—constitutes the decisive event of modernity and signals a radical transformation of the . . . categories of classical thought."[20] There is certainly some slippage here, but it is clear that it is the *entry* of the fact of living shared by all, or *zoē*, into the sphere of the *polis*—which is to say the political sphere that turns life into a public matter, a matter of the law—that produces bare life in the sense that it is most commonly used. Making this distinction is not only essential to careful reading of Agamben's work, but also necessary if we want to use his thought productively and think with it to imagine different, more open and communal ways of living. If we are to attend the biopolitical challenges of the Anthropocene and try to conceive new forms of life then we cannot "[ground] biopolitics in the ontological assumption that political behavior is biologically conditioned." As Ewa Plonowska Ziarek writes, "bare life, wounded, expendable, and endangered, is not the same as biological *zoē*, but rather the *remainder of destroyed political bíos*."[21] That is to say, bare life is not immanent to a woman and/or an enslaved person; life becomes bare life once someone is denied access to *bíos*, to a qualified life, a life that is rightfully theirs.

Life as a continuous spatiotemporal interface with capital is also a critical part of Negri's speculation in which a global process of deterritorialization has led to the creation of a non-place where immaterial labor organizes the relationship between production-consumption through continuous technological innovation and implementation of efficiency measures. According to Negri, the formation of the consumer's cultural imaginary stands out as the contradictory manifestation through capital's strategies of global dominance. In the passage from imperialism to empire, the nation-state loses its preeminent position when supranational and transnational organizations appear, dictating economico-political decisions across the whole world. The notion of a decentered and reticular power echoes Foucault and is conducive to a permeable space through which flows of information, data, monetary aggregates, and migrants concur to the unlimited expansion of capitals. On the other hand, the unlimited margins of the non-place echo Gilles Deleuze and the nomadic movement of capital, which concurrently organizes and shapes itself and this infinite space without asperities. As a manifestation of immaterial labor, affective labor is tasked with constituting simulacra of communities through different industries: Its networking zeal provides a firm structure to post-Fordist methods of production, while the subsumption of personal initiative, intellectual capacity, and emotion into an entrepreneurial subjectivity certifies the permeability of the inside and the outside of work. Biopolitically speaking, the goal of the Empire is to make vital processes coincide with work time by developing control policies that invade all areas of life. As production is transformed into immaterial intellectual output, the nexus between work and its product becomes immanent, in a continuous loop of self-(re)production. In his quest to define a new proletariat, Negri hails the role of unmediated constituent power and its raw, spontaneous emergence and sees a political opening in the Empire's failure to contain the symbolic and aesthetic value of immaterial labor, with the exceedance of the former leading to a new process of accumulation in the common, in turn creating the conditions for a recomposition of labor. Biopolitical production directly affects the so-called "intimate" dimension of beings, and the dynamics of capture that are inherent therein do not consist in a simple substitution of appropriate goods. It is a question not of a mechanical passage from the surplus value extorted in the production process to that extracted in from an entire lifetime, but of an immeasurable surplus labor, because it concerns human intellectual faculties, acquired skills, knowledge, and cooperation in which the whole of life is expressed. Hardt and Negri biopolitically characterize the activities that workers perform as forms of life: It is thanks to these ways of emancipating the self that according to them workers autonomously and continuously bring about "all the capacities for reversal and creating alternative forms of producing and living."[22] For Marx, capital in its continuous expansion had to overcome obstacles of all kinds, from existing relations of production to ground rent, to feudal jurisdictions, to aristocracies. Today, as Negri and Hardt argue, capital is the main obstacle to the unfolding of biopolitical production: in computer networks with patents and copyrights and with the delimitation of enclosures in immaterial property. In their latest work, *Assembly* (2017), Hardt and Negri develop the idea that the processes of production of value in contemporary capitalism have by now become increasingly passive and that they have been reduced to appraise a production process that preexists the capitalist command and organizes itself autonomously (hence the aforementioned emphasis on extraction and not on production, to mark the passivity and the distance from a properly entrepreneurial system).

In closing, the biopolitical paradigm represents the rational field in which power operates and is constituted by the series of subjectivation stages on which, organized like a set of local tactics, it can intervene. Biopower and biopolitics must therefore not be taken as synonyms: The first designates the political technology, methods, and techniques that are concretely aimed at the manipulation of men's life; biopolitics, on the other hand, designates the field of intervention and the forms of rationality that they govern the functioning of biopower. One should speak of biopower to underline its multiplicity, bearing in mind that these singular forms tend to be reabsorbed and integrated into a limited number of strategies and lines of penetration, then subsequently rationalized, and coordinated with each other. Compared to Agamben, Esposito maintains a periodization of biopolitics close to Foucault with an emphasis on modernity, but for Esposito biopolitics is given not only as a seizure of power over life but also as the politics of life itself. Esposito's point of departure is that of the "impolitical," not a category but a stance, an interrogation of the metaphysical interpretation of politics, the emptying out of the political space and its radical boundedness. The impolitical perspective denies politics a relationship with the "good" or other foundational values or ideologies allegedly fueling political action. In doing so, the impolitical returns to the original nucleus of political experience understood as a pure balance of power. Since Esposito's early reflection ran the risk of losing sight of the horizon of transformation, limiting itself to an inquiry into disenchantment and power and resigning itself to the idea that political thought is essentially a philosophy of the established order, the Italian philosopher countered this apparent impasse with the affirmative thought of a different, surging biopolitics. Foucault, according to Esposito, remains entangled in an aporia that it does not in any way allow to resolve, starting from the texts themselves, the fundamental undecidability of the biopolitical paradigm. It manifests itself as the power to produce and at the same time to destroy the subjects on which it is exercised. On the one hand, biopolitics protects and cares for the lives of individuals; on the other hand, continuously exposes them to the risk of annihilation. Esposito manifests the irreparable conflict between sovereignty and biopower and insists on the unintended consequences and the excessive, irrepressible force that life exhibits when it is overpowered, subdued, suppressed. Unlike Foucault's bioideological interpretation of Nazism as an evolutionary perversion of biologism, Esposito's theorization of Nazism as immunization is the same as Nietzsche's ontological substrate. According to Esposito, Nietzsche anticipates the conflict between immunity and community, where the Dionysian would be the excess of life over the individual and over itself, a life that wants to expand, break, and break up to the point of denying itself, refusing to outline forms in which it can reveal itself. By focusing on the vital force more than Deleuze and Foucault, Esposito activates a biological view of Nietzsche's thought. Against the neoliberal appropriation of the *dispositif* of the person, Esposito's concept of the impersonal gestures toward a reconstructive beyond, "a valuation beyond good and evil [that] evades a series of borders the personal self inevitably calls forth."[23] Esposito also offers an affirmative reading of Hobbes's sovereignty, by seeing through the fictional version of the state of nature posited by Hobbes, and instead focusing on institutions and the covenant. Thanks to this form of escape from the alleged state of nature, one may have access to an added value, to a more complex articulation that translates the life of individuals into the life of citizens, envisioning "a more communitarian way of organizing society which is not based on self-preservation."[24]

Cinema, Between Disciplinary Instrument and Affirmatively Biopolitical Medium

Although the term "biopolitics" was adopted in earnest by thinkers in the 1980s and 1990s, its popularity made a significant jump in the late 1990s and early 2000s; it is currently at the peak of its discursive prominence.[25] It is at the beginning of this jump that the "biopolitical turn" in philosophy got fully underway, inaugurating the work of Agamben and Esposito, two of the foremost contemporary theorists of biopolitics.[26] The significance of this coincidence hardly needs elaborating, but it can be sufficiently stated that September 11, 2001, and the resulting so-called War on Terror (which has since claimed 4.5 million lives) and great expansion of the security state, intensified and concentrated the current biopolitical governmentality in the US and around the globe, from everyday life—airport security, for instance—to extraordinary rendition, each of which is produced by what Agamben, after Carl Schmitt, calls "the state of exception."[27] These new protocols emerged as a defense of an American *way of life*—what Hardt and Negri call Empire—that understands itself as a metonymy for freedom and civilization around the world. Jasbir K. Puar eloquently notes that this metonymy functions as much as a biopolitical instrument as population control, coercing "affective investments in discourses of freedom, liberation, and rights"[28] while at the same time denying the potential for more and different life to appear. This rather simple insight is worth noting insofar as it attests that biopolitical thought itself operates on and as a "turning point." Foucault inaugurates two biopolitical turns in his work: The second "turn" is Foucault's identification, at the advent of neoliberalism proper, that is, of the first "turn" in political economy born alongside modernity, which itself marked a reconfiguration of human experience and power. What we call the "biopolitical turn" in contemporary philosophy and critical theory can therefore be considered not only a reflection of new appraisals of Foucault or responses to current biopolitical conditions; it is also indicative of a historical turning point as we move from the twenty-first century into the Anthropocene, an epoch that is occurring in our present, and yet, by its very name, epistemologically reorients temporality away from years and numbers and into an expanse of geologic time inconceivable to the human species that brought it into being and that demands new paradigms beyond species-being. The biopolitical is in constant metamorphosis, adapting, turning into, toward, and out of life precisely because of its proximity to it—that is, as a conjunction of biology and politics, there is a morphogenetic quality to the development of biopolitics proper in addition to its well-reasoned critiques. Foucault's micro-partitioning of power—that series of mechanisms, precisely, of control, management, and exclusion that are internalized in everyone, and everywhere—is introjected by way of representations. In fact, if there are areas of possible resistance and renewal they also originate from mental images—calling them representations dates to the Stoics—within the individual. Changing representations are precisely, attempt to change life, or at the very least to ultimately see things in a different, deeper, more critical and, perhaps, freer way.

As Timothy C. Campbell and Adam Sitze observe, "no point for observing the totality of biopolitics is available to us: there exists *no perspective that would allow us to survey and measure the lines that together constitute the concept's theoretical circumstance.*"[29] In other words, biopolitics and biopolitical thought resists the scientific management and enclosure that they often either mobilize or describe. This self-limitation is weakly messianic, following the foundational biopolitical thinking of Walter Benjamin.[30] Biopolitics cannot be understood, then, as a totality; it is inscribed by a range of relations between the subject and power which change even as they are reproduced. At first glance, this might appear dangerous: after all, if biopolitics cannot be intellectually mapped, does this not attest to its wholesale appropriation of life? This is the pessimism that can often be read in the work of Agamben, for whom "the only hope of living well is through the development of a new political formation that does not partake in the biopolitical capture of life."[31] Even if this is so, it does not obviate the self-limiting capacity just described, which contains its own differentiation. Non-identical to itself, biopolitics is not (necessarily) an irresolvable trap, because it carries the potential to become otherwise.[32] Writing about cinema rather than biopolitics, Adrian Ivakhiv has described this capacity as morphogenetic, borrowing a term from biology, "morphogenesis," to describe cinema's "generation of new forms from old ones, reproduced, recomposed, and reimagined."[33] This insight, which Ivakhiv develops in his work on post-cinematic ecologies, can be detected even earlier in film studies in a way that imbricates biopolitics and cinema on a deeper level. Indeed, one may even turn to Bazin: "The Ontology of the Photographic Image" suggests that cinema has long occupied unsettled territory between life and death. Referring to cinema's "mummy-complex," Bazin links its referentiality, or "indexicality," to the ancient Egyptian practice of mummification. Its aim, Bazin explains, was to "preserve, artificially," the "corporeal body" of the deceased in order "to snatch it from the flow of time, to stow it away neatly, so to speak, in the hold of life."[34] This is easily understood, and one immediately grasps the intended consonance between the preserved body and the photographic arrest of life. But Bazin's crucial insight emerges when he turns his attention from the corpse to the terracotta statuettes placed beside the sarcophagus. It is only at this remove from the body, this level of indexicality, that Bazin indicates a relationship between cinema and biopolitics, which, he asserts, is no less than the foundations of cinematic realism itself.[35] As such, it is also one point at which this relationship overlaps with the vexed and heavily elaborated question of cinematic representation:

> The first Egyptian statue, then, was a mummy, tanned and petrified in sodium. But [it] offered no certain guarantee against ultimate pillage. Other forms of insurance were therefore sought. So, near the sarcophagus, alongside the corn that was to feed the dead, the Egyptians placed terra cotta statuettes, as substitute mummies which might replace the bodies if these were destroyed. It is this religious use, then, that lays bare the primordial function of statuary, namely, *the preservation of life by a representation of life*.[36]

Though it is easy to get mired in Bazin's metaphysics, he nevertheless highlights how cinema oscillates between preservation and metamorphosis. It is famously constituted by a dialectical tension between the empirical and the illusory, that is to say, between truthful representation—what Tom Gunning calls the documentary impulse—and the fabrication of reality.[37] Via its durational motion forms, film catalogues, conserves, classifies, and recreates life; situated between arrest and animation, it explodes still postures into action. Through its synthetic continuity, its mobilization of immobile frames, we witness life persist, transform, adjust, reproduce, and resist in unexpected forms—although this poses the question, "What image of life?" since, when it is caught unaware, the image misses its chance to reply or to recalibrate our investments and expectations; and when it is rehearsed, it stands at indefinite removes from its flagrancy.

Esposito has explicitly acknowledged the consonance between cinema and biopolitics by way of his concepts of immunity and community: "We could say that cinema places itself right on the boundary between these two paradigms [immunity and community] because, on the one hand, it kills, splits, and it presupposes, on the other, however, it exposes through this continuous movement of metamorphosis."[38] Esposito offers this insight—whose full import will be examined later in this chapter—in response to a question posed by de Gaetano, the editor of the Italian film philosophy journal *Fata Morgana*, who, having asked for the philosopher's thoughts on Edgar Morin, offers a précis of the French philosopher's 1956 work, *Cinema, or the Imaginary Man*. While Bazin understands cinema as the preservation of life through representation, duplicating reality in statuette form, always indexed to death, Morin—who likewise thinks of cinema in terms of the afterlife—extends this understanding back into the realm of life again.[39] As Esposito's interlocutor suggests, Morin "sees cinema [as] not only built on the concept of the double, as the immobilization of a reality as pre-existing, but rather, on the principle of metamorphosis. . . . From this point of view, it is a generative principle: an image dies and another one is born."[40] According to Morin, "metamorphosis triumphs over death and becomes renaissance," or rebirth, that once again aligns the conceptual vocabulary of cinema with that of biopolitics. It is precisely this morphogenetic tendency that endows cinema with affirmatively biopolitical potentialities. In what follows, this book argues that cinema can fully progress from the disciplinary to the affirmatively biopolitical when it deploys its reproductive potential to imitate life.

Bringing together biopolitics and world cinema is an admittedly challenging task. After all, it is self-evident that cinema can be used as an instrument of governmentality with its own policing in Rancière's sense of strictly enforcing thinkable roles, from the position of the spectator, whose gaze is necessarily limited to a given frame and perspective, to the range of social categories and perspectives limited by a film's length and scope. Sharing the genetic code of a biopolitical technology, cinema can indeed, as Francesco Casetti writes, be deployed as a *dispositif* for the implementation of a discipline[41]—albeit a "free" one, a discipline of difference and the internal capability of spontaneously deflagrating its ideological embedding—that the task of investigating the potential of cinema to summon governmental and biopolitical experience needs in order to account for contrastive movements. Cinema, as a discipline, functions like an intrinsically falsifying continuum of images, colors, sounds that deceitfully solves the problem of vision and mollifies audiences by virtue of the technical expertise of the manipulators-in-chief. Casetti operates in the wake of Christian Metz's description of spectatorship as a temporal surrendering of one's subjectivity, which traps conflict in the eternal preservation of time and negates the vitality of popular audiences through the "linearization of iconic signifiers" and the "centering of the picture."[42] Viewers are administered a place and a role in the expansion of the bourgeois project, thereby qualifying the "life" the shadows were endowed with as a totalizing illusion with undisguised biopolitical features: how and where and who to meet, with a ready-made set of aspirations, life formalized by the visual as a naturalistic production.[43] To paraphrase Esposito, cinema cuts and kills but also continuously exposes and develops images of life, leaving open the potential for new, radical subjectivities liberated from the limited horizon of thinkable roles; by the same turn, cinema is capable of disciplining the imagination and setting limits on life, naturalizing an imposed reality. This is especially legible, for example, in Italian Fascist filmmaking, which, as Lorenzo Fabbri explains, "had to transform Italian laborers from threats into resources"[44] by way of cautionary tales often delivered through a realistic aesthetic typically associated with Italian Neorealism, which Bazin and countless others have identified with a "revolutionary ethics."[45] Yet, as Roland Vegso and Marco Abel ask, "what is cinema in the age of biopower?"[46] According to them, contemporary "cinema's function is not exhausted in visibility itself: its task, rather, is to tie the domain of visibility to a whole set of other affective domains."[47] Carlos Natalio's own work on the subject complements the task of cinema set by Vegso and Abel, emphasizing that the "splitting" gesture, or procedure, inherent in both filmmaking and biopower must be used "to produce difference, quality, and aesthetic value in the domain of mathematical, repetitive and quantitative process of 'invisible' biopolitical homogenization."[48]

The central claim of this book is not only that cinema captures the forms of life dictated by biopower, but that it can also generate new forms of life that critique, resist, and transform power. Cinema's "deceiving" nature lies in its capacity to create new mental images that could have an impact on physical, worldly life and yet it extends a normative glow as it is inserted into networks of production, management, and exploitation: a process of continuous life formations where "artificiality and naturalness become indistinguishable,"[49] in which their exhibition is always duplicitously destabilizing because of the innate, organic abjection. This apparent contradiction may be reconciled by understanding the cinematic as an affective intensity, a noncognitive investment in certain internal images that, as Hans Belting would say, "both remind us of our body and make us forget it."[50] The biopolitical specificity of cinema as a medium would then lie in its capacity to create images that connect and mediate between the living body and the inert object—although in Belting's wake the cinematic image, the real image and the body are not exclusively separable. It is this double movement between extraction—depletion, coercion, abstraction—and morphogenesis—reproduction, formation, figuration—that endows cinema with a unique capacity to convey biopolitical experience, *which is no less than (contemporary) life.*

This experience has been vividly illustrated in a range of recent films in which the body itself is an infinite site of extraction. Managing bodies by producing their souls as repositories but without stopping to mine their resources: To maximize extraction a rationality needs to process a subject it can concurrently excavate. Anything life can offer: Money, images, labor, lifestyles and biological life itself, conducts spread across the social body: films not simply corroborating or illustrating or questioning a preexistent thought that was born and articulated elsewhere but bringing to life a cinematic actualization of an intuitive and autonomous reality—an encounter between two realms and the implications stemming from their composition. A film like Sean Baker's *Red Rocket* (2021) shows how, in an economy based on extraction—from nature, from other individuals—there cannot be any "new" reconstructed subjectivity other than one based on exploitation. Together with Ben and Josh Safdie, today Baker is the director who most clearly articulates an anthropology of precariousness and instability, in which the factors of an illusory formation—feelings, intimacies, potentialities—are recast as functions of exchange value. In his latest work, *Anora* (2024), the filmmaker again examines the body of a woman as a site of infinite extraction, disguising this appropriation as a screwball comedy in which extraction itself becomes a comedic spectacle. Likewise, in *Sorry to Bother You* (Boots Riley, 2018) we see how the law is no longer the exclusive instrument of sovereign power: Enslavement may no longer be legal but a logic of "whitification" is pervasively in place and occurs at the workplace level. Giving his best broligarch impression, Armie Hammer as the 2.0 evolution of a KKK Imperial Wizard deploys a tech version of white supremacy for the Trump times, a neo-fascist incipient force that acts algorithmically to deprive entire communities of their rights. It is to maximize its effect that the strategy of homogenization begins with dispossessing non-white workers of their communicative tools to ward off the production of a common, to make sure that the workplace can help prevent the formation of cooperative singularities, and to make corporate discourses impenetrable to alternative and critical appropriations by the working class. Like Aristotle's ideas of natural slaves, the "equisapiens" horse-people from *Sorry to Bother You* are the final goal of "libertarian" one percenters by way of intensifying biopolitical logics of dispossession, simultaneously "solving political economic problems of production and the problem of political participation by creating a new slave labor force."[51]

(Whose) World Cinema?

From its inception, the concept of world cinema that circulated in film studies and on the international film circuit has acted as a counterbalance to Hollywood dominance. However, the definition of "world" posed myriad challenges to film scholarship. Can one think of world cinema without either centering the hegemonic core or fetishizing the periphery? As Ewa Mazierska astutely observes, "world cinema" shares the same ambiguities with "world music" and "world literature," each running the risk of establishing a "fake universalism" or a fetishized exotic "other" commodified for Western consumption.[52] Like biopolitics, then, definitions of world cinema tend to produce dichotomies: self/Other, Hollywood/auteur, commercial/avant-garde, First World/ Third World, and so on. There are ethical and political stakes involved in these dichotomies, which often fail to recognize the transnational, global nature of images, capital, labor, identity, and community. Such dichotomies pose, for example, an opposition "between popularity and integrity," "oppression and resistance,"[53] and often pigeonhole "postcolonial diasporic filmmakers . . . as 'native informants' who are expected to provide 'authentic' accounts of their culture of origin."[54] To avoid these schematic reductions and reconcile some of the contradictions inherent in such notions of world cinema, film scholars have been rethinking the relationship between, for example, the global and the local. In their landmark 1994 publication, *Unthinking Eurocentrism: Multiculturalism and the Media*, Ella Shohat and Robert Stam revealed the epistemological and discursive strategies that constructed Europe's putative superiority while at the same time fostering a view of world cinema that focused on its pluralistic versatility.[55] Stephanie Dennison and Song Hwee Lim also problematize world cinema, questioning its very functionality, the cinemas it can or cannot encompass, as well as the power mechanisms embedded within it and its relationship to various audiences; they suggest that film scholars "place more focus on the interconnectedness of cinematic practices and cultures in the age of globalization . . . and theorise world cinema not in terms of 'West vs. the rest' but in relation to notions such as hybridity, transculturation, border crossing, transnationalism and translation."[56] Similarly, Daniela Berghahn proposes an understanding of "local and global spectators not . . . in geospatial terms, but . . . in terms of the locally specific knowledges audiences bring to the reception of a particular film."[57] Still, as Shohat and Stam note in a reappraisal of their 1994 study, such transnational frameworks still tend to center "the Global North [as] the culture of reference" while "the subaltern director is legitimated through a comparison to a superaltern precursor. Thus, metropolitan gatekeepers hail the 'Brazilian Woody Allen,' the 'Cameroonian Spike Lee,' and the 'Palestinian Godard.' "[58]

Reacting against negative definitions of world cinema as not-Hollywood or not-Western, Nagib observes that the "increasingly popular term highlighting the global aspect of film production," or "world cinema," "still lacks a proper, positive definition."[59] Nagib contests the notion, put forward by prominent film scholars like Geoffrey Nowell-Smith, John Hill, and Miriam Hansen, that world cinema and other cinemas and cinematic movements emerge in opposition to Hollywood (American) cinema. "The inevitable result of such conceptions," Nagib writes, "is the reinforcement of the binary division of the world, according to which Hollywood deserves a different treatment from all other cinemas."[60] It is not so much that all other cinemas define themselves in relation to American cinema, Nagib argues, but rather that "analyzing world cinemas through the American perspective is . . . a deeply-engrained habit among writers."[61] This habit has been, as Jeong has succinctly noted, increasingly challenged "as the world's ongoing homogenization blurs old boundaries while causing 'ethical' deadlocks" and "notions of subjectivity and society also undergo new crises and changes," which exceed national and transnational frameworks.[62]

Nagib provides an answer that is both simple and abstract: "World cinema is simply the cinema of the world." One can take this at face value and rightly conclude that all cinema is world cinema, but Nagib is indicating something with much richer implications when she adds, "It has no centre. It is not the other, but it is us. It has no beginning and no end, but is a global process. World cinema, as the world itself, is circulation."[63] World cinema reflects and activates the complex, networked relations of a global world in which neither nations nor their respective cinemas "are confined into tight compartments of their own nationalities, but interconnected with each other according to their relevance at a given historical moment, regardless of whether they originate in the first, second, or third worlds."[64] Nagib has continued to build on the previous paradigm of inclusivity by proposing an overlapping of world cinema and realist cinema, with a certain attention to reality elected as the defining factor and consisting of an ethics of responsibility, space-time wholeness, and "the evidential power of the audiovisual medium (its automatic nature, or ontology, or indexicality)."[65] As also noted by Jeong, Nagib's and David Martin-Jones's *Deleuze and World Cinemas* are interpretations based on totalizing frames that the authors elect as globally recognizable phenomena.

Martin-Jones's approach is not too dissimilar from that of Robert Sinnerbrink, for whom film is ontologically anchored to an ethical interpretation of being and where Sinnerbrink applies the logic of the turn, be it ethical, be it affective, to world cinema in its totality.[66] Mazierska and Lars Kristensen made a direct attack against Nagib's affirmative vision of world cinema for its lack of militant engagement; they equated the dominant Hollywood template of spectacularity and hero-driven narratives with the pernicious machinations of a globalized economy.[67] Moreover, in the introduction to the collection, called "Defining Third Cinema and World Cinema," Mazierska and Kristensen see the falsely egalitarian logic of "diversity and plurality" as essentially compromised with neoliberal agendas, and therefore reject it because of its lack of an anti-hierarchical component.[68] What the two authors may miss is the lack of appeal of Marxism today in terms of a revolutionary perspective, and the fact that political watchwords such as "inclusiveness" and "plurality" may very well be ineffective at dismantling inequality but are a direct consequence of the crisis of classical Marxism. Mazierska and Kristensen's approach is laudable but its prescriptiveness seems conducive to a certain sectarianism, the same that informed Italian Marxist scholar Roberto Alemanno when, to dispense with films by Nanni Moretti and Bernardo Bertolucci that were not considered sufficiently concerned with the condition of the working class, he lauded instead George Lucas's *Star Wars: Episode IV—A New Hope* (1977) because of its honest depiction of a fascist regime and a resistance to it.[69] Possibly, an eclectic, pedagogical approach like that of Katarzyna Marciniak and Bruce Bennett, with its constant scrutiny and subsequent renegotiation of cultural frameworks, breaking the barrier from spectatorship and precipitating students into experientiality, and hints of an irreducible liminality found in even the most "wholesome" industrial product, could provide another step forward in the expansion of world cinema as a discipline.[70] Albeit problematic in its lack of a thinkable, different, counter-hegemonic horizon, Mazierska and Kristensen's emphasis on geographic spheres of influence is still extremely relevant for the direction world cinema has recently taken; in fact, the notion expanded from a geo- into a bio-political domain when, by interrogating Andrew's "global" and "world" cinema phases, Jeong recognized a "concrete universality of the world system," a de facto homogenization of the human condition across the planet brought about by "the vicious interlocking between (neo)liberal multiculturalism and fundamentalist terrorism."[71] Jeong gestures toward a general degradation and disqualification of life into a disposable "asset," a vector where the precipitation of entire populations into societal abjection and the production of bare life meet halfway. This transnational experience becomes then internalized as an affect, a phenomenon that Dominique Moïsi has already backdated to the September 11 attack on the Twin Towers: If, "in an age of globalization, emotions have become indispensable to grasp the complexity of the world we live in," then the reconfiguration of the world order around an American model going through a crisis but still fully hegemonic leads to a concurrent decentering of cultural models and artistic forms.[72] Whether it is turned into a measurable edge to gain advantage in trade flows or an impossibly stable shape for authoritarian regimes afraid of identitarian conflicts, life bounces outside of the self as a projection, a mental image, a form through which the subject thinks and sees. World cinema—and, according to Moïsi, world television, because of its capacity to stretch in space and time new geopolitical challenges—are all merely diagnostic tools to probe new imbalances and containments, as well as the relevant shifts power relations. Liberal, authoritarian, populist—the cinematic subject is one through which the limits of government authority are discerned. It is not, then, unreasonable to suggest that the arrival of streaming services and of Netflix ushered in another phase in world cinema, one that we could call the computerized/remediated phase—computerized because of its algorithmic foundation, and remediated because Netflix, while currently identifiable as "film studio, television producer, home entertainment distributor, internet archive, and provider of web video, films, and television programs" may in fact be the organization initiating a shift whereby "through both the company's innovations and the continued blurring of content, these different categories may soon cease to have any meaning."[73] In the memorable words of CEO Reed Hastings: "We hope to one day become so good at suggestions that we will be able to offer you exactly the right movie or show based on your mood the moment you log on to Netflix."[74] This exemplifies how Netflix fashions itself as a content creator and distribution company, but in truth capitalizes on and performs biosurveillance. It is this "evangelistic and inclusive rhetoric of new media technologies" that Sarah Atkinson warns "should be tempered by considerations of their operational logics of commercialism, surveillance and exclusion."[75] In a more explicitly biopolitical context, this logic is reproduced as DOGE unrestrainedly accesses sensitive data, alters administrative processes, and inserts itself into governance structures without any democratic authority. The reorganization of the State includes an ideological overhaul of research and knowledge production that goes beyond public spending cuts, transforming the State into a tool for politically driven knowledge selection. The government dictates what can be known, who can know what, and reshapes the definition of knowledge to align with a specific agenda that marginalizes those who don't conform to its vision.

Netflix is now present in 190 countries and producing original content in 17 of them; if one looks at their catalog it is not a stretch to observe that the result of the attrition between national "traits" and global domestication is a high number of Netflix-produced works that look more like algorithmically generated assemblages that happen to be visual than like "regular" films. With old libraries co-opted by personalization logic and the new, supposedly disruptive arthouse "masterpieces" certifying the incestuous relationship of many auteurs with the circuit festival and looking more and more like algorithm-generated works, like Ruben Östlund's *Triangle of Sadness* (2022) or Yorgos Lanthimos' *Poor Things* (2023), a film tilting toward "ingratiation"[76] and "appeasement,"[77] the not-so-distant scenario will be that of a population undergoing processes of normalization and normativization in front of the screen, watching the same people try in vain to imagine an "outside" from those same processes: a perfect biopolitical dystopia—or Eden. One could then pick erosion as the master narrative for world cinema with quantifiables on either side of the screen. For the purpose of this book, my interest lies in the interrelation among governmental logics and their techniques, the characters as subjects, and the mental form or image they conjure up to proceed and progress into the next stage of subjectification/subjectivation. In the wake of Belting's work on the nature of images—never fully mental, never fully external, but rather representations that are constantly reinscribed onto themselves and "cannot be extricated from a continuous exercise of interaction"[78]—I attempt to build on Jeong's conflation of abjection and bare life in order to propose a biopolitical interpretation of world cinema where the subject is itself a *dispositif* in which a certain rationality is internalized and negotiated, becoming a site for recreating different life forms and evoking, like a mask, "the simultaneity as well as opposition between absence and presence."[79] World cinema should then be coextensive with a pedagogy for a new materialist universalism outside of a rigid Marxist or purely formalist framework, one that acknowledges that capitalism is not a national asset and therefore each revolution should concurrently involve multiple actors, nations, countries, historicizing and subsequently globalizing cinema by looking at the voices of all its protagonists.

Structure

Since Foucault's formative work on biopower was published in the late 1970s, the management of life as an extractable resource has accelerated. As neoliberal globalization has continued apace, it has reproduced forms of control, violence, and subjectivities across the world. Although cinema as a technology will always have a biopolitical dimension (as both a controlling apparatus and a critical, liberating one), this book is concerned with a specific "biopolitical turn" that can be observed across world cinema between the 1990s and the present day and concurrent with the emergence of the optimization economies. This overall turn can be connected with numerous historical and political transformations, with key coordinates in the late '70s and the '80s, the decades of China's era of opening up and reform under Deng Xiaoping, the Iranian Revolution, the birth of Western neoliberalism under Margaret Thatcher, Jimmy Carter, and later Ronald Reagan and the fall of the Soviet Union. Further coordinates include the

9/11 attacks, the War on Terror, and the resulting expansion of the security state as well as the period between the 2008 financial crisis and the current social, economic, ecological, and humanitarian crises around the world. This is of course a schematic outline that elides innumerable complex, interrelated events occurring over the course of nearly half a century. Paola Colonello sums up this historical trajectory as the promotion of "self-affirmation, competitive spirit and merit, neoliberal stresses and (con)strain(t)s [that] fuel dichotomous relations which see winner opposed to loser, included to excluded, success to failure, profit to loss."[80] Although Colonello's assertion is made in the contact of Iran in particular, her appraisal can be recognized across the world, from China to the United States. Everywhere, this profit motive is not only instrumentalized by the State but internalized by the subject, which tends to "lead to a neglect of the human potential that is difficult to commensurate and make it a tense, daunting proposition to educate the sensitivity of learners to less readily monetizable cultural content."[81] While a full historical account of neoliberalism is beyond the scope of this book, it must suffice to say that 1) as the mass medium of modern experience, cinema is especially suited to represent and interrogate these structuring aspects of contemporary life across the globe in different and important ways; and 2) as the historical and technological conditions that first birthed biopolitics have accelerated and evolved, biopolitical experience is consequently global—although never homogeneous, always reflecting local contexts, uneven development, and shifting positions within the global economy. As an experiential "commons," biopolitical experience is the experience of the body circumscribed, regulated, and disciplined by biopower.

This book therefore aims to demonstrate the unique ways contemporary cinema has engaged with biopolitics and state-sanctioned life forms. Each chapter investigates key aspects of biopolitics—among them, the marriage *dispositif*; the regulation and production of national history whose revisions are written on the body and the self, and which lays claim to everything the population can provide; and the vexed relationship between modernity and reproduction as it regards the artistic image, nature, the neoliberal maternal subject, and the intersections therein. While chapter 1 provides an overview of the current dialogues between film studies and biopolitical thought and a methodological framework for the book, the following chapters represent "case studies," as it were, of biopolitical cinema. Chapter

2 explores the history of post-revolutionary Iranian cinema and its relationship to governmental control more widely by examining the groundbreaking work of cinematic pioneers Abbas Kiarostami, Jafar Panahi, and Mohammad Rasoulof, whose work has registered the history of post-revolutionary Iran and its relationship to governmental control more widely. This discussion will lay the groundwork for an extended analysis of two major works by Asghar Farhadi, a director preoccupied with portraying the coercive, immunizing force of bio-politics as it is scattered and disembodied everywhere, immanent in every interaction, even in moments of possible connection and care: *Fireworks Wednesday* (*Chaharshanbe-soori*, 2006) and *About Elly* (*Darbareye Elly*, 2009) and each of which offers a visual articulation of Iranian political theology as it manifests in the household and family specifically, and how the exertion of biopower on these sites impact solidarity and political subjectivity.

Chapter 3 analyzes the films of directors Sergei Loznitsa, Kirill Serebrennikov, and Andrey Zvyagintsev, seeking to draw out the genealogies of power depicted in films such as *Landscape* (*Peyzazh*, 2003), *The Student* (*Uchenik*, 2016), and *Leviathan* (2014), respectively. Each director engages with the history of Soviet Russian power, how it is justified, recreated, and, more affirmatively, challenged. Chapter 4 examines the biopolitical poetics of post-socialist Chinese cinema, focusing on the work of Wang Xiaoshuai within the context of Sixth Generation filmmakers and their depiction of the cultural and eco-logical afterlives of post-Mao reforms, first exploring the director's earlier film *Frozen* (*Jidu hanleng*, 1997), which outlines the artist's relationship to the State, before examining the biopolitical legacy of the one-child policy in *In Love We Trust* (*Zuo you*, 2008) and *So Long, My Son* (*Di jiu tianchang*, 2019). Chapter 5 probes the biopolitical dimensions of New Romanian Cinema through the films of director Radu Jude, whose work triangulates the nation's complicity in Nazi war crimes and traumatic memories of the Ceaușescu regime, as in *"I Do Not Care if We Go Down in History as Barbarians"* (*"Îmi este indiferent dacă în istorie vom intra ca barbari,"* 2018), or its even earlier history of feudalism and slavery in *Aferim!* (2015), and the country's ambivalent entry into the Eurozone market in *The Happiest Girl in the World* (*Cea mai fericită fată din lume*, 2009) and *Bad Luck Banging, or Loony Porn* (*Babardeală cu bucluc sau porno balamuc*, 2021), the latter of which was filmed in the midst of the COVID-19 pandemic.

While this book has placed its focus on post-socialist and post-revolutionary cinemas, it concludes by forming an eclectic assemblage of films from the West, including the United States, France, and Italy by directors representing various movements, styles, and political reference points: the social horror of new Black American cinema, particularly Jordan Peele's *Nope* (2022); the slow cinema of Albert Serra's postcolonial meditation *Pacifiction* (2023); Alice Rohrwacher's Italian Neorealist revival with magical realist characteristics, *Happy as Lazzaro* (*Lazzaro felice*, 2018); the docufiction of Alessandro Comodin, *The Adventures of Gigi the Law* (*Gigi la legge*, 2023); and the experimental documentaries of refugee life, Sylvain George's *May They Rest in Revolt* (*Qu'ils reposent en révolte*, 2010) and Giovanni Cioni's *From the Planet of the Humans* (*Dal pianeta degli umani*, 2021), as well as Massimo D'Anolfi and Martina Parenti's *Bestiari, erbari, lapidari* (2024). These films are not connected by nationality but instead gesture toward other possible directions in filmmaking that address and respond to contemporary struggles and currents of thought that frequently elude or exceed the present limits of privileged biopolitical discourse, including neo-feudalism, migration, anthropocentric transformations, anti-Black racism, postcolonial history, and the neocolonial present. I propose that instead of resolving the impossible contradictions of biopolitics—its dichotomizing impulse that includes through exclusion, immunizing itself with violence—scholars and filmmakers seek new models of experience, forms of life, and vital relations that may lie beyond the strict horizons of classical liberal thinking.

Thinking Through Biopolitics and Film

An Overview

THE RISING INTEREST IN BIOPOLITICS among film scholars reflects a wider philosophical concern, not just with the imbrication of life and politics, but also with ethics and aesthetics, violence and sovereignty, identity and experience, realism and representation. One of the most comprehensive frameworks for a biopolitical interpretation of world cinema has been laid out by Jeong, who uses Julia Kristeva's concept of the abject, a condition that, Jeong proposes, is now a feature of the human condition.[1] In Jeong's reading, abjection has transformed into a trajectory of expulsion that in turn creates the potential for new avenues of agency. What is clear is that, in light of its mediating potential, the encounter between biopolitics and cinema is in fact a reunion: The medium thinks biopolitically because its genealogy, too, is that of a technology of normalization and surveillance by proxy. Such is, for example, Pasi Väliaho's thesis when he speaks of cinema as one in a series of media—FPS videogames, virtual reality headsets, drone screens—whose kinesthetic elements necessarily regulate bodily gestures under constant states of perceived danger and the production of essentialist forms of vitality.[2] In her review of cinematic practices of representing the manipulation and destruction of human life, Ivelise Perniola offers a taxonomy of the biocratic image based on a Foucauldian catalogue of biopolitical figures: the patient in Derek Jarman's *Blue* (1993), the prisoner in Claude Lanzmann's *Shoah* (1995), and the soldier in Brian De Palma's *Redacted* (2007) provide examples of biopolitical operations aimed at the domestication, mollification, and destruction of life. The three films, Perniola argues, also represent an advancement in their aesthetic politics by stimulating the viewer's critical and creative faculties rather than settling on iconic, euphemistic images that offer pacifying comfort and closure, and that therefore accept the instability of the spectating position. Thus, the filmmakers destroy "the representative logic of cinematic testimony" by purifying and liberating the image from its iconic ballast and eternalizing tragedy as the option that always remains open.[3]

Scholar Rey Chow investigates the condition of, and struggle for, visibility in Chinese visual cultures, unearthing the biopolitical dimensions of assimilation of, for example, Chinese patriarchy in the United States. Chow demonstrates how Wayne Wang's *Eat a Bowl of Tea* (1989) and Ang Lee's *The Wedding Banquet* (1993) each uniquely demonstrate the lengths to which "the non-negotiable imperative to reproduce biopolitically" will go by subsuming differences in ethnicity and sexual orientation into strategies of security and assimilation.[4] At the bottom of the biopolitical ladder one finds a recurring figure: that of the pregnant woman, whose function is to provide the biological substratum necessary to "the redesign of a specific biopolitical investment portfolio."[5] The homogenizing power of an extractive economy can thus successfully integrate and contain any variance; in Chow's specific account of these films, this power is capable of incorporating something foreign and making it Chinese, an operation that can also be seen in Jia Zhangke's *The World* (*Shijie*, 2004), a film that is particularly illustrative of the sharp intersection between capitalism and biopolitical experience. *The World* also features in Sheldon H. Lu's work on the biopolitical nature of Chinese modernity (a subject that is explored in further detail in chapter 3), to which the scholar applies the conceptual apparatus of the "new global biopolitics" or the "neoliberalist economy of affect" in which new exploitative rationalities are applied on a global scale.[6] By establishing a natural progression from Foucault's account of the induced docility of the productive body to Agamben's sovereignty over bare life as foundational politics to Hardt and Negri's postmodern immanentism of affective labor, Lu highlights the intensification of the evils into which global capitalism allegedly intervenes. From Jia Zhangke's film, in which a group of impoverished, uneducated, if not altogether disenfranchised men and women keep a postmodern amusement park running, Lu distills the vertiginous inequality among "citizens who are entangled in the heated games of modernization and globalization."[7] Lu also notes how class consciousness reasserts itself in the post-Mao years, especially in Wang Xiaoshuai's *Shanghai Dreams* (*Qing hong*, 2005). Sociocultural anthropologist Darren Byler builds on Chow's notion of the body as a disposable unit after Mao Zedong's ascent to power:[8] The scholar looks at Xu Xin's film *Karamay* (2010), a testimony on the death of 323 people, 288 of whom children, during a fire that erupted during a performance for state and party officials in the eponymous city. By orchestrating a counterpoint between a necropolitics of disposability and the anthropological concept of "ritual," Byler hails *Karamay* as an example of radical filmmaking that builds on previous works by directors such as Zhao Liang, Wu Wenguang, and Jia Zhangke but proves to be more radical by adding a collective ethos of prolonged trauma. Xu Xin's is a "cinema of witnessing" in which ritual embodiment of trauma and loss and the "weaponization" of affect "undermine the rhetoric of 'free market' success and embody the stubborn shadows in narratives of progress."[9] With its emphasis on the persistence of feelings and the refusal to dwell exclusively on mourning and loss in the film, Byler's approach highlights the tendency in Chinese cinema to privilege durational temporalities in epochs of change whose pace is perceived as inhuman.

Taking a Deleuzian approach, Michael J. Blouin equates the implementation of biopolitical regimes with the practices of schizo-capitalism. Drawing on Antonio Negri's notion of immaterial labor and its idea according to which the post-Fordist trajectory of capital tends to enfold the social horizon and the life processes of workers in their entirety, Blouin sees an evolutionary arc in the treatment of magic on screen culminating in the potential for the people in the audience to "recognize themselves as factories of desire"[10] by exposing the homology between the trickery on the screen and the shenanigans of financialized capitalism: the promised deliverance is negated, and therefore "the act of magic" is presented "as a genuine alternative."[11] According to Blouin, in movies such as *Now You See*

Me (Louis Leterrier, 2012) and *The Illusionist* (Neil Burger, 2006) one can observe parallels between magic and the early implementation of neoliberal policies: Both share a fallacious concept of freedom defined by its limitations, an ephemeral impediment to the power of the sovereign, a covert facilitation of lawful exploitation, all through an adroit conflation of the imaginative potential embedded in the cinematic apparatus and the neoliberal lie of widespread opportunity. Blouin also argues that these two films are structured by a common logic of lack: The audience is "led to invest in a number of absences" according to the neoliberal ontology in which subjectivity is shaped by the doctrine of credit and debt and the Oedipal lack that reroutes desires along proper lines and the will to know is contained by the operations of indebtedness.[12] In spite of their alignment with neoliberal tenets, *Now You See Me* and *The Illusionist* are capable of establishing a creative space for the viewer by aligning our look with that of the victims of an ever-shrinking experiential avenue. Blouin then shifts his attention to a second category of films, most notably *The Incredible Burt Wonderstone* (Dan Cardino, 2014), where the extraction of value is made directly via one's body, human flesh and blood turned into spectacle, and wonderment created through brutal manipulation. The culmination of Blouin's analysis is Christopher Nolan's *The Prestige* (2006), a film that "considers the current ubiquity of the biopolitical dilemma."[13] The film, through several iterations of neoliberal bio-power—Angier's multiplication of his own body, Borden's masochistic creations for purely personal gain, and Tesla's predatory experiments extracting energy from unconsenting villagers—invites "spectators to identify with the magician as a fellow laborer rather than a savior."[14] Such films also demonstrate the potential to orchestrate a move from sovereign biopower to communal biopolitics—that is to say, the power *of* life itself identified by Hardt and Negri's affirmative biopolitics—away from the neoliberal reproduction of lack, scarcity, and impoverishment that leads to schizophrenic results of mutilation, fragmentation, disunity. In Blouin's reading, biopower is coextensive with neoliberalism, while a collective, solidarizing act of realization is the only viable solution to deploy a biopolitics of liberation. The risk of this extreme conflation between the cinematic magic and the "neoliberal illusion" as understood as a magical-symbolic system is the total effacement of political autonomy in the face of economic demands, one criticism already brought forward by Esposito against Negri's system: "Negri tends to superimpose the question of the political on that of work and production, and basically remains adherent to the same liberal paradigm that he wants to criticize, in the sense that it ends up eliminating any element of specificity of the political."[15] In this same vein, a more nuanced interpretation is that of film scholar Dimitris Papanikolaou, who illuminates the medicalization of Greece as a moribund patient of the EU's technocratic architecture. The author emphasizes how the country's condition of deep crisis, from which austerity measures emerged that directly related individual survival to the general management of the population, and the country's concurrent refugee emergency, which accelerated the implementation of camp-like protocols, precipitated Greece into a textbook situation "in which the bodies of people, their disciplining and function, the anatomo-politics of the human body in a spectacular and very public fashion came to be intertwined with the metaphorical constructions of the national body in crisis and with the biopolitics of (a) population."[16] Papanikolaou offers an in-depth analysis of a number of contemporary filmmakers who have responded to the perceived inadequacy of Theo Angelopoulos's high modernism to represent the complexity and the issues such as "exclusion, marginalization, loneliness and abuse" of an EU-affiliated Greece.[17] Papanikolaou regards Yorgos Lanthimos's *Dogtooth* (*Kynodontas*, 2009), which explores the disciplinarian nature of the Greek family, as a biopolitically realist work that intertwines several allegories—of entrapment, of biopower, of docility—which "are managed and mismanaged, transported and repositioned" and then "short-circuit and are put to use again, often in a different direction."[18] By exasperating and breaking up the allegorical circuitry, Lanthimos opens a political dimension, orchestrating "assemblages inside and outside its frame," creating intensities that question the responsibility and the affect toward twitching bodies conditioned by biopolitical rationalities.[19]

Michael Haneke's brutal explorations of the generative mechanisms of violence and power have led him to be one of the more recognized "biopolitical filmmakers." According to Garrett Stewart, *Hidden* (*Caché*, 2005) and *Amour* (2012) exemplify the "analytic of gesture" and its capacity for opening a delay, a trace of discontinuance in the processes of identification.[20] Stewart demonstrates how the protagonist of *Hidden*—Georges, a media personality whose ownership over the image in all its manipulative splendor indexes the colonizing, erasing activity of the bourgeoisie—is remediated by the visual in an ethically charged reversal when he begins to receive mysterious videotapes that indicate his family is being watched. This inciting incident leads to a proliferation of perspectives and optics that erupt from the actualization of the virtual. *Amour*, on the other hand, utilizes the "purely graphic" and virtual dimension of the painted image "as itself a metaphor for lifelessness, the world finalized in its similitude," a suture to a dormant episode, to an unseen event.[21] Haneke's is a poetics of vacillation and refusal, its images persisting in a state of unassigned sense, propelled by arrested virtualities through which cinema is turned into "the potential for an absolute absence to be made manifest," its gestural ambiguity conveyed by the non-linguistic, the unintentional, the obstructive.[22] In his analysis of *The White Ribbon* (*Das Weiße Band—Eine Deutsche Kindergeschichte*, 2009), Kevin Wynter uses Agamben's conceptual apparatus to uncover the ways in which structures of power filiate their own retributive rituals—a liturgy of violence that will eventually supersede and surpass in cruelty the patriarchal rule from which it emanates.[23] Wynter reads the events depicted in *The White Ribbon*—the patriarchs' repressive circuitry of discipline, the children's acts of terrorism as a response to said discipline, the disavowal of the children's responsibility—as a refraction of sovereign power, via its arbitrary amplifications and overreach as well as the continuous integration of exceptions into its domain. Within the interplay between punishers and punished the scholar culls one crucial aspect through which the entire tectonics of retribution can be explored: In the context of Benjamin's explanation of State violence as a self-preserving economy, Wynter designates the monopolistic nature of the sanctions in the intentions of the adults as the monad through which *The White Ribbon* can be interpreted. Wynter argues that the cooperative and performative aspects of the corporal punishment on display in Haneke's film are decisive factors that confirm and sustain a patriarchal—and quite literally proto-fascistic—rule that cannot admit that acts of violence may exist "outside the purview of the law" because in that case "such an arrangement would essentially reveal that the symbolic power of the punisher is illusory."[24] Benjamin features prominently also in Jeong's elegant analysis of mythic and divine violence in global cinema.[25] Jeong's reading of Benjamin hinges on the German philosopher's critique of the law-making violence that institutes systems of power. Opposed to this type of violence, which can also function as a mythical form of punishment to preserve differences and create demarcations, there is a transformational, purifying, "divine" violence, one whose ends are unknowable and whose scope exists outside legality. The scholar sees a competition between these two unstable types of violence in films such as Christopher Nolan's *The Dark Knight Rises* (2012), in which Batman appoints himself as "a sovereign agent of mythical violence" and as a neoliberal, individualistic problem-solver against Bane's ambiguous but anarchically unconditioned divine violence.[26] Power, writes Jeong, is at the basis of the law and sacrifices life to preserve order, producing bare life and *homines sacri* in its operation, whereas authentic and infinite justice may entail blood but it creates death to discover, enhance, and complete life. Thinking with Žižek, Jeong sees an affirmative stabilization of divine violence in the supreme act of retribution carried out by Grace (played by Nicole Kidman) in Lars von Trier's *Dogville* (2003), in which the spectator witnesses a ruthless but merciful revenge that "exceeds the natural limitations of life and embodies an unconditional drive toward the yet-to-come domain of love."[27] Jeong examines the character of divine violence that informs Joshua Oppenheimer's *The Act of Killing* (2012), a documentary in which the brutal anticommunist massacres that occurred in Indonesia in the 1960s following the Suharto coup are reenacted by its perpetrators, including Anwar Congo, one of the leaders of the death squads. For Jeong, these reenactments are not analytically or politically justifiable since, "in the present, they happily reenact the very past act(ing) of killing," an act that reveals and fulfills their "long-repressed desire to be openly acknowledged for their contribution to [their] nation."[28] Jeong notes the crucial irony that, before joining the pro-Suharto paramilitary, Congo and his friends sold movie tickets on the black market; they were even "cinephiles of sorts," drawing on American genre filmmaking (among these are Westerns and gangster films) to narrate their own atrocities, laundering "the act of killing" by transforming it into just that, an act—an entertaining spectacle in the same manner that American Westerns justify and aestheticize colonial violence. As Jeong puts it, "Anwar's squad thus advocates their massacre from a hegemonic viewpoint, reconfirming that a successful coup is unpunishable, as it is no longer an illegal revolt but a law-making revolution." True divine violence in the Benjaminian sense does not exist, Jeong claims, only an ethically questionable "pseudo-divine violence" that nevertheless, as Jeong says, "we may not deny that our nations would not have existed without." True divine violence does not exist; there are only fantasies "of the self as the savior of one's community and the fantasy about the other as the threat to eradicate."[29]

Similarly, Ari Folman's *Waltz with Bashir* (*Vals im Bashir*, 2008), in which one is confronted with the specters of slaughtered Palestinian families of the Sabra and Shatila camps massacre, depicts the emergence of trauma as "guilt for not having recognized their potential sanctity of life as a universal humanity yet to come."[30] The author concludes his review of violence in global cinema by assessing the biopolitical illuminations that the analyzed films represent—the discovery and revelation of the "divinity within humanity."[31] An explicitly biopolitical approach that takes into account the irrepressible excess of life as affect is that of Elena del Río in her essay on Haneke's *Code Unknown* (*Code inconnu: Récit incomplet de divers voyages*, 2000), which she expands on in a book chapter on Carlos Reygadas's *Battle in Heaven* (*Batalla en el cielo*, 2005).[32] The author contends that Haneke's depiction of contemporary life as a nightmare overregulated by passwords and codes is coterminous with an advanced biopolitical regime that has graduated from discipline to control. In the wake of (and in contrast to) Steven Shaviro's *Post-Cinematic Affect*, del Río argues that affects cannot be readily and seamlessly turned into currency—instead, they "function in a double modality, simultaneously as effects of biopolitical subjection and expressions that exceed biopolitical calculation."[33] At the intersection of the affirmative potentialities of a Deleuzian-Spinozist ethology of affects and Agamben's diagnosis of the biopolitical reduction of the human to bare life, del Río demonstrates how Haneke's film is an account of hermeneutic and communicative failures—through faciality, corporeality, gestural diversions—a diagnosis of biopolitical effects on both excluded and included populations. When private spaces are regulated by overcoding and life is appraised in terms of economic and financial capacity, del Río says, the production of bare life concerns not only immigrants and other subaltern categories but potentially every citizen. Del Río identifies the emergence of an immanent consciousness, a pervasive and operative singularity that exceeds the fictional stability with the capacity for affective resistance against biopolitical homogenization. Similarly, in Reygadas's picture, "attention to life entails an impersonal, immanent gift beyond politics and beyond the dispossessing acts and effects of biopower."

According to del Río, Mexico City and other metropolises "transform the spatially regimented model of the camp by giving rise to multiple degrees and modalities of bare life that escape scrutiny and are far harder to detect."[34] At stake, del Río writes, is understanding "the difference between life as vital, resisting expressivity and bare life as the product of biopolitical control."[35] The scholar sees the relationship between Marcos the indigenous proletarian and Ana the upper-class general's daughter as life caught in an untamable immanence and as "a challenge to the controlling, territorializing operations of biopower and to the way these are channeled through the urban space," although Reygadas may be suggesting that their connection is simply a futile diversion within mercenary circuits of assimilation, since it is hinted that Ana is selling sex.[36] The fact that the audience is not made privy to Ana's motivation (it is unlikely out of need, but neither is it explicitly out of boredom) catalyzes the deterritorialization of desire as a category of control. Drawing on Deleuze's aesthetics of the pure event, del Río arrives as a "politics of attentiveness" by virtue of which the gestural emerges as vital singularity "via a slow editing rhythm, an equally slow and deliberate moving camera, and extreme close-ups that magnify the smallest details and movements of the body."[37] Such devices highlight the contrast between affective life and life as lived through a reflexive, subjectified, and all-filtering consciousness that makes itself the exclusive and therefore debilitating measure of experience. Through Deleuze's concept of impersonality, del Río bridges Agamben's notion of bare life with Deleuze's vitalism by acknowledging the affirmative excess of life generated by exclusion in the former and by a "consuming" immanence in the latter. It is worth noting that the characters in both of the films analyzed by del Río dwell in metropoles in which several neighborhoods are covered and sealed by walls of surveillance cameras seamlessly stretching from streets to businesses to public and private buildings, locations that seem to naturally stage revolt—inurement, if not addiction, to capturing mechanisms of discipline and control. An ingenious use of similar locales can be seen in two recent films by Kleber Mendonça Filho, *Neighboring Sounds* (*O som ao redor*, 2012) and *Aquarius* (2016) and, further afield, Bong Joon Ho's *Influenza* (2004), in which life oscillates between *bíos* and *zoē*, between potentiality and something not-yet-fully qualified. Bong's film presents the downward spiral of a traveling salesman in Seoul, who loses his job and resorts to more and more violent crimes. His story is told through surveillance, spy, security, and closed-circuit cameras, in split-screens and all sorts of black and white or color(ized) images, at different resolutions and through an unevenly paced editing. Thus, argues Marco Dalla Gassa, "far from representing the panoptic arm of society that surveils and punishes, superintends and prevents, the whole of the CCTV camera offers itself as an iconosphere inside of which the institution smugly and unflappably attends the show of increasing barbarization."[38] The viewer is thus situated in an uncomfortable position: are the protagonists' seemingly uncontrollable acts of hysterical paroxysm excerpts from newsfeeds, documentary footage, dramatic entertainment, unavowable scopophilic pleasure? Probably a mélange of all the above, and a necessary spectacle of and respite from a hostile society that finds it harder and harder to transfigure the violence on which it is based.

Studies on specific genres as relevant to define the biopolitical anatomopathology of nations have emerged, such as Carla Marcantonio's reading of modern melodrama, particularly the allusion to the reach of modern sovereignty in Pedro Almodóvar's *Talk to Her* and *The Skin I Live In*.[39] There, Marcantonio shows how the almost obscene vitality of Almodóvar's bodies are used to chart the continuous reduction of life to its organic substratum and their concurrent uncanny, never fully explored expressivity. The medicalized processes depicted in the films, Marcantonio argues, probe the biopolitical intensity of the modern body and "open up the possibility of critiquing not just national parameters, but those of modern sovereignty as such."[40] Another, centered on Esposito's doctrine of immunity, is carried out by Robert A. Rushing in his comprehensive probing of the Italian *peplum* as well as other, more recent, cloak-and-dagger pictures.[41] After a painstaking narratological examination, Rushing convincingly argues that the peplum is a genre dominated by the biopolitical paradigm of immunity, which, hiding in plain sight in the peplum tropes, is "above all, immunity from a symbolic, social, and economic castration, a protective sheath of skin without any clefts or fissures."[42] The genre, characterized by its "reliance on slowed or even stopped time to accommodate the spectator's admiring and lingering gaze on the hero's muscled body," its "queer refusal of sexuality, situating itself in a psychic time either before or after desire," and a "seductive expanse of skin" make it a privileged mediator between politics and vitality.[43] Taken to a logical extreme, the immunitarian rationality toward an auto-immunitarian reaction by virtue of which the organism decides to annihilate itself, *pepla* become thanatological, even genocidal, vehicles: "the perfect male body, which stands as a bulwark against the outside, can find its absolute perfection only in death."[44] Since it is "produced at the intersection of the biopolitical and the psycho-analytic," the peplum unleashes a totalizing resentment against not just queering elements whose supposed contaminating potential can drain life out of communities, but against "modernity, effeminacy, civilization, tolerance," and any other phenomena that can generate difference.[45] It adopts the imperative of the antibody and ends up extending the zone of indistinction characterized by bare life to all the other organisms, leading to a protocol of self-cannibalization. Through a similar approach, combining psychoanalysis, biopolitics, and Slavoj Žižek's notion of "ideological fantasy," Hilary Neroni looks at the representation and interpretation of torture in several genres such as documentary, horror, and fictional reenactments of historical events in film and television.[46] The scholar investigates the patterns that emerge after September 11, 2001: Torture is the catalyst of assumptions of the body as a repository of truth, a body from which information can be mined, thereby generating whole rationalities to extract information. Neroni distinguishes two versions of the body: One "manifests itself in the official or accepted justification for torture" and is therefore a biopolitical source; the other "emerges in the failure of the practice of torture to align itself completely with the official justification," and from this misalignment emerges the psychoanalytic subject.[47] By activating two radically different politics, this dual conceptualization of the body also triggers different representations, since desire is irreducible to biological impulses. Such representations "provide the foundation for the contemporary torture fantasy and for the possibility of articulating an alternative that might disrupt this fantasy."[48] The author critiques Foucault's dismissal of psychoanalysis and his suspicion of the idea of the subject as a viable weapon against biopower by affirming that the French philosopher did not see the risk in privileging the ontology of the body—a position that invites practices centered exclusively on the body, among them torture. Neroni is equally skeptical of Negri and Hardt's concept of the multitude, a theorization about the flight from biopower but firmly grounded, Neroni states, in biopower itself: The distinction that the multitude is supposedly capable of bringing about is nothing other than a false perspective, one in which there is no "room for the subject's desire to either undermine [biopolitics] or propel it toward a revolutionary change."[49] Instead, Neroni establishes an affinity with Agamben for his Schmittian emphasis, *contra* Foucault, of the sovereign as the continued "nexus of political power, a power located in the proclamation of the state of emergency."[50] Most importantly, according to Neroni, is Agamben's insistence that the "stripping down to bare life is a constant process, one that therefore can be resisted . . . [opening] up the possibility for creating a contemporary political being that is not reducible to its bare life."[51] For Neroni, depictions of torture in contemporary media are significant because it lays bare the fantasy of the body "as the source of information that explains its own actions"—that is to say, the fantasy of torture is the extraction of truth that verifies and rationalizes the perpetration of violence. Torture, in other words, works as a necessary measure to "size up" a body in order to return it to a biopolitical domain. This is why, Neroni writes, biopolitics cannot undo what biopower implemented: That way, "any insistence on the body as the site of resistance sees a power structure where an ideological structure is actually at work."[52] This, Neroni warns, is the danger of biopolitics, which risks confirming "the system it is trying to contest."[53] Neroni thus stresses the urgency of "seeing the subject instead of a body," which "is the only true barrier to torture."[54]

Campbell offers a different perspective in his work on the biopolitical textures of modernist Italian cinema and its regenerative investment in a form-of-life "who avoids mastery and being mastered because it has opted to grip less."[55] Rather than pursue a direct investigation into the relationship between the apparatus and governmental rationalities, Campbell instead makes a foray into the cinematically rendered effects that a milieu and its layout of forces have wrought on bodies, at the same time providing a framework for an Italian visual thought.[56] Thinking with Derrida's and other philosophies of the gift, and arriving at the monastic—as explored by Agamben in *The Highest Poverty*—as an alternate form-of-life, Campbell contemplates the possibility of a truly emancipatory exchange, one that sees beyond the horizon of the produced thing and does not entrap the participants in a reciprocity that always carries a value with itself. Evoking the figure of the *mancus*, or he who is without hands, Campbell notes a form of resistance in the generosity and gratitude depicted in postwar Italian cinema, especially in films by

Antonioni, Rossellini, and Visconti, who "use the cinematic apparatus to make visible how non-grasping is possible" and, by disengaging cinema from reciprocity, "push the spectator to an identification with a lack that is not her own."[57] Writing of Visconti's *The Earth Trembles* (*La terra trema*, 1948), Campbell stipulates for cinema "the possibility of a commonality between the anthropomorphic potential of the non-actor and of the spectator herself," endowing the cinematic *dispositif* with an affirmative, empowering potential to see the tragedy of failed individuations.[58] Mythic violence underpins Visconti's notion of a salvation that cannot be achieved individually, since the fishermen do not have the necessary distance to intuit themselves as different forms-of-life. Following Jacques Rancière's interpretation of the suicide of Edmund, Rossellini's protagonist in *Germany Year Zero* (*Germania anno zero*, 1948), as an act of both rebellious and responsible self-discovery, Campbell defines Edmund's death as an act of "failed reciprocity" that engenders a newfound awareness of a world in which gratitude is no longer an option so long as giving is opportunistic and transactional.[59] Finally, Campbell turns his attention to Antonioni and more specifically to Monica Vitti, whose "command and evasion of the cinematic apparatus" is understood as a reflection on the connection with the presence of things and the sense of their ownership.[60] In *L'avventura* (1960), through "a phenomenology of different holds, grasps, clenches, fingerings, and touch," Campbell suggests that Antonioni uses a series of transitional objects to register different stages of (more or less illusory) emotionality.[61] Antonioni's non-hierarchical order of images trigger a fetishism that the director keeps at bay by immersing the viewer in a state of uncertain, unfulfilled negotiation whereby cinema abandons a human perspective to rehearse its own stories. In *L'eclisse* (1962), for example, Monica Vitti evades the grip of the financial and cinematic *dispositifs* by embracing vulnerability and alienation: Her ontological status "is not contained or named in a becoming (of animal, of plant, of woman), but rather is markedly different from that form that becomes,"[62] a manifestation of triumphant actuality. Campbell concludes his analysis by noting that, across these films, endings are never definitive; thus, if openness is given as an always present option, their political diagnoses are less desperate than one may expect.

As Maria Muhle has observed in the over-exhibited artificiality of the post-melodramas of Douglas Sirk, Rainer Werner Fassbinder, and Todd Haynes, by creating a textbook governmentally approved definition of life, the filmic melodrama introduces "life as the medium of efforts of formation that it performs on itself."[63] Since cinema offers schemata, produces subjects whose act of contemplation is already inscribed in an inoffensive sociality (or lack thereof), and provides the illusion of recomposition, this book will look at the ways in which the fabrication of truth and of set identities, the translation of political technologies of disempowerment to the visual, and the implementation of life-shaping protocols of inclusion and exclusion are deployed critically in films in which conflict is not neutralized, in which a certain consciousness is displayed and then executes an accepting or a confrontational move. Within this conflict, the subject gains or approaches an understanding of a biopolitical reality that traverses the lines between action and stasis, rebellion and acquiescence, qualified life and bare life.

Modern political thinking is premised on a biopolitical matrix and contemporary biopolitical processes foreground our current individual and collective experience: Political and biological life tend to coincide through production and pleasure, presided over by economies of value together with their logics of optimization and extraction, in regimes where constructional social imaginaries, reinforced by the visual, are part of the biopolitical governance. One can witness a decisive biopolitical turn in world cinema, meaning that the visual articulations of said processes show and define new practices of power, novel processes of subjectivation, and organic forms of coexistence. The films engaging in this struggle show the effects, claims, and counterstrategies, the demands for recognition resulting from devices of regulation and domination as well as experimental ways to found communities where one can *feel* human. Said films, albeit not explicitly adhering to an artistic school or aesthetic movement, still form a cohesive, collaborated body of works by providing examples of biopolitical exposure and distribution. By modulating in different magnitudes the affects and consequences of the biopolitical condition, they help us understand and experience the foundations of the logic of sovereignty, the shifting border between the expanding and the receding in power trajectories, the layers and layers of introjected mechanisms of discipline, the creative and dehumanizing forms of subjugation that instrumentally resurface in order to instill docility into the population. These films think alike in terms of biopolitical preoccupations but maintain stimulating differences even when they engage in the same issues, such as the collision between governmental rationality and freedom, range of political action, and the unintended consequences of biopolitical techniques. Placing the films in dialogue with the scholarship uncovers how a reduction to the biological is an always open possibility; assesses how protocols of seizure and deprivation transform into policies of optimization and restructuring vital forces; shows economic models and a neo-imperial rule that stands for a new form of sovereignty in which vital efforts are subjugated to the law of flexible accumulation; and demonstrates how basic concepts such as security and freedom can only be fully comprehended within a logic of immunity. The biopolitical visual experience not only elicits a philosophical reaction in terms of issues that have become familiar preoccupations but presents itself as an array of exercises in philosophizing insofar as they engage in world-building and think systematically during its construction. Biopolitical readings provide the visual basis for epistemic intensities of negotiation and polarization. If we hold cinema responsible for the reversal of the mimetic deduction between the image and the real and for turning perception into a schizophrenic act of performance, then we must firmly place the medium in a biopolitical protocol. Its protean materiality or lack thereof has become a perfect complement to produce uniformity and homogeneity: Cinema becomes part of a biopolitical instrumentation inasmuch as it exacerbates a certain condition of separation and perceptive forgetfulness.

Rethinking the political as a limit and as a threshold of intensification through world cinema may seem an elusive if not prohibitive task—the very concept of world cinema sometimes resonates as too vague, reductionist, or even haughty in its fraught relationship with Hollywood. A productive way to think of world cinema—without provincializing or defining it in contrast to hegemonic Hollywood cinema—is as a polycentric hub through which cinematic forms are distributed and made available, concurrently generating their own theories and discourses that may challenge canonized approaches, but also as a connection-pursuing practice.[64]

A collision/collapse of political and biological life, understanding biopower as the operative force of contemporaneity, seems the most honest way to stay in touch with the real, turning to the archival breadth of contemporary films to look at the ways in which they register the emergence of new forms of power that mold and manage the living. While avoiding a constraining superimposition of theoretical grids on individual works, this analysis will focus on the idiosyncratic ways in which cinema offers and makes accessible the biopolitical experience and the interconnections of different forms-of-life. If "aesthetic media . . . are uniquely equipped to register, and give symbolic and imaginative expression to, this imbrication of bodies, mind, and power," then film is geared to capture the uncontainable reactions within the fabric of socio-organic transformations.[65] To diagnose the ways in which film thinks about power means to look at how sovereign power, with its banning and excluding attributes, coexists with, and is mutually influenced by, life-fostering practices. Biopolitics as a theoretical development has only recently emerged as analytics with which to diagnose the effects of neoliberalism: In its most compelling forms, contemporary world cinema develops ways of looking at, and representing, biopolitical effects, reacting and responding to neogovernmental projects. The question of power is recurring in the most recent epistemological hypotheses or "turns": Thomas Elsaesser speaks of an ontological turn generating ubiquitous evidences across which characters externalize their subjectivity and consciousness and materializing orders and conventions so that new forms and agreements can be negotiated from an empowered audience; Sinnerbrink posits an "ethical turn"[66] as a most productive engagement through which films not only experiment with theories of morality or political thinking but could also serve as performative vehicles offering transformative options; Nagib interprets world cinema as a manifestation of non-reactive, propositional expressions informed by "an ethics of the real."[67]

Papanikolaou, Sinnerbrink, and Nagib respectively offer three outstanding models for the present study, as well as points of departure. Papanikolaou brilliantly articulates his vision of "biopolitical realism," but this is explicitly represented as a more concretely political analogue to Mark Fisher's capitalism realism rather than to a specific cinematic tradition, although he does nod to Greek realist films, such as those by Theo Angelopoulos.[68] In his book, Papanikolaou emphasizes that his thesis of biopolitical realism is "conceptual rather than cinematic realism";[69] to the extent that he does engage with cinematic realism, his notion of biopolitical realism is squarely predicated on "the weird" as a tone and affect, a "diffuse cultural modality." Unlike Sinnerbrink and Nagib, Papanikolaou focuses on a specific phenomenon within contemporary Greek cinema and its relationship to the country's financial crisis and other political struggles, but one that nonetheless gestures toward "further expansion and different critical openings."[70] For Sinnerbrink, cinema is "a medium of ethical experience"; for Nagib, "world cinema" is "realist cinema." *The Biopolitical Turn in World Cinema* is influenced by the work of these critics; it seeks to engage with and further develop their insights and, at the same time, offer a new perspective firmly anchored in both biopolitical philosophy and film studies. Like Nagib, I explore the definition of "world cinema," an ambiguous and frankly apophatically defined term; like Papanikolaou I examine what a cinema of biopolitics might mean; and like Sinnerbrink, I understand the ethical dimensions of this line of inquiry. But where Nagib finds her definition of world cinema in realism, and where Papanikolaou focuses on the biopolitical realism of recent Greek cinema, this book identifies world cinema as biopolitical cinema. If, as Nagib eloquently argues, world cinema is "committed to reality . . . not as a mere construct or discourse" but as composed of living beings ("people, animals, plants and objects") capable of suffering and dying, this book regards biopolitical experience as the defining experience of creaturely life across the globe.[71]

Like biopower itself, biopolitical cinema is capable of accommodating a wide range of forms; it does not transcend class, gender, nationality, or even genre, but anchors them in a world defined by power. However, this book considers biopolitical cinema as a sort of counter-*dispositif* rather than a priori a medium of discipline and control. Instead, it animates and enacts a mediation of biopolitics and cinema through images and narratives of forms-of-life as they fluctuate, struggle, morph, reemerge, and evolve, as they are constrained and contained by the logic of biopower, which they seek—and succeed, even if only fleetingly—to interrogate, interrupt, and exceed. It is a form of realism that holds in tension the extractive nature of biopolitical management (bare life, capture, exploitation, reduction) at the level of plot and script in addition to the biopolitical foundations of cinema as such; the lines of flight and fractures in cinematic and biopolitical *dispositifs* that dialectically open up new forms-of-life and subjectivities. Put more simply, "biopolitical cinema" names cinema's immanent capacity to counter biopower and its strategies of consensus and adaptability. In the balance of life-shaping protocols of inclusion and exclusion, a governmental rule by design constantly questions itself to mold expectations, manufacture compliance, and evaluate which forms can be more readily introjected and not acquire too much of a life of their own. A functional state-crafting rationality will be able to create grids in which citizens will feel involved, protocols in which individuals will enjoy the illusion of seizing the ghost of political participation. The proud, affirmative thanatopolitics[72] of Maksim Brius and Leonid Plyaskin's *Zoya* (2020)[73] and Fedor Bondarchuk's *Stalingrad* (2013)[74] are, among others, figural anticipations of the Dubrovka massacre by which Russian lives acquire value only insofar as they serve the preservation of the country's elites; the joyful production of neoliberal subjectivities and the enlistment of biological life in contemporary Indian cinema[75] as an accompanying document to monitor the financialization and commercialization of social mobility beyond macroeconomic data; Pixar's *WALL-E* (Andrew Stanton, 2008),[76] in which the decay of a civilization turned into an issue of individual morality lends itself to a sinister interpretation, for example that the exchange of a functioning welfare state and healthcare for the latest technological gadgets[77] stand at one of the extremes.

In this book, I analyze different films that engage at different levels and with different levels of awareness of biopolitical strategies that are creatively compounded in active processes of ruling by design, constantly adapting to new social and economic situations and geared toward epistemic production and the sanctioning of set identities—in short, in the production and management of predictable forms-of-life. In the double movement between form and norm—sometimes a collision, sometimes a dialectical encounter—it is thinkable to unlock the potential for affirmative consistencies in the relation of power to life, thinking with Agamben in terms of potency and resistance works in visual terms. Compared to Foucault, Agamben's approach is decidedly transhistorical, reading biopower as the horizon of Western political thought, embedded in the dominant model of sovereign power. Following Carl Schmitt's definition of sovereignty, Agamben affirms that, through the state of exception, the sovereign continuously manufactures situations that the law uses to justify its own validity. And sovereignty also supposes that the validity of the legal order implies that a demarcation can be established between an inside and an outside of the law, that is to say, between what is included and what is outside the legal order, since the law is justified precisely by that outside, by that state natural, non-social, pre-political, violent, which seeks to repress, eliminate, exclude. *The Jackal of Nahueltoro* by Miguel Littín (*El chacal de Nahueltoro*, 1969) is a study of the irrelevance of the law when an illiterate and uneducated man, "a third-class peasant," as he is called in the film, encounters power. Incarcerated and sentenced to death for the murder of a woman and her five children, the crime becomes an uncertain memory, if not a hallucination altogether. Like Nagisa Ōshima's *Death by Hanging* (*Kōshikei*, 1968), where the Korean prisoner R must be collectively executed to safeguard the notion of Japaneseness in its imperialist and necropolitical meanings, the existence of Jorge del Carmen Valenzuela Torres, the nominal "jackal" of the film, is one that cannot be integrated, but that can serve as an example of the institutional and governmental capacity to produce racialized docile bodies. On the one hand, it is true that "the lack of social care, the lack of a safety net within society . . . leads to the production of individuals such as the Jackal," but the film seems more interested in what might be called post-production, the process of transformation from one from form-of-life to bare life, in which education and citizenship mask the capture of life by the juridical apparatus.[78] The "jackal's" preposterous inclusion is possible only because of his imminent death (figures 1.1 and 1.2).

Figure 1.1. The State as the producer of inclusive death. *Source:* Miguel Littín, dir., *The Jackal of Nahueltoro* (1969; Terra Entertainment, 2006), DVD, 576p.

Figure 1.2. The State as the producer of inclusive death. *Source:* Miguel Littín, dir., *The Jackal of Nahueltoro* (1969; Terra Entertainment, 2006), DVD, 576p.

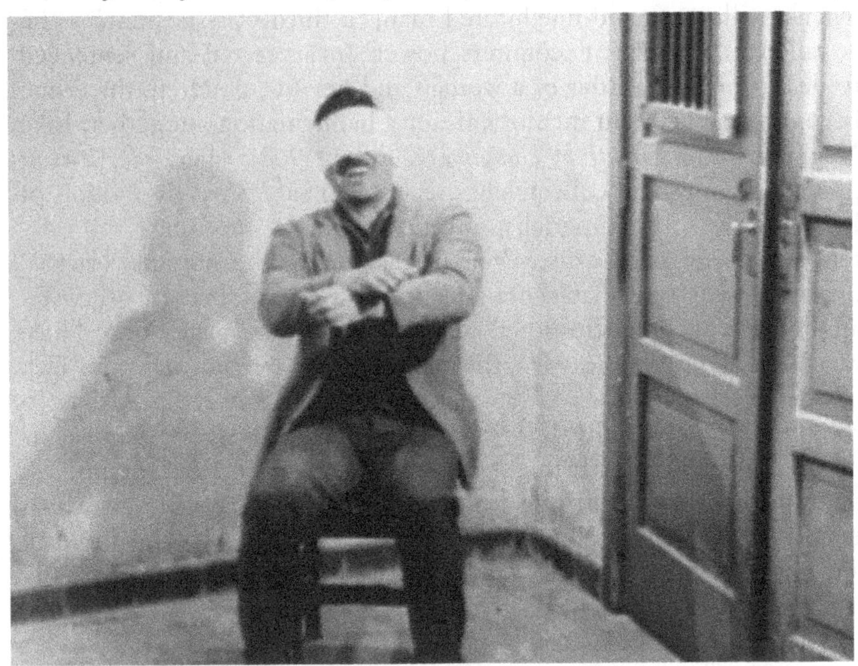

For Agamben, violence becomes instrumental in the generation of power when a constituent power is the one and only legitimized foundation of a constituted power. Violence becomes a relational tool that informs societal order and functions as the divide between the two powers, one generating a separated other as its negative double—or, in the philosopher's words, "true constituent power is not that which produces a constituted power separated from itself."[79] Power will then rewrite biology and deprive man of his natural activities, of productive work, and of the possibility of communicating. The "jokes" uttered by the libertines from Pier Paolo Pasolini's *Salò, or the 120 Days of Sodom* (*Salò o le 120 giornate di Sodoma*, 1975) come to mind, their apparent pointlessness and absurdity implying the negation of the communicative sphere and the expropriation of language, processed and ingested like one's own waste (figures 1.3 and 1.4).

Figure 1.3. The thanatopolitical language of entertainment: the corpse of a young woman contrasted with a wistful joke told by a Fascist hierarch. *Source:* Pier Paolo Pasolini, dir., *Salò, or the 120 Days of Sodom* (1975; The Criterion Collection, 2011), Blu-ray Disc, 1080p HD.

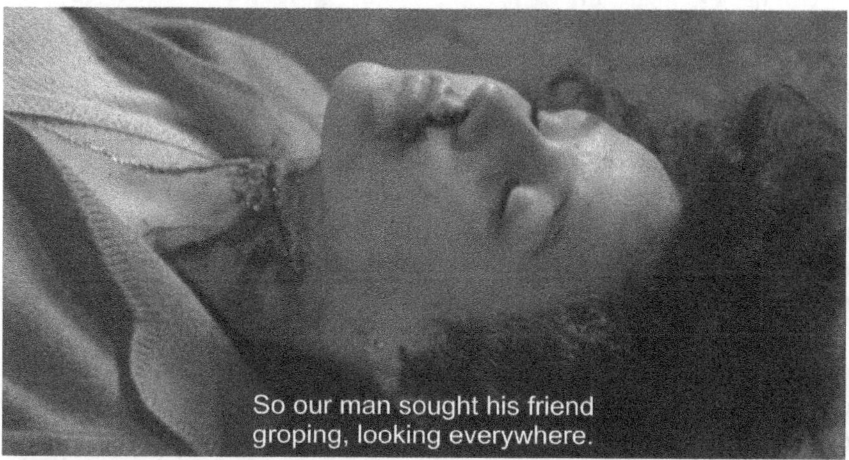

Figure 1.4. The thanatopolitical language of entertainment: A Fascist hierarch pulls at the corners of his mouth with his two index fingers, dirty with feces, as if to make a funny face. *Source:* Pier Paolo Pasolini, dir., *Salò, or the 120 Days of Sodom* (1975; The Criterion Collection, 2011), Blu-ray Disc, 1080p HD.

For the law to be able to prescribe and order, it must calibrate the scope of its capture of life to successfully intervene in and normalize it. But if the strength of the law depends on the relationship of exception, if the application of the right depends on its disapplication, then Agamben says the life that is implicated in its sphere can only be so through the presupposition of a relationship of inclusive exclusion. This means that life is only included by exclusion in law, or that it is only included as naked life, as a threshold that is found simultaneously inside and outside the legal system. Agamben proposes a playful interaction with the law as a way to overcome its transactional pervasiveness, something more far-reaching than just a modification of its letter "since the exception has revealed that the normal functioning of law depends on violent force."[80] Such gratuitous toying with the law can be conceived in terms of Walter Benjamin's concept of violence, but completely disengaged from political ends. An example of this disinterested violence can be found in the pre-finale of Clint Eastwood's *Unforgiven* (1992). At first glance, the massacre carried out by William Munny appears justified by the bounty he is trying to honor, but it soon morphs into an unwarranted act of divine violence—divine like Munny's act of vengeance itself, his specter-like presence in the scene and his superhuman prowess in the duel—whose goal is not to replace law but to bring justice and rediscover humanity. Its counterpart is the moment when Tom Doniphon kills Liberty Valance in the John Ford film from 1962, a disenchanted acknowledgment of the fraudulent nature of "just," law-creating violence (and a dubious way to compensate for the exclusion of African Americans from the myth of the frontier). According to Agamben, democracy does not suppress the assumption of a sacred life but rather ceases to conceive it as a subject, as bearer of sovereignty. This, however, can only entail a contradiction, because at the time it is intended to free the individual from subjection to sovereign power, recognizing his individual liberties, he is once again subjected to the logic of sovereignty, to the repeat the relationship of exception, isolating in it a bare life. Agamben sees a sovereign weaponization of the identification between "man" and citizen, none more evident than in the plight of the refugee. It is also through the refugee and the idea of a state mediation necessary to confer rights that Agamben separates himself from Hannah Arendt, according to whom "human rights can only be recognised within a national polity and can only be realised alongside citizenship or membership within an established political community."[81] A film like Gianfranco Rosi's *Fire at Sea* (*Fuocoammare*, 2016) presents the vulnerability of the migrants trying to cross the Mediterranean and disembark on Italian soil, but also the constant state of negotiation that the encounter with a precarious life sets in motion, and the goals pursued by the State and its officials. Rosi does not directly focus on the transition camps for migrants as sites of exclusion where the uncertainty of the law can lead to violence, but he masterfully orchestrates a spectrum of differing durations—the personnel working in the camp, the migrants, their rescuers, a family living on the island—to show with restrained participation that tragedies cannot be sealed, their agonies ever expanding. Rather than understanding democracy as a constituent process of the political body, Agamben probes it as a governmental technique with its shifting definition of that which should be considered human. If politics has been founded on the assumption of a bare life, this would have to do with the fact that, throughout Western thought, the life-in-common of men has always been thought in terms of identity, that is, in terms of inclusion, of belonging to a life, to a *bíos* according to which men should be able to perform as such.

Identity, the power to establish a condition of belonging, is a constitutive presupposition of the State; in other words, one cannot speak of the State without establishing a condition of identity or belonging. But if this is so, Agamben proposes, it is because the notion of State implies the logic of sovereignty and, therefore, the relationship of exception, and therefore inclusion, or belonging to the political community, supposes, at the same time, abandonment to a power of death. Therefore, by refusing to be included, to be related through a condition of belonging or of identity, men would refuse to be abandoned to a power of death and, therefore, to be subjected to the logic of sovereignty. Hence, according to Agamben, the State cannot allow human to co-belong without claiming for themselves some condition of belonging or identity. And that is also why a politics beyond the factional relationship requires humanity to think beyond all conditions of identity or belonging, no longer as bare lives, but as forms-of-life. A film like John Frankenheimer's *Seconds* (1966) lays bare the violence of a regime in which one cannot break free from the yoke of "juridical-social identities," making the interval between prescribed human living and antagonistic form-of-life close in on itself (figure 1.5).[82]

In the crudest of terms, then, while this book has so far outlined the problematics of biopolitics, it has not yet fully explored a "solution"—if indeed there is one—to biopower's dichotomizing impulse, which separates life from itself in order to constitute the political, extractable subject. The task seems desperate enough, and even more so when the reduction to unqualified life happens horizontally and one does not even need conspiration at the institutional level to make an entire population sacrificeable, as for example in *I Saw the Devil* (*Angmareul boatda*, Kim Jee-woon, 2010), in which Korea's production of an alternate mode of justice based on personal vendetta results in turning scores of citizens into a seamless, casually expendable mass. In biologizing life and naturalizing politics, biopower is the producer, in the most cinematic sense, of images of normative identity; it casts bodies in preconceived roles as it writes a script that lays claim to reality. Moreover, while thinkers of biopolitics have launched compelling attempts to redeem life from its exposure to sovereign violence by positively investing *bíos* with political agency and redemptive potential, it often—despite itself—continues to confirm the language and his-

Figure 1.5. The etatization of life forms. *Source:* John Frankenheimer, dir., *Seconds* (1966; The Criterion Collection, 2013), Blu-ray Disc, 1080p HD.

tory of European political philosophy that provides the grounds for biopower. This reparative approach is inventive and valuable, since it emphasizes that this history and its conceptual language might be reappropriated and reinscribed in order to truly emancipate life, fulfilling the higher ideals of traditional liberalism at the same time as it critiques it—a self-reflexive operation not unlike many of the films explored in the book. However, research outside of this somewhat restricted biopolitical "canon," as it were, offers new yet complementary perspectives with which to look at the connection between life and politics, one that uproots the very grounds of binary distinctions such as *bíos/zoē*, nature/culture, subject/object, among others. Except for Esposito's more recent work, biopolitical thought tends to operate within the confines of the history of European political philosophy from Aristotle onward to Hobbes and Enlightenment *philosophes* like Rousseau, and, later, Carl Schmitt and Walter Benjamin. The reasons for this are practically self-evident, given the history of European political philosophy, which during the Enlightenment gave reason to the European colonial project as much as it gave birth to human rights discourse, a relationship that is co-constitutive, as Arendt, Foucault, Agamben, and others have long observed. Each of these thinkers is vital to the understanding of historical and contemporary biopolitics. However, it would hardly be contentious to assert that a liberatory, redemptive biopolitics will likely not be found in the work of Thomas Hobbes or Carl Schmitt. It is a question not so much of looking away from them, but of opening up to other traditions and disciplines that cross several reference points with biopolitics. This requires that non-European biopolitics be thought with alongside these continental traditions and histories, as their contributions should not, and, importantly, do not even presume to form a normative discourse on these subjects. Such a biopolitics would acknowledge humanity's relationality with itself and with the other forms-of-life in which its own existence is implicated. In order to imagine such a thing, it is necessary to look outside the (white) European and settler colonial context.[83] Critical race studies, Black feminism, environmental humanities, queer theory, Indigenous studies, and posthumanism are among some of the intellectual, political, and scholarly movements outside of the loose discipline of biopolitical thought that have made efforts to do so. Recent studies that have explored the crosscurrents between biopolitics and these other schools of thought include Alexander G.

Weheliye's *Habeas Viscus: Racializing Assemblages, Biopolitics and Black Feminist Theories of the Human* (2014); Mel Y. Chen's *Animacies: Biopolitics, Racial Mattering, and Queer Affect* (2012); *Biopolitics, Geopolitics, Life: Settler States and Indigenous Presence* (2023), edited by René Dietrich and Kerstin Knope; and Jasbir K. Puar's *The Right to Maim: Debility, Capacity, Disability* (2017).

The pathways toward thinking biopolitics beyond the limits of its more dominant Eurocentric genealogy are multiplying; they often adopt a post/decolonial perspective to investigate the racialized and gendered specificities of biopolitical domains; concurrently, there are many points of entry to a more liberatory, affirmative biopolitics. One particularly compelling pathway is the concept of animism. According to Chen, animism or animacy "activates new theoretical formations that trouble and undo stubborn binary systems of difference," including animality, which the author rightly acknowledges is often construed as the "analogue or limit" of the human, but which nevertheless occupies a "richly affective territory of mediation between life and death, positivity and negativity," and other intractable oppositions.[84] However, it must immediately be acknowledged, as Cornelius Borck does, that "animism is . . . rooted in a historical context that now appears highly problematic."[85] While the term is often used to designate indigenous or premodern religions and epistemologies, it is a colonial term coined by nineteenth-century English anthropologist Edward Burnett Tylor—and therefore ensnared in the discipline's racist, colonial origins. It is also necessary to express an aversion to the fetishization of indigenous cultures as an imperialist "fetishization of indigenous difference."[86] The aim of this conclusion's turn toward animism or animacy is not to reproduce a romantic colonial framing of indigeneity, nor to diminish the human as such, but to look toward ways of understanding life that elude some of the pitfalls of a Eurocentric philosophy of biopolitics whose attempts to trace the hierarchical divisions of life tend to end up affirming or reproducing them. Such a form of biopolitics threatens to become the only frame through which we might view life, a reel of domination and subjugation that plays over and over again until it is depoliticized, dehistoricized, regarded as an inescapable reality. This approach is drawn from Federico Luisetti's assertion of the importance of performing "Eurocentric critiques of Eurocentrism" in order to "[deconstruct] attempts to . . . reduce postcolonial perspectives to a denunciation of subalternity and marginalization."[87]

As Anselm Franke clarifies, animism is "a different name for the primacy of relationality, for social immanence."[88] Indigenous writer Louise Erdrich offers compelling example of this concept as a praxis when she relates how, for Anishinaabe elder Tobasonakwut, "His people were the lake, and the lake was them. . . . As the people lived off fish, animals, the lake's water and water plants for medicine, they were literally cell by cell composed of the lake and the lake's islands."[89] The films discussed in this book do not directly engage in traditional animistic practices, but are rather experiments in, as Neera M. Singh puts it in her article on the "non-human turn," "valuing life along and beyond capital."[90] Singh's article provides an excellent account of new directions in animist thinking, by making the compelling argument that the term "non-human turn," a relatively recent movement seeking to elude the philosophical quagmires described above, fails to take into account the "diverse approaches that take vitality and materiality of the world seriously, [or to] encourage attentiveness to deep interdependence and multispecies entanglements."[91] Instead, Singh makes the case for animism or animacy as a movement not toward "decentering the human," as non-humanism suggests, but rather "to displace Eurocentric, modern, capitalist conceptions of the human to allow other ways of being human to flourish."[92] Contemporary animism, Singh suggests, is "not about undermining human agency, but about challenging human hubris of treating the rest of the world as inert and disposable. It is about remembering that other-than-capitalist ways of being often persist despite capitalism's attempts to erase them. Life and conceptions of what it means to be human and to be alive exceed capitalism—and this power of life, or 'biopower from below,' offers grounds for resistance and reimagination."[93] Cinema is one of the grounds for this reimagination. In an essay entitled "An Animist History of the Camera," Teresa Castro writes that "contrary to the conventional understanding of animism," contemporary anthropologists like Eduardo Kohn and Eduardo Viveiros de Castro define animism not "as the (imaginative) imputing of life, soul, or agency to animals or objects: animism now stands for a particular ontology, a way of *being* in the world, whose tenets have become an essential critique of Western naturalism, with its characteristic dualism between Nature and Culture and its opposition between humans and non-humans."[94] Castro's essay, which is equally conversant with anthropology and the history of cinema, stresses early film theory's animistic conception of the camera, from Jean Epstein's 1923 assertion that "the great power of cinema is its animism" to Iris Barry's 1926 claim that cinema had reawakened "a long abandoned animism."[95] Castro does not directly discuss biopolitics in this essay, but it nonetheless demonstrates the compelling, observable bridge that animism provides between biopolitical and cinematic discourses. "The camera [is] caught within a constant exchange of properties within other human and non-human actants . . . the camera came to evolve in an in-between realm where subjectness and objectness are constantly negotiated, uniting 'the camera,' its 'operators,' and 'the spectator' in an intersensory, lived assemblage."[96] This is the redemptive flip-side of cinema as a Foucauldian *dispositif*, which I refer to in my introduction and again in chapter 3. The interdependence between the technical, the operative, and the spectatorial; the tension between the autonomy of the camera and its human operator; the animation of still images, roles, scenes, and objects; are all recognized and accorded with agentic life. This affirms and actualizes Walter Benjamin's assertion, in his famous history on translation, that "the concept of life is given its due only if everything that has a history of its own, and is not merely the setting for history, is credited with life."[97] Life is not bare, biological life; and nature is neither the backdrop to history (as with the baroque period tragedies), nor is it a violent, Hobbesian "state" out of which man leaps; likewise, history is neither a naturalized, inevitable—and therefore justifiable—outcome (teleology), nor, finally, is it a product of a destructive and unalterable "human nature" (nihilism). These are all frozen, still postures, *natures mortes*. The concept of life will *only* attain what it is owed—its freedom from biopolitical reduction and thus its full flourishing—when *everything* is recognized, not as lifeless objects or subjects of history, but as history itself, as becoming, itself. Life cannot be translated by "men" into categories or into history precisely because, if it is "given its due," its protean, dynamic, morphogenetic characteristics would be recognized. Although it cannot be translated, its *intentio* is to express itself, to become legible in relation in new languages, forming new relationships and new forms-of-life. The language that is most legible and most dynamic, I want to suggest, is cinema, precisely because what makes cinema possible is motion, flux, change, differentiation. As Epstein writes: "Slow motion and fast motion reveal a world where the kingdoms of nature know no boundaries. Everything lives. A surprising animism is being reborn. We know, because we have seen them, that we are surrounded by inhuman existences. . . . The cinematographer extends the range of our senses, making perceptible to our sight and to our hearing individuals that we considered invisible and inaudible."[98] In this framework, the spectator is not a passive recipient of the image and its content; the camera is not a simple tool operated by the director but has its own "machinic subjectivity"—not a literal interiority but an other way of seeing and representing life itself. Animism here is not a technological development or an aesthetic movement but a new (or perhaps old) orientation toward the image, one that emphasizes and multiplies relations between nature and life rather than dividing them, almost a cinematic correlative of the Byzantine acheiropoieta, those miraculous images and "shards" of reality, untouched by human hands, spontaneously emerging from the divine—connective, incorporating images which also redefine another border, the one between documentary and fiction. It follows that, as with biopolitics, the philosophy of cinema is dominated by rigid dichotomies of "communication systems on one side and society and its spectators on the other," the latter of which is "dominated by a media monster that imposes its messages with Pavlovian efficiency."[99]

A regime accomplishes its mission when its citizens choose a path of subjectivization by way of subjectivation: Where the conflict between classes has become strategic for the survival of the regime, an intensification in the politicization of biological life has to be expected. The death of Elly in Farhadi's film (see chapter 2) is at the same time a refusal of integration and a supreme act of freedom. It reminds of the reading that Fabio Vighi gave of Accattone in the eponymous film by Pier Paolo Pasolini: an intensity that cannot be contained and remains permanently abject, a defiant fracture of the socioeconomic order daring to be read as the key political event of modernity. By electing to die as a most scandalous sacred event, Vighi writes, *Accattone* "fully assumes the void of freedom, an act that disturbs the socio-symbolic totality and spares him compulsive identification with it."[100] Pasolini freezes the sub-proletariat as a force that cannot and does not want to be assimilated: In his lugubrious, baroque aestheticization the Apollonian forbearance engulfs the Dionysian, centrifugal line of flight. It is unclear where it could derive a degree of political efficacy—a destabilization of the current social order by way of sheer numbers? Still, the question of the symbolic resources feeding the new order remains, the issues of new hegemonic power and a new concept of work and exchange that can be hegemonic linger. Albeit not a defined, transmissible asset, for Foucault power could enhance certain vitals; for Pasolini power was an agent of corruption, and satisfaction of basic needs would lead to complicity and acquiescence. Can power be neutrally (re)created as an encounter? Can maritime spaces testify about organic forms of interconnectedness and not simply be exploited for the passage of "uninhibited capital flows"?[101] *Atlantics* (*Atlantique*, Mati Diop, 2019) treats capital as coextensive with other extractive institutions such as the patriarchal family. The rich husband who can "advance" Ada is one and the same with the entrepreneur who exploits her love interest Souleiman, and when he disappears into the ocean, we realize that water, air, and sand are also one and the same with his pulverized, floating presence indexing the "global interconnection"[102] of enslaved bodies and exploited terrains. From this standpoint, the animistic persistence of the ghosts of the dead hints at a visionary state of limbo in which one can maintain a relationship, a connectedness.[103] For a subjectivity to contour itself against the unnatural rhythms of salaried work and mercenary family ties, life must be lived as a religious phenomenon through an encounter with the sacred. We are at a juncture in which it is unclear what resistance means, and the fact that it often seems too conveniently delegated to the arts speaks volume of the impasse, as if today the revolutionary subject that necessitates a class consciousness could find one only if it inoculated from the outside. One may also turn to the social production of a film like Juliano Dornelles and Kleber Mendonça Filho's *Bacurau* (2019), which adds an ethical instrumentation to the practice of political realism by incorporating every individual insofar as he/she has the potential of helping the community, regardless of other concerns. The unified micro-society of *Bacurau* is in fact a Marxist-Foucauldian utopia, capable of morphing from organic and disciplined unit to libertarian and individualistic anthropogenesis.[104]

2

"The Governmentalization of Social Life"

Asghar Farhadi and Iranian Cinema

If you find yourself in the dream of the other, you're screwed.

> —Gilles Deleuze, "What Is a Creative Act?"

One should succeed in seeing on the screen a sort of documentary of private and public facts.

> —Cesare Zavattini, *Il film lampo*

❧

THE PREVIOUS CHAPTER demonstrated this study's theoretical focus and methodologies, placing the philosophy of biopolitics and film studies into conversation. The present chapter and those that follow it articulate and extend this conversation while staging their own encounters between film and biopolitics. While the following chapters are informed by continental philosophy and film theory, they are not enclosed by these traditions, but rather seek to place them in dialogue with cinemas from around the world whose films, at their most compelling, facilitate—with respect to their unique national context as much as a wider, global one—a richer understanding of the relationship between life and power on and off the screen, with a view toward uncovering forms of biopolitical experience and expression that often elude philosophical elaboration. The aim of this chapter is not to provide totalities or generalizations, but to see how two of Asghar Farhadi's earlier works, *About Elly* and *Fireworks Wednesday*, foreshadow and visually translate what Esposito, writing a decade later, calls "the governmentalization of social life."[1] This chapter begins with an introduction to Iranian cinema as a biopolitical *dispositif* that has elicited a range of innovative cinematic approaches that either explicitly challenge or delicately subvert Iran's Ministry of Culture and Islamic Guidance, which provides strict censorship guidelines, the adherence to which is the difference between production funding and distribution on the one hand, and bans or even arrests on the other. I explore this with reference to three legendary and sometimes inflammatory directors, Abbas Kiarostami, Jafar Panahi, and Mohammad Rasoulof. Having established some of the contours of the politics of cinema in Iran, I turn my focus to the work of Farhadi, who I claim represents a "third way" between Kiarostami's oblique filmmaking and the more politically dangerous cinema of Panahi and Rasoulof. Farhadi's contributions to the reemergence of Iranian melodrama constitute, I argue, both a biopolitical cinema and a counter-governmental artistic practice centered on the political economy of the middle-class family, and whose focus is the forms of life that lie within it and that are captured by the *oikos* (household), the stage and site of relationships between husbands and wives, the state and the population, *zoē* and *bíos*. Iranian cinema as a whole is penetrated by politics, even when its subject matter does not directly engage the operativity of power, past or current scandals and debates, or state and political personnel as such. This has generated strong reactions from scholars, especially regarding director Abbas Kiarostami and his relationship with the Ministry of Culture and Islamic Guidance, which has prompted criticisms of "a refusal to engage with politics . . . in favor of a cinema that is frequently read as either broadly humanist or oblique and formalist."[2] Kiarostami, the most influential director in Iranian cinema, has sometimes been considered escapist or intentionally apolitical; yet the ontic, non-phenomenological movement of his work, which involves the viewer in a relentless reconfiguration of the visual and the real, is quite a radical take on the medium. Nico

Baumbach characterizes this as an art that ecumenically bridges the distance between creator, actors, and audience by positing a community of equals, while Mathew Abbott describes *ABC Africa* (2001) and *Ten* (2002) as Kiarostami's most political works, the former for the way in which the inclusion of the filmmaker himself "points to a way out of the metaphysics of objectivity and subjectivity," and the latter for "how it opens the political, feminist question of the relation between public and private"[3] while at the same time showing a resounding evolution in his use of children insofar as the only male protagonist is a petulant and entitled ten-year-old tragically turned into "the speaker and conduit of patriarchy."[4] This relation between the public and private spheres is a recurring concern across post-revolutionary Iranian cinema, one that reflects and is shaped by the broader organization of Iranian society.

A sudden event taking place outside the visual space of the camera, often accompanied by a key piece of information: This is the dramatic core of Farhadi's pictures. Through this visual conceit, the director is able to demonstrate the futility of coming to terms with the pulsating instability generated by said event. While in his European productions this approach is unsuccessful because the new configuration ultimately relates only to familial dynamics, in his Iranian films it shackles the protagonists to the chain of state power. The most accomplished phase of his work coincides with that which Robin Wright termed as "phase four" of the Islamic Republic's political history. It is a period of political turmoil that began with the "upset election"[5] of Mahmoud Ahmadinejad as president of the country in a transparent move carried out by Ayatollah Khamenei to rein in the apparatuses of executive authority in a moment when Islamic rule and democratizing institutions were on a collision course—a momentous political shift that brought about "a crisis of knowledge" and made it impossible "to discern friends from foes,"[6] making the darkened, crepuscular cinematography of *Fireworks Wednesday* a potent reference to Francis Ford Coppola's *The Conversation* (1974). The actors' dynamic interpretation and Hayedeh Safiyari's fast-paced editing coalesce to bring the viewer to a point of emotional exhaustion—time gets stretched as spaces become narrower; at the end even the open road feels claustrophobic, leaving an impression of extinguished hope. In such a phase of paranoia when traditional ways of dissent are proven ineffective, Farhadi asks foundational questions such as what conduct practices are available to Iranian citizens and to what extent are they independent from each other; what it means to produce a counter-conduct from within a history of invasive governmentality; and how the population deals creatively with the dynamic fluctuation of power relationships. Concerned with the definition of the public and the dissemination of the private in Iranian society, Farhadi's characters are led by events to breaking points in which they are forced to use their ideological capital. Interested in protocols of graduation and participation to the societal order, the director plays with progressions of inclusion and exclusion in the collective domain, showing a conspicuous collision of biological and political life. Foucault saw discipline as a deployable tool of government, especially for Western societies, but its generalizable use has become a precious surrogate of government in states that have not yet reached a mature phase of biocapitalism. He also assessed with great favor in the Iranian Revolution the potential for an anti-imperialist liberation—what struck him was the unpredictability of the revolt and how spirituality seemed to carry it forward, concurrently redefining the previous epistemic regimes.

If "political Islam seeks to reestablish the foundational value of the household by submitting the transaction of pleasure and money to the dictates of divine law,"[7] the space of the household is its most privileged site through which "a natural order, immanent to disciplinable living beings," is established, staged, and confirmed.[8] It is a site through which authority exercises itself, mapping political topologies and a preoccupation through which exercised authority can map the topological partitions of a given political extension—in this case, Iran's tensions and disharmonies at the level of the positioning and apportioning of gendered bodies. One can observe this in the opening of *The Salesman* (*Forooshande*, 2016) in which a young couple, the protagonists, and their neighbors are forced to flee their collapsing apartment building: The home and the security of a family (and therefore the nation) is under threat. This social commentary on the lack of welfare, compensation, et cetera pales in comparison with the symbolic transfiguration of the scene: The Iranian citizenry must constantly demonstrate to earn its place inside the ideological layout disseminated with sudden hurdles, sharp divides, false entries, barred accesses, broken doors. When it comes to political subjectivization, at one pole the Iranian citizenry is the target of internalized totalizing norms aimed at disciplining their conducts and mobilizing them as "a standing reserve of energy to be put to use,"[9] a public resource of loyalty to the revolutionary ideals of the Islamic Republic, at least in the form deemed acceptable by the Revolutionary Guard. This desire for an uninterrupted pretension toward allegiance lies in the nature of the coalition ruling Iran since 1979: By successfully overthrowing the nationalist government led by Mohammad Mossadegh and reinstating the autocratic rule of Shah Mohammad Reza Pahlavi, the United States and the United Kingdom all but killed the consolidation of representative principles in Iran's political system and created the premises for a vengeful wave of nationalist resentment foremostly interested in effective leadership at the expense of democratic entailments. After seizing power in 1979, Ruhollah Khomeini's Islamic Republican Party successfully ousted or subdued all the other formations—Marxist, Islamic, moderate constitutionalist, Nationalist—that were part of the anti-Shah coalition. The suppression of all rival parties essentially turned Iran into a clergy-dominated regime, a de facto minority coalition struggling to gain popular support; hence, the creation of the Revolutionary Guard was crucial to fight "the broad array and strength of the regime's early adversaries"[10] as well as to cultivate proxy militias and oversee military alliances abroad. Another key aspect is the expansive, Pan-Islamic nature of the regime, essential for its survival, pushing its Shiite brand of Islam as an anti-Western, anti-imperialist instrument for regional hegemony. From this standpoint, Iran's internal governmentality and the governmentality aimed at establishing and developing relationships with other Shia organizations such as Hezbollah are tightly connected and predicated on neo-conservative values such as sacrifice, martyrdom, and resistance. Iran's constitution remarkably balances the metaphysical substrate of Islam as a national trait coextensive with the Iranian nation.

Post-Revolutionary Cinema in Focus

In Kiarostami's cinema, which is in its own right an innovative new development in the history of Neorealism—and departure from it, for while Italian Neorealism centers life, Iranian cinema decenters life forms in ways I will elaborate on later—certain principles of the Zavattinian doctrine are radically applied: The goal of the director is to remain panoptically aware of the spectrum of the many potential stories in a narrative. So many, in fact, that the gaze and the *mise en abyme* are inverted as reality becomes the repository of the innumerable virtualities that the camera can intercept and activate. In Kiarostami's films, the relationship between the visual and the real stretches the medium far from the main goal of Neorealism: doing away with Fascism's technicalized mythology. Reflexive turns are only misleading cues whose purpose is to preserve the autonomy of every filmed event. Filming becomes synonymous with reality itself in ways that can be recognized among younger directors in the West, for example Italian director Roberto Minervini, who, like Kiarostami, "provokes" reality by accompanying its embedded stories, actors, and non-actors with his filmmaking presence and craft. This is best illustrated by the Iranian director's description of his casting process: "I sit and talk with them and turn on the camera without them knowing. After seven or eight minutes, once we've found our subject, I pretend to turn on the camera. If you see no difference between the moments before and after this flick of the switch, you know you have a good actor."[11] Kiarostami does not attempt to create convincing illusions—he refutes the reductively platonic charge of art as "false knowledge of reality." The spectator of Kiarostami's films, who has "a hundred years of cinema in [their] eyes," is left constantly questioning reality, situated within what Norma Claire Moruzzi calls "the doubled perspective of reflexive cinema: is it 'real' or is it scripted; is it a documentary or is it 'original?' "[12] His work elicits a new relationship to the real itself, as Alain Badiou has remarked of cinema as such.[13] In this sense, Kiarostami's operation is wholly cinematic not because it offers a totalizing vision of reality, but because of its pure and candid impurity. His films reclaim cinema's specificity as a medium through a coalescence of the aesthetic, the technical, and the ethical, from camera angles, editing, and movement to location and history. This is not a reification of cinema as a "work of art that is separate from the happenstance of the real, no matter how realistic its impression," as Moruzzi elegantly puts it, but as an image of the world looking at itself without a mirror; it does not blur or obfuscate the boundaries between "real life" and film, but, by occupying the very border between them, dismantles it.[14] This does not mean that political censorship and suppression is "good"; it is merely—and no less than—a testament to the creative, morphogenetic potential of cinema, a cinema that exceeds its own constraints by generating new forms.

In his post-revolutionary work, Kiarostami gave life to a new form that would be transfigured by Jafar Panahi, his previous assistant, and Farhadi. Their relationship to the life of this form is as an "afterlife" (*Nachleben*, to borrow a term coined by Walter Benjamin); in their respective divergences from the life of this form, the work of this younger generation of directors might be considered as "afterlives": not as faithful imitations by cinematic "offspring," but as *living after* Kiarostami's enlivened form, modified and modifying as what we might call "life-as-forms." My inversion here of Agamben's idea of form-of-life is intentional, as it reflects the cinematic relations at play between reality, representation, censorship, constraint, and potentiality as well as their political stakes:

> A life that cannot be separated from its form is a life for which what is at stake in its way of living is living itself. . . . [Forms of life are] never simply *facts* but always and above all *possibilities* of life, always and above all power. Modes of behavior and forms of human living are never prescribed by a specific biological predisposition, nor are they assigned by any necessity whatsoever; instead, no matter how customary, repeated, and socially compulsory they may be, they always preserve the character of possibilities; that is, life itself is always at stake in them.[15]

Panahi and Farhadi move Iranian cinema into a more directly political register. Panahi incorporates Kiarostami's use of non-actors, self-reflexivity, autofiction, and docufiction; and while Kiarostami finds formal lines of flight in censor regulations that lead toward new innovations in realism whose politics are oblique and poetic, Farhadi both draws on and breaks away from this approach, offering a social critique on the level of dramaturgy and, while still operating within the letter of the law and sidestepping the censor, transforms its politically indirect approach into an object of fatal knowledge and critique. His exploration of Iranian life as a heavily regulated economy whose sectors proceduralize the extractive logic at the level of the population inspired films such as Rasoulof's *There Is No Evil* (*Sheytan vojood nadarad*, 2020), especially the first segment, and in-depth biopolitical expeditions into Iranian family, commerce, industry, education, bureaucracy, and apparatuses of administration and control such as

Terrestrial Verses (*Ayeh haye zamini*, Ali Asgari and Alireza Khatami, 2023). Rasoulof has continued this investigation with his latest film, *The Seed of the Sacred Fig* (*Dane-ye anjir-e ma'abed*, 2024), insisting on the permeability of every space to practices of surveillance. Whereas Lanthimos's *Dogtooth* presented an image of the family run like the state, *The Seed of the Sacred Fig* shows its dialectical opposite: the state run like the family.

Crimson Gold

Crimson Gold (*Talaye sorkh*, 2003), a film by Jafar Panahi adapted from a screenplay by Kiarostami himself, is exemplary of the director's radical, uncompromising filmic practice. Like Kiarostami, Panahi makes innovative use of cars and driving; both directors also share Cesare Zavattini's Neorealist doctrine of *pedinamento*, or shadowing, a device that involves closely tracking the existence of a character played by a non-professional actor. It is remarkable that the two filmmakers who have not only worked together but share a strong affinity for the same methods should have such dramatically different lives as filmmakers. While critics and scholars tend to overdetermine Kiarostami's success in adapting to the Ministry of Culture's regulations (his work fell prey to the censor several times; *Homework* was banned for three years), Panahi's work is so politically explicit that he has been banned from leaving the country and from filmmaking. Having defied the latter injunction several times, he has also been arrested on multiple occasions. It is not surprising, therefore, that Panahi's work is preoccupied with the collision between the governmental and the subjected individual that generates a form-of-life bordering on the bare and inhuman.

In *Crimson Gold*, Panahi's protagonist is Hussein, a war veteran and pizza delivery driver nearing his wedding day. Hussein, who was injured in the Iran–Iraq War, has literally been re-formed by medication to treat the injuries he endured in the conflict, which have made his face swollen and have caused him to gain weight. Hussein, played by Hossain Emadeddin, a non-actor who in real life struggles with paranoid schizophrenia, a condition that made filming difficult, is not only alienated from his body; when an old boss fails to recognize him, Hussein remarks that he doesn't even recognize himself.[16] Through Hussein's narrative, Kiarostami conveys precisely how bare life can be produced, even cultivated, in incremental measures across everyday life in a contemporary context. The film follows its protagonist on his route, where he encounters a heterogeneous series of Tehranis, one of whom he used to serve with in the military, now a wealthy man, who overtips Hussein out of pity; on next delivery, he finds his customers under surveillance by teenage officers who hang back while their affluent targets throw a lively house party. They forbid Hussein from taking the delivery up to the third floor and even prevent him from calling his boss. Unable to complete his job or even leave the scene, Hussein has no choice but to watch the shadows of the partygoers flicker behind a closed curtain, a vivid evocation of Plato's cave, where prisoners are rendered immobile and forced to gaze at a similar screen. Another customer is a rich playboy who invites him inside, one of the only gestures of hospitality that is extended to Hussein; but there is no connection or friendship to be found—here, Hussein himself becomes a screen as he is obliged to listen to the man's complaints about the women who rejected him. When Hussein and his fiancée (and her brother, who is casing the shop for a robbery that will provide the film's explosive and tragic ending) visit a jeweler in an affluent part of the city, they are rebuffed by the owner, who has ignored them to serve wealthier clientele. As soon as they leave, Hussein, overwhelmed by this humiliating foray into a world that he is neither welcome in nor able to navigate, begins to faint. Because of his injuries, Hussein's every movement is painful, and his affective response to the daily indignities and violence is often a dissociative one: He is not quite present in his life, but his impassive expression holds back the profound insecurity, bewilderment, and shame produced by his precarious existence. Panahi's camera often wobbles to indicate Hussein's point of view or movement, focalized through his distorted state of mind, but also the broader economic, social, and psychic instability that constitutes his life. Yet he appears constantly propelled by an intangible but irresistible power, fully captured by the demands of his boss, customers, the police, and even his brother-in-law; he requires no significant coercion, simply a demand that he responds to with mechanical, automatic, assent. He is treated not like an animal but like a machine: For most of the film, he is on his delivery motorcycle, and it is with this means of transport and minimal subsistence that we can understand Hussein's biopolitical reduction, which so shapes and dominates his life that his body often appears reconfigured by it, centaur-like, until he is finally able to rest in a bed that looks like a tomb. As he lies awake, he hears his neighbor being dragged away screaming by the police, a brutal contrast with their discreet presence in the wealthier parts of town. It is this social inequality that exposes the limits and hypocrisies of theocratic authority in its complicity with capitalism. This cynical relationship between governmentality and national values announces the modernity of Iran, which is as compromised as that of its Western antagonists.

National Security as Sovereign: *Manuscripts Don't Burn*

Rasoulof's explosive 2013 film *Manuscripts Don't Burn* (*Dast-neveshtehaa nemisoosand*) is a brutal, dangerous film that not only flies in the face of state power, but resurrects an officially taboo, unutterable moment in Iranian history: the unsuccessful attempt to assassinate twenty-one Iranian writers on a bus to a poetry in conference in neighboring Armenia. Rasoulof creates a forbidden image of the past that acts as a *j'accuse* to the state and its security apparatus. Part of this film's power is its metatextual component; by re-presenting the writers on the screen, Rasoulof is not only forcing the state to witness its own crimes on screen but also staging a direct artistic confrontation between himself and the regime, which was responsible for his 2010 arrest. His is a frontal attack against a regime whose political justification is theological, and that exhibits the violence at its foundations. One could read the arc of his filmography, which develops from "mystic-realist allegory"[17] to take-no-prisoners thanatological explorations: The entrapped, harassed lawyer from *Goodbye* (*Be omid-e didar*, 2011) could very well turn into the persecuted intellectual from *Manuscripts Don't Burn*. The latter film is as a clear rejection of any naïve faith in political gradualism. As the writers on Rasoulof's screen are hunted and murdered, "the futility of fighting oppression with argument alone" becomes violently clear.[18] Rasoulof and Farhadi share a crucial thematization: the moment in which power, while retaining the sovereign, vertical cut that can cleave its subjects from above, is also put "in relation to the life of those that it governs," in the Iranian case by courting the middle class, cajoling it or blackmailing it into an alliance.[19] Considered a decisive actor in the internal balance of power, the Iranian middle class has recently received stronger attention. It has been historically considered dangerous by the Guardians of the Revolution because of its exposure to Western, liberal values and overall feeble religious devotion.[20] Yet its creation is the result of a necessary exchange of power for modern comfort and relative wealth for which requests for social freedom and individual rights are deferred (such an exchange is recognizable in European social contract theory). This relationship between modernity and religious conservatism is both necessary and contradictory, at once necessary to remain the status quo and legitimacy of the state, and thoroughly unsustainable. This is capitalist modernity, which elicits individualism and a preoccupation with accumulation; in a word, it subverts the values the state claims to defend and protect. *Manuscripts Don't Burn* is a courageous parable shot with experimentation and stylistic contamination, relevant for this discussion because his trajectory both culminates in and transcends "classical" political cinema regarding abuses of power. His first feature, the docudrama *The Twilight* (*Gagooman*, 2002) is an earnest attempt at iterative realism carried out through the Neorealist device of shadowing an inmate through his thwarted attempts at societal reinsertion and social normalization. With this film, Rasoulof proved that he had mastered an early Kiarostami template with a keen eye for relational hurdles and engaging moral dilemmas. *Iron Island* (*Jazireh ahani*, 2005) and *The White Meadows* (*Keshtzar haye sepid*, 2009) are decisive, ambitious allegories with circular narratives of self-contained communities that share a sense of desperation and ineluctable defeat: In the first film, the captain of an abandoned, dilapidated oil tanker in the Persian Gulf supervises the dismemberment of the ship and the destruction of its community; in the second, an empathic and dutiful collector of tears visits several islands dominated by archaic and cruel superstitions that comfort the victims he encounters on his journey but systematically preserve his function. Between *Iron Island* and *The White Meadows* Rasoulof filmed an antagonistic documentary, *Head Wind* (*Baad-e-daboor*, 2008), which drew parallels between the right to free expression and the right to access information. In the latter half of his filmography, Rasoulof has created denser political images that do not allude to or allegorize their criticism of the state but directly engage and disrupt governmental control and biopower. As Rasoulof tackles the political theology of the Iranian regime, his films are not "merely critical of dominant ideology" but, as Baumbach eloquently observes, "create something new out of their transformation."[21]

Apart from the robust drama *A Man of Integrity* (*Lerd*, 2017), Rasoulof's most recent films are situated at the encounter of theological politics and biopower: His protagonists are not citizens as defined by a social contract, but neither they are men—his underlying question is what makes them human in the first place. Rasoulof shows the Iranian state's permanent insecurity regarding questions of its own legitimacy as it relates to the political participation and representation of its people. His insight is quintessentially biopolitical insofar as what is considered human is the concern of the Iranian government, and the filmmaker is mostly interested in what this person is or who they have become. This paradigmatic approach is wholly radical, for it does not call for reform but announces the imperative to "develop strategies to counter specific regimes of rationality rather than countering specific policies within those regimes."[22] Rasoulof appears to marvel at the determination of the regime's executioners: they manifest the same inventiveness and resilience as a state capable of circumventing and mitigating the effects of diplomatic and economic sanctions. His films observe how the drive for sovereign self-protection has turned inward, against the people themselves, whom it sees as a threat: Society must be defended, as Foucault says. But this reveals a crucial truth about sovereignty: It is not the Leviathan whose bodily integrity relies on the hundreds of bodies that compose it, without whom it would collapse; it is Saturn eating his children. Esposito's immunity paradigm is useful for explaining this more clearly, as it is particularly legible in this film: "what is feared, *more than individual cases*, is a weakening of the sovereign power of single states. . . . What is important [to the state] is inhibiting, preventing, and fighting the spread of contagion wherever it presents itself, using whatever means necessary."[23] *Manuscripts Don't Burn* is a film about sovereign decisions regarding the annihilation of three of the writers who were accidentally spared on the bus. One of the writers intends to self-publish his manuscript about the attempt, which implicates a former dissident—now, significantly, a high-ranking censor—as the mastermind of the plan.

It is a political film insofar as it tells its audience which type of society post-revolutionary Iran has chosen to be, which type of pact binds its citizens, and the weight that the constitution carries in safeguarding certain basic principles. It also shows the way real power is generated within and then circulated outside of the letter of the law at the intersection the sovereignty of God and the people, both of which form the basis—and contradictions—of the Republic. Rasoulof is interested in state violence, a form of "immunization in high doses [that] means sacrificing every form of qualified life, for reasons of simple survival." The violence we witness in *Manuscripts Don't Burn* is divine violence: There is no right, and therefore no proportionate punishment. Rasoulof masterfully intercuts chilling scenes of violent interrogation and torture with mocking shots of the two goons Khosrow and Morteza casually grabbing a bite while mosque speakers blare Koranic verses, a background noise that turns tragedy into black comedy as Morteza reassures his partner in crime that what they are carrying out is in harmony with divine law: "We've been given an order and it complies with the sharia."[24] This is a direct reference to the double bind instituted by Iran's "constitutional bodies representing the republican foundation coexisted with bodies representing the Islamic soul," or the Vali-ye Faqih, Guardian Jurist, whose divine sovereignty can supervene positive law.[25] It is through this predicament that a public servant can attribute to himself the right of life and death over others, since what is legal and what secures the integrity of the state are coextensive.

While this film has all the elements of a thriller, it is influenced and nuanced by realism. Khosrow is devastated by his son's medical condition; its expensive care has left him broke and reliant on loans and contract killings. Parallel to the assassination mission is the imminent surgery of Khosrow's son, which depends on the payment he will receive for the job. This becomes the key motivation and justification for his participation in the killings. It is why, despite constantly checking his bank balance, he can tell his accomplice and handler (who is in direct contact with their boss) that he is not taking the job for the money. While this is left unexplained, what he means is that he is selling his capacity for violence in exchange for the life of his son. This element is not a strategy to humanize the story's villains, but to show that the circuit of power is wired such that the perpetrators, too, are reduced to bare life but on the side of the oppressors. Their violence is a divine way to preserve the sacred—without it, there would be no Iran; its continuity justifies itself. The translation of the religious into the political is triumphantly propulsive toward chaos (figure 2.1).

Figure 2.1. Politico-theological musings and law enforcement forces. *Source:* Mohammad Rasoulof, dir., *Manuscripts Don't Burn* (2013; Kino Lorber, 2014), DVD, 576p.

The theological element remains as the element of mediation, the old story of an insecure conscience that transforms into a security system: Religion returns as the transcendental element of politics, its foundation; the political replaces the sacred and vice versa. On the absence of God, one can build a rational state—a utilitarian, representative, nihilistic, optimistic state; likewise, one can rationalize the state by way of the Divine. Rasoulof depicts Iran as a Hobbesian state, indirectly informed by God and directly run by men—and, in this film, by his henchmen. The most dramatic question that the filmmaker asks is where exactly religion is today in Iran—is the country ready for a Kemalist revolution, turning religion into a branch of bureaucracy? The Iranian state is a celibate machine in the Hobbesian declination, founded on the absence of God: If Hobbes showed the difference between the human and the citizen, Rasoulof asks what makes a human a human in the first place. By virtue of this empty presence, God is everywhere in his transcendental absence, guarantor of the functioning of the state, the covenant behind the production of political unity. The last scene—an anxious, inquisitive Khosrow in a crowded Tehran street—reveals the fraudulent nature of the covenant: What is really keeping all those people together? A superstitious executioner with some remote, convenient semblance of humanity, though exclusively for his family, seems to be the most qualified representative to argue for the cause of Iran's social bond: We can be together, as long as we are not ourselves and we erase ourselves by way of the state's nihilistic machine. As spectators, we marvel at the bleak potency of the executioners and the way they fulfill their role of a sovereign who, by virtue of his decision-making autonomy, manages to bring the situation to normality—a normality for which no collateral damage seems too prohibitive.

Rasoulof is aware that there cannot be any real opposition from within, not only as long as the regime's authority is unrestrained, but as long as that authority *rightfully* lies in the hands of violent technocrats who arrogate divine sovereignty. In the film, the technocrat responsible for managing the assassination speaks from an office where, on the wall behind him, a picture of Ali Khamenei hangs poised over his shoulder; the shot suggests that Rasoulof is not concerned with a banal apportionment of criminal responsibility against a single actor, but rather with a whole system of power that limits life. The filmmaker's meticulous narrative of torture and death mirrors the orderly mechanism of power, its rational management. Rasoulof's most powerful move, though, lies in an offscreen decision: The writers may have no chance "except to self-annihilate or to be reduced to bare life assassinated by the state, but their original decision to share the manuscript—whose function is also pragmatic and self-interested; its author wants to use it as collateral to gain a ticket out of Iran to see his daughter one last time—is the founding choice that illuminates the darkness from within. The film's final shot, with Khosrow aimlessly lost in Tehran's indistinct crowd, hints as the routine nature of his assignment and inconspicuousness of his potential targets, implying that in Iran the state of exception would be a step forward. *There Is No Evil* is concerned with the death penalty as an instance of self-preservation and as an act that "becomes merely an administrative decision as significant as any other, utilized for the security and well-being of the State."[26] In these films, Iran seems far from constituting a space where another "us" is possible, and it is made clear that there is a deep divide between the state as a self-generated idea of regional power and civil society. Cinematically, Farhadi shows this anguished and uneasy condition through figures of disconnectedness, exhaustively renegotiating the private boundaries as a paradigm of discipline and control. Rasoulof reaches a similar conclusion via a phenomenological observation of the theological in Iranian rule and its ancillary service to the political. The productive, positive conditioning carried out through aggregative instruments appears to have reached a breaking point.

From Geopolitics to Biopolitics: The Cinema of Asghar Farhadi

On her first day on the job, a housekeeper discovers the infidelity of her employer's husband; a middle-class woman convinces her child's teacher to consider a prospective husband (the teacher's current engagement notwithstanding); a young, untrained, working-class woman works for an unhappy family, nursing an elderly man with dementia; a man learns that his wife has been raped and creates his own retributive justice.

Farhadi's films present the already compromised and fragile (im)balance of middle-class life as it encounters and is encountered by the working class. This encounter instigates a character's confrontation with an almost impossible decision: whether to advance or retreat, confide or conceal, rebel or comply. These somewhat schematic binaries belie the deeply complex and anguished relationship to choice that originates a crisis in Farhadi's characters, who attempt to somehow bridge the gulf between action and inaction, which is as much relational as it is moral: how to deliver an ethical truth when the social order, and one's often precarious place within it, demands dissimulation? Should one inform one's employer about her husband's infidelity, or conceal it, as in *Fireworks Wednesday*? Is it possible to establish a genuine community under such conditions? These dilemmas are not uniquely Iranian and are indeed posed by any society that is sustained by inequality and governmentality. This basic schema, which runs through his filmography, form the bases of Farhadi's hybrid cinema, a fusion of melodrama and social realism, a synthesis that reflects his ability to straddle mainstream and arthouse cinema in Iran and beyond. In his exceptional book on Iranian cinema, Hamid Dabashi writes that "the intersection of art and modernity has made aspects of Iranian cinema signify something beyond itself."[27] Dabashi is referring here to cinema's emergence as the "focal point of an entirely new generation of hopes and fears, attracting an audience that, aware of the modernity of its condition, crowded the theaters."[28]

But his description can be equally applied to Iranian filmmakers' impact on world cinema, of which Farhadi is currently the greatest representative. It would not be too bold to claim that Farhadi, the first Iranian director to win an Oscar, is the country's most important filmmaker since Abbas Kiarostami; to this, I would also contend that he is one of the country's most political filmmakers, not despite his preoccupation with Iran's middle class, but because of it.

Unlike the cinemas of Abbas Kiarostami and Jafar Panahi—or at least their early, formative phases—Farhadi's visual style is the result of a more "written" and less phenomenical approach, in which moral conflicts explode after subtle games of denials and dissimulation. While Hitchcock's films, which Farhadi has acknowledged as an influence, are concerned with deceptive images trapped in the folds of representation, they remain latent in Farhadi. In the British filmmaker's oeuvre, they serve to refract and disguise the manifold, untamable impulses of sexual desire; in Farhadi, these images expose the contradictions of Iran's post-revolutionary social contract that followed the overthrow of the US-backed Pahlavi monarchy. Though it emerged in a different context and tradition, Iran's experiment in democracy grappled with issues of sovereignty, governmentality, citizenship, and law that Western liberalism has faced—that is to say, biopolitics.[29] But this revolution was both a distinctly Iranian and far more contemporary one than, for example, the French Revolution, a detail that was crucial for Foucault, who reported on Iranian revolutionary activity in late 1978. The full complexities of the Iranian Revolution and Foucault's relationship to it cannot be fully explored in this chapter, but it is clear that the philosopher found it significant (particularly after the disappointment of 1968) as a revolutionary event of a magnitude that had not been seen in France for hundreds of years.[30] And although Foucault did not explicitly connect the Revolution and biopolitics, there is no doubt that the post-revolutionary regime faced challenges similar to the ones faced by Western liberalism: how to manage a population when old paradigms of sovereignty, in both cases monarchy, are overthrown by and for the people. How is power reorganized? How is control asserted? Sovereignty as such is not replaced but redistributed and reinvested in the body politic in the form of a social contract that is guaranteed by obedience to the law.

The afterlife of Iran's history is an ambient and motivating force in Farhadi's films. It can be found in the characters' enervated interactions once a topological breach occurs: in *Fireworks Wednesday*, in the kairological phantasm of an allegiance between women; in *About Elly*, when a violation of the segregated space allowed to women occurs; in *A Separation*, when the burden of performing the sacred Law is dumped on the most vulnerable; in *The Salesman*, when a husband takes in his own hands the vindication of his wife's compromised honorability. The disciplinary techniques and apparatuses are parts of their lifestyles, demeanors, behavior—we, as spectators, are left to imagine the might of technology whose only purpose is to impose itself on every becoming and every event and conduct yet to come into existence. The house and the apartment as meta-discursive agglomerates are Farhadi's auteurist signatures: They function as a revealed symbol of the phenomenal world as well as epistemic transformations manifesting themselves as ontological extrusions of actuality, making visible the epistemic a priori in which subjectivization is intertwined with dependence and the undoing of resistance. Foucault famously declared that "the anxiety of our era has to do fundamentally with space," whereby human sites can be finally broken down into exploded views of power relations in order to better understand "what relations of propinquity, what type of storage, circulation, marking, and classification of human elements should be adopted in a given situation in order to achieve a given end."[31] Farhadi's interest does not lie in the types of transactions that occur in institutional buildings or urban environments, although we catch occasional glimpses of such exchanges; mostly, he focuses on the hybridization of private space into something that is not quite public and yet not exclusive, an outside that is not negotiated with an inside, a family space that gets contaminated and becomes a socially tainted living site. Farhadi is a filmmaker of enclosed and partitioned spaces. He transports the meandering, labyrinthine, hostile pathways we see in films by Kiarostami, Panahi, and Bahman Ghobadi from the open landscape into the planimetry of the house—characters seem to be always dealing with an unsettling, unstable aspect of the domestic space, whereby "the circuitous quest makes even the most concrete places fleetingly uncanny—both for the character and for the viewer."[32] Farhadi is one of those filmmakers who, like Rossellini and De Sica and later Cassavetes and Lumet, have reconfigured the notion of cinematic spatiality to show a different correlation between the spatial and the gestural. If with the two Neorealists the very possibility of action was questioned, and with the two representatives of the New York school the urban space becomes the mental and yet already tainted projection of an impossible escape from life's constraints, in Farhadi the hostile and crammed locales hint at the constant need to be at a proper distance and at the right remove. Similarly, he transfers the reflexivity of Makhmalbaf into many of his characters, who at some point turn into skilled liars and manipulators. Hossein Jafarian's cinematography fluctuates between chiaroscuro expressionistic contrast and illumination by way of dark tones, as if the light were constantly suctioned out of the picture.

According to Hamid Naficy, Farhadi's Oscar-winning 2011 film *A Separation* (*Jodaeiye Nader az Simin*) has, "more than any other single film . . . helped globalize Iranian cinema, particularly at a crucial time that the public diplomacy between Iran and the West was at its height."[33] That a film can be at once an incisive, moving social (and therefore political) critique and an object of diplomacy is one of cinema's many "impurities";[34] it is caught not only between art and commodity, but also between art and geopolitics.[35] One of the sites that triangulate this ambiguity is the international film festival. The Iranian International Film Market (IFM) was created in 1998 as part of the more established Fajr International Film Festival.[36] Run by the Cinema Organization of Iran, the IFM marked a new phase of creative exchange between Iran and the West and allowed the country "to market [its] films more aggressively." This exchange "changed the character of the domestic film industry, from one that was primarily government-financed and -controlled to one that moved toward a mixed economy and ideological pluralism."[37] Government censorship still controlled the film industry, but a new set of contradictions were introduced: While the film festival circuit invited cross-cultural exchange both ways, Iranian cinema became caught in the crosshairs of US intervention and sanctions.[38]

At first glance, then, there is perhaps no clearer interchange of biopolitics and cinema than post-revolutionary Iranian cinema, from its mode of production, which includes the role of censorship in relation to financing and distribution, to the language of the films themselves, which are often—but certainly not always—oblique and indirect, even (perhaps especially) when they offer a critique of power and subjectivation. This visual language, epitomized by through-window shots, for example, finds its counterpart in the often indirect and veiled but deeply polysemous communication between characters in the films, which reflects a broader hesitance and taciturnity within Iranian society, as Farhadi has related in a recent interview with film critic Tina Hassannia:

> I love Pinter very much because of the way he uses language. . . . The main trait of his characters is that they say certain things to avoid saying what's actually in their heart. And for us who grew up in Iranian society, this is very tangible. In our literature, elements like irony and metaphor are used very frequently. In a telephone conversation, a lot of people are afraid to be silent and they constantly chat unless the other person is speaking. This kind of talking is often done to conceal something.[39]

Farhadi, who wrote his university thesis on Harold Pinter, evokes the British playwright to illustrate the particularity of Iranian social life and its modes of communication; and while this anecdote is broadly addressed to an English-speaking audience, what it designates is not a universal, transcendent condition that flattens difference and specificity, but a social response to technologies of governmental control that find common ground across the globe. As a director who has made both financially successful and critically acclaimed films in both Iran and Europe, Farhadi has a unique insight into cinema as a *dispositif* or, to borrow from Foucault, a "heterogeneous ensemble" of institutions, law, discourse, technology, finance, bureaucracy, and, among others, ideology:

> I believe there is a big censorship system in the entire world that takes different shapes in different countries. In Iran, the government implements it and it directly tells you what subjects you can or cannot make films about. In other countries, there are implicit systems. They don't tell you what to make or not, but there are subjects that would provoke attacks, so you prefer to steer away from them altogether. That is, unless you have the same angle on the story as the hegemony in society.[40]

In "Confession of the Flesh," Foucault pithily summarizes the *dispositif* in similar terms: "in short, [it is] the said as much as the unsaid."[41]

In the quote above, Farhadi aptly refrains from saying how, exactly, one circumvents censorship, but a close look at his films suggests that it has something to do with the spaces between what is said and what is not said, in an attentiveness to that which is implicit, and in making legible the subtle but violent governmentality that shapes and summons our conduct, our choices, and our dreams, which is to say our subjectivity. While Farhadi's films do not explicitly challenge Iran's religious biopolitics or the principles of state ideology, he problematizes the "implicit systems" that govern contemporary Iranian life through a series of confrontations and caesurae between class and gender, intersections that create biopolitical images of the individual before the law, not in the setting of the courtroom but in the juridical space of the household, what I am calling, after Foucault, the *dispositif* of marriage. In the following sections, I explore this in detail, suggesting that in Farhadi's films, it is precisely this device that excludes women from the *polis* and, following the post-revolutionary repeal of the 1968 Family Act, reinstalls them in the *oikos* as bare life in the realm of *zoē*, the field of living that Agamben's Aristotle associates with women, slaves, and children.[42]

Farhadi has steered Iranian cinema into a more "mainstream," global direction with Tehranian stories of rancor, revenge, and betrayal against the technological-rational background of the regime. However, his work does not diminish its local context, nor does it affirm Western (particularly in the US) stereotypes of an "archterrorist state" populated by religious fundamentalists.[43] Indeed, Farhadi's Iran will be eminently recognizable to his Western audiences: Subjects are urged to side with various epistemic regimes—of gender, religion, class, propriety, among others—that invest in and form people's lives. Farhadi's Iran is a place like any other, a place where social reproduction is continued and maintained by the *dispositif* of marriage. This contrivance is so central to Farhadi's work that it is worth quoting Foucault's definition of it in full:

> a system of marriage, of fixation and development of kinship ties, of transmission of names and possessions . . . it has as one of its chief objectives to reproduce the interplay of relations and maintain the law that governs them . . . it is firmly tied to the economy due to the role it can play in the transmission or circulation of wealth . . . [and] is

> *attuned to a homeostasis of the social body, which it has the
> function of maintaining;* whence its privileged link with the
> law; whence too the fact that the important phase for it
> is "reproduction."[44]

The director's analytics of space involves the link between the spatiality of the house with stories of failed emancipation, solidarity, and forgiveness; how these characters operate through these stories transfigures the possibility of a personal decision into a quiescence that results from or the ways in which he connects the spatiality of the house with stories of failed emancipation, solidarity, and forgiveness, and the way characters operate through them transfigures personal decisions into a quiescence that results from the impossibility of counter-conducts. In those exercises investigating the capacity for equality, Jacques Rancière's definition of the political is apposite here: "the field for the encounter between emancipation and policy in the handling of a wrong."[45] And, as Carol Hanisch famously first articulated, the personal—our interpellations and our conflicts with power that are negotiated through the dynamics of identification and individualization—is political.[46] To elaborate on this a bit further: Our coexistence within power relations and conflicts, whether they are legitimized or contested, is negotiated through the dynamics of identification and individualization. If to recuperate space in biopolitical terms is to recognize it as the site of the coordination and distribution of behavior and then probe and extend its potential as either a private sanctum or a public forum, then Farhadi's films demonstrate the daunting and problematic nature of such a task, which risks painful breaches and excisions among social groups and families.

Biopower, or rather biopowers, are a vast network of environments and social milieux, complex spaces made up of all the material elements capable of interfering with one's life population. Biopowers work through a positive regulation of biological processes scientifically implemented in order to favor them or hinder them. They do not act directly on the element of reality that they aim for, but they "structure a field," they have an interest in related phenomena. The filmmaker illustrates the orchestration of accepted conducts within space—domestic nests turn into deposits of junk, holiday villas into refugee camps, means of transportations double as confessional spaces—and destabilizes its perception by literalizing the ruin contained in violence and exertion. Farhadi insists on its metaphysical quality as the repository where power intensities encounter, a precise diagnostic tool intercepting all the spikes. As Gregg Lambert writes, "The relation of verticality (or the relation of dominator/dominated) will always be a feature of social space, but power does not flow in one direction only, as 'from above,' but also comes 'from below,' since dominated subjects also produce the reality of the dominator-function as a moment of transcendent unification."[47] Viewers are afforded an inside view into a community founded on exteriority: no identification, no harmonization, only a technical operation whereby social belonging functions through practices of self-abnegation such that any recognition of the other's (and one's own) subjectivity becomes an impossible encounter. The point of departure is the restrictions in contact between men and women, and while he is not addressing it from a doctrinal or individual rights standpoint, Farhadi is concerned with the subtraction of collective actions, experiences, contacts, and its biopolitical fallout in Iranian society. Albeit not directly evoking "a distinctive collective project of social-political trans-formation aided by the motivating power of a revolutionary cinema,"[48] Farhadi's early works are preoccupied with a biopolitical provision of social discipline through family life and its destructive impact on solidarity, especially between women. The inciting event of these films is an ungovernable event with subversive potential, which the social body must secure and neutralize, a truly immune response that comes not only from within the family itself—as in *About Elly*—but from the outside, as external actors protect the family in order to protect their own lives, as can be observed in *Fireworks Wednesday*. The stifling, repressive uncertainty generated by unstable rules of segregation creates a vacuum in which "the improvisational nature of space" and the overlapping, capillary diagram of power relations can be bent to one's advantage by an opportunistic negotiation.[49] Space then becomes the figural correlative to Iran's governmentalized social encounters that is threatened by signs of nonconformity to its rules of engagement, and the most revealing locus for the actuality of sanctioned conducts.

Hardly any government officials appear in Farhadi's films, and yet they deal—especially the ones from the 2006–2016 span—with the "political power beyond the state."[50] The filmmaker's operation may not be intentionally Foucauldian in its "view of power as a game between liberties or a structure of action upon the action of others," and yet the films expose an alignment of forces that apparently neutralize the state and its purported sovereignty, only for the concatenation of domination to be reaffirmed traumatically by the characters' impoverished relationality.[51] Similarly, Farhadi's works address key aspects of Khomeini's thought, articulating and exploring the Ayatollah's vision of Islamic integralism, in which religion dictates and permeates the direction of the nation and the behavior of its populace, from communal political space to the home and the self.[52] Though this is far from the liberalism Foucault had in mind when writing about biopolitics (or indeed about the unfolding of the Iranian Revolution), it is nonetheless an excellent illustration of the concept, wherein politics dictate forms of life, where power "acts and assesses the productivity of Islam by its capacity and determination to found and congeal social relations, in other words to institute a society."[53] Unlike Panahi's militant filmmaking or Kiarostami's nomadic, Zavattinian cinema of encounter, Farhadi directs our gaze to the consequences of specific policies that are necessary for the maintaining the ideological integrity of the state and with it the social status quo, further entrenching rigid positions and exacerbating divisions on a class, gender, and individual level. If it is indeed "the state [that] must ideally guard women in the private walls of their homes," the result is the creation of a destabilized area where transgression and punishment are always internal, open possibilities—a monad through which the totalizing reach of tradition can be revealed and is predicated.[54] Farhadi's domestic films are concerned with the subsumption of individual agency bifurcated by theocratic norms and class interest: He emphasizes the technologies of domination that inform the daily negotiations between Islam and qualified life in terms of a collective exposure to laws of orthodoxy.

One can schematically divide Farhadi's output into three phases. The first comprises the TV series *Chashm be rah* (1998) and most importantly *Story of a City* (*Dastane yek shahr*, 2000–2001), in which he mastered unscripted filmmaking by distancing the tales of fictional documentarians from formulaic outcomes and balancing the characters' motivations with keen observations of Iran's societal malaise. *Dancing in the Dust* (*Raghs dar ghobar*, 2003) and *Beautiful City* (*Shahr-e ziba*, 2004) introduce the second group, which comprises his more accomplished domestic works such as *Fireworks Wednesday* and *About Elly* especially, followed by *A Separation*, *The Salesman*, and *A Hero*

(*Ghahreman*, 2021). The third consists of his two projects filmed abroad, *The Past* (*Le passé*, 2013) and *Everybody Knows* (*Todos los saben*, 2018). In *A Separation* and *The Salesman* the collision between middle-class families and a working-class outsider does not fully transcend the dramaturgy.[55] *Fireworks Wednesday* and *About Elly*, however, telescope the immediate, dramatic conflicts to reveal the governmental dynamics behind people getting together, starting new families, and preserving or disrupting preexisting ways of sharing spaces, establishing bonds, and withholding or divulging knowledge. These two films form a biopolitical dyad, complementing and conversing with each other in their respective focuses on the dynamics between Iran's lower class in *Fireworks Wednesday* and the educated, affluent middle class depicted in *About Elly*. Here, the middle class is more of an artificial creation than a spontaneous success of the Islamic Republic, where the nature of the political pact entails an exchange of acquiescence and mobility for wealth and security. That *A Separation* and *The Salesman* won the Academy Awards that eluded the early works (although *About Elly* received a nomination) is worth noting, as it demonstrates what type of pictures Western cultural hegemony demands in order to fulfill the metaphysical equalization requested from art. It is recurring pattern resembling, for instance, the critical acknowledgment of Paolo Sorrentino's *The Great Beauty* (*La grande bellezza*, 2013) instead of his earlier, vastly more radical *Il divo* (2008), a reflection on the nature and necessity of power as part modern Machiavellian prince and part *katéchon*,[56] and possibly a nod to their fulfillment of festival expectations with recognizable and reassuring templates. Farhadi's oeuvre is a sort of "third way" in Iranian cinema: Outside the Kiarostami-Panahi self-reflexivity and Rasoulof's brutal directness, Farhadi undermines Western expectations of "political subversion" whereby viewers obsess more on the film that was not made according to their ideological bias. In his first, more accomplished phase his cinema is uncompromisingly biopolitical in its depiction of the compounded marginalization of poor and working-class women: In its consensus-building strategy, the Iranian regime proposes an exchange between an increase in purchasing power and a concurrent cap in social freedoms and political apertures. The victims of this attrition and its extortive mechanisms are women who cannot enjoy any advantage from this tacit accord and become a convenient afterthought, diversion, recreational pastime, instruments, casualties; the two films analyzed here are the most political because they show how the class that once was the focus of the regime has now become invisible.

Fireworks Wednesday

In *Fireworks Wednesday*, Mozhdeh and Morteza are a middle-class couple on the verge of a breakup. Mozhdeh suspects her husband is having an affair with their neighbor, Simin, a woman who, after her own marital misadventures, has illegally opened a beauty salon in her apartment, a reclamation of public and economic space and an expression of agency that reappears when she breaks up with Morteza near the end of the film. *Fireworks Wednesday* centers on Rouhi, a working-class bride-to-be who travels with her boyfriend from the countryside to the city, where they both seek to find work. Through a temp agency, Morteza hires Rouhi to perform domestic work during the family's trip to Dubai. Although they are meant to depart the following day, upon Rouhi's arrival, it becomes clear that the family's fragile equilibrium has been upset: The tension between the couple is palpable and a broken window signals the anger and turmoil hidden beneath the wealthy family's façade (figure 2.2). Rouhi is soon enlisted by Mozhdeh to observe and report on Simin.

Figure 2.2. Disturbing assemblages and domesticity in Iran: Mozhdeh merging with the domestic space as she strains to hear signs of her husband's other life, just as she is "bound" to the conjugal bed in the final scene. *Source:* Asghar Farhadi, dir., *Fireworks Wednesday* (2006; Grasshopper Film, 2013), DVD, 576p.

Farhadi movingly demonstrates Mozhdeh's desperation to have the truth confirmed, or indeed denied, in a scene where she climbs into the shower and places her ear to the vent, listening out for any sign or clue. Here, Mozhdeh is not merely confined to the home; to be sure, it is not so much that her home constitutes her entire life, but that she is morphing into the home. Rouhi becomes her proxy eye, a watcher whose mobility Mozhdeh later arrogates by stealing her chador. Disguised as Rouhi, Mozhdeh goes to Morteza's office building to see whether her husband is really where he said he would be. Despite her self-concealment, Morteza recognizes Mozhdeh and beats her up in the street as his colleagues look on, scandalized. This violent scene reveals the painful indeterminacy of the truth, which only the viewer and Rouhi are eventually able to see: Morteza's violence is itself an act of concealment, a way of maintaining the social fiction of his marriage.

Though Rouhi is not a natural spy, she soon learns to negotiate the truth within the bio-thanato-political space of the Iranian republic made available to its citizens; by skillfully mastering the information at her disposal, she can successfully graduate to a system of dissimulation and coercion, and take her place as a representative of the government by proxy—for to govern is to structure the options for action left to others, and "it is in the production of a population and of a milieu as natural-artificial phenomena that life becomes governable."[57]

The film opens with Rouhi and her fiancée Abdolreza on a motorcycle, en route to his appointment at a temporary work agency. She playfully looks at photographs the two of them took together—as if trying to catch on a fixed role, an immovable trajectory—until she lets go of one and entangles her chador in the spokes. The fall is of no major consequence, and her main concern is to cover herself and retrieve any missing pictures (figure 2.3). This destabilizing confrontation between the technical movement of the motorcycle and Rouhi's vital reaction to the stillness of the photographic image foreshadows her attempt to reconcile the stillness of her becoming a wife, a mother, fixed into a role, *and* her expectations of life taking her somewhere else. Ultimately, she plays it safe, and the film concludes with her returning to Abdolreza to begin their married life together. Throughout the film, however, Rouhi seeks an impossible assemblage or vital space for her life that cannot materialize because she, as a woman, is constantly under surveillance by a sovereign eye. This can be observed, as it were, from Farhadi's use of several "outside gaze"

Figure 2.3. A tangle between the mechanical and the vital. *Source:* Asghar Farhadi, dir., *Fireworks Wednesday* (2006; Grasshopper Film, 2013), DVD, 576p.

camera shots (figures 2.4 and 2.5), the first of which appears as Rouhi boards the bus to the apartment of her employers, married couple Mozhdeh and Morteza (figure 2.4).

The outside gaze fixes the panoptical relationship to Farhadi's controlled space, generating a type of politicized technology whereby surveillance tasks are delegated to the population at large. Farhadi

Figure 2.4. The impassive gaze. *Source:* Asghar Farhadi, dir., *Fireworks Wednesday* (2006; Grasshopper Film, 2013), DVD, 576p.

Figure 2.5. The fixed outside gaze from within the elevator. *Source:* Asghar Farhadi, dir., *Fireworks Wednesday* (2006; Grasshopper Film, 2013), DVD, 576p.

shows the capillarity of this technology by investing with its mastery anyone who can ride a bus, cutting across locales, classes, social segments; moreover, by choosing not to include any security or government official, he implies the economic efficiency of such a system because it does not necessitate a high number of people occupying positions of power, a sovereignty by proxy embedded in the citizens' individual conscience with no clear observing center. The apparent void of power is a spatial inscription. Incidentally, one may note that this technique has been lately taken up by Ali Asgari and Alireza Khatami, directors of *Terrestrial Verses* (2023), deploying the disembodied eye of the sovereign.

In a surveillance network power manifests itself discreetly: "the subject is watched from multiple and infinite vantage points such that he or she eventually internalizes this process of watching/being watched and self-surveys."[58] It indexes power embedded and rooted in the depths of the social body, a sort of Foucauldian quadrillage that occurs here not in a hospital, factory, or a school but in the open space of a crowded street, punishing Mozhdeh for the very act of moving. At the end of the film the act of concealment will be translated into a practical administration of information and power: Rouhi self-trains in the act of observation and transforms her knowledge into an ethico-political choice, acting as a sort of optical pawn from below, though her allegiances are largely unknown and appear to be in constant flux. Another tracking shot from a distance is offered when Morteza, having learned that Mozhdeh is checking his whereabouts and is approaching his office on foot, temporarily leaves his workplace to intimidate the drivers who are soliciting his wife and then ends up beating her in front of a street crowd. The camera is placed inside the elevator Morteza has just left (figure 2.5).

Unlike the use that Italian filmmakers such as Carlo Lizzani and Pier Paolo Pasolini made of the outside tracking shot as a suturing operation to destabilize, frame, and nail the viewer to a political position of individual responsibility, Farhadi deploys this device to suggest a witnessing presence from a position of authority, the incorporeal but perceived intrusion of the government into in daily life, a pure force of containment that fluctuates toward the inside. Farhadi makes Rouhi neither a victim nor a culprit, but rather a receptor or, in Foucauldian terminology, a relay, as well as an object and an instrument of internal discipline, while at the same time including the hidden face of the sovereign and its segmenting gaze.[59] Her development as a character is subtle but decisive, undergoing several iterations and revisions: first, as a housekeeper, a role she is at first dismissed from, then as a spy when she is hired again, this time by Mozhdeh, to gather information on Simin's whereabouts. In this new role, Rouhi acts as the eyes and ears of Mozhdeh, who instructs her to book an eyebrow appointment at the makeshift salon. Rouhi briefly wonders if she should ask her soon-to-be husband's permission before going, but heeds Mozhdeh's sister's advice: "Don't tell him everything!" When she arrives, Rouhi finds she likes Simin, with whom she enjoys a relatively equal relationship, both of them more or less on the periphery of middle-class life. This generates an ambivalence regarding surveillance on a personal level, where an individual spies on another individual; in turn, it illuminates the biopolitical experience of everyday Iranian life, where the watchful eye of the state infiltrates every relationship.

While she marvels at her new appearance and the sight of exquisite dyes and perfumes, Rouhi becomes aware of a conversation between Simin and the landlord, who questions the respectability of the premises and threatens to evict her. Without prompting, Rouhi steps in and poses as Simin's niece to reassure the owner that the salon is genuine.[60] The space presided over by Simin has a heterotopic quality as a site whose boundaries are uncertain, and where the possibility of an outside becomes clear and where decisions must be taken to redesign our life and its conditions. Her spontaneous fabulation activates a potentiality through which she exposes herself to an existential bond, to a metaphysical common. Far from distancing himself from the political by way of steering clear of explicit conflict with authority figures or definite representations of class, social aggregates, or other political subjects, Farhadi in fact opens an alternative politics: The Iranian filmmaker looks at conflicts that emerge as (un)intended consequences when politics have tried, sometimes in vain, to neutralize other conflicts.

After learning that Simin is aware of Morteza's plans to take his family to Dubai (and their exact time of departure), Rouhi tells her about the earlier interaction with Mozhdeh—she seems to have chosen Simin's side. However, Rouhi immediately returns to Mozhdeh's apartment to report on Simin, visibly and carefully revealing (and obscuring) different parts of their conversation. Rouhi is not a practiced dissimulator, and indeed this may be the first occasion she has been called upon to lie. Torn between her affection for Simin and her duty to Mozhdeh, Rouhi does not yet know what, exactly, she should lie about: She lets slip that Simin knows about the family's impending Dubai vacation, even what time they plan to leave. Mozhdeh instantly interprets this as evidence her husband's affair—who else would Simin have learned it from if not her husband? In this game of shifting alliances, Rouhi's maneuvering, which becomes more agile as the film progresses, reproduces the state within the household, founding a new community "through its destitution,"[61] and generates an internal ramification whereby her move is at once a safeguard of and threat to the monad, the marital relationship, demonstrating that "otherwise deeply private issues of lifestyles and reproductive behavior [are] being elevated to the very top of political concerns."[62] In this circuitous play between trying to be a subject and entering a relation of power, Rouhi becomes a master of herself by choosing not to use the information she has. Was it revenge against the upper class? Was lying all that was left to Rouhi? Farhadi organizes the final sequences around her emotions, alternating between free indirect and reaction shots while she stands at the gate of the apartment building and witnesses the arrival of Simin's ex-husband and their daughter. Serving as the optical center of their comings and goings, we imagine her potentially crafting a plan, imagining options, or maybe coming to terms with her node-like place in this family's network. Being caught in the machinations of so many different families has a cascading effect on her own understanding of married life and parenthood: She is almost in a state of stupor when she realizes how many truces were broken and precarious unities splintered. She determinedly rides the elevator by herself and then, in a state of fear and submission, she ends up concealing the facts. This is precisely the moment in which Rouhi truly accesses marriage as an institution and preserves its statute through a choice of self-regulation motivated by a macronorm, where practicing sacrifice by the subjectified individual is a path toward emancipation and access to freedom. As Morteza says to her in the car, "No one lies just because."[63] It is this transformational moment that springs Rouhi into being as a subject, an example of that moment of failed redirection Judith Butler discusses in an essay on Foucault and feminism. Butler begins by remarking that "self-attachment is socially mediated. . . . We will become attached to ourself through mediating norms." These norms return us to a sense of ourselves and, importantly, "will cultivate our investment in ourselves."[64] Rouhi's hesitation with the truth throughout the film, which culminates in her traumatic encounter with the biopolitical reach of marriage in the elevator, are related to the self-investment Butler describes, a preservation of the position of the self within the social body. Rouhi's moral judgment is transversed by her class, her social status, her gender, and the options produced thereby. To destroy this marriage would be to create a possibly catastrophic rupture in her own life. This is allegorically indicated by the intense feeling of panic Farhadi creates on the two occasions Rouhi loses her chador, a symbol of national belonging, religious piety, loyalty to the state, and her gendered position in public spaces, a necessary passport from the *oikos* to the *polis*. This loss subjects her to a threat hinted at when a neighbor boy in the building shamelessly flirts with her, "as if the missing *chador* were an invitation," since "without it, women are deemed less pure and thus subjugated to all kinds of sexual harassment."[65] Rouhi's act restores the social body within the film to its rightful place; her refusal or failure to speak was a successful immunization of the family. And by saving this unhappy family from divorce, she secures her own future and security. If this act is Rouhi's entry into womanhood and marriage as a form of self-attachment and as a preservation of her self-investment, these choices and transformations are conditioned by strict social norms that guide and constitute the subject. Farhadi is never heavy-handed with this: Rouhi's decision is not premeditated or calculated but second nature, particularly when faced with a kaleidoscope of uncertain truths and consequential secrets. This is not to say that she has no choice or agency; indeed, there are several moments of hesitation, of advancement and then retreat. Preserving the social norms won out, not because Rouhi is incapable of challenging them, but because "what falls outside the norms will not . . . be recognizable": "[It] is precisely that domain of ourselves in which we lived without recognizing, which we persist in through a sense of disavowal, that for which we have no vocabulary, but which we can endure without quite knowing. This can be, clearly, a source of suffering. But it can be as well the sign of a certain distance from regulatory norms, and so also a site for new possibility."[66]

It has been argued that marriage "is used to administer populations through delimiting personal relationships between people, managing the distribution of social goods, the continuation of the population, and the disciplining of individuals through the creation of normative familial life."[67] As I have mentioned before, Farhadi goes further by depicting marriage as a celibate network that prevents other types of relationships and common forms of exchange. *Fireworks Wednesday* depicts marriage as the art of isolating oneself. Her future husband's words, "What did you do? You look even more beautiful," explicitly validate Rouhi's transformation as a subject—she has become a new, "improved" woman.[68] He also asks after her chador. Morteza intervenes here, leaning out of his car window to clarify the situation. All seems well, but there is an undercurrent of tension. This is not necessarily because she is not wearing the chador, but because the missing chador is a metonym for Rouhi's traumatic introduction to married life (and for Mozhdeh's eradication of any middle-class-related hope). This exchange is sincere and unmotivated, but it recalls an earlier moment that day when Mozhdeh's sister advised her, "Don't tell him everything!" Farhadi leaves open the possibility of genuine love while again suggesting that some form of deception is immanent to marriage. What is clear is that in order for Rouhi to invest in her marriage and security, she has also invested a great deal in the marriage of others and in marriage as such, as a subjectifying device (figure 2.6).

Figure 2.6. Morteza explains the missing chador. *Source:* Asghar Farhadi, dir., *Fireworks Wednesday* (2006; Grasshopper Film, 2013), DVD, 576p.

Would a revelation have made any difference? Morteza, returning to the threshold after leaving the two women face-to-face, appears largely unconcerned about the potential disclosure—he casually asks if the wife now knows, half warily, half amusedly: It is a confirmation that "women in trouble in Iran can, in the end, do very little to help one another," as Bert Cardullo writes about Jafar Panahi's *The Circle* (*Dayereh*, 2000) and its depiction of the entrapping nature of structured encounters in Iranian society.[69]

The world around the protagonists is not limited to a panoptical surveillance but engages the other senses as well: "How long since the neighbor's smelled food from our apartment?" If "discipline is a political anatomy of detail," Rouhi and the other plotters of good faith in Farhadi's works are earnest promoters of a consolidation made of "small acts of cunning endowed with a great power of diffusion, subtle arrangements, apparently innocent, but profoundly suspicious, mechanisms that obeyed economies too shameful to be acknowledged, or pursued petty forms of coercion."[70] Rouhi's act may seem at first an innocent act of (self-)preservation, hypostatized by Morteza's lover Simin to end the relationship, but it also works as a foundational event for a communal space where women are humiliated, harassed, attacked, and lied to—thus, "not only is the community to be saved not saved, but, even more, what is not achieved is the safety of the atomized and isolated individuals."[71] In other words, the establishment and empowerment of the community is destroyed from within and transformed into a sterilizing protocol of immunity. Hers is an entry into the practice of correlation by way of the array of options that "constitute, define, organize and instrumentalize the strategies that individuals in their freedom can use in dealing with each other."[72]

The slippage occurs when Rouhi shares something and it turns into a deprivation and a separation, a drawing closer that is resolved in coming apart: Rouhi needs to decide what she has in common with Mozhdeh and the answer is the chador. She chooses an immunization that is also a contagion, quietly approved by the future husband in the final remark about her beauty as a seal of approval to her graduation. As the country's 2022 protests once again demonstrated, the chador is the relay in the microphysical field of Iran's civil life, the aggregator that "covers over the void of sovereign power and the governmental machine," and the point of intersection of the two axes of power that Mitchell Dean has named "the sovereign-reign and economic-governmental."[73] Here, it indexes a failed encounter and confounds the public and the private, the social and the societal, in a way not dissimilar from Simondon's principle of transindividuation or "the mutual points of intersection and transformation" between the individual and the collective.[74] If, according to Esposito, that which members of the same community have in common is not a piece of property or a shared belonging but rather a debt or a suspended gift characterized by absolute transitivity, then the chador, first deployed prior to the Revolution "as an expression of solidarity with traditional Muslims," now acts as a political signifier in Iran, operating as the "gift" of dispossession and expropriation, a reminder that Iranian women are marginalized.[75] Mozhdeh's character represents a double crisis that can inhere in a relatively affluent woman by way of her husband's position, a bourgeois who does not need to work but is still distressed by an economic regime of relegation. It is a bold commentary on the production of a feminine subject, and in this sense one can observe in Farhadi's work many echoes from Bahram Beyzai's films such as *Maybe Some Other Time* (*Shayad vaghti deegar*, 1988) and *Travelers* (*Mosaferan*, 1992) in which women as subjects are folded inside out and subjected to a continuous series of refractive alterations. Moreover, Farhadi doubled down on Beyzai's abstract and mimetic style, a style deployed to reclaim the mythical and ritual aspect of Iran's communality and shared spaces away from the instrumental use made during the revolution.[76] In the last scene Mozhdeh lies on the conjugal bed, the spectacle of a corpse meticulously prepared for viewing: no need to make her die if life is siphoned off of her at every social interaction.

About Elly

About Elly begins with Farhadi's method of intersecting the biopolitical and the topological. The spatial and the ideological overlap most discernably in the home, but it is key to producing and maintaining the integrity of the wider community, and therefore of the nation. Farhadi treats us to a dissolve of an alms box, or *sadaqeh*, with light filtering through its slots, gradually morphing into the end of a road tunnel, approaching radiant sunlight. There is a Persian creed whereby if one helps the poor before a trip, then one's safety during travel—in this case, that of three families on their way to the Caspian Sea—will be guaranteed. The shot is also an internal reference to Farhadi's personal take on slit staging, or the presence in the framing of architectural elements that dissect and shrink the available space—jambs, frames, broken windows, and the like. In Farhadi's filmmaking practice, space indexes the panoptical condition of Iranian citizens and appears to deny the very possibility of performative dynamics of emancipation. The film begins as a group of middle-class friends drive to a vacation rental on the Caspian Sea. With two notable exceptions, most of the group is composed of married couples and their children: Sepideh, her husband Amir, and their daughter; Shohreh, her husband Peyman, and their two children; and Nazy and Manuchehr. Sepideh, the apparent leader of the group and the organizer of the trip, has also invited Elly, her child's schoolteacher, whom she hopes to introduce to Ahmad, her recently divorced friend now living in Germany. While Elly is officially invited in order to look after the children, in truth Sepideh hopes to orchestrate a potential engagement between her and Ahmad.

The alms boxes are an emanation of the charitable aspect of Iran's public welfare, one of the most problematic issues when evaluating the Islamic Revolution as a whole. Raising people out of poverty has been one of its most important tenets, ranging from Khomeini's promise to put Iran's oil proceeds directly in people's pockets to Ahmadinejad's implementation of a basic income. All endeavors have failed to varying degrees, not only due to US-led efforts to impose sanctions since the very outset of the Revolution, but through de facto privatization of public assets in the first case and heightened inflation in the second. Farhadi does not abuse the trite truth that governmental control has taken over personal decisions; rather, the idyllic atmosphere of the seaside vacation becomes the occasion for an assessment of the consequences and an evaluation of the margins inscribed in individual initiative. It is the nature of that embrace that interests the filmmaker, and not merely its repressive essence; in *About Elly*, Farhadi appears to suggest that solidarity does not exist outside mechanisms of control brought about by the apparently liberal prism of the extension of mobility and economic rights.

The view from the alms box that initiates the film is a clear suggestion of the panoptical eye of the Iranian state. It soon opens out onto a tunnel, where Sepideh, played by Golshifteh Farahani, leans out of a car window (figure 2.7). In front of the car, the opening of the tunnel can be seen, recalling the previous shot while mimetically reflecting the woman's scream. It is the most joyous scene in the film, first appearing as a cry of liberation and pleasure. However, on further

Figure 2.7. An aleatory reclamation of space. *Source:* Asghar Farhadi, dir., *About Elly* (2009; The Cinema Guild Home Video, 2015), Blu-ray Disc, 1080p HD.

inspection, it is far more ambivalent than this. Is it joy? Abandon? Rage? Hopelessness? The true nature of her emotions and desires is never fully clarified—similarly, Farhadi does not give the audience the satisfaction of "knowing" Elly, who becomes the central mystery of the film. While the scene's brilliance rests on its ambiguity, the scream, whatever it may mean, is the assertion of a voice, a middle-class voice that is understood to be exempt from the laws of propriety and could claim some control—over space, over bodies, over legal status. As the film unfurls, we see the group of friends arrive at the realization that despite their class privilege and relative wealth, they are not immune to the Law. There is a sense of diffuse unease in Elly's interactions with her hosts, which the film traces and draws out. The following, unstaged footage of families camping and walking by water and trees hints at an experience that instead of being communal results in further atomization. Farhadi shows that even though citizens are afforded the opportunity to interrogate state doctrines—and in fact, "each individual, even the most stupid, when placed in a conspicuous space can exert a form of normalizing and homogenizing social control"[77]—they are reminded the hard way that a minimum slippage in the sanctioned interpretation can result in tragedy.[78] Once the friends arrive at the seaside villa, they are informed that the owner will return home the day after, thereby cutting short a stay they thought would extend over the weekend. Sepideh pleads with the family that manages the properties to find alternative accommodation, persuading them with a decisive, dishonest detail: that Elly and Ahmad are newlyweds and need a proper arrangement for this escapade. Elly's imagined marital status becomes the founding lie of the entire group's experience, ominously foreshadowed by a shot and counter-shot showing the group's laughter and the stern look returned by the boy of the local folks who look after the villas. While the contemptuous stare may at first be considered a result of class difference, as Godfrey Cheshire explains in his insightful review of the film, it also hints at the performative nature of the urbanites' existence, enjoying the perks of a relatively wealthy lifestyle: The child is not convinced by it and the audience is led to scrutinize the true nature and extent of these relationships.[79] Farhadi not only showcases the divide between the middle and the working class; he also exposes the weakness of the doomed reformist thrust of the former, whose "growing tendency toward individualism and de-politicization,"[80] lack of cohesion, and dependence on the state for job security and welfare ensures tacitly submissive exchange of freedom of expression and civil rights. The picture hints at a vertical movement of power, with Elly being on the receiving end of an act of dissimulated, "soft" coercion, the display of a preying enforcement that results in the exertion of pressure on subalterns.[81]

Farhadi is interested in how the reality of how societal microcosms like the family are diminished and destroyed when institutionalized abuse becomes a form of governmentality. Farhadi's *About Elly* conveys the articulation of power being encapsulated then inscribed inside a group that exchanges material resources for other types of participation. It may seem a cynical proposition, but it is at the heart of the strategies carried out by other players in the region—see for example the discussion of the "Turkish model," which opts out of Western-style consumerism and foreign investments in exchange for the promotion of Islamic expression and conservatism in the public domain, all the while failing to account for "the complexity of Turkey's political climate and democratic development."[82] Used as a pawn, or rather as a commodity, it is futile to determine the direct responsibility for Elly's death, just as it is in Antonio Pietrangeli's *I Knew Her Well* (*Io la conoscevo bene*, 1965). Hers is a second disappearance, a fundamental rejection of the enactment of a role she has been coerced to play, a rejection as a Foucauldian "leaping out the window" when the space for resistance is dramatically diminished.[83] The film then becomes a tragic commentary on its title through the blindness of its middle-class protagonists: "To know her is to love her," says Sepideh, implying that the group is interested in imposing its performative fallacy instead of carrying out an honest epistemological exploration.[84]

In *About Elly*, the detonating rupture of the economic order happens through the nominal protagonist, officially engaged but trying to get out of the relationship. Ominous camera swings index frustrated attempts to gain acceptance—following the party, then lingering in the emptiness of the beach house; escorting the group as they connect and bond, then pursuing some of its members as she tarries near thresholds, openings, frames. Elly is invested in the matchmaking ploy and seems content with having just a glimpse of a different future, but that circumstance does not seem the most hurtful to her; it is when she strongly expresses this intention to return home and is nonchalantly dismissed by Sepideh, who even hides her phone, that she seems to get to a point of no return. She enjoys a fleeting moment of abandon helping one of the children disentangle then fly his kite, only to disappear shortly afterward. A creeping atmosphere of dilapidation swiftly leads to a state of frozen impairment: The violation of the economic space in turn deteriorates physical spaces, relationships, even nature. *About Elly* takes no prisoners when it comes to destroying the veneer of stability that the middle-class status guarantees in Iran. What it allows is an unsteady supply of services and consumable products, but any other foray into an expansive, vital outreach is foreclosed. It is in the commentary on this lack that Farhadi's films intercept Foucault's biopolitical project: The college friends seem content with a type of participation to a sociality where rules are not questioned, and Elly's function is to stabilize that which can never be stabilized. While Jacques Derrida is concerned with fraternization as the privileged pattern for relationality, one should nonetheless think of the other's presence "as exceeding cognition, such that the other's singularity exceeds the thematic or designative grasp of the subject."[85] Foucault's approach to friendship focuses on amicability as a locus where similar technologies of the self meet each other: Self-mastery is a collaborative effort, and the practice of self-formation cannot take place in an ascetic vacuum but calls for the determination of "admissible and acceptable forms of existence or political society."[86] Foucault, though, also recognizes creative potential in friendship by affirming its relational asymmetry, by refusing binary categorizations, and by emphasizing "the invention of particular relationalities" and the acceptance of its singularities.[87] Thus, the ethical nucleus of friendship is grafted into the political tissue. Subsumed by domestic recognition and routed through expected codes of behavior, membership to the type of friends' club depicted in the film appears to be awarded via strict adherence to an orthodox codification. Elly's disappearance and death cannot do anything to stop the perfunctory coercions she had to endure when she was alive: New forms of disfigurement take over as she is mischaracterized, slandered, and betrayed by her traveling companions. The second half of the film is a calculating, bureaucratic negotiation turning Elly into dross, an unfortunate but necessary residue of another of the group's games—hence "resist[ing] the prospect of granting Elly's probable death any sacrificial or transcendental meaning" takes a more ambiguous and sinister turn.[88] Ahmad then calls a number on Elly's phone and reaches Elly's fiancé, Alirezah, who pretends to be her brother. The group, which is beginning to unravel, play along despite knowing, as Sepideh tells Ahmad, that Elly doesn't have a brother. Deception occurs within and outside of the group: Sepideh conceals, and later reveals, her knowledge of Elly's intention to break off her engagement; Ahmad, who also learns of the engagement, wants to protect her from the group, who he is certain will judge her. When they are confronted by Alirezah, they give him a sanitized version of Elly's motives and actions, a panoply of lies that alert him to the fact "that some significant truth is being withheld from him."[89] Under pressure, Sepideh, until now the keeper of secrets, relents and tells Alirezah that Elly accepted the invitation.

Farhadi indulges in the group's lapses in judgment, obedience to marital law, inane attempts at self-preservation. Is Sepideh's revelation a darkly ironic twist or the definitive lie told to her grieving fiancé? Is she using Elly as a proxy for her own rebellion? Sepideh cannot bring herself to tell the fiancé how tormented and anguished Elly really was: Creating a fictional, daring Elly is another testament to the impossibility of solidarity and open understanding. Through her one understands the perverted nature of the exchange in Iran's political economy: The regime ensures rights insofar as those who enjoy them do not try to alter its DNA—those, in turn, become complicit enforcers helping to break down the barrier between public, private, and political. The tension between freedom and conservatism reaches its extremes: The friendship is exposed as an inventory of domination mechanisms, and it becomes clear that what we are witnessing is more of an opportunistic alliance than a union, one that does not ask for a sacrifice from within, and that operates through co-opting mechanisms and not through engagement. Farhadi does not spare the regressive nature of the bond and its totalizing foundation, also showing how apparently harmless pieces of information trigger spiritual dilemmas that can be actualized through the thriller form. The filmmaker looks at transfer mechanisms, not via indoctrination, but by way of dissemination/assimilation and how they successfully operate in protocols of totalization. In his films we see the depiction and subsequent unfolding of "processes of subjectivization bring the individual to bind himself to his own identity and consciousness and, at the same time, to an external power."[90] Always in a state of interrogation, Farhadi's tragic heroes are victims of a strangling finitude, an immanent state of displacement, struggling to "learn how to make spring their way of life from the laws of life that is their own."[91] *Fireworks Wednesday* and *About Elly* are films that mirror each other phenomenologically: In the first instance, we see the negative polarity affecting the marginalized when they decide to confront class differences and inequalities; in the second, the depriving stance of the middle class is made explicit when targeting its subordinates. In 1973, the second issue of the *Quaderni di lotta femminista*, entitled "Il personale è politico," brought attention to the ideological use of categories such as the "pre-political" as well as the "private" in order to expose the bad conscience of the "institutional" Marxist political formations of the time in Italy, uninterested in the servile condition of the woman in every aspect of her life.[92] Farhadi's *Fireworks Wednesday* provides an answer to those concerns by showing the inception of political in the personal, and its morphing into the social. The films of this quartet (the other two being *Dancing in the Dust* and *Beautiful City*) all end with failed encounters, with all the transient opportunities missed: Farhadi shows us a society that slowly but surely is running out of options—its space weaponized, its marital bond informed by a biopolitics of exclusion.

Each of the films discussed in this chapter functions as a critique of power. They do not "save" their characters or enact alternative communities because such communities do not yet exist. Such a community requires a new language of relationality, new forms of contact and social antagonism, new ways to understand the use of resources and modes of production as organic totalities, and possibly even a way to dissolve supranational organizations. That new form might be cinema itself and its transformative effect on the constitution of the self. Whether it guarantees a radical response is an open question, but it presents its characters' dilemmas as ethical ones. The viewer is not asked to approve of or identify with their struggles or transgressions, their flaws, but is rather invited and persuaded to witness the crisis for what it is: the struggle to expose and deconstruct the technologies of the self in search of new political possibilities, the peril of confronting a sometime disembodied but potentially reemerging sovereign that institutionally nests itself in the weak seams of the social fabric, the fight against the osmotic infiltration of the economy into governing techniques.

3

Russia and the Use and Abuse
of Genealogical Authority

Wars are no longer waged in the name of a sovereign who must be defended; they are waged on behalf of the existence of everyone; entire populations are mobilized for the purpose of wholesale slaughter in the name of life necessity: massacres have become vital. It is as managers of life and survival, of bodies and the race, that so many regimes have been able to wage so many wars, causing so many men to be killed.

—Foucault, *History of Sexuality, Volume 1*

If there were a modern political cinema, it would be on this basis: the people no longer exist, or not yet . . . *the people are missing.*

—Gilles Deleuze, *Cinema 2: The Time-Image*

～

AN ENGINEER GETS STRANDED in a sleepy, provincial town a few hundred miles from Moscow; after many other bizarre events, he witnesses the suicide of a cook who had earlier served him for dessert a platter of sponge cake that, incidentally, was the exact copy of his head. In the futile and desperate search for a train that will take him back home, the engineer runs into a subterranean museum. A venue that one would barely expect to hold a few local icons and relics from Soviet party activists suddenly transforms into a trove of treasures and *tableaux vivants*, transforming the museum into a marvelous phantasmagoria: Romans reporting to Nero, Priam's grandson Dardan, Attila and his cohorts had all picked that small town for their epic battles, heroic deeds, settlements, migrations. It soon becomes clear that this underground museum acts as a compendium of Moscow's State Historical Museum and the St. Petersburg's State Museum of Political History: the engineer witnesses the False Dmitry, Minin and Pozharsky, Vladimir the Great and Stalin, blended with local celebrities in a dazzling display of homogenized absurdity. Karen Shakhnazarov's *Gorod Zero* (*Zerograd*, 1988), almost a cinematic companion to Venedikt Erofeev's Perestroika-era prose poem *Moskva-Petushki*, illustrates and mocks two of the most represented aspects of centralized power in Soviet and Russian cinema. The first is the return of fictive genealogies of imperial reach whose goal is to neutralize the everyman and then insert him in a grandiose narrative; to normalize, to make power seamless, invisible, and natural; to dissolve the average citizen's pushes and thrusts for a different type of utopia into an unmodifiable and inevitable history that they are forced to welcome as their own. The second, exemplified by the city museum as the biological freezing of the historicized form, is the inescapabilty of power as sovereignty—a rule that never graduates to life-fostering processes but is synonymous with domination, and whose immutable goals are submission and seizure. Working together but more and more out of sync, these two aspects conjure up a desacralized image of power, whose mechanisms to justify its absolute nature are jammed, and whose absurd manifestations—the naked secretary, the "schizophrenic" cake—are the symptoms of an increasingly difficult task to hide the void at its core; incidentally, it seems that the fictional evocation of Troy is enough to legitimize power, as Foucault mentions in regards with the French monarchy.[1] The local prosecutor shows the engineer how the law permanently becomes the norm, and the engineer accepts his defeat; the film introduces the interplay between power as repression and power as production.[2] As Anton Weiss-Wendt has pointed out, the transition between Soviet communism and neoconservative, authoritarian nationalism has been seamless: It is a unified, bureaucratic view of history showing a heroic and bound-to-be victorious Russia where loyalty to its leaders is the architrave holding the architectonics of the State, and feeding an ongoing process of "cumulative radicalization"[3] aimed at monopolizing research and production of culture from above.

Among both late Soviet and contemporary Russian cinema, there has been a significant tendency to attempt to counter the state-sanctioned genealogies of the nation with a more radical Foucauldian genealogy, offering a critique of power's consolidation and its permeation of daily life, probing and deconstructing the internal logic of Russia's imperialist vocation. If *Gorod Zero* encapsulates all the neuralgic passages neutralized by legitimizing normalization, films such as Alexei Popogrebsky's *How I Ended This Summer* (*Kak ya provel etim letom*, 2010) problematize the traumatic transition from pre- to post-Soviet Russia, allegorizing the unspoken as the only true, negative connection that links different generations all but exemplified by films that deal, critically or complimentarily, with the extractive logic to produce Russia's revanchist, nostalgic exceptionalism.[4] Two undercurrents characterize recent Russian cinema. One is a wave of works deploying the kind of abstract imagery that Vlad Strukov analyzed under the guise of the symbolic mode, post-evental non-time and non-space where phantasmatic meaning explodes into multi-valent, schizophrenic identities to which only a posthumous subject can relate. The other wave more directly engages with the biopolitical generation of the "Russian man" and the problems of articulating a new and exportable ideology after the demise of the Soviet project. Often focused on the Stalinist period, scholarship that analyzes the relationship between Soviet and Russian cinema and its representation of history has insisted on strategies of concealment, reassessment, and reinvention.[5] Under Vladimir Putin, Hollywoodization has extracted the entertainment and propaganda value from certain historical events to such an extent that some scholars have talked about it as an "ontological change" of the image in Russian cinema, an industry that distances itself from novel relationships with history and society and is confined to the immunized ward of generic conventions.[6] The orange and teal coating of formulaic Hollywood stories in Russia varnishes grotesque, funereal, and yet festive celebrations of death, a colorized correlative of the necrorealism of Evgeniy Iufit and Vladimir Maslov taking itself seriously about thirty years later. Some filmmakers have sought to counter these sterilized historical adaptations by proposing different perspectives, frames that may delegitimize that essentialist scripting of the past. This state has brought the film industry in Russia to a standstill: The freedom, in terms of available options for fundraising, interactions with European cinema, and other artistic expressions declined rapidly after 2012. The democratization of the film industry attempted by Sergey Tolstikov ended abruptly when Putin's return as president of Russia brought policies of vertical integration, first with Vladislav Surkov and later with Vladimir Medinsky.[7] Revenue from domestic productions fell sharply, covering only one-third of the total in recent years, the Cinema Fund fell under direct control of the Ministry of Culture, and filmmakers ended up pleading their cases at the Culture Committee of the Russian Parliament.[8] As a result, the acculturation strategy carried out in this retrenching phase of Putin's power hinges on the following actions: 1) complete exclusion of international films from domestic theaters during holidays, in order to maximize the largest portion of time Russian citizens can spend in movie-houses; 2) total oversight of fund allocation, resulting in a de facto monopoly of domestic productions, directly via control of the Cinema Fund and indirectly via symbiotic—or perhaps parasitical—relation between the various holdings with media-related interests and the Kremlin; 3) seamless administration to the public of Kremlin-approved projects, such as Russian versions of the Marvel multiverse in the form of sport epics, or a return to the Russifying historico-hagiographical biopics of the 1930s and 1940s, with titles such as *Admiral* (2008) or *Kalashnikov* (2020) taking the baton of *Chapayev* (1934), *Admiral Nakhimov* (1947), or *Michurin* (*Life in Bloom*, 1949).

The ultrarealism of the aforementioned *Zoya*, as well as of films such as Andrey Bogatyrev's *The Red Ghost* (*Krasnyy prizrak*, 2021) and Kim Druzhinin and Andrey Shalopa's *Panfilov's 28 Men* (*28 panfilovtsev*, 2016)—the latter, produced by the videogame company Ganjin Entertainment, was explicitly used as a sort of cultural brokerage with Kazakhstan[9]—are part of an attempt to re-ideologize the historical past and conjure up a shared heritage via one-sided, lugubrious propaganda fantasies. *Zoya*'s titular character is the figural correlative of Putin's zig-zagging policies from biopolitical enhancement of life—his vision, repeatedly mentioned during public speeches, of "500 million Russians," the criminalization of abortion, and other policies—to its necropolitical deprivation—the same lives rescued from abortion are sent to the Ukrainian trenches or to Russia's own "African Corps" and other military contingents (figures 3.1 and 3.2).

Figure 3.1. "Defend me today and I will be able to defend you tomorrow." Russian-style natalism that regards children as military resources and women as procreators of new white crusaders. *Source:* Vkontakte.

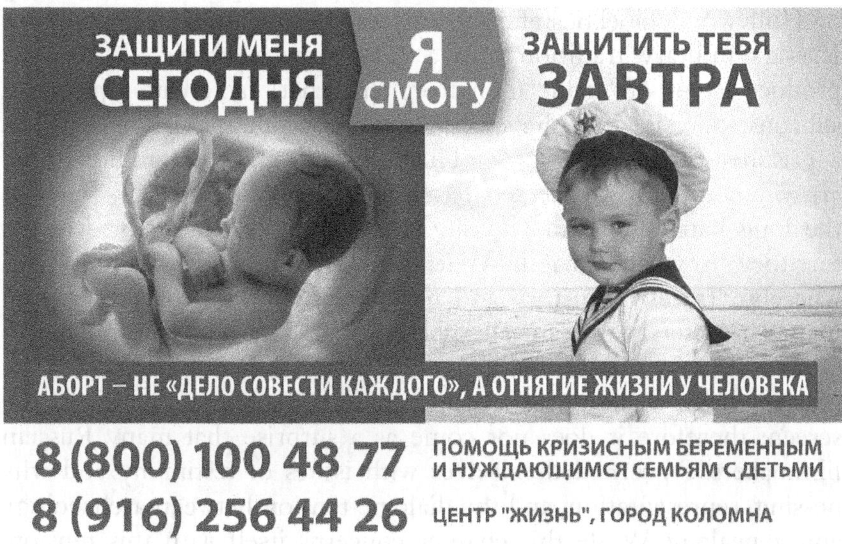

Figure 3.2. Necropolitics and state-sanctioned arts. *Source:* Label: Splav Slov.

In its emphasis on the production of a patriotic spectatorship, these fantastic incursions into the painful stories of World War II recall the kitsch of socialist realism: By parroting the color grading of Hollywood blockbusters and injecting the "power and glory" of Russia's military tradition into a videogame aesthetic, those films produce a type of "artificial environment [that] can create a powerful subconscious effect on the spectator, who becomes a visitor to, if not a prisoner of, the artwork."[10] This Russian version of militainment art, often directly connected to current geopolitical affairs such as the long battle to claim Ukraine as a "natural" part of the Russian territory, is what Mariëlle Wijermars calls the omnipresent past, whereby "traces of history and narratives describing its events and main characters permeate all spheres of society and cultural life."[11] Such a drastic and carefully crafted exercise in biopower is coextensive with the disappearance of ordinary Russian people from the screen; therefore it does not come as a surprise that many Russian filmmakers concerned themselves with issues of testimony and witnessing, representation, and the dialogic tension between archaeology and genealogy. While this chapter concerns itself with this tension, critiquing Russian biopower, it is nonetheless not credulous when it comes to liberal democracy; rather, it examines the enormous effort at producing narratives, anachronistic ideologies, national fantasies, and racial mythologies that emerges to conceal the absolute power that the political class exerts. Directors such as Kirill Serebrennikov, Andrey Zvyangitsev, and Sergei Loznitsa invite an examination of the effects of governmental techniques on the subject that are located in the cultural and cinematic production of menacing externalities. These external threats are connected with allegedly anti-Russian qualities but are in fact xenophobic fantasies laundered by national self-defense. Even *Brother* (*Brat*, 1997) by Aleksei Balabanov, one of the most luminous achievements in articulating the sanctity of the national idea, had to rabidly pit its folk hero against internal and external obstacles, articulating an idea of Russia as an alternative to the West, which is characterized as an existential threat. As scholars such as Nancy Condee have probed the imperial vocation of Soviet-Russian filmmakers, it is in fact remarkable that Balabanov, who would later volunteer a decaying, nihilistic portrait of Soviet times in *Cargo 200* (*Grus 200*, 2007) cannot help but project externally Russia's existential need for power and influence (figure 3.3). Two years after the first Chechen campaign and the approval of a constitution that borrowed elements

Figure 3.3. Bagrov, after learning jihadism during his deployment in Chechnya, is bent to annihilate the "Collective West." *Source:* Aleksei Balabanov, dir., *Brother* (1997; Tartan Video, 2003), DVD, 576p.

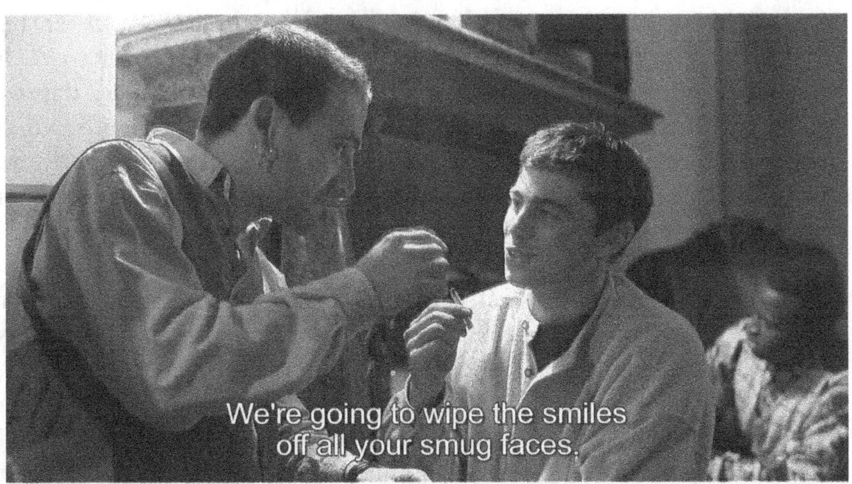

from the French semi-presidential system and the American judiciary, Balabanov unleashed his legendary protagonist Danila Bagrov against the Chechen and other exogenous threats. *Brother* offers a hybrid of familiar genre cinema—the action movie, a recognizable film genre with an "authentic" national ethos, thereby providing viewers with a vision of "an imaginary totality and fictive collective body."[12] Balabanov's approach to "generational" filmmaking is to turn the figure of the lone antihero, which emerged from late Soviet, perestroika-era cinema exemplified by *ASSA* (1987) and *The Needle* (*Igla*, 1988)—particularly the latter's anti-Soviet nod to peripheral autonomy—into a hero driven by nostalgia and *ressentiment*. In doing so, Balabanov produces a politically aggregating emblem that transforms an "action" film into a fantasy of reactionary national identity that is both a diagnostic of the chaotic situation of post-imperial Russia and a prognosis of its Eurasian destiny. For example, in a shot occurring at 55:23, Bagrov basically shares the frame with an American and a Frenchman, representatives of two *"ethnoi"* targeted by the fascist thought of Lev Gumilev, an antisemitic Soviet Eurasianist and ethnographer whose spurious ethnological history and its pseudo-scientific discourse are now popular among the Russian ruling class.[13]

Bagrov, firmly devoted to a suprematist preservation of his culture, and blessed by the exceptional drive that his Russian superethnos is endowed with, notes that between the two there is no difference: "Soon," he says wrongly addressing the Frenchman, "your entire America is going to bite it . . . we're going to wipe the smiles off all your smug faces." An avid consumer of Russian rock music, Bagrov stands for Russia's failure at persuasive power. Bagrov scoffs when a girlfriend points out that he was addressing a French person and not an American, retorting, "Big difference!"—a stance that accords with Gumilev's views of the French and the American revolutions, whereby both nations have been degenerated by "a parasite ethnos, one that has lost its ancestral land and survives leeching on another ethnos."[14] This further racialization of Eurasian thought, which is now used for geopolitical purposes that go beyond Europe and Asia, is a form of Russian white supremacy whose analog can be found in white nationalism in the United States. While Balabanov has declared himself completely uninterested in politics, his "Russian Rambo" is not merely a genre film (a category the director often highlighted when asked about his body of work).[15] Indeed, as a genre film, this thriller provides the perfect ideological framework for Balabanov's revanchist protagonist, the ordinary Russian man who is transformed into a "heroic actor" who "[stands] away from the masses" as an exceptional, racially superior body in whom *ethos* and *ethnos* are undivided, a body that is "distinguished as a sort of superperson."[16]

So far, this might describe any number of American action films, but Balabanov's hero is in direct conversation with an idea that was born in a Soviet labor camp and ended up occupying a crucial place in conservative nationalist Russian politics: *passionarnost'*, or "passionary." *Passionarnost'* is a critical concept in Gumilev's thought. A combination of cosmology, mysticism, genetics, and the Stalinist epistemology of "the new Soviet person," *passionarnost'* was, again according to historian Mark Bassin, a special kind of energy derived from cosmic radiation only certain "mutant" individuals—"passionary individuals"—are able "to absorb and convert in [great] amounts" and whose "capacity for sustained labor output" is "entirely exceptional." *Passionarnost'* confers an "'insuperable inner striving' for some sort of 'purposeful activity.'" Following Gumilev's eugenic mysticism, passionary individuals include Genghis Khan, Alexander the Great, and Napoleon Bonaparte. This energy, which is invested in such individuals, allows them to form ethnic groups whose destinies continue to be propelled and influenced by that transformative biological gift.[17] Even if Gumilev's theory were not a pseudoscience that rationalized its own antisemitism, it is easy to discern how, by this definition alone, the concept would appeal to Putin conservatives (including neo-fascist Aleksandr Dugin) in the twenty-first century. Indeed, Putin has used the term in his speeches; almost a year to the day after Russia's invasion of Ukraine, Putin declared in an address, "I believe in passionarity [*passionarnost'*], in the theory of passionarity . . . Russia has not reached its peak. The feeling of patriotism . . . is the core of our future. . . . if you do not love your Fatherland . . . it means not to believe in the future either. . . . We have an infinite genetic code. . . . All this can be united in one word—patriotism."[18] Russian scholar Sergei Medvedev has called Crimea "a territory of the subconscious," suggesting an ideological coup in which never-resolved destructive impulses—post-imperial resentment, authoritarianism, insecurity with regard to the West, especially the US, historical denialism—take over and mobilize the entire energy of a mind and its body—the entire Russian body politic.[19] From this standpoint, Russia has found renewed comfort in the Soviet kitsch representing its leaders as being a mystical coextension of its culture and history and outweighing in wisdom and knowledge its entire population. The nature of this endeavor was foreshadowed at one of the most significant sites of Russian national identity, the main Cathedral of the Russian Armed Forces, from which a mosaic depicting the country's 2014 capture of Crimea was hastily removed in 2020 (its whereabouts are still unknown).

In the mosaic, surrounded by *babushki* and other aging citizens, Putin is accompanied by Minister of Defense Sergey Shoigu, Minister of Foreign Affairs Sergey Lavrov, Federation Council Speaker Valentina Matviyenko, and State Duma Speaker Vyacheslav Volodin, as well as FSB Director Alexander Bortnikov and the head of the Army's General Staff Valery Gerasimov (figure 3.4). In a country whose demographics were already catastrophic before the invasion of Ukraine, the absence of young men in the mosaic is a sad omen of what would happen two years later, with an egregious number of men of serving age either fleeing the country or being used as cannon fodder for ultrasophisticated Western weaponry in the trenches of Donbass and other regions. Internally, it was necessary to quash dissent, as young people, who disapproved of the general direction of

Figure 3.4. Novorussian kitsch. *Source:* BBC News.

the country, let alone the war, became disposable.[20] What this situation reflects, and which is so relevant to contemporary Russian film, is the State's biopolitical understanding of the population "as secondary to the territory of the country" and its national resources.[21] Indeed, in this configuration the population itself becomes a means to an end, a resource to be extracted for the production of a national fiction. The war also gave Putin the opportunity to ponder a final move from an authoritarian to a totalitarian, neo-fascist state with a conservative religious component, a return to the centralized planning of Soviet times and a generic anti-West platform at its core—before resuming profitable business partnership, that is—producing himself as the leader in which the mysticism of Russian Orthodoxy, the Russian "gene pool," and Russian military might intersect.[22]

The strategy by which this has unfolded has involved the systematic military occupation of any venue in which information and culture are not sanctioned by the State, going so far as to occasionally kill their representatives as a warning to others. Revised and uncritical versions of centuries-old artists and their work are deployed to enclose the population in a fictive national narrative and remove any elements of Russian culture or history that might challenge it. This is the context and frame of reference within which the filmmakers discussed in the remainder of this chapter operate.

Sergei Loznitsa's Cinema of the Crowd

The restoration of Russia as a global power was an issue that concerned the country's political scholars and the intellectual class as soon as the Soviet Union collapsed. One of the most productive concepts was that of *sobornost'*, the ecumenic, spiritual union of peoples. Emphasizing Russia's spiritual reserve as an antagonist to the decadent, individualistic, and aloof West, together with a dismissal of parliamentary culture, practical emphasis on military might, and strictly Russocentric interpretation of the tenet, scholars such as Evgenii Troitskii paved the way for a political deployment of the concept, while going as far as saying that "the *sobornyi* consolidation of the ethnos is more and more becoming the categorical imperative of our time."[23] A similar mysticism can be encountered in Putin's production of Russia's military aggression as the inevitable fulfillment of Russia's exceptionalism, with a crucial difference: While intellectuals like Troitskii saw the Soviet period as an aberration and an "immoral" phase because of the dissolution of the family and other theological concerns, Putin's shrewd approach was to resituate the Soviet era, Stalinism in particular, within a greater narrative of Russia's manifest destiny—a *sobornost'* for the current era serves as a guiding principle for both internal and foreign affairs, the former in terms of cultural homogenization, the latter in terms of presenting the country as engaged in a struggle against the West and also as a model of development (and concurrent with Donald Trump's attack against the secular state). Albeit critical of Russia's autocratic and xenophobic overtones, it could be argued that Sergei Loznitsa's archival understanding of Russian history hints at a similar continuity, only this time to deconstruct it, by looking at the constant production of self-serving scenarios justifying the idea of Russia's inevitable superiority over Europe's democratic institutions.

The Ukrainian Loznitsa, born in Soviet Belarus, raised in Kiev, and now living in Berlin, occupies a position as both an insider and an outsider. Drawing on this ambivalent yet mobile position, Loznitsa has constructed, over the course of his career, a visual ethics based on a witnessing perspective that is engaged in the removal of distances, one that seeks to arrive at new forms of epistemology: "I strive to eliminate everything that might be a hindrance to knowledge." Known for both documentaries and fictional films, Loznitsa straddles the divide between truth and fiction, exposing the gulf between them that is often disavowed by nationalism. This ethos has elicited the ire of both Russian and Ukrainian critics. For example, Shakhnazarov, as chair of the Kinotavr Film Festival, at which Loznitsa won an award, accused the direct of anti-Russian sentiments.[24] Meanwhile, Loznitsa was expelled from the Ukrainian Film Academy in 2022 following the 2021 release of his film *Babi Yar: Context* for his "cosmopolitan" failure to demonstrate his commitment to "his national identity."[25] This alone makes his work vital for understanding the complex relationship between biopower and the population, but it is his preoccupation with groups, institutions, and crowds that is particularly relevant and radical, from his early short documentary *The Halt* (*Polustanok*, 2000), which focuses on a train station's waiting travelers, to the explosive fiction film *Donbass* (2018). Taken together, Loznitsa has created his own cinema of the crowd, one that reaches back to the earliest moments of filmmaking while remaining uniquely attentive to the urgency of his contemporary moment.[26] His films are at once autopsies of (post-) Soviet histories and living archives of the present. The documentary aspect of these films participates in the filmic conversation between reality and the represented, but it has a more specific significance, as it poses the genre's claim to truth against the dreamscape of state propaganda and immanent, "genetic" patriotism.

The director's 2003 film *Landscape* (*Peyzazh*) offers a vision that runs counter to nationalist fantasies, a biopolitical image of a depressed post-Soviet Okulovka, a small town in Novgorod Oblast, and its dispirited residents as they wait for a bus to come. Although they are not dissidents, the viewer hears fragments of conversation that are inherently political and critical. As they stand in the snow, the people complain about the hospital and the reduction or cancellation of their social benefits, and testify to domestic violence, alcoholism, drug addiction, and general malaise. Life in this place, which might stand in for similar towns across the country, is peripheral, inert, and residual thanks to state neglect and economic exclusion. The film functions as a sardonic allegory of Russia's homogenizing policies, so pervasive that even its utopias feel mass-produced: First we hear a man dismissing any perspective for decades to come, skeptical about a potential Chinese takeover, then one woman recounts how she was taken in by the hospital after bringing her husband, hinting at the precarious fungibility of the bodies on screen. Apart from a few young men with few prospects but military service (more on this shortly), the people in this "landscape" are national resources not because their identities can be exploited, nor can their bodies be fed to the war machine; instead, the population of *Landscape* is useful to the State only insofar as they do not pose a threat—they have been deprived of any mode or resource to do so (figure 3.5).

The film bears a resemblance to *Las Hurdes: Land Without Bread* (*Las Hurdes: Tierra sin pan*, 1932), Luis Buñuel's only "documentary" (in truth more of a reenactment of an ethnographic study by Maurice Legendre), which observed daily life in Las Hurdes, one of Spain's poorest regions at the time.[27] The extreme misery it depicted caused controversy, and the film was banned in Spain. Both directors blend the techniques of phenomenological realism with avant-garde aesthetics that depict the "strangeness of everyday life when viewed through the camera's lens, whereby it becomes an ethnographic object."[28] *Landscape*,

Figure 3.5. Locals comment on themselves as production of unqualified life. *Source:* Sergei Loznitsa, dir., *Landscape* (2003; New Wave Films, 2013), DVD, 576p.

however, contains one crucial difference: here, the commentary originates from the people themselves. The blob of bored, often old and often sick travelers appears far from motivated by *passionarnost'* or other semantic pirouettes of Russia's manifest destiny—when the bus finally comes, the crowd shove one another to get on. Unlike *Las Hurdes*, the Russian folks in Loznitsa's film are "living" because their bodies refuse to die, made to look like the titular landscape.

This film can be placed in dialogue with Didi-Huberman's pluralist ethos of observation, which Alison Smith describes as an orientation toward "unexceptional individuals who make up a collectivity but should not be simply subsumed into a mass."[29] It is the exclusion of the people we sort of spy on in *Landscape* from the tightly controlled political sphere and oligarchic wealth that link Loznitsa's crowd to a figure Didi-Huberman has outlined as central to the history of cinema itself: the "extra." Loznitsa deftly triangulates the seams of bare life that run through the political and cinematic subject, actor, and "extra," which in *Landscape* are intimately linked. Didi-Huberman traces the extra back to the earliest moments in cinema history, the famous *Workers Leaving the Lumière Factory* (*La sortie de l'usine Lumière à Lyon*, 1895) which showed "for the very first time on screen the lower classes in full movement," originating "a history of exposure of the people: it is the social body in its entirety that, at the end of the nineteenth century, becomes the principal object of this new atlas of the world in movement."[30] Here, one can readily determine the significance of a concept as resonant as "exposure" in relation to *Landscape*: The film exposes the would-be passengers to film, connecting their image to a global audience as the Lumière film did, to be sure, but in exposing its "lower classes" alongside their voices, the film "exposes" their biopolitical exposure to sickness, physical violence, emotional trauma, and material deprivation. This correctly suggests elements of ethnographic cinema, which *Landscape* projects against the spurious ethnocentric logic of the State. If we take root of the prefix of both terms, *ethnos*, what this film seems to be saying is that an *ethnos* is not constituted by a mythical "ethnic" identity but is more fixed to is essential etymology: the *ethnos* as a band of people or a flock or swarm of animals—we might also add "extras." What connects this group is not national identity or ethnicity, though they may be Russian, but forms of struggle and suffering as "beings whose life is irremediably and painfully assigned to happiness," a condition that challenges the very notion of the nation, which can withdraw its privileges and protections at any time.

In addition to the Lumière workers, Didi-Huberman cites further examples of the documentary nature of early film, which depicted "bull races and baby competitions, political demonstrations . . . fruit and vegetable markets; dockers at work," and so on.[31] As cinema continued to develop into a *dispositif*, the depiction of such social bodies literally faded into the background. Those that once populated the bull race or the vegetable market as a collective and who, together, composed a moving, living world as the camera's subject, became *extras* operating in the scenery, objects that lent a mute verisimilitude to the main performance of the actors, the stars. Didi-Huberman observes that the French word for extras is *figurants*, which is always a plural noun (from the verb *figurer*, "to appear, to represent, or to be an extra"), indicating a dis-individuated mass—when a single extra must be referred to, he says, it is as "*un simple figurant*, meaning 'a simple or mere extra.'" What's more, *figurants* is French slang for bodies in a morgue awaiting identification.[32] Although Didi-Huberman does not draw this parallel explicitly, it is clear that the extra is the "bare life" of cinema, constituting the main action, and leads by their exclusion from the narrative, their subjection to "shouted orders and to military discipline." They must remain fixed, immobile, mute or else it will threaten the very reality they exist to uphold: "the setting parks him . . . submitting him to shouted orders and to military discipline. Should he step out of line, *he will put the set in danger*."[33] This, I suggest, is the key to understanding the title of the film *Landscape*, whose main visual focus, after all, is the crowd.

At this point, it should be acknowledged that the figures in Loznitsa's film are not hired extras but real passengers waiting at a real bus stop. Their voices rise above a murmur, every expression of quotidian distress indexed to a life and a history that will go on (must go on) beyond the screen. People are shot in close-up or from a distance depending on their proximity to the camera, which never stops its attentive but even rhythm to linger on one face any longer than another, either from a height or lower to the ground in a properly "optical" manner. But on closer inspection, the viewer will notice that the sound of these voices, which Loznitsa recorded separately from the footage, does not match up with the movements of his subjects' lips: the speech is out of sync with the speakers, and it is unclear whose life and whose voice the words belong to. One is never sure who is really speaking—a brilliant sonic duplication of the camera's elliptical, kinetic panorama. This formal intervention carries a special significance, as it divides the subjects' bodies from their speech. Just as the extras merge into their setting, allowing the stars and plot to stand out in relief, the body of the crowd—crucially, as a whole—becomes the landscape of the voices. From this disembodied soundtrack we gather that these people often live in states of relative poverty: Loznitsa's point seems to be that once a general state of deprivation is maintained and the citizenship is already accustomed to a low standard of life compared to many Western countries, then it is easier for Putin or whoever sits at top positions of power to perpetuate a politics of Russian exceptionalism that blends identity and distinction, through which they establish an imaginary relationship with the leaders, who also protect them against the menace of liberal democracy and all their cultural baggage (let us not forget that Putin banished gender studies on the basis that they are a threat to national security).

Just as Didi-Huberman's extras merge into their setting to allow the stars to stand out in relief, the body of the crowd becomes the landscape for the voices of the "extras," both compositionally—the moving images are the background for the audible voices—and politically, for they also disturb the image of the nation's potency and the legitimacy of the State; that is, they *put the set in danger*." The voices that populate this landscape discuss amputations, house fires, spoiled meat, and beatings, and wonder when the bus will come. A few teenagers stand against the wall, drinking beer as a woman off-camera discusses her contempt and fear of her husband, who "goes completely off the deep end" when he is drunk.[34] Recent deaths, drug problems, alcoholism, theft, and deprivation are recurrent topics of conversation that indirectly testify to the "uneven development" and consequent "temporal unevenness" of a community that has been forgotten.[35] Loznitsa's bus stop is not simply an ideal place to observe daily life; it is also the site of something much more complex and paradoxical: The bus stop is a locus of immobility, the passengers suspended in an arrested, arbitrary temporality that may or may not transport them to what is left of their lives. The people waiting at the bus stop are aware of this condition. When the bus finally comes, the crowd shove one another to get on.[36] Men and women talk among themselves about when, and if, the bus will arrive. One man says, "Two hours waiting for fuck-all. There's no fucking bus either," and begins to relay a darkly comic anecdote about being picked up by the drunk driver of a tractor—its seat covered in agricultural excrement—instead.[37] At another point, a woman says that the bus will arrive at three o'clock. "Three?" another woman asks. "That's right," the first woman replies. "One day it comes at three, one day it comes at five."[38]

Loznitsa shares more with Gogol than with Ilya Repin: a similar sense of dark absurdity, both unafraid of human vulgarity. And indeed, the crowd at the bus stop more resemble "dead souls" than fully living beings, recalling Gogol's novel of the same name, in which the unscrupulous bourgeois Chichikov buys the rights to dead serfs (as property belonging to their landlords, they were called "souls" when they were counted as chattel), which he intends to leverage for a large mortgage. A little less than a century later, Trotsky would use the term to criticize Stalin, who, he wrote, "collects dead souls for the lack of living ones."[39] "There will be no prospects for the next thirty to forty years in Okulovka," says a member of Loznitsa's crowd, offhandedly summarizing the town's terminal, almost post-nuclear decline, and with it the suggestion that the "souls" of this post-Soviet town are trapped in the death not only of a place, but of a time (one might also add an identity). The figures in *Landscape* speak of a generalized order of corruption and exploitation, establishing a history quite apart from the transcendent national destiny that animates Putin's neo-imperial incursions precisely because they move themselves from the periphery and into the center of history. For example, one woman tells a story about "some lads from Chernobyl" she once knew:

> I used to know some lads from Chernobyl, twelve of them at least. Lovely looking lads they were. "My god, look at the state of you," I said. They were lying there, complete wrecks. And now our lads are dying in Chechnya too. It's so terrible it doesn't bear thinking about. When I went in, they were all sitting against this wall. "What are you lot doing?" I asked. And they said: "We can't sleep because of the pain." They're just buried and forgotten. I can't bear to think about it.[40]

In this narrative, the woman speaking above links her connection to the 1986 disaster with the—at the time *Landscape* was filmed—ongoing

Second Chechen War. This war, as the polyphony of the crowd suggests, has claimed or ruined the lives of the dwindling "supply" of young men in the town—a vivid and precise example of the extractive nature of biopolitics I have sought to outline throughout this book. This is something Loznitsa's films index again and again: The nation produces citizens whose freedom consists in dying for the motherland, extracting and mobilizing lives militarily, managing life as source of available deaths. Throughout *Landscape*, the military abuse of young men is known to the members of the crowd. At another point in the film, a man can be heard saying, "They don't give a damn about people." A woman answers him: "We were afraid, and we'll be afraid our whole lives long," marking this condition as the continuity between the past and the future.[41] If one traditional aspect of spectatorship is to recognize and, in the act of watching, convert a body, its movements, gestures, and speech, into a more or less legible person (this is the case with both fiction and documentary film), Loznitsa does not permit it in this film. He insists on the alienation of life from itself, separated within itself in a way that illustrates the production of bare life without also affirming it. This is inscribed in the composition of the film itself: Long tracking shots are separated either by seamless hard cuts or by black leader emulsion, imparting a sense of constant movement at a slow but measured pace—not a walking pace, but a *looking* pace, a rhythm proper to the image itself.

In *Austerlitz* (2016), Loznitsa turns to another crowd, this time the visitors to three different Holocaust memorial sites: Auschwitz, Sachsenhausen, and Dachau. Like his historical documentaries—such as *The Event* (*Sobytie*, 2015) and *Babi Yar. Context*—*Austerlitz* is concerned with the ontological (re)construction of images, but here these are dialectically juxtaposed against more "profane" medialities and images: smartphones, selfies, poses. *Austerlitz* is not so much a documentary as a fragmentary chronicle, a stream of depurated images. In this black-and-white film, Loznitsa's camera records visitors to former Nazi death camps, their indexical insufficiency now in painful display. The film begins with a long, wide shot behind a small grove of birch trees, through which a group of visitors can be seen, obscured by leaves and branches at various points. Their backs are turned to the camera as they sit on the wide stone benches typical of museums, but we can see a man turn to another person and speak. There is no audible dialogue, only a few murmurs, the sound of birdsong, and the wind. They do not appear to realize they are being filmed. With this image, Loznitsa initiates three orders of observation: the camera, the visitors, and the viewer of the film. Memory is both reconstruction and forgetfulness—we yearn for every visitor to look deep into their selves, we painfully try to guess if they are affected at all, what their role will be in a future construction and propagation of knowledge: The film captures what Dennis Walder called "an uneasy sense of the past as the source of endless layers of destructive human impulse that will and indeed must be remembered for survival in the present."[42] Thus, while tourists stream through barren locales that can only barely evoke tragedies for which there are no words, one dares to go beyond that dubious experience, even if it means to seize a specter with one's own bare hands.

Loznitsa not only borrows the title of this film from W.G. Sebald's novel of the same name but even asserts that it is an adaptation of the German writer's work. However, film critic Luca Malavasi reasonably suggests that Sebald's novel tells the viewer relatively little about the film or its subject, instead offering Didi-Huberman's *Écorces* (*Bark*, 2011) as the true companion to the film, emphasizing the position of liminality the observer must by necessity take and the severed temporalities in which "the Camp must lie to tell the truth, simplify to be understood, be didactic and welcoming in order to constitute itself as 'the locus of memory.' "[43] In the wake of Esposito's disaggregation of the subject–object divide into a mélange of human, material, and animal as living entities, *Écorces'* main point of interest lies in its biopolitical overcoming of the human as the only category capable of producing and experiencing affect. According to Didi-Huberman, sensations and gestures are still nested in *materico* surfaces, in the context of a general rethinking of "memory studies through a non-anthropocentric lens."[44] Loznitsa documents the collision of a continuous stream of visitors against an immovable structure, in space and in memory (perhaps a direct reference to certain scenes in Lanzmann's *Shoah*).[45] It is the chronicle of a disaggregation, of a collision between two antagonistic durations—one, that of the daily flow of tourists, reconciling their forward movement and mediated entertainment with the other, the fearsomely solemn immobility of the camp as the life, death, and memories that reside within it come apart in real time. The filmmaker's sharp irony is present as ever in his exposure of the visitors' apparent inability to recognize their proximity to the pain and death that reside within the camps still; they prefer to experience their visit to the death camps as a touristic excursion, viewing the piles of shoes and gas chambers through their phone cameras rather than witness, unmediated, sites of world-historic suffering and cruelty. In one particularly shocking scene, a tourist takes a selfie in front of the notorious sign, "Arbeit Macht Frei," at the gates (figure 3.6). After being shown a set of posts to which prisoners were tied and tortured, a tourist poses in front of it, mimicking the imagined posture of a dying inmate.

In Loznitsa's documentaries multiple planes, perceptions, and senses come together, often parodying the possibility of new kinships. In *Life, Autumn* (*Zhizn, osen,* 1998), the inhabitants of a remote Western Russian village in the Smolensk area, humans and animals, are transformed into a fluid form-of-life. The filmmaker's humanism is not a way to place man outside and above the animal world and therefore to exclude someone or something from the human condition, starting from animals up to the same people whose underdevelopment is postulated. If we recall the constellation of Aristotle, Foucault, and Agamben, we may readily say that it is the distinction between the human and the animal that truly founds biopolitics, and the anthropocentric *dispositif* of the human. This anthropological *dispositive*, one of the foundational moves of Western philosophy, has allowed the recursive and intractable exclusionary

Figure 3.6. Tourists gather around the entrance to Auschwitz. *Source:* Sergei Loznitsa, dir., *Austerlitz* (2016; déjà vu films, 2016), DVD, 576p.

mechanism that has not ceased to devise new forms of dehumanization by which a human's existence is brought into the field of animality. Within this view, the animal is always defined as a subtraction from the imagined superiority and plenitude of the human. The animal, or whoever is made to occupy its position, is structured by something that is always missing; this lack is the principle of every animalization, that is, of every degradation. However, Loznitsa's comment is not simply an "animalization" of the village's inhabitants. The camera frames goats as well as dogs comforting humans, to such an extent that the distinction between animals and humans seems to be called into question by the species themselves, and "life" seems to escape the biopolitical and turn into an intensity that can be shaped and constrained in different ways—recall the earlier discussion of ethnos as a general designation of any collective of people or animals.

My Joy (*Schaste moe*, 2010) asks the same question about the real options one Russian man has when it comes to "life." Russia is the space of anomic violence—a land where "a pre-political universality has already determined our social order," in other words, a perfect expression of Hobbes's interaction *more ferarum*.[46] In fact, Loznitsa subtracts from his world any evidence of juridical mediation; by showing the spontaneous interaction of individualities—the village scene in *My Joy*, the bus scene in *A Gentle Creature* (*Krotkaya*, 2017)—he pushes his criticism to the farthest end of the spectrum: the centralized, iron leadership of Putin is all but a façade for the Western media, while at the periphery of the empire, his subjects are victims and perpetrators, *chinovniki* or petty administrators of a symbolic stand. In a way, Loznitsa's works are stringently materialist films: Putin, who acts as guarantor for his circle of oligarchs, cannot govern a country but simply lets his people reproduce at the local level the predatory dynamics unfolding in Moscow, and from the same standpoint one could expect the nature of every "abuse" of power, of every act of oppression to be in deep consonance with the ruling *siloviki*. The two films can be read in a dialogue with other contemporary Russian filmmakers, such as Zvyagintsev and Serebrennikov, to establish the state of things in terms of sovereignty, state of nature, and population control. Compared to Loznitsa's take on bare life as the material fabric of Russian politics, Zvyagintsev's Hobbesian reading may be too optimistic, since the emergence of political power, albeit tyrannical and arbitrary, seems to thrive on the anarchic condition it supposedly replaces.

At first sight, *My Joy* deals with a sovereign exception, a protocol of degradation unleashed on its protagonist, a truck driver named Georgy trying to find his way in contemporary Russia. But the film does not depict the production of bare life and its consequences for the human, but rather of that "particular driving force of politics" that regulates the exclusion and insertion into "socially qualified existence."[47] It shows, in fact, an ironic collision between a purely physiological existence and the bliss of the redeemed body, the ecstatic plenitude whereby our singularity is fully realized as openness and potentiality. Only once Georgy's body is beaten, exhausted, assaulted, and exploited and descends into a state of pre-, or rather post-linguistic indifference can he finally encounter redemption: "the only ethical experience (which, as such, cannot be a task or a subjective decision) is the experience of being (one's own) potentiality, of being (one's own) possibility—exposing, that is, in every form one's own amorphousness and in every act one's own inactuality."[48] There are two flashbacks in *My Joy* of a time both historical and affective, as if the eruption of the past that *Austerlitz* leads on toward finally breaks through: a Red Army soldier killing an NKVD officer after the latter tries to steal his belongings while the former is on his way back home from the front; two fleeing Red Army soldiers killing a teacher in his home after the latter openly expressed his hopes for a German victory. Here time first appears to accumulate, then to rewind on itself. The images burst forth from the present, not as actively and willingly evoked memories but as natural reactivations: When confronted with them, the present of *My Joy* appears to be an impoverished actualization of those inhuman acts of annihilation—the present is but a depleted synthesis of a deterministic history, a vector launched at full speed toward a disastrous final crash. But there is a coexistence that is also a persistence of present and past, whereby the two hold hands and get confused in their dance. Loznitsa appears to suggest that the status of citizen in Soviet Russia and in contemporary Russia is a simulacrum of any statutory right, anybody can be indifferently victim or perpetrator, at any given time; that history is used productively as a splitter, a separator; and also, following Carl Schmitt's classification of enmity during times of war, the forays into the past are ruptures that precipitate Russia into a state of constant and absolute antagonism whereby absolute enmity is "a form of enmity that loses all containments of time and space."[49] At the end of the film, a gunfight erupts and Georgy not only executes the two brutish, beastly policemen, he also murders their victims, a major from Moscow and his wife. To borrow from and abbreviate Benjamin's famous theses on history, in this film, images of the past flit by, flash up in moments of danger, never to be seen again unless the present recognizes itself in those images.[50] There seems to be no possible redemption of historical time; the last murders will open up more baleful options—or, the driver being the only one acting politically (Loznitsa makes the point by showing him picked up by another driver, who states decisively the merits of a lay-low philosophy), his message is that for Russia to again enjoy a civic society and elaborate political thought not exclusively geared toward geopolitical domination, one must first rid it of Russians. The point is elaborated in *Donbass*, where Russia's vampiric sovereignty is put on display through multiple modalities of extraction of resources from the occupied Ukrainian regions. Unlike *My Joy* and *A Gentle Creature*, in *Donbass* there are no recognizably central protagonists, which emphasizes the assembly-line quality of the Russian occupation, a hell carnival where, under the surveillance of dead-eyed *chinovniki* and military goons of the Russian Federation, the population is constantly fooled and plundered. The use of violence is aimed at showing the failure of Russia's concurrent symbolic codes: Its dehumanizing tactics bring us back to an idea of politics in which absolute power is necessary to ensure certain outcomes that otherwise would be impossible and whose primary goal is to prevent confrontation. This comprises what I call the Loznitsa universe—an enclosed system in which every film coexists with the other, together with their tropes and their mythologies, and which contains the historical truth of the relationship between Ukraine and Russia.

Such a relationship is an extractive one: At first one's image is appropriated—in the film's opening scene, actors impersonate Russophone locals asking for protection; then a performance—in another early scene, an administrator fakes an anti-corruption inspection at a hospital; following this, the occupying separatist soldiers extract personal belongings and money—a local business owner's car is expropriated by threats to his daughter's safety (figure 3.7); then a spectacle is extracted from the body as a Ukrainian fighter is tied to a pole and beaten; finally, when there is nothing left to appropriate, life: The same actors of the first episode, now eliminated for their corpses to pose as victims of a Ukrainian attack, are wrenched from the local

Figure 3.7. A Novorussian soldier articulates the main reason of the invasion to a Ukrainian citizen. *Source:* Sergei Loznitsa, dir., *Donbass* (2018; Salzgeber & Co. Medien GmbH, 2022), DVD, 576p.

population to fill the unbridgeable gap in the Russian self-image. The business owner sequence is particularly telling in how seamlessly and with what precision the military personnel move from one resource to another—property, family, assets: Everything is free for the taking. It is a pure, contemporary historical expression of what Hardt and Negri call extraction and its intimate links to colonialism.[51] Loznitsa articulates how the production of externalities like "the Russian idea," militarized institutions and affiliations, and techniques of accumulation converge to create a modern-day serf, pushed so close to the edge of citizenship—a citizen only insofar as one "belongs" to the nation that claims ownership of them—toward a zone of indistinction. *Donbass* resonates with *The Trial* (*Protsess*), a documentary Loznitsa released that same year. *The Trial* is a montage of archival material from the "Industrial Party" trial, in which, in 1930, several Soviet economists and engineers were accused of plotting a takeover of the country's institutions through sabotage. The trial had all the Foucauldian ingredients of the power display, from the compelling scripting of the conspiracy to the nonchalant issue of the pardons: the juridico-theatrical liturgy of the confession, the smooth ritualization and detailed narration of the alleged crime, and the irrelevance and fungibility of the defendants, with all the mechanisms working in perfect sync to confirm the ruthless precision and the unchallengeable might of the Soviet machinery of justice. Loznitsa suggests that nothing has changed in these mechanisms to produce truth: The simulacral state of political activity in Russia cannot be separated by its own gestation of hyper-reality, one that apparently does not need the logic of late capitalism to be prosperous and a liberal economy to consider prisoners as collective property. Also, Loznitsa marvels—sometimes humorously, sometimes cynically—at how Russians' common language may very well just be lent to them from an outside—unless we interpret the throngs of people, loitering or waiting for buses, as in *Landscape*, or the crowds in *My Joy* and *A Gentle Creature* as ironic counterpoint to Neorealism's doctrine of encounter. In *Landscape* in particular, the disembodied, out-of-sync soundtrack signifies a continuously failing adaptation, displacement, a mockery of change and progress—no matter the human "material," the ontological placement is already provided by the soundtrack, a sardonic implementation of that "hyperaudibil-ity" that Fatimah Tobing Rony has called one of the crucial facets of visual biopolitics and its patterns of symbolic deprivation.[52] Here, we can sense an affinity with Aleksandr Sokurov, for whom Loznitsa has shown great appreciation:[53] If, for Sokurov, the moribund feeling of dilapidation is a function of his cinema of "transcendental evocation, guessing and anticipation,"[54] then Loznitsa likewise prods his audience to look and find itself in the indistinct crowd, with our wretchedness, repulsiveness, empathy, and the absurdity of Russian historical time. *Donbass* has been criticized for failing to emphasize significant geo-political and historical complexities that led some parts of the local population to join the Russian attempt to destabilize the region and transfer power from Ukraine to Russia. However, Loznitsa's interest lies not in synchronic history but in the internal logic of radical exploitation: *Donbass* puts on display the sovereign's total power through spectacles of punishment and terror to confirm his overwhelming authority and ability to crush any popular resistance. The Ukrainian filmmaker's nihilism is not just a sadistically humorous commentary on Russian identity or a naïve inquiry into the absence of a middle class whose upward trajectory could bring about a set of democratic checks and balances as well as an implementation of the rule of law (of course, this does not necessarily follow, as can be seen in both chapters 2 and 4).[55] Therefore, the sovereign's system of terror not only does not come under pressure, but is fomented by the very classes that began to challenge such a system in Europe more than three centuries ago. His genealogy of Russian power comes full circle with

State Funeral (*Gosudarstvennye pohorony*, 2019), a montage of archival footage of Stalin's funeral. The mummification of the leader's body marks a decisive stage in the aestheticization of Soviet politics as an attempt to thwart the decomposition of the very premises—rhetorical, ideological performative—upon which the cult was based.

Hobbes, Serebrennikov, Zvyagintsev and the Russian Leviathan

Orthodox Christian theologian Pavel Nikolaevich Evdokimov wrote that the "Orthodox faithful never liked the summae theologiae, nor scholastic systems. Every formulation or excessive definition led to instinctive distrust. Orthodoxy does not need to formulate, it needs not to formulate."[56] With *The Student* Kirill Serebrennikov revives the political allegory, a genre popularized since the 1960s by film traditions in countries ruled by military juntas and other dictatorships, like Brazil and Eastern European nations. If, for Brazil, the allegory of underdevelopment was a figure of historical and political difference, "a desirable antidote to illusionary organic cohesions and regressive mythologies,"[57] in Eastern European art it stood as a figure of political apathy and moral stagnation. Serebrennikov's film acts as an iteration of this genre, a device that roots contemporary Russia into a backward current and invites an exploration of its oblique senses; it is a work that successfully manages "to condense an endless number of questions and experiences into a few individual characters whose life courses, nevertheless, represent a national fate, the destiny of an ethnic group or of a class."[58] Or of a nation, one may add, engaging with the notion of subjecthood in its most thanatopolitical dimensions.

The Student may be regarded as a biopolitical reflection on the introduction of Western values such as individual rights and personhood in contemporary Russia, an allegorical commentary on a political system that, to sustain itself, must produce new forms of bare life. According to Serebrennikov, political activity in contemporary Russia is predicated on creating states of exception, on pushing those who can serve as an example to gray areas of suspended law. The entire legal system—thanks to a balanced constitution perennially contradicted by bills and pronouncements issued by the executive power—is structured in a way that begets unpredictability and instability at best, biased outcomes warranted and safeguarded by political patronage at worst. Such a situation leaves the law open, if it is not an invitation, to sovereign intervention, indicating the immense tension between a normative biopower and a transcendental sovereignty.[59] A different, more pronounced exception is instead granted to the Orthodox Church, which, despite a guaranteed plurality of confessions protected by the constitution, conquered a space of absolute privilege and power.[60] The reasons are multiple and largely motivated by waning consensus. At the onset of his political career, Vladimir Putin "represented the widespread yearning for stability in a society traumatized by disintegration and decline."[61] Then, the need to enlarge his coalition led Putin to forge a steel pact with his remaining constituencies—"elite cronies who benefit from the status quo, conservative voters, state bureaucrats, and workers in import-competing sectors."[62] Among those conservative voters were also those who clung to an idea of might traditionally associated with the Soviet Union. The necessity of this pact steered the Putin rule toward an original, efficient brand of nationalist populism. For Putin, nationalism became an unavoidable means of producing political mobilization to secure legitimacy: Defined as "a collective movement to repair pride by reversing the evaluation of national attributes," nationalism empowered the Russian executive to reinvigorate the Soviet past as a moment of collective jubilation, in which the nation was able to celebrate its power.[63] That way, the Molotov-Ribbentrop pact becomes "a tremendous success of Stalinist diplomacy"[64] and, following a geopolitical doctrine aiming at reassert influence over large swaths of Europe, each act of aggression is disguised as either an act of peace or a preemptive measure to counterbalance the evil intentions countries west of Russia have against it.[65] Therefore, even a purely aggressive unilateral act such as the invasion and annexation of Crimea, indispensable to feed and sustain the Putin doctrine, will be presented a defensive maneuver, a necessary gesture to ward off "an existential threat to Russia."[66]

Internally, conservative think-tanks and associations gained the upper hand in interfacing Putin with Russia's people, while internationally Russia sought a leadership role in anti-EU organizations in order to influence and destabilize European institutions, coagulating in a hybrid ideology that stressed "the tradition of a normed family, the appreciation of hierarchy and religion, and an unquestioned belonging to larger collectives (class, nation), industrialism, scientific and technological progress."[67] The *manu militari* occupation of culture with preemptive censorship, homogenizing guidelines, and general repression of unsupervised artistic creation followed in an attempt to rein in any voice critical of the governing alliance. By way of identitarian rallies aimed at orienting them to symbolic constructs via affect and emotion, the citizenry is in a perpetual state of mobilization to draw new confinement policies for those who try to infringe the coalition pact subscribed by the forces in power. The distance between "the *People* as a whole and as an integral body politic and, on the other hand, the *people* as a subset and as fragmentary multiplicity of needy and excluded bodies" becomes an uncertain quantity, a moving target that citizens must be able to situate if they do not want to lose certain privileges.[68] Serebrennikov uses the student and martyr as a mystical instrument of sovereign rule, an agent that has determined the distance between the people and Being and works relentlessly to see a topological *collapse* of the two, recognizing that "*bíos* is situated in those totalitarian or fundamentalist states whose task it is to exclude the improper from the mode of living that is proper to the State."[69] His agitation reminds us that populist power will use its finest specimen to test the boundaries of the enclosure where civil society is bound for captivity. By creating a separation "between self and enemy based on racialized norms of identity and ways of life" and amputating the Jewish teacher from the healthy Russian body, the film shows a successful protocol of adjustment and reintegration into Russian society at the expense of ethnic and religious minorities and queer individuals.[70] In a comparison with the now rehabilitated Stalin, Putin's course of action appears as wanting. Stalin's was a productive, expansive, and generative biopolitics, while Putin's is intermittently effective but essentially nihilistic. Stalin's biopolitics was anti-immunitarian, in the sense that since no pre-existing, idealized form-of-life was the base for the immunitary action, his regime was led by "the drive to give life to what does not yet exist."[71] Serebrennikov depicts Russia as a vast zone of indistinction "in which subjects' recourse to conventional legal and political protection is curtailed"[72] and a model of limited pluralism is practiced through the law and apparatuses of policing, whereby the population can repeat and exercise all that which is not forbidden. A new push, and scores of citizens who are deemed unassimilable are conveniently marginalized under the approving eye of the central authority: The whole society feels cleansed from the contamination of the ethnically impure, sexually undecided, and physically challenged.

The Student

Veniamin, the subject of *The Student*, is not a religious fanatic; like Putin, he is a layman who uses religion to fulfills its historical mission—that is, prevailing against an enemy, be it globalization, technocracy, neoliberalism, external conspiracy—while at the same time building a bridge between the present and its tradition, also the Communist one, by diffusing the political into a performative affect. Serebrennikov shows how Veniamin recreates and galvanizes his people, but the director separates him from the Orthodox Church: The recruiting attempt carried out by the priest, a faculty member at the high school where the events take place, is frustrated, meaning that the "official" church must fall in line and react to the new grassroots instances injecting fresh forms into the formless soul of the nation. However, the two overlap in their nefarious judgment of the biology teacher: The priest is a gray stand-in for patriarch Kirill, whose emphasis on the sheer illegitimacy of freedom of consciousness and the baleful effect of separatism between church and state has characterized his tenure. The partnership between political power and Orthodox Church in Russia is not a renewed version of the Byzantine symphony of orders; it is a natural convergence of rules that envision an anti-West, Slavophile destiny for Russia, and not too different from the current version of the United States where the population is co-opted into permanent culture wars.

Veniamin acts as a true proxy for the sovereign because he convinces the others that there is chaotic state of things and he is the solution, the only one who can neutralize the danger and remove the threat. While inserting sexual frustration as an ahistoric motif at the heart of Veniamin's fanaticism, Serebrennikov turns him into a more complex character—a true believer outside a structured and therefore bureaucratized Church, a stormbringer of another potential wave of counterreformation capable of displacing, subjugating, and ultimately replacing the religious authorities, and a spontaneous, grassroots activist who reminds the people of their ultimate populist call, finding an internal enemy at regular intervals.[73] Originally based on the play *Märtyrer* (2012) by Marius von Mayenburg, *The Student* abandons the concerns of the original work—the permissiveness of rights in a modern, liberal multiethnic and multireligious state—to focus on the mechanisms of political redistricting in what Serebrennikov deems a de facto tyranny. Von Mayenburg said that at the core of *Märtyrer* were concerns related to Islamic fanaticism and the literal application of the Koran: Its protagonist being an Old Testament Christian, the author seems to consider dialogue with the most enlightened part of Islamism a possible trajectory to contain then evolve out of fundamentalism. Instead, by featuring the racial element in the final confrontation between the biology teacher and Veniamin, Serebrennikov follows a different path. The filmmaker is not interested in the way religion and science short-circuit during times of religious integralism and "clash of civilizations"; rather, he shifts the focus to the use of fanaticism as a political tool to disintegrate internal enemies. Serebrennikov accomplishes that by way of a substitution—replacing the "racist" of the original text with "fascist"—and a strategic addition, that of virulently antisemitic passages from works of John of Kronstadt and from the homily *Against the Jews* by Saint John Chrysostom read by Father Vsevolod, the religion teacher of the high school. It is the racist turn that Foucault mentioned in *"Society Must Be Defended,"* the move "from a political-military discourse into a racist-biological one."[74] The Russification of the text is carried out by those references—in particular John of Kronstadt, because the Eastern Orthodox Church saint is the type of cultural warrior that needs to be evoked then mobilized when a racial norm must be defended.

Through the ideological filter of John of Kronstadt—a nineteenth-century Orthodox priest known for his anti-Communism and antisemitism, canonized during *perestroika* and popular among nationalists—Serebrennikov gives to the "martyr" of the original title a new meaning, ironic and sinister at the same time: in the miscellaneous volume entitled *Ya predvizhu vosstanovlenie moshchnoy Rossii* (I foresee the restoration of a powerful Russia), a 1907 manifesto that resonates with the type of Russian citizen that Vladimir Putin has tried to construct, John of Kronstadt envisions a Russia where everyone can be expendable: "On the bones of the martyrs, as on a strong foundation, a new Russia will be erected."[75] Thus, if in the text the real martyr was the teacher who nails her foot to the floor as a final gesture of defiant sacrifice, here Veniamin and Elena are both necessary actors in the protocol of exclusion. When an anomaly arises in the biological spectrum, supposedly authentic national forces remind the impure element of its exceptionality by cleansing the organs of their presence and thereby assuring the continuity and strengthening of the race. The *yurodivy*, the fool in Christ, founds a new authority that does not go against the king, but reinforces his sovereign domination. Veniamin is the space for initiative in Russia's theological politics and the annihilation of the teacher allegorizes the permanent and indispensable state of danger on which the State is predicated. The character who stands for Christ is in fact the Jewish professor, Elena, who evokes the martyrdom of crucifixion by nailing herself to the floor after she is fired from the school. It is not only an ethical investment in the conduct of the character, who like Socrates chooses death because politically it is the best and most appropriate choice. She puts the best before life and she is the only true politician, because when an individual tries to act for the best of all, she does it before the others by example. The pursuit of happiness and the rights of one are never separated from the life of society at large; it is an ethical attitude, one in which it is hard to distinguish between public, private, collective, and institutional (figures 3.8 and 3.9).

The films by Serebrennikov and Loznitsa deal directly with life and the way it is managed, mollified, molded, and exploited through violence: We sense the permanence of the sovereign and recognize the biopolitical reverberation. In Andrey Zvyagintsev's works the

Figure 3.8. Management projects in Putin's Russia. *Source:* Kirill Serebrennikov, dir., *The Student* (2016; Matchbox Films, 2018), DVD, 576p.

Figure 3.9. Management projects in Putin's Russia. *Source:* Kirill Serebrennikov, dir. *The Student* (2016; Matchbox Films, 2018), DVD, 576p.

abandoned child and his ghostly circulation are the figural correlative of a country with a declining demographics and a desperate need for youth, echoing the representation of children in other cinemas as foreclosed potentialities.[76]

Leviathan

Leviathan, Zvyagintsev's most explicitly political film, is a mercilessly pessimistic statement that regards power as a vertical line, a blade that cleaves through the flesh of Russian society and articulates how the sovereign uses conflicting pronouncements in the legislation to accommodate a political agenda, or to elevate to the rule of law pronouncements confined to other spheres.[77] *Leviathan* transposes to Russia the story of American Marvin Heemeyer, who, motivated by grudges against local officials and business owners, spent months modifying a bulldozer he would later use destroy various properties around his Colorado town, including the former mayor's house, before killing himself. In Zvyagintsev's adaptation, the Job-like figure of Nikolay, a car mechanic (like Heemeyer), is driven mad by local government plans to expropriate the valuable coastal land his house is built upon. Unlike Heemeyer, Nikolay does not shoot himself but is arrested on suspicion of murdering his wife; meanwhile, his house is demolished, to the delight of the local mayor. At the end of the film, Aleksey Serebryakov's Nikolay learns that he will finish his life in prison. Given the systematic rape and torture occurring in the Russian penitentiary system—Wagner's recruiting success was predicated on the convicts' hellish conditions, so much that a quasi-certain death on the Ukrainian frontlines was preferable to serving one's sentence—it is easy to imagine the same happening to him, made into an example of Putinite sovereignty, for which no property, no recess, no bodily cavity is off limits. *Leviathan* thus investigates the sovereign pact that holds the country together, its organization of violence—the modality through which aggregation, operativity, and common goals are possible. But are they? The self-legitimizing sovereign power depicted in *Leviathan* is, by all means, a brutal and unsophisticated one, based on a subtractive logic of interdiction and repression: In the Foucauldian evolutionary scheme it comes before disciplinary power and biopower, and resistance to it seems straightforward, coming in the guise of "revolution, social movements, terrorism."[78] Still, at first glance, Hobbes's premise may not seem completely relevant for Zvyagintsev: If Hobbes's remitting covenant, far from warding off war and conflict, institutionalizes them, it originates from a historical trauma—based on fear of war, conquest, and violent laceration of the population in general—that does not offer immediate similarities with contemporary Russia. One possible similitude is the function of the Law in Hobbes's architecture of the state, not as an instrument with which to homogenize the population, but rather as the procedures through which a series of relationships that are not of sovereignty but of domination are transmitted and implemented. It is a poignant incursion into the negative inclusivity of Russia's legal system, a country where "legal repercussions stem from loss of political status, rather than vice versa."[79] The state of things sketched in *Leviathan* is that of Max Weber's patrimonial society, in which the boundaries of power relations are under constant stress and always in flux and, to return to Hobbes's book, a pact between a despot and his subject. The loss of property and the loss of familial bonds are one and the same because in a patrimonial society there is no difference between a personal appropriation, a personal conduct, a personal sphere and an official one. Unlike countries like China, where a strategic hybridization of the Gandhian concept of Satyagraha and the "assumption of bare life"[80] has emerged as one of the few remaining options for an emancipation from within, in contemporary Russia the lack of a comprehensive, alternate political elaboration at the collective level is apparent. The interest lies in the filmmaker's evaluation of Hobbes's applicability and relevance when analyzed against the power structures in place under Putin, a leader who has so far successfully wiped conceptual alternatives and charismatic candidates off the political spectrum. In Hobbes, the Leviathan is an assembly that turns men into citizens—sovereignty is a transformational representativity, not a supreme power but a state in which one must obey, no questions asked, no matter what is ordered. The film's point of departure is a juridical conception of power, "a scheme of analysis and evaluation that interprets power in legal terms, above all: laws, prohibitions, censorship, constraints and so on."[81] After all, the protagonist enlists the help of a legal counselor to avoid being dispossessed of his property by the municipality; the two sides, though, practice a law that is not based on a code. They are instead driven primarily by methods of domination, and the film shows that the law is practiced as an extension of *dominium* and slavery as political obligation. In fact, the politics of property depicted in *Leviathan* seem lifted from another of Hobbes's texts, specifically *On the Citizen*: "If ownership consists in having preeminent power in conjunction with a natural right to exercise that power . . . then it follows that sovereigns, by virtue of their sovereignty, own everything in the commonwealth that can be owned, including the citizens themselves and all that they possess. In showing that citizens cannot hold any property rights against the sovereign . . . *On the Citizen* develops a powerful and coherent defense of despotic sovereignty."[82] Another link between Hobbes's thought and the film is the ferocious move against the religious principle of authority, which precedes the citizen. The film is concerned with the unbalanced and the excessive, the incongruity of power, its superabundance and deficiency, as well as the question, "Who makes the Law?" The filmmaker at times has a Hegelian view of the Russian State, as if it had incorporated religion as its transcendental masterplan, as its will toward the absolute to justify and exalt itself. It is Hobbesian in its rejection of the contract as the foundational moment of the State—here the commentary is bitterly ironic, since a lawyer is the one who is called to verify the voidness of such pact and certify the equivalence of law and sovereign will. In the film, Zvyagintsev anatomizes the legal system of a totalitarian state: police that do not answer to the judiciary and can autonomously and freely incarcerate and send people to death; judges that are brought under complete control of the executive branch; laws that do not respect the principles of generality and non-retroactivity; a juridical doctrine according to which the will of the people is incorporated in Vladimir Putin and emanates directly from him. In Hobbes, the Leviathan is an assemblage that turns men into citizens, but it is not a power standing above its subjects—it is unpropped, a necessary, levitating fiction. All power is just: if politics is given in the emptying out of all that comes before it—religion, tradition, national soul, and so on—then *Leviathan* shows the futility of that law, sealed by none other than a lawyer. It was Locke who said that man does not carry with himself anything from the state of nature except for the right to property; according to Hobbes, the only thing that the state cannot tell its citizens is to suppress their own lives. Zvyagintsev replaces the seventeenth-century Church with the contemporary Russian Orthodox one and its grifting appetites, implying that ownership of private property is the preferred way for Orthodoxy to stay relevant, and that the law in Russia operates in the name of religious truth and as a general means to satisfy the humming of the state machine and its vertical hierarchy of power, whereby if one condition for the good outcome of the presidential agenda is to assuage the Orthodox Church, then it is necessary that "every level of the regional state apparatus is working away on its respective set of responsibilities."[83] More than a filmic rendition of the book, the picture then seems to resonate with Paolo Virno's historical-naturalistic interpretation of Hobbes's metaphysics: Precisely because man is "naturally evil" in his state of nature, this "should not at all imply the formation and conservation of that 'supreme command' that is state sovereignty."[84] Hobbes puts the community as the foundational move of civilization—and only if the citizen is freed from the ghosts of the past, he graduates to that phase of rational mediation that is the true entry into modernity; Zvyagintsev's Russia, on the other hand, is a criminal free-for-all suspended in a durational state of lawlessness.

The film has been criticized for its overt "festival aspirations" and for the implacable bluntness with which it tightens the grip on the protagonist: Its aesthetic, illustrative qualities notwithstanding, the story of inescapable collusion between political and religious power seemed too predictable and convenient without really providing new insight or usable strategies against said complicities.[85] Power appears as a given, leaving no credible options for revolt—unless we consider killing the mayor and his bodyguards in cold blood a suitable one, which, as Zvyagintsev seems to imply, is the way the president *wants* power and opposition to it to be understood. However, as with *Manuscripts Don't Burn* and its limitations as a "classic" political film, it is their existence we have come to question, in a Russia whose current spiritual and military horizon is that of a perpetual World War II.

4

From Biopolitics to Ecopolitics

The (Un)intended Consequences of Biopower in the Cinema of Wang Xiaoshuai

I have never contemplated suicide myself, but I feel that apart from being alive in the physiological sense, apart from breathing and eating, there is a social life for everyone.

> —Wang Xiaoshuai, interview with Michael Berry, in *Speaking in Images: Interviews with Contemporary Chinese Filmmakers*

It's like a scientific experiment. Your feelings now are the outcome of the experiment.

> —*Frozen* (Wang Xiaoshuai, 1996)

IN KANBASHI, AN ENORMOUS crane suspends a tree high against a blue sky; as it carries building supplies along a narrow road in Inner Mongolia, a semi-truck, from a distance, looks more like a toy than a vehicle; a lush architectural model lights up against a panoramic screen to reveal a sleek presentation for Ordos, a magnificent city of the future; a lush rendering of a rocky grotto with small, serene human silhouettes adheres to an unfinished gray wall, presiding over a disarray of steel beams and pipe scattered in the sand. In Yumen, a flock of sheep files across a ruined landscape populated by derelict apartment buildings; a faded municipal mural evokes ancient frescos; the sheep wander onto the stage of an abandoned movie theater before running off into the distance. These scenes are taken from *Man Made Place* (*Renzao kongjian*, 2012), a student film by Yu-Shen Su for the Academy of Media Arts Cologne (figures 4.1 and 4.2).

Figure 4.1. The "playfulness" of Chinese ghost towns. *Source:* Yu-Shen Su, dir., *Man Made Place* (2012; Film- und Medienstiftung NRW, 2022), online primer, 1080p HD.

Figure 4.2. The "playfulness" of Chinese ghost towns. *Source:* Yu-Shen Su, dir., *Man Made Place* (2012; Film- und Medienstiftung NRW, 2022), online primer, 1080p HD.

Both locations in the film are "ghost towns." One, Ordos, is a new hypermodern city without any apparent residents, except perhaps the crews of construction workers building the newest parts of the city; the other is Yumen, an abandoned town at the edge of the Gobi Desert, an area once rich with oil and ore deposits.[1] Ordos is a future built so quickly that the present has not yet reached it, while Yumen is an abandoned past whose mineral and social resources have been tapped out. A few years later, Zhao Liang reprised this theme of extraction in his Dantean nightmare, *Behemoth* (*Beixi moshou*, 2015). While *Man Made Place* is uncanny and disquieting, *Behemoth* relocates the *Divine Comedy* in industrial Northern China and Inner Mongolia. The film, which was banned in China, depicts the infernal coal industry in the region, wherein the destruction of the living has no boundary, destabilizing the very concepts of life and nature.

Both films may be considered potent, highly legible (and very beautiful) introductions to what has by now become a necessary platitude in analyses of China's ascent, since the mid- to late twentieth century, to global economic and political dominance as a major superpower in an increasingly multipolar world: It happened so fast. It is well known that the share of global investors in the Chinese financial market is growing; that US pension funds are heavily invested in China; that China has adopted new data protection laws that strengthen the public monopoly on data acquisition and processing. What may be less known to the Western reader is that one of the country's ambitions, announced at the CCP's Twentieth National Congress—to overtake the United States in the global economy—has been jeopardized by the faltering health of small banks, a property crash, and ballooning debt. China is between a rock and a hard place, or *zuo you* ("left right"), to borrow the title of Wang Xiaoshuai's 2008 drama, whose rather misleading English translation is *In Love We Trust*. When Xi Jinping recently pledged to redistribute wealth and admonished corporations and the super-rich "to return more to society," many analysts saw it as a belated moment of recognition for the Communist Party.[2] It was the result of the *enrichissez-vous* race that has been actively promoted by the Party leaders since the time of Deng Xiaoping, and, with it, inequality—which, as in the United States and elsewhere, the advent of tech platforms has accentuated.

A perhaps lesser-known part of this history is that Milton Friedman, one of the most prominent neoliberal economists of the Chicago School, delivered several lectures to Party leaders at the invitation of the government. As economist Isabella Weber succinctly puts it, "The reformers replaced the Maoist slogan of revolutionizing social relations with the idea of making up lessons from capitalism in order to achieve historical progress through market reforms. Consequently, a technocratic policy agenda became dominant, and China became amenable to what Foucauldians call neoliberal governmentality."[3] Friedman endorsed and influenced aspects of China's economic policies under Deng via General Secretary Zhao Ziyang, except, of course, when it came to China's insistence on state control of the market and the issue of private property.[4] In this way, China became "integrated into the global market while the Chinese state [reserved] its rights to control the economy."[5] Deng's reforms, which included abandoning Mao's planned economy, making the country's workforce available to foreign investment, and moving toward owner cultivation in the agricultural sector, created an enormous shift in the conditions of Chinese people's existence, and a consequent transformation of family life, perspectives on work, and political engagement. Mao famously wrote that the Cultural Revolution was a repressive operation carried out in the open.[6] Deng's economic input retained the same top-down, vertical approach aimed at setting in motion a social movement, creating partners from within said movement while at the same time avoiding widespread diffusion of political power—a strategy of mass activation and revitalization via mobilization and power dilution. Opposition to an approach to economic growth that immediately appeared disorderly at best and unsustainable at worst—for instance pathologically tied to sectors such as real estate—took different forms. China's GDP enjoyed a peculiar form of distortion: Setting a predetermined target, it retained the constrained nature of planned production, thereby forcing local administrations as well as, for a long time, the property sector to deliver enough economic activity to meet said target, facilitated by the loose nature of soft budget constraints. China's way to growth via real estate development resembles certain the policies of the West—securitization, bailouts carried out by state banks—emphasizing the most pernicious ones such as a political centralization of investments and a de facto nationalization of the sector via the creation of bankruptcy-remote entities. Thus, China's road to urbanization was accomplished from a distance, like Yu-Shen Su's long shots of the desert expanse and the tiny, toy-like truck that traverses it. This chapter explores Wang Xiaoshuai's filmography, which, including his most recent work, *Above the Dust* (*Wotu*, 2024), insists on the pernicious consequences of displacements on different levels, from those illustrated by Zu's images to the far more intimate, social repercussions of modernization.

Sixth Generation Filmmakers

Wang Xiaoshuai (b. 1966) is a member of the Sixth Generation group of film directors. His work, like that of his contemporaries, Jia Zhangke (b. 1970) and Wang Bing (b. 1967), emerges from the conditions and consequences of the transitional period between the Cultural Revolution and Deng's reforms. Though the generational moniker is neither fixed nor taxonomical, it designates a set of shared concerns regarding these changes, which scholar Yingjin Zhang so eloquently describes: "Sixth Generation directors tend to evoke perceived binary oppositions between rural and urban, romantic and realistic, subjective and objective, allegorical and existential, mainstream and marginal."[7] Further, as Xiaoping Lin writes, "the work of the Sixth Generation filmmakers is in general a study of China's painful transformation from a Soviet-style social state into a new global capitalist country."[8] The categories of capitalism—market, competition, efficiency, professionalism, performance, entrepreneurship of the self—became categories of a single, comprehensive way of thinking: They took by storm the most diverse fields, from public services to domestic life, from school to health, from cultural initiatives to religious practices forcing entire generations to rethink individual perspectives, familial bonds, and political engagement. The techno-scientific and sociopolitical aspects of population control then became entangled: Administration of life in China became a different form of dominance, the articulation of a governmental biopower. After what was understood to be the heroic years of ultraliberal reengineering of the economy, China focused on optimizing mineral extraction, exploiting natural resources, maximizing energy reserves—in other words, integrating the technologies for the individual with the technologies for the ecosystem.

The cinema of the Sixth Generation of Chinese filmmakers is transitional in style, linking to broader collectivities and staging collisions between individual agency and events in which "characters are conduits for articulating the collective nightmare of history."[9]

Men and women tend to the death of natural landscapes, plants, families, other men and other women—cycles in which death not only appears to be the only reasonable output, but is produced at record speed. Based on the experience of "fragmentation, instability, and social change," with the Sixth Generation the task of filmmaking is to equip a whole new sensorium.[10] An emphasis on the immediacy of the filmmaking process as a capture or a seizure—the "on the scene" nature, or *xianchang*—often invested in showing the erosion of the shared space or *gong kongjian* is a fundamental feature of Sixth Generation pictures. They do not, however, completely abandon the choral narratives of the preceding generation, but when they do tackle the Cultural Revolution—as in Wang Xiaoshuai's *11 Flowers* (*Wo 11*, 2011)—or internal migration, they tend to move from the historiographical to the individual inscribing their country's history, memory and myth into intimate political stories. This movement between (but not fully "from") collective history to individual story reflects China's own movement between Mao's Communism and its emphasis on the collective to Dengist capitalism and beyond. Because of the concurrent phasing out of Mao's socialization of labor relations and the implementing of post-socialist planning rationalities, the biopolitical instrumentation has been particularly useful at penetrating the idiosyncrasies of China's governmental project. Wang Bing films, for example, articulate a granular anthropology of Chinese men and women—survivors, witnesses, laborers, migrants, workers, and others—caught between the defunct mastodons left behind by the abandoned centralized planned economy and profit-driven reconfigurations put into effect at breakneck speed. Wang Bing presents the reconfiguration of human life—or its annihilation—within "the effects of the biopolitical arrangement"[11] and finds how the human "waste materials" resulting from the state analytical management of its population expand and morph into forms of life that are uncontainable even by the most capillary securitizing institutions. From this standpoint, his documentaries have been considered an invaluable integration to Foucault's account on the systematization of power relations when considering "a type of governmentality that is both non-Western and non-democratic."[12] For instance, in *'Til Madness Do Us Part* (*Feng ai*, 2013) thanks to the lives suspended in the concentrationary environment[13] of the mental asylum, some of them without names, we see an unforgettable gallery of bodies and faces emerge from an institution whose goal is to extract the residual sanity still left in its patients-prisoners and turn them into bare life. In the films of Wang Xiaoshuai and Jia Zhangke, instead, extraction is a mode of representation, illustrating China's intense economic transformation through its social and actual landscapes. While Wang Xiaoshuai's recent films address the history and consequences of China's one-child policy and internal migration, Jia Zhangke's works present the predacious excavation and defacement of the landscape. Their commitment to the concurrent representation of people, landscape, and technology as complex and unnegotiated coordinates on a continuum puts him in a political and technological tradition of filmmaking to which directors such as Vittorio De Seta, Giuseppe Taffarel, and Michelangelo Antonioni also belong. Even though China has been in continuous economic expansion for decades, the three filmmakers analyzed here all belong to a phase that, in his survey of industrial and infrastructural films of Italy's economic boom, Pierpaolo Antonello has described as a "more critical, reflexive aftermath."[14] While this chapter does not overdetermine the relationship between Italian realism and Chinese cinema, it is an important link, one which Wang Xiaoshuai, Wang Bing, and Jia Zhangke are each in dialogue with, but not in thrall to. The quotation from Antonello is relevant in the sense that the anxieties that were thematized in Italian cinema during the heroic years of the economic boom—development without progress is repeatedly mentioned by Pasolini and De Seta, whose films depict the psychological consequences of a state of failed negotiation between men and women and the new industrial landscape—resurface in China at the onset of Deng Xiaoping's reforms. In these films, economic freedom appears to bring about a fundamental disconnection between environment, communities, and life. For example, in Wang Xiaoshuai's *Drifters* (*Er di*, 2003), "America" is a potent agent of social disintegration even from thousands of miles away, while in *Beijing Bicycle* (*Shiqi sui de dan che*, 2001) it is simply the know-how necessary to extract even more profit from untrained labor. Sovereignty as the monopoly of violence and life-fostering come together in Wang Xiaoshuai's cinema in composite, hybrid ways. Richard Letteri was quick to point out that the *paterfamilias* Lao Wu in *Shanghai Dreams* was a "victim of history, his own identity being written and re-written by the political and economic forces that he once, according to his friends, believed were best for his nation" and yet, given his stern Confucianism, he functioned as a power conduit between the family, the factory, the workers, and the State.[15] He performs an unrelenting, authoritarian version of Confucianism: He is a tormented, memorable character in a schizophrenic bind, "his own identity being written and re-written" as he tries a painful synthesis between political loyalty and economic opportunity, among failed dreams of modernization and impossible obedience to abstract moral imperatives.[16] In *Red Amnesia* (*Chuangru zhe*, 2014), Wang Xiaoshuai takes a step further by starring an elder as the main protagonist with an unflinching moral compass and a particular dedication for worship towards ancestors and dead family members—a practice that "highlighted the family and kin relationships, as a model for society," and yet could not definitively yield the fruits of "order, benevolence, harmony and reciprocity" to a community unable to deal successfully with biopolitical control.[17]

The protagonists of these films are often people who should be the beneficiaries of material progress and who feel pressured to provide for themselves and their families but are caught in a no-man's-land where their efforts seem incommensurate with what is requested from them. A Pasolinian affection for the dropouts who cannot participate in such economy is shared by Jia: In his early films the characters played by Wang Hongwei are a pensive iteration of Truffaut's Antoine Doinel and his rebellious but ultimately stagnant attempts to escape, but also of Bonifacio, the character played by Sady Rebbot in Tinto Brass's *Chi lavora è perduto* (1963; also known as *In capo al mondo*). They all share centripetal breakouts, a deep and sardonic bitterness about suffocating societal norms and, most importantly, values such as rectitude and altruistic integrity that are laughed at, dismissed as quirky eccentricities if not altogether ignored.

Jia champions affective histories told in an adventurous style reconfiguring established visual strategies to uniquely express that which is perceived as a tragic transition in China. In *Pickpocket* (*Xiao Wu*, 1997) Jia's camera lingers in an almost unintentional way on a New Year poster. The fish and magpie are common in this type of poster (figure 4.3). Fish in Chinese is 鱼 (*yú*), which sounds the same as 余, meaning "abundance, surplus, or more than enough"; and magpie in Chinese 喜鹊 (*xǐquè*) is literally "happy bird," symbolizing good luck or happiness. The cat is known as a good catcher, and the text reads roughly, "Wish you good luck year after year like the cat that catches big fish." Here, Zhangke sardonically juxtaposes the outsider with

Figure 4.3. Chinese New Year poster. *Source:* Jia Zhangke, dir., *Pickpocket* (1997; Curzon Artificial Eye, 2012), DVD, 576p.

the stylized graphics of a kitschy poster evoking the mass-produced optimism of festival decorations: from one subspecies to another, lying outside the segmented social groups, Xiao Wu is forced to drop out and contemplate "year after year" the grim continuity of poverty, where luck never arrives, or where poverty can only be avoided through luck. In this film, a petty thief with a moral code—an individual trying to inhabit an anthropological model different from those laid out by the State—has little room to operate in post-1979 China, as its governmental rationality was transitioning from the predictability of the plan to the extractive speed of the market.

The Work of Art and the Art of Government

Wang Xiaoshuai's early films interrogate foreign influence, an external force—Western business practices, neoliberal entrepreneurship, abandonment of traditional forms of solidarity—that China cannot simply assimilate and seamlessly "make Chinese." In *The Days* (*Dong chun de rizi*, 1993) one of the protagonists, Dong, is an artist who paints according to Western representational canons and tries unsuccessfully to sell his work to Hong Kong clients. When his wife Chun leaves him and moves to the United States, Dong has a violent episode, gets diagnosed with a "light form" of split personality, or *jingshen fenlie zheng*, "mind-split-disease," the Chinese term for schizophrenia. He is caught by the camera as he morosely dons the "Zhongshan zhuang" uniform, associated with Sun Yat-sen, the first president of the Republic of China, which became a symbol of both the Chinese and the modern in the early republican era.[18] In the Maoist period, it was an everyday garment for men of any social standing. After the 1980s, it was largely replaced by the Western-style suit (although today restyled *Zhōngshān zhuāng* is again fashionable in formal settings). The use of the uniform at the end of the film is deliberate and meaningful but is far more significant than simply mocking the party line. As with many Chinese artists who, in the reform period from the late 1970s to the early 1990s, often looked to the West for both inspiration and recognition, the expression of their artistic imagination and creation did not always integrate smoothly into the structures of everyday life in Chinese society. The old, uniform Western oil painting in the background indicates a conflict or split: past and present, Chinese and Western, the individual pursuit of self and collective, national identity. This struggle is also inscribed in the lived environment and landscape: Wang masterfully captures the "necessary" but breakneck speed of the growth and the victims it leaves behind when Dong and Chun visit his family, who live outside of Beijing in the Northeast. When they go to the local cemetery to pay respect to Dong's deceased brother, they find the graves covered by plants and sprouts, since every available strip of land must now be put to some extractive, productive use—an image that will reoccur a quarter century later in *Chinese Portrait* (*Wo de jingtou*, 2018) and *So Long, My Son* (2019). Throughout his work, Wang upholds this tension between the stillness of the people as life forms and the changing countryside around them, the speed of "progress" threatening to colonize and sequester even one's memories. In each film, this stillness acts as the resistance to gaining edges, optimizing land and life, and an entrepreneurial investment in the self.

Throughout Wang's oeuvre, one can detect a movement from a genealogy of the modern subject to a genealogy of the modern space that makes the inextricable overlap, or rather, the ecological connection between the human and the natural landscape (figure 4.4). Wang's characters may not directly engage with the "idleness as resistance" makeshift manifesto of a Chinese youth tired of competition against peers in a perverse cycle of "self-improvement," but they definitely engage critically with the third evolution of biopower, a state-sanctioned rationality that Davide Tarizzo calls the "society of optimization," a designation that seems very much in sync with China's anarcho-capitalism, and against which the few remaining options are "inactivity . . . but also the temptation of the risk, or the dark, or the harmful."[19] This is further developed in his subsequent films, *Frozen* (1997), *Beijing Bicycle*, and *Drifters*. *Frozen* is perhaps Wang's most explicitly biopolitical film; it crystallizes the politics of life and the representation of life, a dual and dueling account of the political subject who forms the body politic and the highly individual,

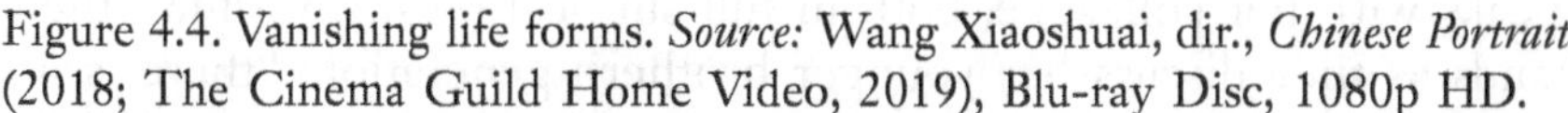

Figure 4.4. Vanishing life forms. *Source:* Wang Xiaoshuai, dir., *Chinese Portrait* (2018; The Cinema Guild Home Video, 2019), Blu-ray Disc, 1080p HD.

inward-looking (and in truth solipsistic) artist. Wang's film follows Qi Lei, an artist who performs four acts depicting his own death based on the seasons and their elements: in autumn, an Earth Burial (buried alive); in winter, a Water Burial (the artist jumps into a frozen lake); in spring, a Fire Burial (he sits inside a circle of flames). The film focuses on Qi Lei's final performance of the year, an "Ice Burial" for the summer solstice, which he intends to culminate in his death. Discouraged by his family and girlfriend, Shao Yun, Qi Lei plans his suicidal performance in secret, with the help of gallery owner Lao Lin, who acts as both mentor, accomplice, and villain. For Lao Lin, Qi Lei's performance is a philosophical, even metaphysical "experiment." However, it becomes clear that the socially alienated Qi Lei turns his performance into something so disconnected and disengaged from the materialism that causes this alienation that it leads toward death. The film provides a new twist on the idea of art for art's sake—and indeed, critic Wang Xiaoping has compared the film to the paradig-matic fin-de-siècle work on the subject, *The Picture of Dorian Gray*.[20]

Qi Lei lives with his sister, a doctor, and her husband, both of whom are bewildered by his plan. In a key scene, Qi Lei's sister speaks with her colleague, both in full surgical outfits, washing their hands as they discuss her younger brother's generation: "there is no material or social basis for their depressions."[21] Here, biopower is fully articulated as the coincidence of medical rationality and state ideology. The film therefore establishes two essential modes of existence that result from competing histories and changing conditions: Qi Lei and his community of artists and misfits, a sort of generational "accursed share" that embodies nonconformity, individuality, and inquiry, while his sister and others—for example, the police, or administrators at a psychiatric facility—represent a "social normality mainly embodied by the medical community."[22] Concerned by Qi Lei's obsession with death, Shao Yun convinces him to undergo a medical exam at a psychiatric hospital. As Qi Lei, Shao Yun, and his best friend (credited as "Longhaired Guy") walk through the institution, they pass patients dressed in identical striped uniforms who watch over them as they wait to be seen by a doctor. The characters lose their identity almost as soon as they enter the building: As Longhaired Guy lectures Qi Lei that "the hygiene of the mind is more important than keeping China's streets clean," a doctor emerges and forces him into a room despite his protests.[23] Longhaired Guy attempts to convince the doctors that he is not Qi Lei, pointing out that they are each from different regions, and speak with different accents. When he offers to show them his ID, he finds it is missing from his wallet, a further indication of the population from the perspective of the art of government.

This anonymity is dialectical, for although it indexes the subsumption of the individual within the anonymous mass of the population as a whole, it can also be used to subvert government incursions on artistic freedom. During the shooting of *Frozen*, Wang also worked on another film, *So Close to Paradise* (*Bian dan, gu niang*, 1998). Concerned that the former would endanger the production of the latter, Wang directed the film as "Wu Ming," or "anonymous" in Chinese. In an interview with Michael Berry, the director explains the affinity he felt with the Chinese performance art scene after he was blacklisted by the Film Bureau for *The Days*: "performance art was quite popular in China in 1994; however, there was only a small circle of artists working that field, their situation was not so good either." Wang recalls further:

> There was a performance art exhibition around the anniversary of the Tiananmen Square Incident. I had heard that some performance artists were arrested after the show because of the sensitive timing. The incident left me very depressed, a feeling that was only enhanced by my own experience making films. I felt that the entire atmosphere was terribly disheartening—it was an atmosphere in which art was being suffocated. It was during this time that people started talking about a young artist who had committed suicide. Was this real? Or was it part of a staged performance?[24]

In *Frozen*, Wang explores the cinematic and philosophical possibilities of this final anecdote, incorporating the arrest of the performance artists—a real-life event, itself entangled in a wider historical moment—that so depressed him. The "young artist who had committed suicide" was a performance artist called Qi Li, a model for Wang's near-identically named protagonist. As Silvia Fok's research has demonstrated, there is very little material information on Qi Li, but an account of his own original "Ice Burial" is attested to in a Chinese literary journal, *Tendency Quarterly*.[25]

When Qi Lei's group of artist friends and fellow misfits witness the arrest of a performance artist, it is shown from the perspective of a photographer's eye and lens, the camera clicking and flashing on the police among other young people with cameras. Though ostensibly about the arrest of an artist, it would not be too bold to venture that it acts as an assault on the police (and thereby authority). After an officer says "No pictures!" the disparate group of photographers swarm and outnumber the three or four cops on the scene, literally destabilizing the film itself as the camera shakes, sways, and veers with the action. Afterward, we see an officer's hand block the lens before the camera pans down to the grass underfoot before cutting to the hallway of an apartment building. Inside, Qi Lei and his friends discuss the event: The performance had only just started before it was broken up by the police, who claimed it "threatened public security." Qi Lei and his friends sit on the floor of a small apartment, drab but for a few photographs on the wall and a canvas in the corner, drinking beer. Longhaired Guy tells Qi Lei that although it's been a full day since the arrest, the artist's whereabouts are still unknown. Most of the group think the arrest is ridiculous—and compare it to a similar arrest years before—but one of them, offscreen, gives his own cautious take on the matter:[26] "They chose such a sensitive moment"—echoing the phrase Wang himself used to recall the rationale given for arresting performers on the anniversary of Tiananmen Square.[27] This undisguised and journalistic confrontation between art, discipline, and governmentality is imbricated with Qi Lei's final and fatal performance, which might itself be identified as a biopolitical product of history, particularly that of Tiananmen Square, an event that "massively converted [China's population] to a worldview oriented essentially toward economic growth" at the expense of human life.[28] The outcome of this worldview is reproduced when Qi Lei's brother-in-law takes some of his paintings despite the protests of Qi Lei's sister: "I've heard that if a painter becomes famous, the price soars."[29] It illustrates in images an insight made by scholar Jing Nie: "If China was under the supervision of ideological powers from its establishment in 1949 to the 1970s, then contemporary China is operated by economic forces, which dictate the ordering of the other dimensions such as ideology and culture," to which we might also a fraught relationship with nature as a site for extraction.[30] If *Frozen* is, in many ways, an allegory of post-Tiananmen China, it is also a meditation on the nature of representation and performance, where nature itself serves as a mimetic, a political, and an ecological index. While most of the film takes place in the city, the contrast between urban and rural landscapes (an important motif in Chinese cinema in general and Wang's cinema in particular) only emerges after Qi Lei's Ice Burial finally takes place. During this last performance, the artist hugs a large block of ice to his chest; it is later broken up and scattered over his body. At first, it appears that he really has died, but soon it becomes clear that his death was in fact a performance. Not only that, but a forgery, since we later learn that Qi Lei's sister counterfeits his death certificate with her colleague. The audience learns this after Qi Lei's "death" at the hospital, when he is shown in the courtyard of a large, traditional house on a hill overlooking the city. Here, Qi Lei and Lou Ling discuss the afterlife of artist and performance. Qi Lei remarks, "I don't feel anything. Before, I worried what it would be like after my death. Now that I've done it, I feel quite used to it. The air here is excellent." Lou Ling responds, "People adapt very easily to their surroundings."

They speak as if Qi Lei truly has died, and that this hilltop retreat might be some corner of the afterlife—identified with non-urban nature—to which Qi Lei is adapting (figure 4.5). At the same time, it is quite clear that the death was a production: Qi Lei asks Lou Ling if many people visited his exhibition, whether anyone "expressed doubt" about his death or not, whether they cried or cursed his name. This dynamic, which in lesser hands might be a self-reflexive but simplistic exploration of "the real" versus "the fake," is here a radical assertion and actualization of cinema's essential impurity, which makes it as much a part of nature as a technology. Qi Lei returns to the city for a final time to haunt his old life, checking up on his sister and, from the shadows, his girlfriend, who runs outside to follow his apparition.

When Qi Lei performs his death, what is he performing? This is the first and most essential question of the film, a question that frames the narrative from the very beginning as the voiceover asks, "Nobody could say exactly what his motives had been. Wasn't a life too high a price to pay for a work of art?"[31] This question is fore-shadowed early in the film, when a fellow performance artist, a young woman, jumps off a building and falls to her death.[32] In fact, there are three suicides encoded in *Frozen*: first, the anecdotal suicide, the real-life Qi Li; second, Qi Lei's performance of death, which is linked

Figure 4.5. Lou Ling advises Qi Lei after his staged death. *Source:* Wang Xiaoshuai, dir., *Frozen* (1996; Fox Lorber Home Video, 2001), DVD, 576p.

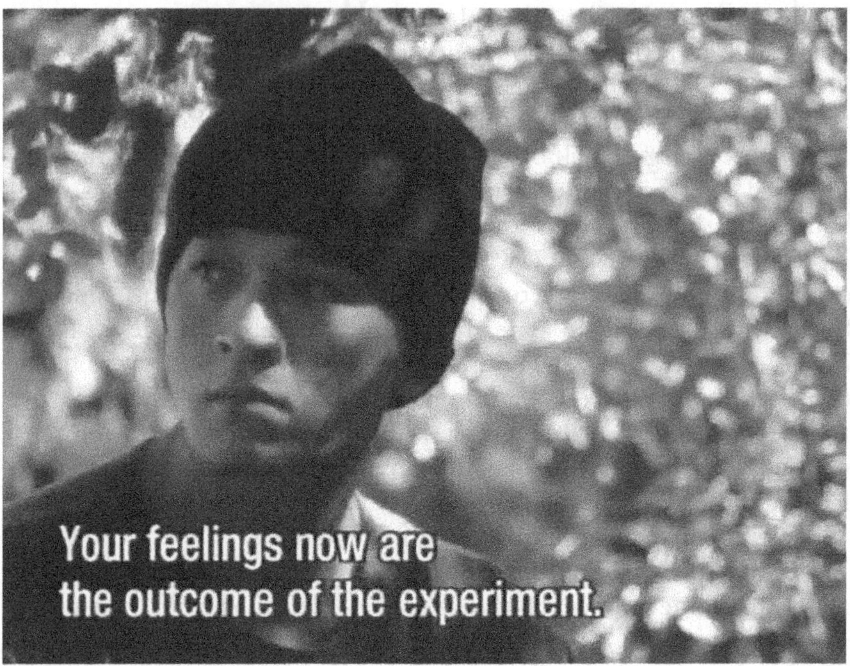

to his own forged death certificate, raising enigmatic questions about art's ability to reflect life; and, finally, Qi Lei's "real" suicide, which occurs without an audience, three months after his performance on the summer solstice. The latter is introduced by four different shots of an autumnal, rural landscape. On the fourth shot, the viewer sees a tree with Qi Lei's lifeless body beneath it as a voiceover explains, "Three months later they discovered his body beneath this tree. He had used a knife to cut his own wrists. The fresh blood had tinged the earth around the tree red."[33] The narrator takes care to note that while "it was officially stated that the day he killed himself was the first day of autumn . . . for most people, he had already died on 20 June during his Ice Burial."[34]

In his article on the cinematic *dispositif*, critic Juan David Cárdenas uses Wim Wenders's 1982 film *The State of Things* (*Der Stand der Dinge*) as an example, writing,

Art, commodity, industry and ideology: everything is involved in a film. [*Der Stand der Dinge*] is perfectly inspired by this insight. A movie that is being filmed, in Wenders' movie, is shown as crystallizing different levels of production such as artistic creation and factory functions, different social dimensions like the work of art and commodity, different conditions such as time of creation and time of factory production and finally, when the filmmaker in the movie films his own death, it becomes clear how impure cinema is as art. A film is rooted in material life so much so even life itself is in danger. The basic dangerous condition of cinema is its own impurity.[35]

Though Cárdenas references a very different film, *Frozen* can be regarded in light of this cinematic capturing maneuver. If we continue this thought experiment, *Frozen* has something unique and nuanced to say about the context of its own production in China, as a Chinese film, and the broader context of film as a medium. The entanglement of history, memory, and the free market that Cárdenas identifies in his article is especially potent in Wang's film, reflecting both the Foucauldian mechanism of cinema as such *as well as* its biopolitically meaningful local context. It is this, and nothing less, that Qi Lei performs when he produces his own death(s). Two death certificates; two suicides; a life and death divided into two forms of biopolitical production: the performative spectacle of death and the corpse of the artist. It cannot be, though it is tempting to speculate, that Qi Lei's "real" death connects reality with nature, with something as visceral as blood sinking into the ground, into the root system of the tree, because this, too, is an image. When Wang shows us Qi Lei's body beneath the tree, when he tells us blood stained the earth red, he suggests that art—that cinema—and nature are both animated and killed by one another; that this impurity, whose locus is the body of the artist itself, is both its peril and its potentiality. Qi Lei creates a work in which the body and its representation become fused together, fixing the mortality of the body to the indexicality of the image. Life becomes a pure, absolute form "whose value consists therefore of its inutility and whose use consists of its intangibility" as an index to the pernicious consequences of sacrificing everything to materiality.[36] The death of the author is quite literal in this film, for the artist writes and paints with his own life, effecting the coincidence between the artistic body and the corporeal body. In this sense, Qi Lei provides a commonality between Pasolini and Foucault, for whom revolutions and counterrevolutions are created by and transit through the body. Qi Lei's artistic struggle wrestles with the conviction that an art that truly lives must coincide with the life and death of its creator. For this new form of art, an art that lives and dies, death is not the end but rather something that propels the work of art, along with its artist, into the future, potentially forever. For Qi Lei, the task of the artist is to remain elusive, unseizable, impossible to trace back to other molds, to old provocations, to past events. At that point, *bíos* and *zoē* will also be indistinguishable and tend to coincide as qualified life is inscribed into bare life.

Reproducing China in Wang's Later Work

If *Frozen* is indissolubly preoccupied with the death of the artist, two of Wang's later works, *In Love We Trust* (*Zuo you*, 2008) and *So Long, My Son* (2019), operate on the same continuum but shift their attention from the artist to the child and to the bioethical and biopolitical dimensions of the family, particularly pregnancy. The first of these films focuses on a divorced couple, each now happily re-partnered, who attempt to cure their terminally ill daughter by conceiving a second child to be a bone marrow donor. The second explores the afterlife of China's one-child policy over the course of thirty years through the lives of two families. Both films register the (un)intended consequences of China's one-child policy and the privatization of property, which are linked in materially and historically significant ways. These films center the pregnant feminine body under biopolitical protocols that limit reproductive autonomy. In *In Love We Trust*, pregnancy answers the moral imperative to save the modern bourgeois Chinese family and maintain the growth of urban development. In *So Long, My Son*, women's fertility is regarded as a threat to modernization, which requires reproductive limits in order to flourish.

By contrasting the one-child policy and the grief over lost children with the *topoi* of China's economic success—dense cities, skyscrapers, construction sites—*In Love We Trust* and *So Long, My Son* unambiguously link the restriction of human life and bodily autonomy with modernity and globalization. It should be noted that this is neither controversial (it was approved by official censors) nor even necessarily subversive, but rather a visual and dramatic articulation of Dengist policy, which explicitly recognized population control as "a central fact on which future development strategy must be based."[37] Indeed, these policies were devised to address "the population problem," a term used by the CCP that uncannily echoes Foucault's assertion that biopolitics emerged to address the "problems posed to governmental practice by . . . living beings forming a population."[38]

The control of the (potentially) pregnant body exerts a historical force that not only affects the past and the future but also enters and alters (cinematic) time itself. In *In Love We Trust*, pregnancy and impending death create a moral dilemma located within the family, which will impact the lives and futures of five people, including the dying child, and which gestures beyond the horizons of the film itself, leaving the matter unresolved, ambiguous, and open. While this film takes place in the present day and reflects looser policies of family planning, *So Long, My Son* is in many ways an epic history of the one-child policy from 1982 to 2016, when the limit was increased to two children, though this latter reform is not mentioned in the film.[39] Both films also highlight the intersection between wealth, class, and reproduction, most notably *So Long, My Son*, which features Liyun, a woman forced to abort her second pregnancy because she cannot pay the prohibitively expensive fines imposed on parents of second children. By contrast, *In Love We Trust* features a blended middle-class family—the protagonist is a real estate agent, and her ex-husband is a property developer, professions that are significant to the film and its dialogue with modern China. In what follows, I take an approach that is both anachronistic and chronological, examining Wang's latest film, which spans the 1980s to the present day, before turning to *In Love We Trust*, an earlier film that exclusively takes place in contemporary, urban China. In doing so, I suggest that the films are two "volumes" of what I am calling Wang's genealogy of natality, which traverses revolutionary and capitalist China. With these later works, Wang reintegrates the upheavals of Chinese history into his canvas, into which he embeds the lives of ordinary people at a deeper level. His lens is as much focused on the unexpected consequences of the Cultural Revolution as it is on the possibility of new subjectivities and communities, both of which respond to the biopolitics of birth and natality.[40] Both films situate "'reproductive life' . . . at the intersection of thanatopolitics and biopolitics as these relate to women's bodies," in ways that correspond to both China's Communist past and its capitalist future, and which are plotted and located in the classed and gendered body.[41]

"We're Rich Now. No Need to Be Afraid": Natality, Urban Development, and Landscape in *So Long, My Son*

In *So Long, My Son* biopolitics and ecopolitics intertwine in the image. This section examines some of the key images in this film to better illustrate the constellation of concepts described above. The film opens with the *Rückenfigur* of a child, Haohao, looking out at the manmade reservoir that stands placidly between him and an expanse of sunbaked, rolling hills dotted with trees and foliage. A group of boys below splash in the water. When Haohao turns, the camera follows, revealing another boy in a blue tracksuit, Xingxing. The boys, who share a birthday, are best friends whose parents are also best friends, more like brothers. Haohao tries to convince Xingxing to join him and the other boys in the water, but he refuses. Haohao storms off, running down the embankment toward the water. Soon after, we see a reproduction of the opening scene—this time the camera frames Xingxing from behind, an outsider looking on as the other boys play without him. It is later revealed that these are Xingxing's last moments—caving in to the pressure, he will soon enter the water and drown. Like many other chronological details in the film, this fact is deferred, buried in the narrative, a latent devastation waiting to erupt. Instead, the film immediately cuts to the next scene, where Xingxing appears to return home and eat dinner with his parents. What follows this is perhaps the most pivotal scene of the film: A long shot of tiny figures dotting the distant banks of the reservoir, where a group of adults, including Xingxing's parents, factory workers Liyun and Yaojun, rush toward his body, too distant to see. A woman, Haiyun, notices her own son, Haohao, on top of the hill again, shivering in his bathing suit. In the next scene, Yaojun, followed by his wife and several other adults, including Haohao's parents, races through a tunnel with Xingxing's limp body as a train screams past them in the opposite direction. Here, Wang contrasts the industrial future with the drowned child, mechanical speed with the propulsion of the human body. Unlike the train, Yaojun cannot cross the distance between the tunnel and the hospital fast enough to save his child, who was likely dead before he was even found. Reviving Xingxing would require no less than breaking through time to prevent him his drowning. The camera frames Yaojun, his wife, and others from behind and from the front, offering the viewer both the perspective of the runners and of the train. The dark tunnel frames a bright, curved view of its exit, operating as if it were a screen pierced by the oncoming train. The scene unavoidably recalls the infamous Lumière Brothers' 1896 film *The Arrival of a Train at La Ciotat Station* and the terror it allegedly evoked in the audiences of the time.[42] As Barbara Mennel points out in her discussion of this early film, "the moving train embodied the changing perception of time and space in modernity; space as urban versus rural and time as modern versus pre-modern. Films manipulate space and time, whereas trains collapse space and require the concept of universal time."[43]

The train here similarly heralds modernization, which, as Hongbing Zhang notes, "has long been understood in China . . . as a temporal movement in which China will be improved from its old tradition to the universalized ideal of a new tomorrow, now globalization is broadly perceived as a spatial movement in which the improvement of China means its integration into the . . . market."[44] *So Long, My Son* internalizes these rapid movements of time and space—not through ruins and slow takes, as Wang's contemporary Jia does, but through active development—as it is registered by the both the landscape and the family—and nonlinear cuts: the film is almost entirely made of flashbacks and flash-forwards (figure 4.6).

I have recounted the opening scenes in such detail to illustrate that it is precisely at this point, at the inception of the film, that Wang begins to close the circle between social production and the production of industrialized space.[45] In this film, the train that rushes past the protagonists links the speed of modernity with the trauma of a lost child, both of which distort, or perhaps redefine, time. The narrative does not follow a progressive, traditional structure. Only at the very end of the film do Wang and his audience arrive at the present day, a further temporal and self-reflexive complexity that refuses a neat, orderly history and epistemology. The temporal

Figure 4.6. Xingxing's parents run for help through a train tunnel. *Source:* Wang Xiaoshuai, dir., *So Long, My Son* (2019; Curzon Artificial Eye, 2019), Blu-ray Disc, 1080p HD.

distortion of this film is indexed by the train, but its true origin can be traced back to the first scene: Between Xingxing's first appearance at the reservoir and his death, Wang intercuts scenes from ambiguous temporalities, a disjointed mixture of flashbacks and flash-forwards. The second scene, described above, which suggests that Xingxing returns home from the reservoir, appears to follow on from the first, but the next few scenes—of his parents rushing to the banks of the water, running through the tunnel with his body—suggest that this was merely a memory of an earlier moment. Although I have referred to Xingxing's death throughout this section for ease of reference, the film does not immediately disclose his death. Wang merely shows us Xingxing rushed down the hospital corridor, where a frenzied Yaojun is held back by orderlies. Next, Wang cuts to the reservoir, which is violently bifurcated by the train as it races across the foreground.

The viewer is then transported to the coast of Fujian, where the dinner scene is reproduced in a new setting, a spacious but rustic home near the coast. Here, Liyun prepares a meal for a teenage boy she calls Xingxing. The warmth and ease of the previous scene are absent, and when Xingxing storms out of the house, it is evident that his relationship with his parents is far from idyllic. Soon after, it is revealed that this Xingxing is a local boy Liyun and Yaojun adopted and named after their dead son, an identity he can never usurp and whose absence he can never replace. It is here that the concept of reproduction is not only complicated but acts as a reference point for Wang's larger inquiry into the possibility of representing history as an image. This inquiry is not simply poetic or intellectual, but practical: "China is changing so fast that it is really hard to find the old things my movie required."[46] In terms of production, "China's accelerated economic growth even affected filming, necessitating the construction of sets to mimic less affluent eras of the country's history."[47] The friction (or fiction) between the teenage Xingxing and his adoptive parents derives from his intuition that he is a copy of the original child, a representation Liyun and Yaojun desperately want to counterfeit to appease their hungry grief. In this way, the film makes the radical suggestion that nothing can be recreated; that every representation is an inimitable, singular act of creation with its own past and future. Liyun and Yaojun can no more "reproduce" a replacement for their son than Wang can reproduce or return to historic China—the referent has been destroyed. Wang's narrative continues to oscillate between different time periods before and after Xingxing's death. Wang's refusal of a progressive narrative and his insistence on nonlinear editing makes it clear that as soon as Xingxing goes to the reservoir, temporality explodes, becomes fragmented.

The rest of the film follows both the aftermath and the lead-up to this event, centering on the relationships between Liyun and Yaojun, Xingxing's parents, and Yingming and Haiyun, Haohao's parents, as well as Haohao himself, whose guilt and grief become living things that reside within him. As the film continues, it becomes clearer that the link between Chinese modernity and parental trauma is far less figurative than it might initially appear. The drowned Xingxing is not the only lost child in the film: The teenage Xingxing runs away from home after a fight with his parents, whose expectations he feels incapable of meeting. A flashback reveals that Liyun became pregnant before her first son's death but was forced to abort the pregnancy. Complications from the abortion—instigated by her best friend, Haiyun, an officious local Party leader—have made it impossible for Liyun to conceive children in the future. This creates a latent biopolitical economy of loss and substitution that is fully activated by the loss of Xingxing's life, which neither the past (a potential sibling) nor the future (an adopted son) can stabilize or repair. One striking example of this occurs when Yingming gives Yaojun a cleaver and begs him to kill his own son, Haohao, as a kind of payment for Xingxing's death.

The film reproduces a question Zhang formulates as the challenge of modern China: "What and how to integrate, what to be left behind, who has the power to integrate what and whom, and how to define the relationship between the integrated and disintegrated?"[48] If *So Long, My Son* answers this question, it does by presenting the very disintegration that eludes integration, formally reflecting the palimpsestic marks that history, memory, and trauma inscribe on the lives and bodies of human beings. This does not mean there is no logic to the narrative; far from it. The discontinuous temporality of Wang's film offers new opportunities to connect individual memory and collective history without necessarily privileging one over the other, but by demonstrating how they coincide in the most striking of ways. About two-thirds of the way through the film, Yaojun carries Liyun to the hospital after she attempts to commit suicide. As he sits in the hospital waiting room, the film cuts to a series of MRI images of a brain. A young doctor, who later turns out to be Haohao, says, "Her condition isn't looking good."[49] The MRI results belong to Haiyun, who is dying of cancer. This and the previous scene are likely separated in time and certainly in space, but they are visually imbricated such that one tragedy "leads" into the other; this is not a causal relation, but a mimetic and mnemonic one where one memory resembles or provokes another. The film cuts to a private party at an upscale restaurant. Haohao breaks the news to his father outside a restaurant. Inside, Haiyun—who has long since exchanged her modest Maoist uniform for expensive evening wear—shares a toast with other fashionably dressed, affluent guests. Near the end of the film, Liyun and Yaojun return to Beijing at the invitation of Haiyun, who wants to see them before she dies. When they arrive, the landscape has drastically changed: It is now a bustling capitalist metropolis; most of the old buildings have been demolished to make way for enormous tower blocks in various stages of completion. As they drive to their old apartment, Liyun remarks, "There's almost no trace of our past." A moment later, Yaojun waves at a statue of Mao situated outside a busy shopping center called "Victory Mall," a strikingly postmodern image that suggests a metastasizing past that never stopped happening.[50] They return to their old apartment building, now somewhat dilapidated and neighbor to a massage parlor; they drive past. Once they reach Haiyun, she is nearly unconscious in a hospital bed, but manages to tell Liyun, "No need to be afraid. We are rich now. No need to be afraid. We can help you pay the fine for a new baby" (figure 4.7).[51] At Haiyun's funeral, we learn that Yingming's source of wealth is real estate development when he offers to set them up in one of his apartment buildings.

These two scenes occur sequentially and consolidate two strands of critique in Wang's film. First, that reproduction was always a class issue, even before China turned to capitalism; factory workers could not hope to afford the prohibitive fines for a second child, but those with wealth could. This has resulted in a kind of class eugenics, as reproduction rates relate directly to economic inequality: a "class hierarchy of reproduction" that reveals an uneven biopolitical relation to state policy in which the fine, or "social compensation fee, acts as a severe punishment, while for the wealthy it is a trivial expense."[52] Second, by linking this with urban development, *So Long, My Son* suggests that China's one-child policy has successfully enabled the country's rapid modernization, its entry into the global market and the profits therein; the struggle, sacrifices, and suffering of Chinese workers has not resulted in the revolutionary dictatorship of the

Figure 4.7. A dying Haiyan tries to make amends with Liyun. *Source:* Wang Xiaoshuai, dir., *So Long, My Son* (2019; Curzon Artificial Eye, 2019), Blu-ray Disc, 1080p HD.

proletariat, but "a capitalist machine decorated with socialist orna-
mentation that violently crushes any expression of labor organization
and working-class solidarity."[53] This has reasonably resulted in a gulf
between the state-sanctioned, disciplined history of China's development and individual memory.

"This Place Is So Strange No One Wants to Rent It": Family, Private Property, and the State in *In Love We Trust*

Though filmed in 2007, *In Love We Trust* foreshadows and often
elaborates the concerns and motifs of *So Long, My Son*, released over
a decade later: In both, the narrative engines are history, pregnancy,
the dead or dying child, and extreme attempts to forestall or repair
such a loss. Indeed, although it is far less epic in scope than *So Long,
My Son*, *In Love We Trust* may be read as a retroactive "sequel" to
the former film. Focused fully on contemporary rather than historical
China, the film addresses bioethics, modernity, and natalism from a
strictly middle-class perspective. And while *So Long, My Son* concerns
the disciplined, socialist maternal subject, *In Love We Trust* follows Mei
Zhu, a character who represents the neoliberal maternal subject, a
woman with a much greater, although somewhat ambiguous, degree of
bodily autonomy.[54] In each film, reproductive desire is disciplined and
motivated by biopolitics, but never exactly or apparently constitutes
a free choice, and in both cases is framed as a political (*So Long, My
Son*) or ethical (*In Love We Trust*) imperative.

Mei Zhu is professional real estate agent for an overseas landlord, divorced and estranged from her ex-husband, a *nouveau riche*
contractor, with whom she shares five-year-old daughter, Hehe. Mei
Zhu and Xiao Lu have since remarried, the latter to Dong Fan, a
young flight attendant, and the former to Lao Xie, a sensitive software
developer.[55] The film is an acute observation of these characters—particularly Mei Zhu—as they are each captured by an impossible but
undeniable proposition when Hehe is diagnosed with leukemia: To
save Hehe, Mei Zhu and ex-husband Xiao Lu must have another
child, a "savior sibling" to facilitate a cord blood transplant. The
family itself and the home become the sites of an ethical dilemma
with such strong resonances that it is unclear whether Wang's film
wants to conserve the traditional family or destroy it. It is precisely

this contradiction that makes what appears on the surface to be a rather soapy melodrama in fact a radical political work, an extreme melodrama that heightens generic conventions to such a degree that they transcend reason. The predicament in *In Love We Trust* isn't really an ethical problem to reason through and solve, but the unassailable ethical demand of life that must be obeyed.

The film is an intense, uncanny melodrama that has, reasonably, been read as a "main melody movie"—propaganda films that extol the virtues of the State and Party ideology. Scholar Wang Xiaoping writes that while Wang Xiaoshuai's early work criticizes the hypocrisy of the country's movement from "socialist collectivism to a materialistic individualism," *In Love We Trust* should be nonetheless considered a "main melody" or propaganda film: Wang Xiaoshuai "buys the ostensibly altruistic rhetoric of the authority, which essentially calls for the willing cooperation of the populace to put aside the (socialist) ethics and morality in favor of a particular, 'sublime' goal; by which adulterous relation (both literally and allegorically) is perpetrated in the name of love . . . falling into a politically conservative mentality which self-willingly caters to the interpellation of the authoritative power."[56] While this analysis is well-founded and compelling, my own reading aims to attend to what Wang Xiaoping admits are the "self-deconstructive elements within [the film], some of which even evoke our supposition that these might be deliberated arranged" in a more dialectical fashion.[57] For instance, the restrained performances are mediated by unusual angles and distant wide shots that often limit the viewer to a voyeuristic or often surveilling position, sometimes even high-angle shots in tight spaces. Similarly, the use and control of mobile phones in the film are deployed as the central setup and payoff of the film. Early on, Mei Zhu accidentally "pocket dials" her husband Lao Xie. This is a habitual occurrence, as the audience learns when Lao Xie suggests that Mei Zhu lock her phone screen to prevent these uncontrolled and unconscious transmissions—she replies that she doesn't know how to do it, and the matter is forgotten until the end of the film. I will address this in more detail shortly, but for now it will suffice to say that *In Love We Trust* is not a straightforward melodrama nor a wholly successful a political film, but something stranger and more intractable, what one might loosely call the "social gothic," reprised as social horror in *Red Amnesia*, one of Wang's other films.[58] The film opens with the mechanical view of a taxi dashcam as a vehicle conveys unseen and unspoken occupants past tall, well-to-do Beijing tower blocks. The next shot is an over-the-shoulder shot that reveals Mei Zhu as the passenger and an unnamed driver. In the next scene, Mei Zhu shows a young couple around a spacious but unusual apartment. Though there are three bedrooms, the only bed in the apartment is located in the larger of the two living rooms, an unusual detail the potential tenants remark upon. Mei Zhu replies, "The landlord put it there, but if you rent [the apartment], you can rearrange the room later." The couple is perplexed at the lack of furniture—in addition to the bed, there is a standing mirror, floor lamp, and an armchair, with a modest glass table and chairs in the adjacent dining area. Mei Zhu concedes the point, but reassures them: "Yes, but everything is brand new. The landlord just renovated it and he's out of the country now." The couple is not quite convinced, and Mei Zhu fails to lease the property. Strangely, and importantly, real estate dominates a film that is ostensibly the saga of a family and their heroic attempts to save their daughter's life. But these two elements are not disconnected, and indeed dovetail in meaningful ways throughout the film (figures 4.8 and 4.9). Mei Zhu's "unleasable" apartment plays a pivotal and structuring role in the film. During the first apartment viewing, Mei Zhu receives a phone call from Lao Xie, who tells her that Hehe has another fever—the inciting incident of the movie and the first indication to the audience that something is wrong.

Figure 4.8. Mei Zhu and the hostile functionalism of middle-class interiors. *Source:* Wang Xiaoshuai, dir., *In Love We Trust* (2008; Film Movement, 2011), DVD, 576p.

Figure 4.9. Xiao Lu placating disgruntled workers at a building site. *Source:* Wang Xiaoshuai, dir., *In Love We Trust* (2008; Film Movement, 2011), DVD, 576p.

Mei Zhu's job as an intermediary for an overseas client is an important part of the film's socioeconomic context, as Wang Xiaoping has also noted. Xiao Lu, too, acts as an intermediary between developers and workers. When he receives Mei Zhu's call about their daughter's illness, he is on a large urban building site arguing with workers, who threaten to walk off the job over missed paychecks. Xiao Lu cannot afford to have building stop, but neither can he afford to pay his workers, because he relies on the developers to pay him for the labor. Throughout the film, this conflict becomes a parallel plot whose economic and metaphorical significance transverse the wider struggle to keep Hehe alive. The progress of the building site—and therefore the growth of Beijing and China more generally—becomes visually linked to Hehe's survival; both child and building site must continue to grow and flourish at any cost. If the means of these tasks is somehow immoral, that is overwritten by the transcendent morality that motivates it: one the one hand, preventing the death of a child, which is abhorrent and unnatural, and on the other hand, maintaining the health and growth of the economy. This relationship is the structuring example of what Shuqin Cui broadly and perceptively identifies as the more general "strong woman figure in family melodrama [which] mirrors diminished masculinity in a market economy and recuperative power of female sexuality."[59] Indeed, whereas Mei Zhu is motivated by a singular, obsessive purpose, an active agent who expands the borders of what is accepted and the possible, Xiao Lu struggles to achieve harmony and stability at work and at home, relying on short-term promises and manipulation. For example, he pays his workers part of their wages to get them back to work for a few days. But, as his assistant tells him, "The problem is still there." Xiao Lu responds: "Can't let construction halt."[60] The imbrication of Hehe's life and the future of the building site becomes visible in this scene, as Xiao Lu receives a call from Mei Zhu, who tells him that neither she nor he is a suitable donor. Wang Xiaoping offers a valuable further insight into the slippage between natality and development when he explains that the privatization of state-owned enterprises in the 1990s is "often allegorically designated in the official rhetoric as a resurrection [of the businesses] through [a] 'blood transplant,' " suggesting a mimetic relationship between Mei Zhu's pursuit of life-saving cord blood and the neoliberal turbocharge of what was once a socialist economy.[61] Over the next several scenes, Hehe undergoes chemotherapy, which fails, leaving a bone marrow transplant as her only hope of survival. A doctor tells Mei Zhu that a sibling would be the most likely match, mentioning that he recently met a patient whose sister was a perfect match. "Of course," he concedes, "for a one-child family, this is more difficult."[62] The next day, Mei Zhu shows the same apartment to a family with two children, who become the film's first legible signs of (exceptions to) the one-child policy. Mei Zhu remarks on the clients, and the woman happily responds that while she had not even considered it at first, her husband's family encouraged her to have a second child. The couple are polite about the apartment but complain about the lack of furniture. Catalyzed by this encounter, Mei Zhu meets with Xiao Lu to persuade him to conceive another child with her. When they propose this plan to their respective spouses, new anxieties and desires leak into their conversations, as it becomes clear that the issue of children in these new relationships has always been unsettled: Xiao Lu has been avoiding the subject with Dong Fan, who desperately wants a child; and while Lao Xie is more accepting, he asks frankly, "What happens if you and I want another baby later?"[63] Although both partners ultimately agree to the plan, it significantly lessens their chances of having their own biological children because of the one-child policy, not to mention the general material cost of supporting three children.[64] Nevertheless, Mei Zhu and Xiao Lu embark on a series of artificial insemination attempts facilitated by the state hospital. In a later scene, a doctor tells Mei Zhu that the method isn't working. While it is "hard to tell" why, the doctor asks Mei Zhu if she has ever had an abortion. Mei Zhu says yes: "I didn't think I would want children after my second marriage. So I did it. Afterwards, I felt guilty, so I tried to have children again, but I miscarried all of them."[65] Revealing this painful, personal history makes Lao Xie's earlier question to her even more meaningful. The doctor replies that she is "just worried about habitual abortion," adding, "You are not young." Mei Zhu's history of miscarriage ups the stakes, and while the doctor is only concerned with "habitual abortion," the specter of abortion looms large. This scene suggests an uneasy slippage between bodily autonomy and state mandates on procreation—a biopolitical juncture further defined by the doctor's reply to Mei Zhu's request to try one more time: "That's not possible. It's against hospital policy. We have already let you slide on the rules."[66]

Having exhausted the possibilities of artificial insemination, Mei Zhou convinces a reluctant but stoic Xiao Lu to pursue what she understands to be a more viable alternative—sexual intercourse. His initial response to her request, "This scandal will get us on TV!" is, in addition to one of the few humorous moments in the film, one of the frankest articulations of the challenges Mei Zhu's course of action poses to social norms: In her attempt to save her daughter, she threatens the institutions of monogamy and the traditional family such that it could destroy the reputations of everyone involved.[67] As Wang Xiaoping perceptively writes, both couples "have to give up their interests, including the most cherished one for the middle-class: family value[s]. . . . What makes them hesitate to do [so] is not merely the inexorable result of losing their 'face' in public, but also an over challenge to the ethical custom of society."[68] Mei Zhu's reproductive goal is both the highest moral cause and the most dishonorable act. It is morally upstanding to save one's child at all costs; yet cheating on one's spouse, no less than conspiring to conceive a child with another partner, is traditionally considered wicked—and yet these describe the same act. Wang Xiaoping regards the whole scenario as a coercive "main melody" film rationalizing China's move away from socialism toward neoliberal capitalism, in which "the ethical-moral dilemma is pushed step by step to its foremost." "By forcing every person to make their most difficult choice," Wang suggests the film privileges an extreme ethics of mandatory self-sacrifice as advocated by the CCP.[69] Cui reads it in terms of power relations, noting that Wang's film "turns the life-and-death issue into the single force driving both the narrative and power negotiation."[70]

Mei Zhu vows to keep their plan secret from Lao Xie to spare his feelings, while Xiao Lu tells Dong Fan, who leaves him that night. The next day, Mei Zhu returns to the unleasable apartment for another viewing, this time four young women, possibly students. They comment on the "weird" design of the apartment and joke about sharing the property's only bed in the living room—unremarkably, they also decide against renting the apartment. Meanwhile, Mei Zhu calls Xiao Lu, who agrees to go ahead with the plan. In the next scene, Mei Zhu is back home, about to rush out the door—she tells Lao Xie she has an appointment with a client, a lie. She and Xiao Lu arrive at the apartment in the same taxi. She directs the driver: "Left," "right," an evocation of the film's title.[71] It begins to make sense not simply in its designation of a moral dilemma, but also as a structuring principle: left, right; action, reaction; throughout the film, the characters shuffle left because they cannot go right, and right because they cannot go left, shuffling back and forth between the corners they are each pushed into. Here, the recapitulation of the idiomatic title underscores the moral and ethical stakes, which reach their highest point when the ex-couple enter the apartment In this scene, the curious state of the apartment fulfills its unsettling potential. The unsettled, uncanny qualities of the space, its resistance and even hostility to habitation, contains and reflects the ambivalence and anxiety that animate Mei Zhu's and Xiao Lu's reproductive encounter. In the space of about two minutes, all of the narrative elements collide and coalesce. Once inside, both are visibly nervous.

XIAO LU: There won't be anyone coming?

MEI ZHU: No. The landlord is out of the country, the place hasn't been leased yet.

XIAO LU: This place seems strange.[72]

Between this exchange, Wang cuts back to Lao Xie, who answers a call from Mei Zhu. The "pocket dial" from the beginning of the film recurs once more here. Lao Xie says "Hello?" into the receiver, but hears nothing but the conversation between his wife and her ex-husband. The camera cuts back to the apartment.

> MEI ZHU: This is a living room. The landlord put a bed here. That's probably why it seems strange.

> XIAO LU: There's someone living here?

> MEI ZHU: No. There isn't. These things are all brand new. I bought some quilts. There are personal products back there too. The furniture is so strange, no one wants to lease it. So I leased it for a month. Take off your clothes.[73]

I have included this dialogue and a detailed description of these scenes in order to demonstrate how, although he does overdetermine these elements, Wang takes great and subtle care to create a rhythm of affective responses to the space. The apartment function as a theater of biopolitical desire and fear where three acts play out: the first viewing, which establishes the strange place where Mei Zhu receives the call about Hehe; the second, which takes place after Mei Zhu learns that sibling is Hehe's best hope, and features the family with two children; third, the viewing with the four students, during which Mei Zhu calls Xiao Lu; and of course the final act, where Mei Zhu and Xiao Lu try to conceive a child through sexual intercourse.

The dilemma presented in this film extends to any critic trying to make sense of its ethics. While Wang thinks it is a neoliberal utopia that embodies the coercive rhetoric of the state, Cui understands the film to offer a utopian vision of life beyond "cultural conventions and heterosexual constraints."[74] In the first instance, the film is criticized for its capitulation to the party line and a tacit endorsement of Chinese capitalism. In the second instance, the film "mocks the one-child policy" and balks at traditional values. Does *In Love We Trust* affirm neoliberal ideology or does it subvert gender norms? This chapter suggests the film does both and neither simultaneously, whereby a possible strategy of survival and resistance is a theologically secularized reinvention and de-securitization of life. The film's protagonist develops from a real estate agent into an entrepreneur of life, becoming both its agent and its medium. It is in this sense that Mei Zhu is, as described earlier in this chapter, a neoliberal maternal subject. Indeed, when the characters in this film discuss the hoped-for child, it is not as a future person with a speculative identity, but as the bearer of raw material—cord blood—to be extracted and reinfused into a body assailed by cancer. This is an uneasy analogy indeed. On the other hand, it might be presented in a far more affirmative light if one focuses on the fact that, in order to protect and contribute to the flourishing of life, Mei Zhu redefines Chinese middle-class ethics and reconfigures the family structure, making room within its now expanded boundaries for new models of coexistence beyond the *dispositf* of marriage. It is this more affirmative orientation, which neither ignores the insinuation of capitalism, nor fetishizes monogamy, that may best describe *In Love We Trust*.

In each of his films, Wang uncannily presents post-socialist capitalism and its attendant anxieties and horror as biopolitical in nature. He shares with other East Asian directors—such as Hirokazu Kore-eda, with his reinvention of families that cannot be straitjacketed in any institutionalized definition—a faith in the human, which hardly breaks through but finally emerges like in the heartwarming ending of *So Long, My Son* when, despite all the deaths and the pain, the protagonists still find in themselves their nurturing voice. The past is inscribed on and carried within the human body, whose life is marked and managed by governmental technologies. In blurring the difference between qualified life and biological life Wang is not far from Hannah Arendt's notion of natality as the basis of the political, in the words of Miguel Vatter, "after all the illusions of the earth as a *Heimat* are laid to rest, after all attempts to think the political starting from or returning to the familial have shown their barrenness, and, perhaps, even after the passing away of all political form or organization as such."[75] With the destruction caused by the one-child policy and the furious and absurd rhythms and demands of housing and real estate construction in the background—their lingering presence as a convenient obfuscation of historical traumas, as in *Red Amnesia*—the decision to bear a child in *In Love We Trust* is existential. It may not concern the fabric of political demands, of rules and democratic principles, but it points to a kairological way to seize control of one's life by creating life through, in the words of Adriana Cavarero, a "surging" move, a sudden gesture in "the phenomenology of political experience."[76]

5

Allegories of Extraction

Radu Jude and the New Romanian Cinema

"ONE SHOULD LOVE ONE'S OWN people, of course, but not feel hatred for other races, should one?"[1] This question, posed halfway through the World War I novel *Forest of the Hanged*, adapted by Liviu Ciulei in the eponymous film (*Pădurea spânzuraților*, 1965) hints at the conflict not as an epic of decisive strategies, assaulted borders, or heroic warriors but as a machine that, thanks to the political invention of arbitrary "races," utilizes and consumes life. Romanians against Russians, Romanians against Italians, Romanians hanging their Czech comrades, and finally Romanians against fellow Romanians in an immunitarian craze that ends in autoimmune destruction, similarly to Francesco Rosi's *Many Wars Ago* (*Uomini contro*, 1970) when Gian Maria Volontè's Lieutenant Ottolenghi shouts (deploying a Gramscian lexicon) "Enough with this war of *morti di fame* [starvelings] against *morti di fame!*" In war's incontestable horizon, sending soldiers to certain slaughter in pointless assaults is simply a stress-test to prove the capacity and strength of the military institution as biopolitical institution, a way to make sure that the hierarchies in place during civil life remain the same during warfare, while destroying lives of potential revolutionary "subversives" for good measure. War is the biopolitical logic that makes power a modifier of human life, and the infantryman is among the purest of the state-sanctioned life molds

171

because of its fungibility and disposability, to the point that the foot soldiers depicted in *Forest of the Hanged*, *Many Wars Ago*, Joseph Losey's *King and Country* (1964), and Stanley Kubrick's *Paths of Glory* (1957) feel like an iteration of the *Muselmann* in a similarly concentrationary environment. But to witness the struggle of a subject who strives to be autonomous or at least find his own breadth against an authorized and established episteme, one does not need to look at his being torn apart in a military logic, since the civil domain is itself "an order of battle."[2] Battling hostile networks of power relations, individuals are implacably probed and prodded until a satisfactory, docile conduct is activated. The biopolitical excavation into the subject until life fits into an expected form is one of the recurring templates throughout Romanian cinema, with Radu Jude's "rehearsals" of extraction among the latest examples. Jude also emphasizes a racializing tendency that seem to transcend the periodization of Romanian history as pre- and post-Communist rule.

The manipulative intervention of power into the body politic and the pliability of images as if they were originated from the archive of an omniscient authority appeared in world cinema after the perspectives of political renewal collapsed. In Europe in 1970, Greek director Theo Angelopoulos's first feature film *The Reconstruction* (*Anaparastasi*) presented a mélange of realism and modernism: The "verifiable" premise—a homicide carried out in the mountainous northwestern region of Epirus—and the aesthetic—location shooting in poor, dilapidated locales, the use of nonprofessional actors in choral scenes—could evoke for the audience a Neorealist propensity with its Rossellinian ruins and Viscontian landscapes, whereas the collision of temporal planes and the negation of privileged epistemological avenues were those of an advanced cinematic modernism. In fact, Angelopoulos's formal influences in this first film do not belong to a strictly Neorealist framework but instead embrace Italian post-Neorealist tendencies toward the Oedipal search for fathers, the problematic inhabitation of one's identity as opposed to socially expected "roles" and conducts, as well as the undecidability of already mythologized historical "facts," closely linked to works by Bernardo Bertolucci and Michelangelo Antonioni. The impossible and futile "reconstruction" of the crime (and yet malicious for its exculpatory purpose, nailing the villagers to an irreversibly "backward" condition that not even the state could redeem) carried out by the judiciary and enforced by the police is in truth an attempt to fish for the most convenient narrative, specifically one that excludes power from culpability and designates the perpetrators as less-than-human creatures, incapable of exerting moral judgment or controlling their vicious depravity. By intersecting the plot with events staged by the prosecutor and materials collected by a crew of journalists, Angelopoulos exposes the entire police procedural as nothing more than scheming, with all the structural problems—among them the abandonment of the countryside, controlled immigration, widespread destitution in a general atmosphere of backwardness and political oppression—unaddressed in the film. By layering the event with references to Aeschylus's *Oresteia*, the director also situates *The Reconstruction* as an inquiry into the meaning of ancient myth for contemporary Greek culture, probing its continued relevance as well as its pernicious power when its inscrutability is fatalistically used as a privileged instrument to understand and appropriate the things of life as quintessentially immutable. Of the two suspects, Eleni emerges as a woman dispossessed not only of basic properties but also of a sense of herself, as Vasidas Karalis writes: "The image of her existence never appears completed in her own conscience; it is centerless, mediated by mirrors, and obfuscated by un-thinking. Society conditioned her not to be herself, but to become her anti-self, unable to have any rational or cognitive understanding of who she is and what she is doing."[3] I took this detour because a few years earlier Romanian cinema also presented its reconstruction to world cinema, with the same prodigious assemblage of realism and modernism with the release of Lucian Pintilie's own *Reconstruction* (*Reconstituirea*, 1968), a film that not only provides a commentary on the perversity of subjectivation, but also examines the biopolitical techniques of the Romanian state: the regime that was not satisfied to simply clear itself of wrongdoing while destroying the periphery of its nation, as in Angelopoulos's film, but also needed to extract a surplus to produce a docile form of life. Whereas in Angelopoulos's film a murder is committed to conceal an extramarital affair, Pintilie's *Reconstruction* depicts the reenactment of a brawl for a dubious didactic short film on the consequences of alcoholism. Pintilie single-handedly brought Romanian cinema on par with its European neighbors by synthesizing the tendencies from previous phases of the country's cinematic history such as a brilliant Neorealism-inspired phase, specifically in a De Sica declination, lauded by Cesare Zavattini himself during his 1957 trip to Bucharest—and by turning them into ironic, self-reflexive devices. For instance, the entire premise of *Reconstruction* could be read as an "exploded" take on Zavattini's *film-lampo*, that is, a film based on an event that took place in real life and interpreted as nonprofessional actors by the same people who happened to be part of it.

The atmosphere of Pintilie's film is one of gregarious control: a controlled playfulness, a farce that turns into tragedy, a failed liberalization that can be withheld from the subject in the span of an instant, just like in those years the process of de-Stalinization had been controlled by the Romanian Communist Party and the Securitate. In another short-circuit between produced reality and representation, the militiaman tells the two youths who must restage the brawl to do everything exactly as it was and "make it reality."[4] In spite of the apparently mellow tone of the harmless reconstruction, what one witnesses is the relentless advancement into a state of aggression via constant extraction. It could be argued that the characters are too conveniently selected and bring a certain allegorical heaviness to the picture: The old, alcoholic teacher protests the futility of the whole enterprise but is not directly involved and almost remains an extra; the prosecutor and his blasé but threatening demeanor at some point has his face turned into a death-mask while sunbathing with a handkerchief on it; the militiaman plays the good cop part and is the real agitator behind the scenes; the operator, from the German minority, shouts at the youths to hit harder; the old woman herding the geese barely speaks, while the young, bikini-clad woman is at some point assaulted by one of the youths and seems to confirm the infamous patriarchal rule by virtue of which a "no" will eventually turn into a "yes" provided that one injects enough coercion into the approach. The two women represent the audience of the educational film and are mostly depicted as passive and indifferent, possibly, as Monica Filimon argued, "to pique viewers' interest in them" and to enhance "their entertainment value for the narrative."[5] Despite this figural clumsiness, *Reconstruction* demonstrates the inescapability of power transmissions from vertical output to horizontal propagations that encroach upon subjectivity and the ways such power manufactures a created life for its citizens to be enjoyed as spectacle, occasionally turning them into a mob when release is needed. It is worth noting that other commentators have compared that mob to the crowds that, in Timișoara, Bucharest, and other Romanian cities, finally revolted against the decay of the last years of the Ceaușescu regime in 1989;[6] here, however Pintilie's mob better connects to the puerile gregariousness founded on simple slogans and intellectually infantilized life which is a mainstay of Fascism and other authoritarian regimes. The film reveals how docility is instilled into the population to create an artificial, yet more "authentic," life repository. In terms of the symbolic kernel that anchors these strategies to reproduce and keep life under the control of state-sanctioned codes of conduct, *Reconstruction* does not directly address the emergence of a certain radical nationalism but hints at rural-patriarchal values as a breeding ground for the conformist cronyism of socialist ideology. Pintilie's boisterous filmmaking, his sharp criticism against state-mandated surveillance and its grotesque disciplinarian techniques, as well as the fragile forms of life they produce whose façade is always in danger of crumbling, also inform the current phase in Romanian cinema. In the absence of a manifesto or a commonly shared platform or program, the New Romanian Cinema (NRC) does not yield itself to well-defined and diverse interpretations, as is the case for previous waves, such as an intellectual or aesthetic dissatisfaction with "old-school" cinema, transformed conditions in production, technical training completed abroad, political antagonism against ruling parties and bureaucracies, and a stream of new themes and challenges that concurrently appear in other creative fields. However, while drawing the contours of an emerging cinematic wave and setting an artistic and cultural "perimeter" around it, the NRC presents us with an immediate, privileged access route, the double historical trauma of emerging from the Communist regime, especially under Nicolae Ceaușescu, and the country's almost immediate adhesion to EU institutions and entry into its advanced market economy.[7] After this double earthquake, in terms of its own political imaginary it appears that Romanian nationalism is capable of wearing different masks and resurfacing as the official discourse, as in terms of institutions, as Lucian Boia writes, "Romanians seem to be more attracted by symbols specific to national cohesion and authority than to those characteristic of democratic life."[8] Although Boia references polls from 1996 with the Army scoring at 92 percent and the Orthodox Church also very high at 89 percent, in the 2023 poll those two institutions have remained in the top two spots at 70 percent and 62 percent respectively, while dissatisfaction with the Parliament and political parties in general has declined even further, from 28 percent in 1996 to 17 percent in 2023.[9] The political fallacy of national unanimity resurfaces in several (often farcical) forms: an awkward concealment of the Communist past; a similarly puzzling, mythologizing rehabilitation of King Michael and Marshal Antonescu; a struggle to deal with the country's nationalism born—because of its precarious geographic position and the upper class's rejection of authentic, peasant Romanian culture—as "a national inferiority complex."[10] This devotion to constituted power—or, rather an adaptability that veers into resignation—is the cipher of the cooperative project that established a sort of historical outlook on the relationship between the population and the state, that of *Tales from the Golden Age* (*Amintiri din epoca de aur*, 2009), a comedic dramatization of urban tales from Communist times: The five directors draw different but converging arcs, aimed at exorcising the specter of a still relatively fresh dictatorship, in which the stories follow a bottom-up trajectory to flesh out the corpse that history has made available to them. Ceaușescu's specter emerges vividly only at the end of the film, after each tale has taken care of the litany of party officials, secretaries, administrators and anything and anybody else that was part of the mammoth Romanian state machine. More than the dictatorship, therefore, *Tales from the Golden Age* addresses the imposing bureaucratic apparatus set up by the regime, all reconstructed and "reconstituted" à la Pintilie by controllers, managers, inspectors, and various other figures of uncertain definition who try to oil a rusty celibatory machine that could be activated only in topsy-turvy ways, since there is a rule for everything, and therefore every rule can be broken by exchanging various favors and bribing the right people. Francesco Saverio Marzaduri has inscribed this stupefied docility into a larger philosophical question regarding the issue of who was—and is—the true "maker" of history in Romania: In line with Corneliu Porumboiu's affectionate look at the provincial town of *12:08 East of Bucharest* (*A fost sau n-a fost?*, 2006), whose citizens are still uncertain whether or not they really made a revolution in 1989, a good 16 years after the fact, those people "do not even imagine any rebellion, nor do they desire it."[11]

Doru Pop was the first to analyze the NRC in concert with other "rupturing" movements and stated that the Romanian case should be understood as an additional member of the European and International waves of the 1960s and '70s.[12] Pop identifies several similarities between preceding film movements now labeled as new waves, but even he must acknowledge that any homogenized categorization is unfeasible: "Even if they are not a film school, they represented a school of film for many of their fellow filmmakers."[13] Of all the film movements Pop analyzes in relationship to NRC, the most apposite is Italian Neorealism. What the two have in common is not the realism of the profilmic per se, but realism as a new way of looking, and therefore of experiencing, the world. This is particularly observable in *The Death of Mr. Lazarescu* (*Moartea domnului Lăzărescu*, 2005) and *Aurora* (2010), two films by Cristi Puiu. In both films, Puiu orchestrates a series of haptic recognitions through reframing and point-of-view changes, seeking to triangulate the spectator, the characters in their hapless act of looking, and the others caught under both gazes to precipitate the viewer into a transformative, experiential dimension in that resonates with a "cinematic rendering of a new epistemological attitude,"[14] an anxious desire to tell stories after the double disruption of the end of Communism and the entry into Western European political and economic practices. It is in situations like these that cinema serves as the aesthetic proxy for a new threshold of intolerability. The aesthetic congruity with Neorealism, taken as a measuring stick against which each new wave should be compared, was explicitly invoked and further investigated by Elena Roxana Popan, as if a category that is proving to be critically more and more tenuous could provide a template for other emerging movements in world cinema that wanted to experiment with film form and challenge the "conservative paradigm."[15] In an exchange with Cristian Mungiu, the director lamented that during Neorealism's times film could have a different social impact, something that today is amiss also for the lost experience of watching films together: Film as debate-generating medium is gone and the main preoccupation for a filmmaker should be to reach as many people as possible.[16] However, due to a national film industry that, as late as 2000, was not able to produce a single work,[17] it is better to use NRC as a general category for thinking about the output of Cristian Mungiu, Cristi Puiu, Corneliu Porumboiu, Radu Muntean, and other filmmakers as a collective cinematic ecology. Moreover, as Pop writes, even though works by Pintilie, Liviu Ciulei, and Mircea Daneliuc may have felt like "too rare and incoherent incidents," they were regarded as equal to other European cinemas, which elevated the country's reputation within the European culture industry and decisively necessitated the designation of a first, "proper" Romanian

New Wave that emerged in parallel with other modernist innovators of the 1960s.[18]

In an attempt to provide an analysis of Romania's national DNA as a productive matrix for its film output, scholars such as László Strausz and Dominique Nasta have interrogated the old folktale "Miorița" and the serene passivity of its male protagonist who, after being informed by one of his ewes that two of his fellow shepherds are scheming to murder him, simply accepts his fate and instructs the sheep to see to his after-death affairs and inform the family. While according to Strausz, the mioritic matrix generates a stance toward events based on a dithering temporization, a state of quasi-stupor elaborated on indecisiveness and second-guessing,[19] Nasta hails the ballad as a pure geography of the Romanian soul, its stoic resignation a decisive factor in orienting the national spirit because "fatality is indeed at the core of the Romanian psyche, precisely counterbalanced by a lot of black humour, spontaneity and ironic wit."[20] Lazar and Gorzo have dismissed such interpretations as an "obsolete, essentialist view of Romanian identity and culture"[21] and have provided a political-governmental précis of the New Romanian Cinema:

> Formal rigor; a mixture of dramatic immediacy and emphatic ordinariness; a Frederick Wiseman-like feel for the workings of institutions, and an emphasis—also documentary-like—on process and procedure, depicted in what approximated 'real' duration; a sensitivity to matters of ethics, both personal and institutional; a witty, caustic sense of how citizens interact with representatives of the state, and also of how neighbors or strangers interact with each other in contemporary Bucharest; and an awareness of social and professional hierarchies and their corresponding tensions, of the pervasive fault lines of class and caste.[22]

What transpires from the directors of the NRC is a constant state of atomization, thanks to which multiple structures of power—economic, political—may easily succeed at manipulating people toward their own ends; a resigned feeling of disenfranchisement; uncertainty regarding what values, narratives, and communities are available to be reappropriated; the presentiment of an impossible arrival derived from the failed suturing of historical wounds. People find themselves compounded into disciplinary devices, while the pressure of preying enforcements is put on display, as in Cristian Mungiu's *4 Months, 3 Weeks and 2 Days* (*4 luni, 3 săptămâni și 2 zile*, 2007), where the young female protagonists seamlessly move from one disciplinarian institution to another—dorms and hotels as extensions of the prison, families in which they are produced as obsequious, mediocre, and lacking—before putting their lives on the line to challenge the protocolization of their existence. Or, rather, it is the film's protagonist, Otilia, whom we follow across a city in which one always feels under surveillance and who shows us a real, unconventional energy as she rams through every obstacle. She does not publicly or openly confront the state as an institution, but her head-on resolve in each encounter accrues a political intensity by which she turns into a force who writes with her own body across space as an overarching institution, engaging "both the horizontal plane of society and the vertical line of generations" (figure 5.1).[23] Mungiu mentioned that when it comes to depict the "breeding ground" of power, his poetics is to "confront the materiality of things and human relations without technical distraction, montage, artifice"; he repeatedly uses the Rossellinian word "rhythm," meaning that he tries to capture the soul of a location by letting the location and the set he build within and around to dictate camera placement and angles.[24]

The long take of the dinner scene is the creation of a space where characters are entrapped. We are challenged by the frontal

Figure 5.1. Family and state proxies at the dinner table. *Source:* Cristian Mungiu, dir., *4 Months, 3 Weeks and 2 Days* (2007; The Criterion Collection, 2019), Blu-Ray Disc, 1080p HD.

perspective of Orthodox icons, which reject the natural or central perspective that issues from the standpoint of the beholder and chooses what Pavel Florensky called the reverse perspective, which forces the beholder to surrender his own standpoint and sense of distance.[25] In a personal conversation with the author, Mungiu stated that his is a cinema that tries to break a distance and achieve a certain degree of objectiveness and auratic thingness to show the breeding ground of power relations.[26] Stylistically, Mungiu's long take is a device of entrapment. *4 Months, 3 Weeks and 2 Days* is a film about the ineffable decentralization of control made immanent in all social relations. Labor time and nonlabor time, social life or individual life: there is no respite, no freedom or break from external patterns of intimidation once the choice of incorporating them has been made. Totalitarianism is possible only after the social contexts of privacy have been atomized: When there are no cultural alternatives offered to individuals by economic endeavors, religion, or kinship then the roots of the will to resist despotism are concurrently eradicated. With the following *Beyond the Hills* (*După dealuri*, 2012) Mungiu composes a potent allegory of Romania as an orphan country: When one of the two protagonists dies at the end of the film the mood is that of despair but also resignation, for her exuberant physicality just proved too much for institutions that are obsolete and unprepared. The hospitals—among them the one in which Alina arrives already dead—are shown as diagnoses of the Romanian present: for Puiu, places in which one can unleash economic frustration and reaffirm power hierarchies; for Mungiu, triages run by bean-counting medical personnel where men and women have finally completed the transformation from human beings to patients to numbers, Alina's life crunched and then compounded into a statistical figure (figure 5.2).

Language itself is an instituted power and can be deployed to straitjacket an individual with a state-sanctioned role, as in Porumboiu's *Police, Adjective* (*Polițist, adjectiv*, 2009). Anna Batori, who holds panopticism as the defining characteristic of the NRC, considered *Police, Adjective* the perfect example of what she calls "vertical enclosure," or the mélange of "the omnipresent camera technique and the socialist representation of space," a vertical vector that initiates a top-down process of subjectivation.[27] Porumboiu shows the sardonic dissimulation of language, a constraining logic in which biopower and the power of euphemism march in sync, examples of which Perniola

Figure 5.2. Life as statistics in post-Communist Romania. *Source:* Cristian Mungiu, dir., *Beyond the Hills* (2012; The Criterion Collection, 2018), Blu-Ray Disc, 1080p HD.

had already found in *Redacted*. *Police, Adjective* is a game of shadowing: The camera tails a policeman who in turn tails a student who occasionally uses recreational drugs. The film depicts "characters being trapped by language structures"[28] and concurrently installs a panoptic apparatus pursuing bodies in drab interiors and gray exteriors: The atmosphere is depressing, the details circumscribe a feeling of inescapability whereby each individual has a predetermined mold to fill, that the surrounding landscape—human and not—will "help" codify once and for all.

Thus, the NRC is a cinema of extended historicity, of the rhetoric of clean slates and new beginnings and the inadequacy of national mythology, and a biopolitical cinema of institutions—courts, hospitals, schools, police, but also family, and religion, the Orthodox Church, as well as film itself—deployed as control devices whose commands violate bodies, phagocytize life, and extend the nation's (a)historical depravities. Compromise, corruption, and decay are so pervasive that reality is ruptured by their uncanny, ebullient intrusions—mysterious aggressions, random acts of vandalism outside the frame, the mediated suffocation of Mungiu's *Graduation* (*Bacalaureat*, 2016). The prodigious journey of perdition of the "precariat"[29] in Puiu's *Stuff and Dough* (*Marfa și banii*, 2001) is a masterful contribution to the allegorical tradition of many Eastern European cinematographies. Films such as *Life Is Beautiful* (*Život je lep*, Boro Drašković, Yugoslavia, 1985) and

Calamity (*Kalamita*, Věra Chytilová, Czechoslovakia, 1982) bleakly—or, in Chytilová's case, more playfully—portray societies whose functionality is predicated on vertical (state toward people) as well as horizontal, reciprocal surveillance (people observing and being observed), with the time image-digressions such as *When I Am Dead and Gone* (*Kad budem mrtav i beo*, Živojin Pavlović, Yugoslavia, 1967) and *Identification Marks: None* (*Rysopis*, Jerzy Skolimowski, Poland, 1965), and involve trains that cannot be operated, or that go nowhere, or take the protagonists back to square one, or simply stop and never restart, as if the focus on aborted projects and failed expectations were the only aesthetically viable solution. The very structure of the allegory—that of stagnating condensation—was the privileged form to mirror the stasis encountered in the arts, in institutions, in society, mirroring that suspension of duration that Katherine Verdery has called the "etatization" of time, a biopolitical intervention on the citizenry that "flattened time out in an experience of endless waiting."[30] In Jude's *The Happiest Girl in the World*, the young characters' dull banter about cars often mentions the Dacia, once a national embarrassment turned industrial pride: "I did 170 km/h on a Dacia," boasts the young man at the wheel, as if escaping but at the same time nostalgic for the mass blue-collar life now lost in Romania except for jobs offered by foreign car manufacturers.[31]

Referencing Neorealism may feel like a reductionist move insofar as its theoretical legacy was more radical than the actual works it produced: to name just a few of its directions, among Luchino Visconti's anthropological otherness, Vittorio De Sica's phenomenological explorations, Roberto Rossellini's stratified temporalities, Antonio Pietrangeli's montage of affects, and Vittorio De Seta's early deployment of *cinéma vérité* techniques, it prefigured many a new wave, and it should be mentioned in the perspective of a debate on collective identity.[32] What was shared by Neorealist directors was the dismissal of Fascism's technologized mythology and the attempt to imagine filmmaking as a practice that would not reduce the other to state-sanctioned behavior and conducts. It can thus be argued that films of the NRC were attempts to honestly portray the country as it was, exposing past crimes and hypocrisies and thereby imagining a reborn nation to which all the citizenship should aspire—especially the early films from the original "core." Radu Jude took the early stage of New Romanian filmmaking to a different, evolving direction by including/

superimposing to the reality on the ground the imaginary specter of the nation with all its fragments and figments coming from a past that cannot go away, even in a globalized present. With their emphasis on racist dehumanization and exclusion, Jude's films ask a question that rings true also with *Reconstruction*: What does it mean to be human and to consider another individual as human? After all, Pintilie's startling capture of a passing train full of pioneers singing a song about squirrels and rabbits, together with the geese that are finally corralled at the end, almost feels like an inside joke about another type of reproduction, while Vuică, one of the two youths, jokes that the difference between a man and a monkey is that the monkey does not need an ID card. Vuică, the most disenchanted and resigned of the two, he who cannot follow orders and turns every situation into a playful desecration, is the "sacrificed": Pintilie's portrait of the disciplinarian rationalities resonates with Fabbri's definition of state power in many Fascist films, solving the conflict between creative and created life "as a life-shaping authority, a saving power able to reconcile factory productivity, social reproductivity, and individual happiness."[33] Radu Jude operates a subtle reconfiguration of the historical film: He does not deconstruct episodes of national "greatness" but rather looks critically at the degenerating evolution of Romanian nationalism and intervenes to "explode" its often grotesque symbology to paroxysmic extremes. During an interview regarding the film, Jude stated that he was not interested in recreating a state of illusion and immersion into a precisely recreated nineteenth century, yet he successfully aimed to make the film historically authoritative by way of an archaeological method of discursive investigation.[34] Further evidence of Jude's biopolitical sensibility is evident in *Aferim!* (2015), a film about the condition of slavery of the Roma people in early nineteenth-century Romania. The film follows local constable Constandin (Teodor Corban) and his son Ioniță (Mihai Comanoiu) as they pursue Cartin (Toma Cuzin), an enslaved Roma man who has run away from a local boyar's estate. We follow their journey across through the countryside, rendered in observational, suave panning shots that first allow people in the frame and then accompany them as they depart. The tirades we hear on the Roma throughout the film, steeped in bigotry, superstition, or basic stupidity resonate with contemporary European governmentality, according to which the "gypsy" is the quintessential biopolitical other, a non-citizen characterized by traits all carrying negative moralized values, and the first victims of the logic of encampment and containment, a living testimony of "how powerfully tight the connections are between nineteenth-century racial doctrines and contemporary segregation."[35] One of Jude's central artistic endeavors is to find ways to repoliticize Romania's cultural memory: The filmmaker does not hide the constructedness of his historical images and actually exposes the cannibalization that cultural practices, national mythologies and various ideologies have carried out at the epistemological level—it is almost as if he is proposing a pedagogy of visual literacy applied to the construction of history, with direct references to contemporary inurement. Jude is interested not simply in recreating an event that a certain episteme made possible, but also in measuring the distance with current epistemic lines, hence the jump cuts with old films, other media and various types of footage, fellow directors, characters from popular culture and real public figures, stimulating a rehistoricization of the past and a critical stance toward the present. In his works, the shadowing of characters who travel by car, by horse, or on foot indexes biopolitical journeys into social totalities and racial imaginaries that Jude tries to split open by way of accumulation, annotation, and cultural and literary asides until a sort of explosive saturation is reached. Apropos the present condition of the Romani people, their communities often incur what Ayten Gündoğdu described as a radical form of desubjectivation as humanity is extracted from individuals to produce a life that is not designated as human, whereby "the unmaking of legal personhood often goes hand in hand with the destruction of political and human standing."[36] The film invokes parallels not only between past and present marginalizations but, by foregrounding an active spectatorship and subverting its expectations, Jude's method in *Aferim!* may be applied to current and future historical amnesias. His approach is not dissimilar to that of the Greek historian Thucydides's organic appropriateness, that is, preserving credibility and verisimilitude by intercalating the narrated events with made-up but plausible dialogues, speeches, proclamations, and so on. Jude's account aims for historical legitimacy by involving scholar Constanța Vintilă-Ghițulescu, whose research has touched topics such as the sociological transformation of the visibilities of bodies and the politics of the public spectacle of punishment. The garrulity that infests the film illustrates the problematics of the Foucauldian relationship between subject and power, the articulation of verbal discursive practices based on accepted "knowledges" through which individuals compel themselves to rationalize, justify, literally talk themselves into subjectifying restrictions while reestablishing the "truth" at every utterance (and at every act). As Mihai Dan-Cirjan writes, "Throughout the movie almost every character is eager to explain, clarify, and in the end legitimate the social tragedies surrounding them: slavery, patriarchal violence, xenophobia, antisemitism, crude racism, or dizzying social inequalities."[37] Gorzo and Lazar were quick to point out similarities with films by Anthony Mann and Hal Ashby: *Aferim!* also resonates with Sydney Pollack's western *The Scalphunters* (1968), which presents a similar situation of an uneducated white man on a horse carrying around a witty, better-traveled and very intelligent enslaved man, not to be returned to his owners, but to be used as a pawn for certain furs that were stolen from him. The Burt Lancaster vehicle treads the dangerous territory of the comedy–western hybrid; however, despite the fealty it pays to Hollywood conventions (its hero is eventually redeemed), every exchange throughout the film is motivated by an unassailable logic of material transactionality. Similarly to *Aferim!*, which takes place in 1835, when "some boyars set about the transformation of their slaves into profitable capital,"[38] *The Scalphunters* presents people as well as objects "as commodities which continue to be traded and stolen, exploited for their commercial and sexual value."[39] This automatic and automated reproduction of social value is also observed by Judit Pieldner, who writes that in *Aferim!* "almost every member of the nation (with the exception of those in the lowest position in the hierarchy, the Gypsy slave and the child) reproduces the experienced social relations of inequality at the first available opportunity."[40] What the Roma people endured as enslaved people from their arrival to the principality of Wallachia—the first evidence of their presence in Romania is found in the fourteenth century—until the promulgation of the "Law for the Emancipation of All Gypsies in Wallachia" in 1856 (1855 for Moldova) can hardly be put into words. Gifted to monasteries, offered as dowries, exchanged for cattle, tortured in the most gruesome ways, the Roma were the test subjects for the most despicable dehumanizing practices one can think of. As David Crowe bluntly writes, "In the long course of the Gypsy experience in Eastern Europe, none has been worse than that in Romania."[41] One of the key moments of the film involves an encounter with a priest (Alexandru Bindea) who delivers these lines:

> Each nation has its purpose. The Jews, to cheat, the Turks,
> to do harm, us Romanians to love and suffer like Christ.
> And each has their habits. Hebrews reads a lot, Greeks
> talks a lot, Turks has many wives, Arabs has many teeth,
> Germans smokes a lot, Hungarians eats a lot, Russians
> drinks a lot, English thinks a lot, French likes fashion a lot,
> Armenians are lazy, Circassians wears much lace, Italians
> lies a lot, Serbians cheat a lot, Gypsies get beaten! Gypsies
> must be slaves.[42]

The priest is a casually crusty man of the Church busy at reaffirming the current state of things as immutable—one may say God-created—with all the benefits and privileges of the Orthodox Church included. The use of long and wide shots allows for more landscape to enter the scenes and create a disquieting contrast between the placid rustling of leaves and the historical tragedies—justified, and surrealistically "rationalized"—that unfold in front of our very eyes. The priest's encyclopedic knowledge antagonistically racializes all the peoples that at one time or another have crossed into Romania; the result is hilarious and chilling, immobilizing the other in a dismissive if not entirely dehumanizing state of inferiority and by contrast almost elevating the Romanian people to the status of chosen one. His taxonomic thinking exposes the Church as an immunitarian institution whose aim is not to make the Gospel popular, help your neighbor, or study the Holy Writs, but to produce surrealistically biased knowledge just to defend its properties and inoculate its faithful. Jude cast Victor Rebengiuc, the most distinguished actor in Romanian film and theater history, as the small landowner who hides the enslaved Roma. Rebengiuc starred in the film I mentioned earlier that brought Romanian cinema to international attention, *Forest of the Hanged*, as Apostol Bologa, the World War I lieutenant who experiences a Christian rebirth and refuses to fight and condemn his fellow Romanians and is hanged as the result—in much the same way as the Czech officer that he had helped condemn. Now playing as a past iteration of his old character, Rebengiuc's Stan Paraschiv is one through whom viewers can experience the abysmal distance between the message of the Gospel and the clerics who interpret and spread it for and to the people, in the Romanian case complicit in the tragedies suffered by Roma and other minorities. It is not an exaggeration to consider Rebengiuc the national consciousness of Romanian cinema, and the weaponization of his relevance in Romanian history at large is a stark reminder that the Orthodox Church has so far "failed to provide any sort of apology that would help bring about genuine healing and reconciliation,"[43] especially after enjoying centuries of labor from enslaved Roma. Jude inserts the son of the constable as an audience stand-in for literal educational purposes and titillates Romania's bizarre nationalism by exalting its "achievements" as if they belong to an upside-down world. At the end of Jude's film, the boyar eviscerates the slave as a punishment for creating his own form of sexual value. Aside from the special familiarity that Pintilie and Puiu, and later Puiu and Jude, enjoyed thanks to mentorship and collaboration, it is thinkable to establish a line among these filmmakers that deals specifically with the role of violence in the organization of society—as an unintended, but ominously expected, consequence of state policies during the "nationalization" of time (*Reconstruction*), as numbing and banal as the other aspects of daily life (*Aurora*), or playfully disguised as cultural trait to reveal a concentration camp mentality (*Bad Luck Banging or Loony Porn, Babardeală cu bucluc sau porno balamuc*, 2021).

We have seen as the New Romanian Cinema is characterized by reflexive cues destabilizing the epistemological position of the viewer in the interpretation of the historical past and the moral evaluation of current Romanian society. While rejecting the "new wave" label, Radu Jude is the filmmaker who has turned the *noul val* into a shockwave. Jude's biopolitical filmmaking deals with a people that seems hopelessly conditioned, whose protocols of marginalization and dehumanization of minorities are impossible to break through. If Mungiu's formal gestuality aims at creating a continuous oscillation between diegetic characters and audience for a productive interpretation of historical and social landscapes, Jude reconfigures techniques of *cinéma vérité* by injecting almost intolerable durational vectors into the profilmic. Often metatextual, his films deploy reflexivity as a critical weapon for absorption and distanciation; his trenchant modernism uncompromisingly confronts historical responsibility, institutional ignorance, societal malaise. For instance, in *Bad Luck Banging* the first part of the film is a redesigned version of the Zavattinian device of tailing with a Dadaist shake-up. The protagonist moves in a disfigured city with no principle of cohesion, where brands, ruins, fictional showbiz characters of various origins, media personalities, and common and clichéd denizens compose a purulent imaginary through which our *flâneuse* must push through before the showdown with her equally monstrous inquisitors. Through Jude's lenses Bucharest and Romania by extension turn into a grotesque non-space where schizophrenic accumulation and crass exhibition of narcissistic incivility mask an ethical wasteland and, even more tragically, a resolute anti-historical deliberation: Let's not revisit critically any of our pasts and let's wallow in a state of paternalistic stupor. Jude takes the viewer into Jamesonian territory: The fraudulent and parasitical DNA of the postmodern is decompounded through the postmodern itself, parsing through the pastiche with its own instruments, while a moment of truth is achieved by exposing the type of mediation affecting that experience. The educator, the disciplinarian use of historical heritage, the Jew: The similarities between *Bad Luck Banging* and *The Student* are remarkable, exemplifying Jude's greatness as a filmmaker who can evoke the transformation of the human into residual life without explicitly referencing the camp. The third finale, when Emi turns into a Wonder Woman/Predator/Alien hybrid, brandishes a huge dildo, and goes trawl fishing among her colleagues while forcing them to fellate the sex toy, feels like the tremor needed to destroy repackaged history sold as a brand, cultural misery, camp-thinking attitudes—in a word, an antidote against a biopolitical race to the bottom, which strives to produce its single and unified Romanian people adopting an ur-Fascist toolkit.

In *Bad Luck Banging*, Jude shows that once that logic is institutionalized hospitals can easily turn into morgues, schools into courthouses of inquisition, churches into Fascist indoctrination camps, and reenactments of the mass murder of Romanian Jews by Marshal Ion Antonescu into celebration of the national spirit, as in *"I Do Not Care If We Go Down in History as Barbarians"* (*"Îmi este indiferent dacă în istorie vom intra ca barbari,"* 2018). *Barbarians* has been examined as a contemporary iteration of modernist politics[44] and as a post-postmodern metacommentary on the pitfalls of history understood as pedagogical effort.[45] In effect, the sudden move at the beginning of the film from the National Military Museum to the Buftea studios in Bucharest, and the passing reference to *Oglinda* (1993) and Sergiu Nicolaescu's penchant for reactionary and jingoistic filmmaking, frames it as a multi-layered pastiche where "official" history, its sedimented memory, and its propagation as spectacle converge and collapse into an inextricable clew: Historical representation and its legacy understanding are like threads of yarn with multiple beginnings and even more, frayed, ends. Jude's criticism is not only directed against the negationist, celebratory nature of Nicolaescu's picture but also against the very idea of a truthful and transparent historical film (see *Oglinda*'s other title, *Începutul adevărului*, or "The beginning of truth") and the emphasis on the "reconstruction" of past events via authentic firearms, uniforms, et cetera. Mariana and her crew in fact are not sure about the real provenance of the military gear (from actual on-field action? from *Oglinda*?), and adding to the general atmosphere of confusion, reticence, and removal is the fact, as Ludmila Martanovschi and Dana Mihăilescu have noted, that the museum is located on a Bucharest street named after Mircea Vulcănescu, an undersecretary of the Antonescu government and staunch supporter of antisemitic views.[46] Instead, Jude allegorizes the agony that creating a shareable event for collective memory entails, a path that will become almost inaccessible, so much that Mariana will have to put almost everything on the line, and fight against elected officials, her cast of reenactors, even the man she may call family in a not-so-distant future—and yet the end result may be interpreted as a confirmation of the very evil she wanted to expose. Trivialization, reverse-victimhood complex, cherry picking, racial conservatism—Jude shows the ways through which a nation chooses to evade responsibility; by contrast, in his documentaries on the role of Romania and its people in the Holocaust, *The Dead Nation* (*Țara moartă*, 2017) and *The Exit of the Trains* (*Ieșirea trenurilor din gară*, 2020), he chose a layered montage comprising all the pictures, all the voices, all the witnesses, all the collected materials about the victims, precisely because for each painstakingly recovered testimony there is a corresponding perpetrator that deserves equal attention. Around halfway through, Mariana reads an excerpt—about the "fabrication of corpses" by "conveyor belt"—from Agamben's *Remnants of Auschwitz*.[47] The line that runs across *Aferim!*, *Barbarians*, and *Bad Luck Banging* is that of an immunitary construction of "deservedly" abjected and "unnatural" forms of life—ethnic, immoral, dangerous others—through which Romanians can conveniently consign to oblivion their historical shortcomings and responsibilities. The value of security—one of the determining purposes, from Hobbes onwards, for the legitimation of sovereignty—has been subjected to an increasing absolutization, freed from a rational, measurable, and demonstrable analysis of actual dangers. It has turned into an a priori, a mental structure through which to organize ways of thinking and living. The fruit of this obsession for security is the production of the enemy and its criminalization. Jude shares with Agamben the idea that biopower institutes a continuity between a totalitarian and a democratic state, that certain interruptions in the circuit of thinking are spontaneous outgrowth of Romanian "civil" society (figure 5.3). By eliminating the Jew—produced by Romania's people in uniform as a formless entity, the very negation of the human—Jude shows how the pitiful bunch of judges representing Romania's institutions try to acquire a form of their own, regenerating a view of Romanian nationalism through suppression and the threat of extermination. The oxymoronic creative destruction that is advocated here is the objective that animates the camp after the camp—conceived and operated by Nazi criminals in the past and now eternalized by followers of Antonescu and their always resurfacing coalitions of the willing.

Jude has no qualms at implicating his own people in this painful but necessary process of rebuilding and rehistoricizing of social memory, pointing to "Romania's commitment to openly and publicly acknowledging itself as a perpetrator in World War II not only at an institutional level but also at a more grassroots, popular culture level."[48]

The Happiest Girl in the World follows one day in the life of Delia, a girl who has won a Dacia. Defying her parents, who wish to sell the

Figure 5.3. The racialization of education. *Source:* Radu Jude, dir., *Bad Luck Banging or Loony Porn* (2021; Magnolia Home Entertainment, 2022), Blu-ray Disc, 1080p HD.

car and use the money from the sale to finance other family projects, Delia decides to keep the vehicle. As part of the prize package, she is also required to shoot a promotional spot in which she is repeatedly asked to drink the soda produced by the company that raffled off the car and utter a few promotional lines. The prodigiously layered picture has been hailed, among other things, as a vehicle to empower women by resisting to "authority, manifested in the form of male authoritarianism";[49] a "contrapuntal modernist . . . version . . . of the intermedial carnivalesque . . . bringing to the fore the post-Communist crisis of patriarchal authority and the disintegration of traditional family";[50] an instance of the deconstruction of male authority, in which family leadership is shown as "the subject of a bargaining process";[51] a showdown against an "ominously complex father figure";[52] "a contemporary poke at the country's attraction to celebrity and filmmaking";[53] and "another ordeal story"[54] in the vein of similar pictures made by Puiu and Mungiu. All these interpretations seem appropriate—especially that of Lazar and Gorzo, who adroitly point to "the unpleasant discipline of bodies and movements"—and yet, they possibly need an integration that deals more directly with the economic aspect of the film, the relationship between a subject and material goods: *The Happiest Girl in the World* could also be viewed as an ironic essay film on the nature of contemporary market economy, the prism through which every decision on one's existence must be made, the locus of survival, the scope of the decisive relation that one entertains with a piece of property.[55] It is a sardonic, less bloody, but equally violent counterpart of films such as Paul Thomas Anderson's *There Will Be Blood* (2007), where the extractive logic is the destructive principle that governs and organizes every aspect of one's life. By mocking regional mannerisms and cultural idiosyncrasies and making them look hilariously backward, Jude masterfully creates a sense of vertigo for a viewer who questions the position of countries braving a global economy. Jude shows how the coming-of-age works in a market economy: On paper Delia is a winner, but she must acknowledge a number of exchanges, giving up more—family, friendship, education—that she bargained for. The time of production and consumption—and of filmmaking—is not commensurate with the ease of chronological time: It hurries and hastens Delia until she accepts that being part of the economy and the value chain means accepting their trade-offs and being already in debt. While for her, she desperately insists, the car is coextensive with the experiences and friendships of her formative years, for the world around her it is just a value (the parents) or a tool conducive to more value (the soda company and the production crew they hired for the shoot). The car can be turned into money, but—following Guy Debord—the spectacle of the commercial is just one and the same currency: a forced fiction where "qualitative human becoming in time has become subordinated to the quantitative accumulation of capital."[56] For Debord, when capital dictates one's exposure to time we are in a tyrannic condition of non-life, a condition in which a community is not the master of its own experiences. With its promise of abstract social time (Delia) or accumulation of money (her parents), the car—of which the production of the commercial is an allegorical projection—imposes its own inanimate will on the community around it, a type of circulation "marked by a form of temporal domination: a mode of biopolitical control over lived time" (figure 5.4).[57] In fact, Jude turns the tragicomedy of the continuous shot into a microcosm of an array of neoliberal extractive practices: just as ex-socialist workforces integrated by corporate businesses in Romania, as Liviu Chelchea writes, "reskilled themselves through various training programs . . . faced individualization techniques orchestrated by the management, and subjected themselves to subtle disciplining

Figure 5.4. The society of optimization, Romanian-style. *Source:* Radu Jude, dir., *The Happiest Girl in the World* (2009; Thunderbird Releasing, 2010), DVD, 576p.

actions" leading to a category of painfully uncertain deferment that the scholar calls "virtual time," or "the intensive elaboration and subsequent relocation of various personal plans to an indefinite future," Delia's bona fide transformation into an entrepreneur of the self is a figural omen for a country that is being asked to do just the same.[58]

With *Do Not Expect Too Much from the End of the World* (*Nu aștepta prea mult de la sfârșitul lumii*, 2023), Jude appears to join other filmmakers of the (sur)real in an impasse of sorts. Like in *Anora*, a trip through hell disguised as comedy, Jude's camera follows Angela around Bucharest as it followed Emi in the anti-city symphony *Bad Luck Banging*. (Angela might also be regarded as an adult version of Delia, one who "made it" and now takes advantage of the things she previously learned while on set.) Throughout the film, a sleep-deprived and precariously employed Angela drives between the city and its periphery, stopping to interview injured workers for a workplace safety film produced by their employer, a multinational corporation based in Austria; it becomes clear that each of the workers Angela interviews need the paycheck they will receive if their audition is successful. Unlike Delia, Angela is not the protagonist of the grueling series of takes that occupy the last thirty-five minutes of the film, but the device is the same in terms of grooming and extracting. Her sleep deprivation may very well amount to torture, while her toxic, misogynistic alter ego Bobiță—a vitalist iteration of the Andrew Tate life-form, a dimwit double who parrots his misogynistic rants and concurrently reveals himself as a fitting allegory for the country—is the natural evolution of a corporate experience where one can only be in control or on the receiving end of the exploitative game. The juxtaposition with Lucian Bratu's *Angela Goes On* (*Angela merge mai departe*, 1982) reads the country's evolutions from a feminist standpoint and highlights the "trade-offs" in freedom of expression, latent fantasies of domination over the female body, and power dynamics related to exploitation. No surprises from the cold-blooded executives, or from Dorina Lazar's Orbán-worshipping husband; at the end of the film, the impatience of accumulation to reinforce certain political points such as the atomization of Romanian society and the absence of subtlety are remembered more than the bravura performance of Ilinca Manolache. Jude seems to imply that "kinetic" hypercapitalism has already blurred all the distances between past and present, real and fake, organic and inorganic, where everything can or rather *must* go viral and fractal—but Romania as a country already had a good record for it. In fact, it is not that the simulacral ways of global capitalism destroyed the country's soul—its dubious historical record, in which you can casually call Fascism "anti-Fascism" and antisemitism "friendship among peoples," made it a perfect host for such practices. Therefore, *Do Not Expect Too Much from the End of the World* appears to be a work of marginal gains, implying that, for a confused Romanian people, "political" or clique-dominated capitalism—a "state of affairs in which the prevalent notion is that all individuals are out for themselves, and everything—from public offices to public assets—is for sale"—is neither a curse nor a blessing, but a natural destination.[59]

Almost 25 years after *Stuff and Dough*, the NRC has not lost its propulsive boost but is still a festival phenomenon. Some of its nominal initiators are going through a phase of creative impasse, to the point that even the reception in the awards circuit is cooling. For example, despite its bravura sequences and the honest depictions of biopolitical prejudices against immigration to Europe, *R.M.N.* (2022) by Cristian Mungiu was received with only circumstantial interest during its screening in Cannes, its symbolic weight just too much to be supported by the film's narrative arc. In Romania, only Bucharest, Timișoara, and Cluj have something resembling an arthouse circuit. In a country of about 20 million residents, films by pluri-awarded directors such as Puiu, Mungiu, and others rarely break 20,000 views in theaters; the only films that can reach a vast number of households are those produced and subsequently broadcast by HBO. If the outlook may not seem too bright, there is indeed at least one story that bodes well for the future of Romania's film and quality television: the ongoing sitcom *Las Fierbinți*, still running after twenty-four seasons on national channel PROTV in a sea of Indian, Turkish, and Latin American soap operas—among its directors, Constantin Popescu of *Tales from the Golden Age*. With its humorously self-orientalizing domestic ethnography and its deconstruction of rural stereotypes *Las Fierbinți* has worked as a training ground for technicians, writers, production executives, and filmmaking professionals, and one can only wish that its interplay of farce and political observations will inspire future generations of Romanian directors.

Conclusion

New Directions in World Cinema— The Animist Turn

Every attempt to rethink the political space of the West must begin with the clear awareness that we no longer know anything of the classical distinction between *zoē* and *bios*, between private life and political existence, between man as a simple living being at home in the house and man's political existence in the city.

—Giorgio Agamben, *Homo Sacer*

One of these *sadhus* [holy men] must be willing to feed his own body to starving tigers. So far, no such situation has occurred. However, should it occur, I think that is what should happen. That is how I, too, should behave.

—*Sadhu* interviewed in *Notes for a Film on India* (*Appunti per un film sull'India*, Pier Paolo Pasolini, 1969)

⌒

"WHAT'S A BAD MIRACLE? They got a word for that?" asks OJ Haywood (Daniel Kaluuya), a protagonist of Jordan Peele's 2022 film *Nope*, a hybrid of Western, science fiction, and horror genres. With *Nope*, Peele continues his project of social horror, further developing a critique of spectacle, visual witnessing, and surveillance that began with the director's debut film *Get Out* (2017).[1]

195

Jordan Peele's 2022 film *Nope* illustrates well the tension and difference between cinema as *dispositif* and cinema as a "lived assemblage," a network of interacting animacies: the agency and action of animals, people, and extraterrestrial forms of life that demand to be, but are not yet, recognized. *Nope*'s monster, Jean Jacket, shifts between the terrifying monster of Debordian spectacle and a form of life that, like the film's human protagonists and its animals, seeks to survive. Jean Jacket's oscillation between an allegory of the spectacle and creaturely life reflects the impurity of cinema, which has the potential to be either a technology of control or a medium capable of crediting everything with a life and a history of its own.

Nope begins with an epigraph, a quote from the Bible: "And I will cast abominable filth upon thee, and make thee vile, and will set thee as a spectacle."[2] The spectacle thus becomes a Biblical curse—and what else is a curse but "a bad miracle"? This becomes the film's main inquiry, which Peele explores with postmodern nuance and self-reflexivity, well aware that his $68 million production participates in the industry of spectacle at the same time as it resists and critiques it. Its acknowledgment, via quotation, of the "abominable filth" of the spectacle can, therefore, be related to Badiou's relation of cinema as an "impure" art. Peele takes care to show the viewer the spectacle's modes of production from the very first scene, which features the set of *Gordy's Home*, a metafictional television show that parodies the range of American family sitcoms over the last forty years. The scene is filmed not from the point of view of the live studio audience, which is not shown, but from the perspective of Jupe, a Korean American child actor who plays the adopted son of a rocket scientist and an astronaut.[3] He watches as Gordy, the titular chimpanzee, murders almost all of his fellow cast members. The scene ends with Jupe hiding under a table as Gordy approaches him. The film then cuts to a scene that features Black animal wranglers OJ and his father, Otis Sr. (Keith David), training their animals for their latest role: A group of horses tread easily in circles, each attached to the spoke of a horse walker. Nearby, Otis Sr. teaches another horse to play dead, a subtle act of foreshadowing. The first indication of an alien life form (later named Jean Jacket, after one of the Haywood's horses) is money: In the same scene, a nickel apparently falls out of the sky, piercing the eye of Otis S. and killing him. After his death, X-rays reveal the shadowy image of the coin lodged in his skull. Money, Debord writes, "presents itself as an emissary armed with full powers who speaks in the name of an unknown force."[4] The film flashes forward six months to a scene that opens onto another film set, this time the set of a commercial. OJ stands in front of a green screen with Lucky, a horse with strips of gaffer tape affixed to his body. The scene establishes and emphasizes OJ's skill and attunement with animals, a connection that in some ways takes precedence over his uneasy human relationships. OJ's discomfort with people can be observed in his stilted, quiet interactions with the crew. He stays close to the horse, mirroring its shy movements. His sister, Emerald ("Em," played by Keke Palmer) arrives late, rushing in front of the green screen to deliver a safety briefing. She speaks directly to two cameras: Peele's camera, of course, and that of the advertisement's white director, Holst, who sits behind his camera while a mostly white production crew stands in the background. Em addresses the crew:

> Now I know you guys know Eadweard Muybridge, the grandfather of motion pictures who took the pictures that created that clip, but does anybody know the name of the Black jockey that rode the horse? The very first stuntman, animal wrangler and movie star all rolled into one and there is literally no record of him. That man was a Bahamian jockey that went by the name of Alistair E. Haywood, and he is my great-great [great] grandfather. That's why back at the Haywood Ranch, as the only Black-owned horse trainers in Hollywood, we like to say, "Since the moment pictures could move, we had skin in the game."[5]

In truth, the real-life jockey in Muybridge's photos still remains anonymous, for while the photographer included the name of the horse involved in the pictures, he failed to designate its rider.[6] By framing the story with the famous image of the jockey, by giving the jockey a name, and by presenting both image and jockey in terms of inheritance and ancestry, Peele explicitly asserts the Black presence in, and claim on, the history of cinema—in addition to reclaiming and reappropriating white images of the Black body. The body of the jockey, Peele seems to be saying, animates cinema's origins, while his anonymity haunts its present, demanding the return of his proper name. With *Nope*, Peele effectuates the return of the repressed image through his critique of the Debordian spectacle that not only saturates everyday life, but thoroughly mediates it.[7] Indeed, there is a double mediation at play: the general spectacle that mediates everyday life and, specifically, the violence that further mediates life, particularly Black life. This mediating violence is itself mediated by the spectacle, and often even coincides with it. It would not be possible, for instance, to list all of the police violence and killings that have either been captured by cellphones or indeed police body cameras (when they are turned on). The panopticon evidently fails to elicit self-discipline from biopower, of which the police are a primary agent.[8] Although this is not explicitly referenced in the film, its approach to visual recording and spectatorship is highly ambivalent as well as self-reflexive.

As one of *Nope*'s metatextual frames, Muybridge's images of the Black man riding a horse establish a link between biopolitics and spectacle. Everyone in the film is involved in cinema in some way, from Gordy, the murderous sitcom chimpanzee, to the Haywoods' horse-actors. Indeed, the human protagonists of the film working behind the scenes as animal wranglers, production crew, and camera operators is significant, indicating a complex, if not exploitative, relationship to nature. A significant scene during the commercial shooting sequence occurs when, without warning, a crew member holds up a reflective VFX mirror ball to Lucky's face. Confronted by his own image reflected in the mirror ball, the horse panics, kicking up sand from the platform, and ruins the shot. With this violent encounter between the image and the real, Peele continues to ask the questions that film studies has been grappling with since the nineteenth century, doing so this time from the perspective of an animal. Peele's film suggests that there is something deeply debased, even deadly, about the extraction of images from living beings for profit. Gordy responds to the exploitation of his image by creating a bloody spectacle. The spectacle itself has no loyalty; it cannot be tamed, and will, ultimately, return to destroy its makers. Gordy's violent refusal to cooperate suggests that not even the image itself can be domesticated, that nature and its materiality can never quite be assimilated, which contains the latent potential to undo the spectacle. Peele's film implies that a genuine image, or rather, a non-spectacular one, will demonstrate these contradictions not by denying or avoiding the spectacle, but by reappropriating it in order to assert the interconnection, rather than the commodification, of life and nature. Amy Bridges persuasively reads Jean Jacket in terms of Donna Haraway's concept of tentacular thinking, asserting that Peele

> appears to suggest that we have reached the ultimate end stage of capitalism's infiltration into every single aspect of our daily lives. . . . [Peele] implicates [Jean Jacket] and us in this chain of consumption that sees money paid for suffering witnessed. . . . The irony of OJ's reaction to Jean Jacket, "don't look him in the eye," is thus laid bare as the monster octopus presented as an evil capitalist symbol that is both dangerous to look at and impossible—[or] unprofitable—to look away from.[9]

Going one step further than Bridges, it would not be unreasonable to suggest that in this sense Jean Jacket represents a kind of capitalist animism, one in which everything is interconnected in its capacity for commodification, an idea supported by Peele's assertion that "the villain is this otherworldly threat. And it is also something that everyone has in common—everyone's relationship to the spectacle."[10] One of *Nope*'s decisive moments occurs when OJ suggests that Jean Jacket is not, as it was first assumed, a spacecraft in the shape of a traditional postwar sci-fi UFO, a vehicle operated by an alien species, but is itself an animal made of flesh, one that hunts, eats, and excretes its prey (note that it cannot digest money). Importantly, Jean Jacket is alive as long as it can elude its conversion into an image. The film's protagonists soon learn that Jean Jacket disables electric devices, including digital cameras, necessitating a return to pre-digital cinematographic apparatuses, such as Holst's vintage 35mm camera. What's more, OJ soon realizes that Jean Jacket, like Lucky the horse, reacts violently to any direct gaze: "I don't think it eats you if you don't look it in the eye. . . . You don't look at it unless you want its attention." It may be hunting the residents and tourists in Agua Dulce, but it, too, is hunted. Jean Jacket is lured by an array of colored air dancers—dynamic, tubular simulacra of human beings most commonly placed outside used car lots as visual lures to potential consumers—that it mistakes for humans. In turn, the human beings in *Nope* are lured by Jean Jacket's visual reproducibility. The film is about looking and looking away, drawing attention and avoiding it, representation, decoys, simulacra—all in the service of reproducing an image (preventing Jean Jacket from killing more people and animals is secondary to this goal).[11] Jean Jacket's physiology, its entire existence, appears to be devoted to resisting mechanical and optical detection, which makes the capture of its image even more enticing. Yet, as Jupe insightfully observes, Jean Jacket (whom he classifies as a member of a species he calls "The Viewers") is itself engaged in acts of surveillance. Surveillance and consumption are conjoined here, as Jean Jacket devours anything it sees, whether it is human, animal, or inorganic material like flags, plastic, money, even a wheelchair. Jupe believes he has an understanding akin to a contract with Jean Jacket, to whom he feeds the horses he has bought from the Haywoods in exchange for its performance at Jupiter's Claim, a struggling Wild West-themed park. But Jupe makes the same fatal mistake as the producers of *Gordy's Home*. As OJ later proclaims, Jupe tried "to tame a predator." In the end, Jean Jacket reproduces Gordy's bloody spectacle on a vast scale, devouring the entire audience, including Jupe and his entire family.

In contrast to the aforementioned capitalist animism is a far more redemptive, if ultimately unfulfilled, animism. It can be found in a flashback Jupe has, just prior to his death, of the *Gordy's Home* massacre. His memory returns the viewer to the very first scene of the film, resolving the cliffhanger that ends on a young Jupe cowering beneath a table as Gordy approaches. Rather than harm Jupe, as he has the rest of the cast, Gordy reaches his out to Jupe, offering his fist for their signature exploding fist bump. Jupe reaches out too, but before they can connect their fists in solidarity, Gordy is shot in the head. In the very moment when Gordy has liberated himself, ready to transmit his newfound sense of freedom to others, he is killed by a power geared at destroying potential alliances. The chimpanzee is killed not because he massacred the entire crew of the show, but because tried to share an experience with Jupe. Gordy's revolt may be violent and, ultimately, unsuccessful, but it is a meaningful, if visceral, example of what Singh calls "biopower from below."[12] Such an animism holds the promise of a more horizontal relationship with others that markedly contrasts with the verticality of the capitalist spectacle, embodied by Jean Jacket, which is unable to comprehend others, including animals, as living beings. If, as Bethany C. Morrow has astutely observed, Black American social horror is "an indictment of the American imagination and of American mythology,"[13] with its disturbing assemblages and technicalized mythology that occlude and deny the reality of white supremacy and racialized violence, then this is deeply true of *Nope*, which creates new hybrid forms of the Western and science fiction genres as the fitting mise-en-scène for a film with such insight into the horror of the American spectacle, with its long investment in racialized violence, which capitalizes on everything, not only converting flesh and blood into profit but also directing the viewer's gaze toward—or, as the case is here, away from—an extractive, life-denying image, where anything can be consumed. Yet *Nope* is exemplary of cinema's affirmative, critical capacities that do not underestimate the medium's ability to discipline life.

Coloniality, Negative Animism, and Unmotivated Life

Several recent French films have shown how the morphing contours of the immigrant-refugee carry on themselves the writs of biopolitical misappropriation and dispossession. If in Ladj Ly's *Les Misérables* (2019) one could observe the production of race at the administrative level—the racist cop calls the black youths "microbes" and the people he arrests and intimidates "clients" as if to congregate in one stance the biological and the businesslike, a transactional model in which normativity is dictated racially and "entrepreneurially" like in a market-based approach—Bertrand Bonello's *Zombi Child* (2019) establishes an even more sinister conflation of imagined identity and subjugation. Bonello weaves together the colonial past and the neocolonial present with two parallel narratives: The first is based on the real legend of Clairvius Narcisse, a Haitian man who was purportedly transformed into a zombie and forced into slavery on a sugar plantation; the second follows Mélissa (Wislanda Louimat), Narcisse's granddaughter, a teenage girl who attends an elite, majority-white boarding school in Paris. The film's protagonist, however, is Fanny (Louise Labèque), a popular white student at the school who befriends Mélissa. Fanny quickly becomes obsessed when she learns about Mélissa's tragic past—her parents died in the 2010 Haiti earthquake—and her connection to Haitian Vodou through her family. Soon, Fanny's desire to benefit from Vodou power drives the film. Desperate for the affections of Pablo, a boy from her hometown, Fanny financially manipulates Mélissa's young aunt Katy, a Mambo (Vodou priestess), into performing a ritual to exorcise her of her heartbreak (figures C.1 and C.2).

Figure C.1. Via reverse-victimhood Fanny manipulates Mambo Katy into performing a ritual. *Source:* Betrand Bonello, dir., *Zombi Child* (2019; Film Movement, 2020), DVD, 576p.

Figure C.2. Via reverse-victimhood Fanny manipulates Mambo Katy into performing a ritual. *Source:* Bonello, Betrand, dir. *Zombi Child.* 2019; New York: Film Movement, 2020. DVD, 576p.

Pleading with a reluctant Katy, Fanny asks, "Don't I count cos I'm white and healthy? Can suffering be ranked?" Here, the figure of the zombie imbricates the undead past and the repressed history of French colonialism that lurks beneath the patriotic, revolutionary history of *liberté*, *egalité*, and *fraternité*—the film opens onto a class-room history lecture—at the same time as it illuminates the new, neocolonial relations of power that extort and extract culture, labor, and natural resources from former colonies in the Global South. Bonello extends the necropolitical process of zombiefication beyond the soulless counterpart of prolonged consumerism, revealing it to be a relentless project of racialization and othering, an itinerary of subjugated subjectivity in which the transition between the two states stands out as the real moment of loss and the fact of having turned into a zombie not being in itself the worst part of the event. It is then "the death of death," the colonizing West's final achievement, an eternal youth predicated on the extraction of life, a colonial version of the Nazi "less life for you is more life for me." At the level of plot, Bonello depicts what is superficially a thoroughly careless teenage folly, a selfish but innocuous request motivated by unrequited romantic love. But by convincing Katy to conduct a serious Vodou ritual as though it were no more significant than a dating app, the film reveals the "compulsion to return repeatedly to the original site of the trauma," an intemperate agony that "continues to chase humanity's collective subjectivity, with no healing in sight."[14] However, Fanny doesn't just want to resolve her love life with magic; she wants to extract Mélissa's inheritance, to lay claim, however childishly, to part of what makes Mélissa powerful and instrumentalize it to her own desire. At the end of the film, Katy's ritual backfires, leaving Fanny possessed by Baron Samedi, a powerful Haitian spirit or *Iwa* of Haitian Vodou. Bonello brings this extractive logic to its extreme with his adaptation of Henry James's *The Beast in the Jungle*, taking place in a dystopian future where, to be considered completely human, already molecularized individuals must turn into de facto lobotomized lower-status beings. The world depicted by Bonello in *The Beast* (*La bête*, 2023) is one that strives to be emotionless, detached, and as near to the machine ideal as possible and where autoimmune practices of emotional mutilation are the natural outcome for an enervated citizenry that cannot connect anymore "with other human beings who very much resemble them in terms of ethnicity, class, and social affiliations."[15]

This dissolution of regulatory regimes and the points of cleavage in thanatopolitical normativities has been the object of a recent wave of catastrophic films depicting the Anthropocene as a phase of lethal endangerments, untenable immunitary logics, and über-neo-liberal horror—but film can materialize the excess of life it seizes on other meandering, affirmative potentialities.[16] As early as the 1990s, Daniele Ciprì and Franco Maresco provided with the *Cinico TV* shorts a biopolitical visual account of the different, failed models of predatory development that Sicily experienced through representations that were not simply, as often described, post-apocalyptic, but post-everything, post-human and post-nature, and in which life "tends to the inorganic"[17] and indexes one of the many existential enclosures made visible by biopower, in line with Elizabeth Povinelli's reconfiguration of the distinction between Life and Nonlife in *Geontologies*. This is especially evident in Serra's recent film, *Pacifiction* (2023). "I need to take a step back," says Benoît Magimel's De Roller, the High Commissioner for French Polynesia (figure C.3). A white French colonial administrator, he wears a white suit, surely a nod to Werner Herzog's *Fitzcarraldo* (1982).

De Roller, the protagonist of Serra's *Pacifiction*, looks at the sublime blue water from a light aircraft. "You can't reason if you're emotional. It's not possible. You have to abandon your body entirely. With enough distance, you can make decisions that benefit the many. And not get caught up emotionally."[18] With this image and these lines, biopower speaks through a colonial government functionary suspended thousands of feet in the sky, surveying the Edenic spoils of Empire (what Serra calls a "rotten paradise") with the omniscient eye of a body in flight: From an aerial perspective that reminds the viewer of similar points of view from films by Leni Riefenstahl and Roberto Rossellini reclaiming the land below as righteous property

Figure C.3. De Roller's view of French Polynesia. *Source:* Albert Serra, dir., *Pacifiction* (2022; Grasshopper Film, 2022), Blu-ray Disc, 1080p HD.

of the sovereign and colonizer, De Roller is a person who has "abandoned" his body so "entirely" that it floated above the clouds.[19] The polysemous title of Serra's work perfectly encapsulates the relationship between life and biopower: The former is subdued, pacified, by the latter through the fiction of protection and security. In Serra's film, the fiction is a colonial one: a lush, tropical paradise, the kind printed on mid-century postcards and replicated in tiki bars. The Pacific-fiction is a pacifying-fiction which the viewer is invited to read and identify, encouraged by the film's affective paranoia. This "fictional" quality is manifested in the unsettling and uncanny undercurrent of violence as truly breathtaking shots of the Tahitian landscape are juxtaposed with the dark, alluring, and yet sickly interior of a local nightclub that is filled with European customers (diplomats and sailors) and Tahitian staff (bartenders, servers, and entertainers). Film critic James Slaymaker makes this juxtaposition even clearer when he writes that "*Pacifiction* paints a portrait of French Polynesia as a land suspended between indigenous agency and external mechanisms of control and dehumanization," adding that it is "an area still overcoming the trauma of its brutal colonial past and looking toward an uncertain future."[20] The plot and tension of Serra's film centers around the possible conspiracy by the French Navy—whose submarines have been popping up nearby—to conduct nuclear tests in the area. De Roller shapeshifts between diplomat and detective, investigating a conspiracy that is no less than the return of the colonial past (in which he is squarely implicated), the specter of nuclear testing that at every moment threatens to return (figure C.4). *Pacifiction* has been

Figure C.4. De Roller in shadow against a bright orange sunset. *Source:* Albert Serra, dir., *Pacifiction* (2022; Grasshopper Film, 2022), Blu-ray Disc, 1080p HD.

most consistently deemed an apocalyptic film and a paranoid thriller, but the extent to which these genres index it as an ecopolitical film has not been fully explored.

The nuclear bomb is an exemplary figure of imbrication for biopolitics, ecopolitics, technology, imperialism, and the potential devastation of human beings and their environment, the simultaneous destruction of both *zoē* and *bíos*. Between 1966 and 1974, France carried out forty-one nuclear tests across the French Polynesian islands, and while the government insisted these were done safely, declassified documents have demonstrated this to be a gross lie: Indeed, the tests exposed 90 percent of the French Polynesian population to radioactive fallout.[21] The concealment of this information resulted in the rejection of thousands of compensation claims—by 2021, only sixty-three Polynesian citizens had received compensation.[22] Furthermore, between 1975 and 1996, France resumed its nuclear testing program; and though these tests were kept below ground, the explosions still released radioactive material, causing even higher rates of cancer and other illnesses linked to radiation.[23] These tests also, of course, had a negative impact on ocean life, coral reefs, and other ecologies. In Serra's film, De Roller mediates between anti-nuclear Tahitian activists and shady business and military interests. This mediation is the extent of his capacity for action; De Roller is the highest government official in French Polynesia, the living representative of the President of France. Enjoying unparalleled mobility within the island, De Roller (French for "rollerblading") is a man who circulates between dark nightclubs, churches, luxury hotels, and government buildings. When the heir to an unnamed fortune asks for De Roller's investment in an abandoned hotel built on a *morai* or sacred cemetery ("people with money help each other"), De Roller responds ambiguously, "I'll be someone you can count on if you need help," managing to signal his own importance without explicitly agreeing: The implication is that he may not invest himself, but he will facilitate it. When asked if he has been invited to the club, De Roller boasts, "I invite myself. I don't need anyone. I utilize my privilege maybe too often. I just make sure everything's okay. People know me. They know I'm very involved with everyone." He continues, "I'm pretty proud. They've proven their trust in me many times," before breaking the fourth wall as he says, "which is nice."[24] This reflexive disclosure to the *viewer* redoubles De Roller's easy, seductive charm, while also highlighting the more sinister subtext of exploitation and abuses of power that runs like a current through the film.

Where can animism be located in this film? On the one hand, *Pacifiction* is full of eerie, beautiful shots of intense orange and pink sunsets, lush vegetation, and, importantly, the sublime ocean. In an early scene, De Roller presides over a surfing competition at Teahupoʻo, or "place of skulls," a town known for its enormous waves (figure C.5). This extraordinary sequence cements the film's slow, wave-like pace, a contrapuntal exchange between awe and danger. Speaking on a jet-ski as colossal waves roll toward them, De Roller offers a local surf prodigy favors: "If there's any way I can help you, just let me know." When the surfer asks if he is in the competition, De Roller replies that he "competes in a different realm . . . I compete in politics." Afterward, he chats with the man operating his jet-ski. "Not much happens in my job," De Roller says. The man responds, "Well, this is my office and it's always trying to kill me."[25] A clear if asymmetrical analog is set up between the surfers and skippers and De Roller's life of politics and intrigue.

But more than this, the waves are a real presence, evoking a relationship between humans and nature that is only superficial (or, we should rather say, it is not "productive") if such relationship is exclusively based on domination and exploitation. Even so, De Roller cannot domesticate the trees, waves, or vegetation on the island; and amid the seedy neon lights of the nightclubs and the commodified culture of luxury hotels, these elements of the landscape represent

Figure C.5. Wide shot of the massive waves. *Source:* Albert Serra, dir., *Pacifiction* (2022; Grasshopper Film, 2022), Blu-ray Disc, 1080p HD.

some of the few sources of direct experience on the island. The border between subject and landscape becomes blurred; it is as if the life force of man transmigrates into nature (figure C.6). This force has the potential to circulate, to remove its division from nature and join in the animacy of its fellow beings—water, plant, animal, human—but the onus is on "man" to find a way to balance and channel it properly. The ocean is a constant reminder of this onus; not a threat but an omen.

We (and very likely De Roller himself) do not know exactly what is really happening outside of the neon darkness of the club, whose flashes of color and whispered conversations hint toward, and distract from, a hidden catastrophe that is only incomprehensible because it is alive in every single atom. While De Roller is shrewdly cynical, grasping at heroism as he assures locals that he will fight for them, this fight manifests as intrigue rather than action. In the last half of the film, he attempts to dissuade a French admiral from resuming the tests. Diplomatically, elliptically, De Roller mentions a man whose mother had thyroid cancer, breast cancer, and throat cancer, "one after another": "That's why people are a bit nervous. You could call it paranoia, but isn't it common sense? . . . I think it would piss them off if we did it again."[26] If there is a form of animism in Serra's film, it must be understood as radioactivity. "Radiation is colorless and odorless, yet capable of affecting living beings at the genetic level. In this sense, nuclear materials produce the uncanny effect of blurring

Figure C.6. French Navy sailors mingle with locals and blend in with the surroundings in *Pacifiction*. *Source:* Albert Serra, dir., *Pacifiction* (2022; Grasshopper Film, 2022), Blu-ray Disc, 1080p HD.

the distinction between the animate and the inanimate, and between the natural and the supernatural."[27] Is it paranoia, or is it common sense? Paradoxically, radiation reminds us of the animist order of life in which everything is connected, from the coral reefs to the High Commissioner. Intent on uncovering a nuclear conspiracy, De Roller looks through binoculars at the Day-Glo orange horizon, adjusts his blue-lensed sunglasses, shines a large flashlight on the dark water in search of submarines. In a long, brilliant monologue, De Roller holds forth as a large, white man in a Hawaiian shirt struggles to stay awake:

> Politics is like a nightclub. They call this place Paradise, but they're idiots. It's a party with the devil. They're all there together, with lights beaming into their faces with strobes in the dark. It's flashing, they've lost their bearings. They lose their bearings . . . their balance, their memory . . . their common sense. There's no more day, no more night. There's no more time. That's politics. People in the dark who don't even look at each other anymore. Completely cut off from reality. . . . They think they control everything. They control nothing. Not even I control anything. It's just an illusion. I'm gonna go into that club, turn on the lights, turn off the music, and look into their defeated faces one by one. . . . That's politics today. There's nothing left. There are no more men. . . . It won't be tests. They'll drop the bomb. You'll see.[28]

De Roller never elaborates on what he will do once he turns on the lights and looks into the faces of his fellow men and women; he never spies what he is looking for through the binoculars; his flashlight never illuminates the nuclear submarine. The conspiracy is not visible—it is instead the failure of the visible, more specifically the failure of empiricism qua the visible. It is colorless, odorless; it is light. De Roller's failure was the belief in his own (bio)power. In the end, his political position is meaningless. Even the High Commissioner is replaceable. De Roller's backward revolution, from loquacious diplomat to a paranoiac who might just miss the last boat off the island, hints at the fungibility of the Western experience. On reflection, the film allegorizes a frustrated mission to renew a bygone (and wholly deluded) vision of benevolent colonial paternalism. Also denied is the mythic, Edenic state in which man and nature are so indistinct, so enmeshed, that their relationship transcends ethics and politics; even, perhaps a prelapsarian temporality before the violent caesura between *zoē* and *bíos*. In reality, the intermingling power of the state and capital won't consult with him before the bomb drops. But in the meantime, he will continue to entertain the tourists and use his friendly charisma to placate the people who actually have a stake in the world he—and by extension France—occupy. Modernity failed, the Enlightenment failed, but colonialism continues to affect the island like radioactive fallout, insinuating itself into commodified, indigenous bodies and the landscape itself.

Alessandro Comodin's docufiction *The Adventures of Gigi the Law* (*Gigi la legge*, 2022) features another figure of authority and his encounters with animacy. Gigi, a police officer in a small village in northern Italy, is in pursuit of his own conspiracy: a wave of suicides that have hit the town. As in *Pacifiction*, there is a blurring between reality and the protagonist's own worldmaking whose boundary seems to lie between Gigi's hypervegetative, jungle-like garden and the dusty roads he patrols in his uniform. In Comodin's and Serra's films the encounter with the environment unfolds as a dynamic perception of the organisms and natural phenomena that constitute their organic milieu, an ongoing and—sardonically—Anthropocenic interrogation of the specificity of human activity in the natural continuum. Gigi is played by non-professional actor Pier Luigi Mecchia, Comodin's uncle, a former cop, further blurring the border between "naturalness" and fiction and the lives that inhabit their corresponding forms. Oscillating between uniformity and nonconformity, Gigi tries to bring, and find, the garden's vitality in his working life, where he seeks connection and community. There are moments when he is nearly successful. In one of the earlier scenes, Gigi comes across a teenager whose motorbike has broken down. Gigi manages to restart it, then rides it himself, driving in ecstatic circles in a field surrounded by dry crops. He gives the young man a ride home; they chat amiably about school. Gigi's tentative but enlivening romance with Paola, a new female dispatcher, germinates over the radio, but never fully flourishes (figure C.7).

The film conveys a relationship between man and technology through Gigi's use of the radio, through which he has conversations with his colleagues, including Paola. While Comodin's visions of Gigi's technology-mediated encounters are suffused with irony, we

Figure C.7. Gigi flirts with Paola over the radio. *Source:* Alessandro Comodin, dir., *The Adventures of Gigi the Law* (2022); courtesy of Shellac Films. Used with permission.

learn that that mediation can be a totalizing one, one that excludes other connections with other symbolic orders such as nature or music. Gigi's staunch refusal to cut his trees, and the ghosts and songs that unexpectedly appear and erupt in the film, signify the need to restore the link with something spontaneous, magical, fertile.

Gigi manages to inhabit a new subjectivity, one in which the subject looks for his soul outside of himself. There is a creaturely vulnerability in Comodin's film that is purposefully absent from *Pacifiction*, and is reflected in the difference between that film and *Gigi*'s more naturalistic, documentary style. The latter possesses an autofictional, documentary veracity and a far more provincial, yet less restrictive form of life. While De Roller is able to access forms of sensuous ecstasy with the ease of a diplomat accustomed to state-level privilege and transport, Gigi cannot even bring himself to cut the branches in his garden, which has made him a pariah to his next-door neighbor; and whereas De Roller is trapped in his tailored, archetypal suit, Gigi steps in and out of roles, reinhabiting old pop songs, changing scenery and uniform as he sits in shorts and sneakers, made smaller in relation to the enormous, almost prehistoric trees he has lovingly cultivated, and against which he derealizes himself. Gigi's forest is the luxuriant vehicle that allows him to make connections between real and imagined events and to harness the dormant energy connecting humans to other realms. This recalls Didi-Huberman's concept of "phasmid thinking," based on the mimicry of insects in Paris's Jardin des Plantes. The viewer "witnesses [the] disappearance both of clear-cut boundaries of identity . . . as well as the subversion of customary concepts, such as the distinction between animal and milieu and between life and inorganic environment" (figure C.8).[29]

Even so, both figures constantly interrogate their position as well as that of the spectator, who is never surer of the limits of the real than Gigi or De Roller themselves and gets involved in their acts of rediscovery and recuperation of a vital substrate. Each character heralds what might be called an inoperative, or disguised, form of life that is always on the move. This movement is not forced or fugitive (as it is for the young refugees in Sylvain George's films, which I will explore shortly), although it is a form of life that eludes captures, refuses its own shell, nest, or uniform. De Roller and Gigi are characters that mark the endpoint of figures like Federico Fellini's Marcello or Michelangelo Antonioni's death-driven clairvoyants. Their unmotivated mobility no longer entails ennui, but a mode of seeing a new world all the time, a world in constant metamorphosis that at every point

Figure C.8. Gigi in his forest-garden. *Source:* Alessandro Comodin, dir., *The Adventures of Gigi the Law* (2022); courtesy of Shellac Films. Used with permission.

threatens to overwhelm them with. It is worth noting that both De Roller, an ineffectual diplomat in the face of the military arm of the state, and Gigi, an aging beat cop, connote a roller skate (in French) and a spinning top (Italian) via the evocation of *Gigi la trottola*, the Italian translation of the Japanese manga *Dash Kappei*, signifying the torsion that characterizes the movement of their lives. Ineffective authority figures that should in theory govern and orient, De Roller and Gigi both constitute a tongue-in-cheek mockery of the frustrated attempt to define the border between subject and other, as with De Roller's colonial decay, and between civilization and wilderness, as with Gigi's forest. Nevertheless, they are characterized by an unqualified movement in the sense that *zoē* is unqualified life; however, this is generated not by biopolitical exposure or political nakedness, but by the fig-leaf of a declining, peripheral, provincialized authority that has become less relevant to the global administration of the anthropo-capitalocene. Neither free nor entirely purposeful, they are propelled by an inert, habitual force, perhaps the force of memory, veering toward territories of wonder and intrigue, "natural" fantasy—in De Roller's case, made possible by the threat of nuclear annihilation—and nightmare, without successfully transcending their point of departure: To be inoperative, they move all the time, propelled by the steam of their own privilege. Their animism, still anchored in Western power structures, is avuncular rather than fully paternalistic, though they try with all their might to enact a connection with the "other." In *Pacifiction*, for example, the "uncontrollable" waves imply a fracture, a wound—France's imperial past—that De Roller attempts to repair and suture in his awkward and bumbling way. The problem is that this hoped-for relation remains mystified, reinforcing the split between self and "other" that maintains the distance they seek to overcome. And yet, as Gigi's ontological status demonstrates, the destruction or the emptying out of the subject can be concurrently experienced as its fictional expansion, as its own negative re-apparition as a specter, by way of which the subject reconfigures itself in another place, in other organic or inorganic realms, a "requalification" of subjectivity on a different place. He abhors the cutting of his trees not because they are decorative, but because he feels that they are really a part of himself. Gigi's garden represents the yearning for, and possibility of, a (re)connection that is "more-than-human," a community of the *plan-thropos* which can equally accommodate plants, animals, and people.[30]

Permanence of Italy, or the Sovereign Panhandler

As the Thirty Years' War destroyed the imperial foundations and states in Central Europe began competing differently, the birth of productivity and the concurrent emergence of political economy as the necessary scientific justification led to a growing politicization of biological life.[31] The first level of this stabilization of power was the detailed and the individual, taken over by the disciplinary systems studied in *Discipline and Punish: The Birth of the Prison*, while the second was the mass, managed via the regulatory operations analyzed in *The History of Sexuality—The Will to Knowledge*. Schools have often been featured as the breeding ground for personal dramas and sentimental or, in the case of Italy, smutty comedies, while barracks in war movies are often the background to individual tragedies echoing the bloodshed of the frontlines: Marco Bellocchio instead treated them as purely agonistic repositories for power struggles. The repeated gestures and the spasming bodies of *In the Name of the Father* (*Nel nome del padre*, 1971) and *Victory March* (*Marcia trionfale*, 1976) are analyzed, mocked, criticized, but nonetheless presented in their positive and productive function—they could be from a factory and an assembly line. Automatization, leadership, the pulverization of the collective into a plethora of petty demands, the rejection of the unscientific, uncertain action of parliamentary procedures replaced by problem-solving leaders—all concur to establish a stifling, Right-leaning political stability, as if the only unifying motifs for the country could be the authoritarian regressions of Fascism and Catholicism (figures C.9 and C.10).

Visual studies scholar Giacomo Tagliani engages the biopolitical dimensions of Italian cinema by interpreting its long tradition of biopics as intersections of life, history, and politics. Biographical films directed by Francesco Rosi, Marco Bellocchio, Paolo Sorrentino, Gianni Amelio, Susanna Nicchiarelli, Nanni Moretti, and Alessio Cremonini deploy the actorial body as "a surface on which processes, tensions and dynamics that traverse the social body are inscribed," clarifying the nature of the exercise of power and the relationship between life, politics, and praxis.[32]

Among the directors Tagliani mentioned, Cremonini's *On My Skin: The Last Seven Days of Stefano Cucchi* (*Sulla mia pelle*, 2018), the story of Cucchi's brutal beating and subsequent death in prison after a brief detention, seems the most qualified to engage with governmental practices. In it, the police are depicted in a Foucauldian

Figure C.9. Marco Bellocchio and Italy's permanent Fascist vocation. *Source:* Marco Bellocchio, dir., *Victory March* (1976; Rai Cinema; 01 Distribution, 2020), DVD, 576p.

Figure C.10. Marco Bellocchio and Italy's permanent Fascist vocation. *Source:* Marco Bellocchio, dir., *In the Name of the Father* (1971; CG Entertainment; Cristaldi Film, 2013), DVD, 576p.

mode, appearing as a regulatory technology—after all, they kill an unemployed person—whose only way to reaffirm a lost authority is to target vulnerable people in its care and close ranks to demonstrate impunity. The other pictures confirm a different tendency, which is to say that the representation of power per se has always been problematic for Italian filmmakers, who have often treated it as an essentialist conduit, like a weapon to be wielded, an impending punishment, a foreclosing blow. Its reticular visualization is even more uncertain, and the preferred strategy is that of the "arbitrary act, control, domination" or "as machination, as secret, as conspiracy," thus betraying more than just occasionally an imperfect knowledge of the sociopolitical processes, if not even a direct responsibility in the events.[33] One possible exception is director Francesco Rosi, who throughout his filmography has pursued an inventory of powers and an investigation of the ways they claim ownership over bodies: The hyperconstellation of powers has become so vast and extensive that power is everywhere and cannot be located and seized with certainty.[34] Italian directors have excelled at depicting the reverberations of politics as a key element of human experience and the crisis that comes when such participation in militancy becomes futile. In a review of Nanni Moretti's *Bianca* (1984), Alain Carbonnier wrote of the main character's fear of loving, of being together with another person, as a "refusal to believe," adroitly drawing a line with Moretti's previous works about a disenchanted generation that had lost all political coordinates and all faith in political engagement: The hopelessness caused by that traumatic lacuna seeps into one's inner life, into one's intimate sphere—a vertiginous plumbing of political, social, and private.[35] However, in films that entertain a more indirect relationship with power one can see ways in which life is partitioned and disqualified. For instance, Alice Rohrwacher can be situated between Pasolini's doctrine of dispossession, Sergio Citti's cinema of the hungry Italian wanderer, and magical (anti-neo-) realism of Ettore Scola. All of Pasolini's films confront aspects of Italy's contemporary political and social problems related to the country's postwar industrial boom, its economic transformation, and the abandonment of its people, dialects, and customs in the countryside and on the city margins, where traditional sacred rites still played out in ritualistic fashion. Pasolini's *The Hawks and The Sparrows* (*Uccellacci e uccellini*, 1966) exemplifies the trajectory of the Cold War subject as postulated by Hannah Arendt: embarking on a journey with no destination, excluded from all traditions, his energy scattered throughout a bunch of delusions, but compulsively "programmed" to take on new challenging paths. The movie seamlessly glides from a postmodern present (the youths clumsily dancing outside a tumbledown "Las Vegas" bar in the outskirts of Rome) to an austere past (comic actors Totò and Ninetto's medieval quest of evangelization) to a messianic future (the street signals evoking the humble figures of street cleaners and tinsmiths, in the hope of a recognition of the quasi-divine greatness of simple man). In Totò, Pasolini saw a representative of that "modernity of the people" as he writes in the poem "Il canto popolare," in which modern equals authentic. Scola mutates this authenticity as being of the people, as in the opportunism of the people, the cynicism, the capacity of adjusting to adversity, to improvise among chaos, and the spontaneous ability to perform. Citti's *Il minestrone* (1981) is the director's most ambitious and complexly woven story, about the eternal and atavistic hunger of a proletarian class that has lost any coordinate, be it geographical, political, or moral. The Southern Rome bridges of Laurentino 38 on which the film opens, as well as Sasso Marconi, which almost closes it, are non-places, neutral spaces that the three protagonists, and the barbarically hungry horde that they drag behind, cross without connoting them, incessantly and relentlessly guided only and exclusively by their own stomach.

Rohrwacher draws on these traditions to create her own unique, contemporary style and philosophy. *Happy as Lazzaro* (*Lazzaro felice*, 2018) is her most legibly biopolitical film. Set on an Italian estate called Inviolata, isolated since 1977, fifty-four sharecroppers work on a tobacco farm, where they are kept in debt, in miserable poverty, forbidden from leaving the estate without permission from its owner, the Marchioness—a request that is always denied, as the film quickly establishes when a young couple wish to start a new life elsewhere. The protagonist of the film, Lazzaro (figure C.11), is the opposite of Melville's Bartleby: Instead of "I would prefer not to," Lazzaro assents to every command, whether it is from Tancredi, the young heir to the estate, or his own family, who, though they themselves are burdened with work, order him around with a frequency that surpasses his own share of the toil. If, according to Agamben, Melville's Bartleby could be a new messiah by disrupting the ontology of potentiality, Lazzaro, with his "I'd rather yes," his affirmative reply to every demand, is a

Figure C.11. Close-up of Lazzaro in a tobacco field. *Source:* Alice Rohrwacher, dir., *Happy as Lazzaro* (2018; 01 Distribution, 2018), Blu-ray Disc, 1080p HD.

moving but grim commentary on the emphasis of self-improvement and entrepreneurship so ingrained in our societies of optimization. The very nature of Lazzaro's resurrection is a kind of excavation, an extraction from the ground, plucked from the earth like the tobacco leaves he and his fellow sharecroppers cultivate. Lazzaro's inability to refuse any demand soon places him out of proximity of the human and within range of a host of biopolitical, perhaps even what we might call "bio-religious" figures: feudal serf, saint, animal, and *homo sacer*. Besides resonating with Agamben's ontological warning on the existential trappings of potentiality, with his private revolution of the "yes" Lazzaro looks like the emptied double of the revolutionary subject, a figure that economic forces have long ceased to produce. By turning his private life into work, Lazzaro becomes a pure distillation of productive relations, separated from the human element of life and dominated in every capacity and every sphere. However, even though the social root of Lazzaro's exploitation grows into a real political form, that is to say, an ahistorical and omnipresent rationality of serfdom, a revolutionary option remains very abstract in Rohrwacher's film. As a political subject, Lazzaro has no choice in terms either of political representation or of revolutionary praxis.

Rohrwacher's most radical stance in this film is her Pasolinian approach to filmmaking, where "history . . . is always now."[36] The viewer is almost immediately immersed in an uncertain temporality, a living palimpsest of history where almost medieval, and certainly feudal, life coexists with electricity—in the first scene, Lazzaro's family carry a single lightbulb into a bedroom, screwing it into an unexpected light socket, while other items that come into view—a Walkman, an early cell phone—make the temporal space even more uncertain. Rohrwacher shows how problematic it is to carve out an economy of personhood among practices aimed at gaining profit: She highlights the class differences not only through a juxtaposition of work and leisure but, more meaningfully, through a paradigm of extraction that is exemplified, for the peasants, by a debt that cannot be extinguished and, for the landowners, by the game of kidnapping, in which resources pass from the rich to the rich. Soon, Tancredi befriends Lazzaro, forcing him to neglect his duties on the farm. Bored with his life on the estate and in search of a way to upset and extract a ransom from his mother, Tancredi forces Lazzaro to help him fake his own kidnapping. During this time, the two young men form a strange but close bond as "half-brothers." While the Marchioness orders the peasants to carry out an exhaustive search for her son, the only person who takes action is Maria (the daughter of the Marchioness's right-hand man), who, having found the only signal on the estate, uses the enigmatic cell phone to call the police, who soon arrive by helicopter. What shocks them is not the "kidnapping," but the backward conditions of the estate and the extreme poverty of the laborers, who, along with the audience, are suddenly thrust into the present: When the officers ask them why the children are not in school, they are absolutely baffled. Meanwhile, Lazzaro, distracted by the novel sight of the police helicopter, falls off a cliff and "dies" in a ravine. Many years later, Lazzaro wakes up, having not aged a day since the accident, and walks for miles into the city, where he remains a servant to the whims of others. He wanders over to a large group of workers, many of them migrants from outside Europe, who are bidding for poorly paid jobs on farms and in factories. Here, he is united with one of the survivors of Inviolata, Antonia, who takes him in. He joins Ultimo, her gruff partner, and her son, as well as some of the old people from the village, who barely survive by scamming passersby. The scam—for which Antonia, unbeknownst to him, leverages Lazzaro's honest, trusting face—involves selling fake reproductions of an antique music box, forged from the original artifact, stolen from the estate. But Lazzaro's real talent—a skill that, like Lazzaro himself, is raised from the dead—is identifying edible plants that grow at the edge of the railway near his family's squat. Ultimo, a hardened criminal, is struck with wonder: For him, the existence of living things that may freely nourish him—that require no exchange, and indeed, in their wildness, no cultivation—is miraculous.

This film is a fairy tale, a slow ballad, a film about inhospitable lands and uncertain borders, from a historic to a human Middle Age. But it is also a spiritual fantasy with a modern St. Francis, a picture about the damned of the earth in the wake of predecessors such as Pasolini, Citti, Scola, Comencini, Taviani, Olmi. In *Happy as Lazzaro*, Rohrwacher's dispossessed vagrants found their community in solidarity and a Christian form of dutifulness. What are the modern serfs teaching us about power and its rationality? Are they—and Rohrwacher—hinting at a possible resistance? *Happy as Lazzaro* highlights the continuity of old forms of serfdom under advanced capitalism and triangulates a spatial-temporal inevitability of exploitation and privilege, at the same time testing the regressive risk of theorizing new subjectivities. Rohrwacher shares with Pier Paolo Pasolini the impossible, synthetic reconciliation between different worlds as well as a common sentiment on the old, heroic resignation and submission of the Italian people. For Pasolini being modern means not having a culture, and the only resistance lies in the body itself. In *Petrolio*, Carlo the protagonist is split between and doubled into a bourgeois fascination with traditional power predicated on reassuring values and uncorrupted sexual availability and promiscuity. His second incarnation uses sex to reconnect with the hunger, the vitalism, the honesty of the people. The journey is successful: by the loss of his sexual marker, the entire economy of desire based on ownership and consumption is destabilized. *Happy as Lazzaro* is Rohrwacher's most ambitious film after the 2011 coming-of-age story of *Heavenly Body* (*Corpo celeste*) and the rural elegy of *The Wonders* (*Le meraviglie*) in 2014. Transfixed by the decaying mores of the present day, she shares with Pasolini "a burning nostalgia for the premodern world."[37] In Pasolini's practices of transformation Carlo turns into petroleum and changes sex, then the Fascists rot, while in Rohrwacher's film Lazzaro goes from man to corpse to man again and also, like St. Francis, befriends a wolf—or, at the very least, has a peaceful encounter as in the book by Chiara Frugoni that is among the materials for the script.[38] Rohrwacher lifts the moralizing, instrumental evocation of the wolf that in the legend of St. Francis is the taming of a metaphysics of violence and robbery enabled by Christianity and turns it into a symbolic (non)representation of economic injustice caused by an unrepresentable financial power. Apparent becomings pervade the transmutations—from human to animal, from young to old, from alive to dead—but there really is no emancipatory political space. There is only one explicitly affirmative moment in the film: when Lazzaro forages the wild plants and weeds growing near the train tracks at the edges of the city. Ultimo is overwhelmed with emotion to discover that the urban wasteland could provide such a bounty, exclaiming, "all this stuff just growing everywhere, for free!"[39] The resurrected Lazzaro and his Pasolinian ethics of dispossession—giving oneself up to the tiger, or to the bees—points to a community of homeless people with a wealth of edible plants and vegetables growing in the interstices of the urban spaces, a concrete gesture toward a cooperative society in a non-market economy.

By the end of the film, Lazzaro and his comrades return to Inviolata. Now abandoned, the farm from which they were liberated becomes their inheritance: They plan to squat there, reclaiming and cultivating the land. Like Pasolini, Rohrwacher in her film privileges a break in linear temporality, forgotten subaltern cultures, erasures, and a non-hegemonic "peasant" temporality dictated by the rhythms of nature, of the earth. However utopian Rohrwacher's vision of their future may be, it is also problematic—a temporality of resignation, deep necessity, and scarcity. While it boldly inscribes a relationship with nature that is not extractive, it fails to elude the petrified trap of nostalgic archaism. Yet there is what Benjamin might call a weak messianism in Lazzaro, a faded but potent possibility of a subject with the "ability to see and bring animation into any form of being" and a notion of life that is "not bound by the partition of Life and Nonlife, the contemporary and the archaic."[40] In a stunning coda, Lazzaro and his community of peasant workers-turned-squatters stroll down an elegant Milanese gallery (figure C.12) to buy pastries for a dinner with an adult Tancredi who, they learn, even impoverished, has not abandoned his arrogant and profiteering ways. For many of us, Rohrwacher seems to say, not even death will suffice to throw off the ahistorical yoke of serfdom.

Figure C.12. Taking a stroll downtown and yet expelled from the polis across centuries. *Source:* Alice Rohrwacher, dir., *Happy as Lazzaro* (2018; 01 Distribution, 2018), Blu-ray Disc, 1080p HD.

Is it fair to say that like *Gigi*, *Happy as Lazzaro* fails philosophically but succeeds as a film, testing the boundaries of an affirmative biopolitics? Regardless of the genre—arthouse parable, comedy, music clip turned documentary—a sort of vital nihilism appears to emerge as the dominant technology of the self, to conform to sanctioned forms or to flee from them—for instance, the neoliberal schlemiel played by Fabio Rovazzi in Gennaro Nunziante's *Il vegetale* (2018) and the two Bresso youths from Alessandro Redaelli's *Funeralopolis: A Suburban Portrait* (*Funeralopolis*, 2017). Nunziante had directed the first four vehicles for Checco Zalone, supremely reassuring pictures in which critique of homophobic practices is eventually reabsorbed into a heteronormative foundation that denies any possibility of queer transcoding. Zalone plays with clichés dialectically, apparently exploding them from within only to feature them comically and finally reaffirming them in a false synthesis. Undergoing all the humiliation of a cruelly flexible, turbocapitalist economy but ultimately triumphing thanks to his upright and high-minded choices, the protagonist of *The Vegetable* is not dissimilar to the formulation of the films with Zalone. The out-of-place-ness of Rovazzi's lanky body and his stoic demeanor have a Keatonesque quality: He faces every hurdle, disappointment, and piece of bad news with unpretentious indifference. At the same time, he builds his community, regains his place in the family, and finds his love interest through all the work-related misadventures—the preposterous way in which *The Vegetable* establishes a happy ending for Fabio makes viewing the film an even more disquieting experience because the fragile packaging of the fabula reveals a managerial reality where work is coextensive with life, as theorized in the studies of Luc Boltanski and Ève Chiapello. This new culture, Boltanski and Chiapello write, criticizes the separation of work life and relationships from private life, family and personal relationships; it substitutes the hierarchical organization with the fluid organization of networking; it rejects the planning of hierarchies, the protection of permanent jobs and linear careers in a single organization that enhances, on the contrary, flexibility and mobility, the capacity to change and adapt to change—to go through several segments at once and to jump from one segment to the other.[41] In the new managerial culture one no longer speaks of a worker but of a person, meaning that marks the indispensable psychological, social, linguistic and communicative, affective, cognitive, narrative factors to the networking of the subject. Every subjectivity connected to a network is active and participating and, with the transition from vertical to horizontal organization, the subjects are ideally involved in different and multiple relationships. Finally, each individual weaves relationships of different kinds as they become involved in other relationships. Such a network is made up of mobile and flexible connections that intertwine, which appear well characterized by the notion of the project: From this standpoint, *Il vegetale* makes light fun of neoliberalism's social atomization but ultimately refuses a full reconciliation and hints at a community of the destitute based on sharing as our only way forward. Originally conceived as a loose collection of lived moments from which the filmmaker Alessandro Redaelli would later extrapolate different fragments for a music video clip, *Funeralopolis* blossomed into a full-fledged documentary on the two wannabe horrorcore rappers Lorenzo "Vashish" Passera and Andrea "Felce" Piva and their environment—the fellow drug users, the small town of Bresso near Milan where they hail from and spend most of their time, as well as their homes and families. On *Esquire*, Violetta Bellocchio mentioned Claudio Caligari's cult movie *Toxic Love* (*Amore tossico*, 1983) as the most relevant antecedent to

Redaelli's picture, but because of a similar *vérité* approach its closest cinematic relative is actually Nico D'Alessandria's *The Emperor of Rome* (*L'imperatore di Roma*, 1988).[42] Both films show users who live, or rather float, in a temporality made of preparation of the daily doses, continuous bargaining and scavenging for more and different substances, petty thefts, random vandalizing and lawbreaking, but also extraordinarily raw moments of love, friendship, and other emotional attachments and connections. What we see are lives of people who did not have any expectation to begin with; they are already resigned without complaint, there is nothing romantic, epic, or even vital about their condition—they simply keep going. Rome and Milan lose their respective façades. In *Funeralopolis*, the places where Felce and Vash hang out look like a desert but with sharp concrete edges: It is not that their lives are necessarily produced by that uninspiring, ultimately hostile space, but they provide the third dimension by virtue of their marginality and their uncertain status—they are not citizens, not workers, but a segregated "something else" at the mercy of the police and other instruments of security because a hierarchy of space corresponds to a hierarchy of life. Outlawry, drug use, being incessantly on the move because they do not belong to any place in particular: These are not the issues depicted in *Funeralopolis*, but simply the ingredients of Vash and Felce's existence, a dough that is continuously kneaded and in which there is no special ingredient. The two colleagues on the rap scene often ask friends and fellow users whether they have someone who cares for them, almost to ward off the dispensability and precariousness of their own lives: They seem to be insulated from any circuit of reproduction—of capital, of heteronormativity—and their uncompromising vitalism is an answer to a logic that sees the drug addicts as not fully human insofar as they produce themselves as bare life. Vash and Felce still see themselves as people, but they are in a state in which it becomes harder and harder to remind themselves that they are still alive, still living (figure C.13). For them, life appears to be something that one cannot really lead or even live: Too many of its aspects are predetermined; they cannot be consciously nor deliberately pondered or put in some "rational" order. With its biopolitics of social suffering and exclusion, *Funeralopolis* presents a likely futile nihilistic resistance to atomization that ends up as self-production of lawlessness, marginality and subsequent loss of citizenship.

Figure C.13. Vash and Felce bring life to the cemetery and vice versa. *Source:* Alessandro Redaelli, dir., *Funeralopolis: A Suburban Portrait* (2017; Twelve Entertainment; Terminal Distribuzione, 2019), Blu-ray Disc, 1080p HD.

Dissolving Borders: Biopower from Below

In his writing on animism, Anselm Franke asks, "If things become active, alive, or even person-like, where does this leave actual humans? Animism in this sense is greeted by the Western mindset as the threat that we must exchange positions, for now we can only imagine ourselves as annulled, in the role of the inert, passive stuff that was previously the thing-like 'matter' out there."[43] In a very real sense, then, animism—and an animist biopolitics of cinema—means interrogating the "proper" boundary between self and world. To conclude this book, I turn to three recent films that speak of the desire for and urgency toward dissolving, in a sense, these "proper boundaries," which manifest both phenomenologically and materially: Giovanni Cioni's *From the Planet of the Humans* (*Dal pianeta degli umani*, 2021), Massimo D'Anolfi and Martina Parenti's *Bestiari, erbari, lapidari* (2024), and Sylvain George's *May They Rest in Revolt* (*Qu'ils reposent en révolte (Des figures de guerres I)*, 2010), all of which engage with and address the thanatological barrier(s) among territories and species. An animist biopolitics of cinema can be characterized as a line of inquiry into artifacts that, in the wake of de Castro's multinaturalist ontology, postulate and evoke "a spiritual unity and a corporeal diversity,"[44] and aim to outline the contours of subjectivity or personhood in species and things that do not look human. An animistic perspective, as Marta Segarra writes, is often deployed "to counter the effects of the Anthropocene or the Capitalocene, especially the global climate crisis and the extinction of so many species."[45] While Segarra applies this interpretation to, among other films, Apichatpong Weerasethakul's *Tropical Malady* (*Sat praalat!*, 2004), Lav Diaz's mournful epics on the implementation of intensive cultivation and other ludicrous, tentacular forms of sovereign domination over the Filipino population and soil also show a concurrent, pernicious colonization of the landscape and the senses. It is of particular interest, though, that animist perspectives in the three films I mentioned activate sociocultural relationships among all the thinkable realms and can also make us reflect on the ways in which states manage racializing mechanisms, as biopower differentiates among those who are worthy of moving, living, and congregating and those who are not.

The violent maintenance of state borders physically divides life into citizen and non-citizen; by virtue of this demarcating function, the border produces the refugee, who, in turn, unsettles the anxious border and its claim toward circumscribing and containing the citizen. In other words, the refugee disturbs the legal fiction of the border and throws the "originary fiction of sovereignty to crisis."[46] The ultimate divider and arbitrator of *zoē* and *bíos* in contemporary life, the border is the most crucial illustration of Esposito's concept of immunity. Immunity, in both the biological and political senses, is itself a border, as Esposito defines it: "immunization identifies the threshold beyond which the protective apparatus attacks the very body it should protect."[47] Instituted to "limit reciprocal violence" between different communities—or, rather, *similar* communities, since Esposito, writing after René Girard, asserts that "human beings fight to the death not because of the differences between them . . . but because human beings are alike or even identical"—the border further reproduces the division between life and nature that encloses the landscape and distinguishes the qualified life of the citizen with the mere, or bare life. The border designates, in order to punish and deprive, the form of the refugee.[48]

Cioni, D'Anolfi and Parenti, and George interrogate the border in very different ways, but all do so by way of radical engagement with the documentary form. One may judge their musings on nations and territories as unbalanced if not too abstract or, worse, naïve, but their exploration of the ethical breadth of the medium deserves recognition, venturing into the "future beyond the nation-state and its destructive exclusion of non-citizens."[49] For three years, George embedded himself with a group of refugees, young men from a range of countries, such as Kurdistan, Bangladesh, Iraq, Somalia, and Sudan, among others. Shot in black and white, George's film documents these undocumented young men, acknowledging their lives through the eye of the camera, which they speak to directly, without any apparent influence by an interviewer. D'Anolfi and Parenti's point of departure is a stark distinction among different domains that end up blurring such confines and maps a non-anthropocentric zone of interest by cataloging film experiments, from early twentieth-century zoos to contemporary X-ray imaging (animal sphere); studying plants, which highlights encounters between incommensurable lifetimes (vegetable sphere); and allegorically looking at stones, construction materials, and rubble as fossil memories for the future (mineral sphere). Cioni uses archival footage from the past in conjunction with his own material, which he filmed at the Italian border with France.

In Cioni's film, the border itself is animated by its history as a route taken by refugees from World War II to those fleeing war, persecution, economic deprivation, and climate collapse today. The director walks across the Italian–French border, talking to migrants, learning their stories, trying to help, and treading the same hidden and dangerous paths above the Riviera that Italian Jews also traversed as they fled the country during Fascism. This border is also the site of the village that was once home to Serge Voronoff, a Russian endocrinologist who performed "rejuvenation" surgeries on hundreds of men during the 1920s and 1930s, grafting monkey testicles onto rich patients in search of renewed sexual vigor. These experiments reflected the general obsession with renewal and triumph over decay during the Mussolini regime. Interspersing excerpts from old films—among them the original *King Kong* (1933) and Edward Dmytryk's *Captive Wild Woman* (1943)—Cioni conjures up both the Frankensteinian and vampiric project of biopower, its thrust to control, enhance and then spectacularize life through film. His call is for a form of life that refuses to be straitjacketed: Be *new life*—new family, new community, new ways of bonding—but for someone, like when he decides to "turn" into the brother of one of the immigrants thus trying to be a producer of new, supportive forms. Although the film is narrated by the director himself, Cioni entrusts one of the most captivating elements of the narrative to a chorus of frogs whose habitat is concentrated around the wetlands of the Franco-Italian border. In a series of exchanges I had with Cioni, the Tuscan filmmaker explained that for him frogs are liminal creatures, living between the light and the dark, animals that we don't usually see but are always present and resilient, Egyptian symbols of fertility, a tongue-in-cheek version of the Spielbergian "life finds a way," but who, in their water tanks, represent the isolation created by social media and screened life in general (figures C.14 and C.15).[50]

Revisiting archives is also a strategy to remind ourselves of how the materiality of the medium affects the organic nature of the subjects and phenomena on film. Concurrent with Eadweard Muybridge's experiments on animal locomotion—but distancing itself from his unmotivated and serendipitous "inoperative images"[51]—a strand of "scientific" filmmaking studied animal behavior to control the human species even better or, in the worlds of Massimo D'Anolfi and Martina Parenti, to "invent new cages"[52] as stated in their biopolitical review of animal, vegetable, and mineral manifestations on the planet, *Bestiari, erbari, lapidari* (figure C.16).

For D'Anolfi and Parenti, film exposes its double vocation of capture and liberation when it is confronted with recurring anxieties, such as the place of man on earth and the distinction—or collapse—between organic and inorganic matter. While observing the interactions between humans and other domains, the filmmakers suggest that our species is far behind others when it comes to adjusting and contributing to a biological and material equilibrium: By revolting instead of adapting, as opposed to plants and other, more "patient" forms of life, humans demonstrate that they have not yet found their proper space and role on the planet, their extractive practices just a desperate form of guessing.

Visually, all these films oscillate between images of stillness and motion. George's film is filled with shots of the port of Calais, train tracks, and semi-trucks, underlining it as a place of transport, one where goods and capital may flow, but which offers no safe route

Figure C.14. Post-organic assemblages at the border. *Source:* Giovanni Cioni, dir., *From the Planet of the Humans* (GraffitiDOC, 2021). Courtesy of Giovanni Cioni.

Figure C.15. Post-organic assemblages at the border. *Source:* Giovanni Cioni, dir., *From the Planet of the Humans* (GraffitiDOC, 2021). Courtesy of Giovanni Cioni.

for asylum seekers. An early scene documents a local park, cutting between shots of border police trailing a small group of very young refugees, mixing traditional, steady documentary shots with those of a shaky, handheld camera that is often held as waist height and even

Figure C.16. Dog obedience training in the military. *Source:* Massimo D'Anolfi and Martina Parenti, dirs., *Bestiari, erbari, lapidari* (Montmorency Film, 2024). Online primer courtesy of Massimo D'Anolfi and Martina Parenti.

sometimes drops its focus to the ground as though interrupted. Freeze frames, slow motion, and unsteady shots show the police chasing the boys through a park, eventually catching up with them. Here, too, George includes long, handheld shots of the park's trees and foliage. Fountains in the park, birds in flight, trees blowing in the wind, a full moon rising—not descriptive, filler shots but indexes of as many broken links in the environment, in the social fabric, in that which we haphazardly still call nature. It contrasts with the lives of these men, which lack nature's elemental freedom to circulate, but also serves to emphasize their exposure to a state of nature in which the rights and protections of citizens are denied to them. The young men are often shown running, but this is a forced mobility rather than a free one, a mobility that must elude capture but never reaches its desired destination outside of the liminal, fugitive existence whose presence within European borders is illegal. Sounds of movement, like the crunch of gravel or the scream of a truck, emphasize the sensory contours of forced mobility. It becomes very clear that these young men occupy a completely parallel world to the local French citizens, or even tourists. Inhabiting a zone of exclusion, they are unable to live a settled life. In one decisive scene, a man, his face and body out of the frame except for his hand, describes this state of existence. As his hand gestures back and forth, he tells his interlocutor, also off camera, "*Comme ci, comme ça*; fifty-fifty; so-so; not dying, not living. I exist, I don't exist. In between. Not human being, not animal. In between."[53] With this statement and this gesture, the young man demonstrates the fundamental absurdity of the Cartesian and other splits, and, we might speculate, of the biopolitical episteme that has "guaranteed for centuries the translation and transition of persons into things, oscillating between them and allowing the proliferation of multiple thresholds."[54] A scene like this could easily precipitate an analysis of the refugee as *homo sacer*, or even Agamben's figure of the undead *Muselmann*. Such an interpretation would be missing the point, however, of George's film: of the shots of nature, the varieties of motion, the food the men share with one another and, in what was called the "Jungle," the shelter they shared. Even so, it would also be mistaken to read these moments of solidarity as transcendence. Rather, such moments of camaraderie as well as of despair must be viewed as distinctly political. George's film calls Agamben's bluff, so to speak, when it represents refugee life as political, capable of resistance, definition, and meaning, outside of the *polis*. One might even go so far as to say that political transformation can only occur, paradoxically, outside of, even against, the political process, the protections of the nation-state and its rapid rejection of weakening institutions like the UN High Commissioner for Refugees. In collaboration with the young men on the screen, George's camera deconstructs the visual normativity of the generic documentary and the linear, rigid narratives expected of asylum seekers in favor of an openness of relations, dispensing altogether with the idea of "otherness" and moving, together, toward a notion Esposito calls the impersonal. Informed by the work of Donna Haraway and Simone Weil, the impersonal deconstructs the legal fiction of the "human person" invoked by the Universal Declaration of Human Rights, on its recto a document of civilization and on the verso a document of barbarism, and which, in any case, grows dustier with each year and each massacre that goes unnoticed and unpunished. The impersonal represents a counter-*measure*, one that blocks the *dispositif* of the person and its juridical division of the human. As Timothy Campbell writes, "in the move toward an impersonal perspective, justice is reached when one no longer erects borders but grows 'feelers' instead for all kinds of life."[55] The impersonal is not a form of division but a form of "relationality to other forms not limited to the person—be they plants, bacteria, viruses, or animals." Put differently, the impersonal "names an openness to relationality with forms not limited to the person."[56] In a particularly disquieting sequence in *May They Rest in Revolt*, one can find a viscerally persuasive illustration of the impersonal that the men in George's film all but explicitly describe as a counter-*dispositif*. Two men stand together, shot from a somewhat low, almost submissive angle. The older man uses a razor blade to methodically etch cuts into his fingertips. It is hard to watch. The camera cuts to another low-angle shot, this time of a young Eritrean man named Temesghen. He leans into the lens and says, "Survive. You have to survive."[57] He holds out his own hand and proclaims, "This is a virus. HIV virus, you know? This is [a] virus, in Europe," then looks away in disdain. As Debarati Sanyal insightfully notes, Temesghen's gesture and designation of his hands mirrors "contemporary rhetoric on the migrant as a figurative and literal contagion."[58] The older man explains that in Europe, there are "systems for [the] circularization of fingerprints in order to know how the man will arrive and when he will go. The Europeans have developed their techniques and we have our techniques to hide our fingerprints." Following this thoroughly Foucauldian assertion, Temesghen adds, "If it was possible to cut this [hand] and throw it and bring another hand, I would [do] that. But it is not possible. I'm just burning my hand. I don't know what happens to my hand. They are making us slaves, you know? Slaves of their own country, by these fingerprints. They destroy our lives. We can't go. We can't [pause] change our lives" (figure C.17). When Temesghen pauses to look away, the film goes into slow motion, emphasizing the stasis and immobility that prevents him and his friends from changing their lives.

In another sequence on the outskirts of Calais, two other men lean over an open fire on a length of railroad track, which the camera films at ground level. Planks from an old pallet burn next to pieces of scrap metal. No faces are shown in the sequence; the only close-ups

Figure C.17. The defaced fingerprints of a migrant living at the Jungle refugee camp in Calais. *Source:* Sylvain George, dir., *May They Rest in Revolt (Figures of War)* (2010; Potemkine Films, 2016), DVD, 576p.

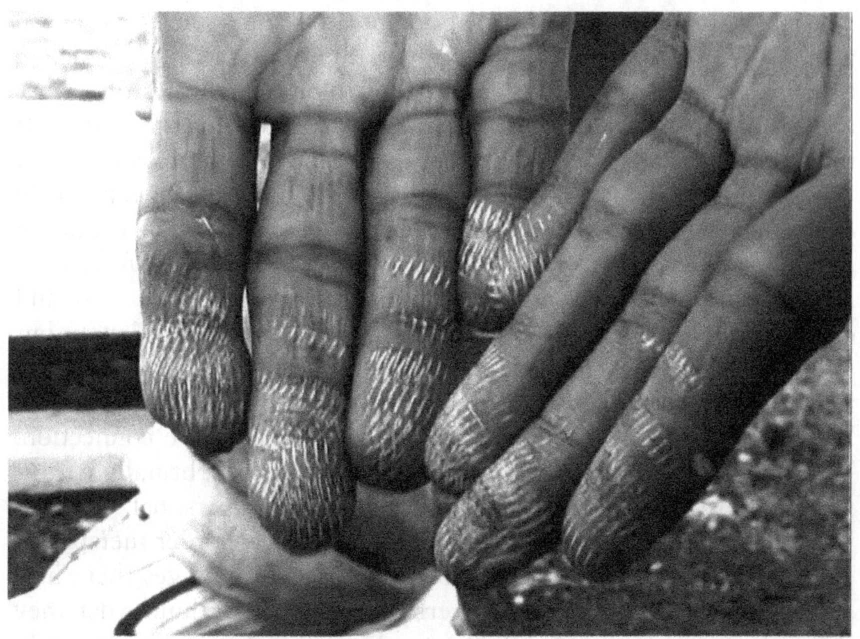

are of their hands. One man pulls something out of the fire: a thick steel wire of some kind wrapped around a screw like bait on a fishing line. When it is hot enough, the camera closes in tight as the man deftly, quickly taps his fingertips against the searing hot screw. "I say this is our tradition. Because white men did it to our great grandfathers [laughter]. Now, we are not going to wait [for] somebody to pain [hurt] ourselves. We will pain ourselves," the man says, referring, Sanyal writes, to the past branding of slaves—recalling Temesghen's earlier words—emphasizing that this reference to slavery is "not symbolic, but utterly material," as an extra dose of biometric regulations mark their bodies.[59] To elude capture by the immigration police—again, unsettling indexes of white "slave catchers"—it becomes necessary to "brand" their own bodies. With his face offscreen, he holds out his hands; his fingers have neat rows of white burn marks from the screw. "We are suffering," he says, adding, "Anyway, it shall stop one day. For I believe one day Africa shall become Europe and Europe will become Africa." "These are our prayers," another man adds. They laugh. "Yes, these are our prayers. One day, we shall see Europeans migrating to Africa to go and look for a job."[60] As Sanyal again astutely notes, this sequence "visually recalls Benjamin's dialectical image," illustrating the collision of "global memories of slavery and colonialism" with "the present of postcolonial migration."[61] It might also be added that it presents a (messianic) future not just of "transnational liberation," but a radical upturning of the current world order, not just a decentering of Europe's global position (acquired through colonial extraction), but a complete reversal of fortune, a tragic *anagnorisis* whereby white Europeans are forced by war and other circumstances to seek new lives in Africa. The men laugh, but it invites the viewer (in particular white, Western viewers) to close the distance between oneself and the real people on the screen, to lower the border between spectatorship and imaginative connection. The stateless men's destruction of their fingertips is a brutally corporeal demonstration of Esposito's *dispositif* of the impersonal, one that wrenches the philosopher's conceptual boundaries, border metaphors, and figures of the self out of their abstraction and plunges them into actuality. By scorching their fingertips, the men continue what they themselves call a tradition, which is no less than what Benjamin would call a tradition of the oppressed—not an unbroken, conserving tradition, but a dialectical one in which the past is visibly marked by the present. Crucially, this tradition separates them from their biometric capture by a state that refuses to recognize them as human persons in precisely the sense inhered by the legal discourse of human rights. By de-personalizing themselves from the state, they are not only taking extreme precautions to avoid being stuck—or sent back to—the first EU country they entered according to the Dublin regulation; they are also defiantly writing their statelessness on their bodies, making visible their audacious de-personalization by the European nation-state. They are also, moreover, attempting to create new indices for new selves so that they might retain control of their own fate and apply for asylum again, maybe in another country, "like a new person."[62] As a counter-*dispositif*, the scarred fingertips of the refugee thoroughly expose the contradictions of the logic of the person. While the latter, embodied by postwar, post-nuclear human rights, nobly claims to "reconstitute the broken link between human being and citizen, spirit and body, right and life," recent rights declarations have patently failed to prevent their gross violation. According to Esposito, this failure is the result of the category of the person itself, which "produces and even enlarges . . . the gaping hole between rights and humanity."[63] The current juridical system of rights, designed to aid the millions of displaced people after World War II, produces statelessness; for, as Esposito observes, "it isn't possible to personalize someone without depersonalizing or reifying others. . . . Silhouetted against the moving backdrop of the person looms the inert figure of the thing."[64]

The defacement of fingerprints is thus a multivalent, highly political act. It operates outside of and against the juridical realm and invites one to consider the famous Bazinian relation between the real, objective world and the world of the photographic image. While the men in *May They Rest in Revolt* reject the use of their most singular physical attribute, their fingerprints, they clearly consent to be recorded by George's camera. In this film, young, stateless men like Temesghen grasp their own "biopower from below." This is, in a sense, quite literal, given the many low, almost reverent camera angles throughout the film. It is worth recalling again for a moment Muybridge's pre-cinematic picture embedded in *Nope*, a very different film but one that shares George's devotion to animacy and the subversion of the coarse, diffuse spectacle that pervades contemporary life and biopolitical experience. In this film, George's camera reasserts the origins of cinema and intimates the medium's most redemptive future: creating life-forms that defy cinema's institutional vocation by extending the borders they temporarily inscribe, and admonishing that natural and human histories should be rewritten together.

Notes

Introduction

1. Giorgio Agamben, *Homo Sacer: Sovereign Power and Bare Life*, trans. Daniel Heller-Roazen (Stanford University Press, 1998), 85.

2. Eric Hynes, "Interview: Sergei Loznitsa," *Film Comment*, May 16, 2018, www.filmcomment.com/blog/cannes-interview-sergei-loznitsa-donbass.

3. Kyle Chayka, "Watching the World's 'First TikTok War,'" *New Yorker*, March 3, 2022, www.newyorker.com/culture/infinite-scroll/watching-the-worlds-first-tiktok-war.

4. Caryn James, "Donbass: The Ukrainian Satire That's Too Real," *BBC*, April 7, 2022, www.bbc.com/culture/article/20220401-donbass-the-ukrainian-satire-thats-too-real; Shaun Walker, "Donbass: True Lies from the Ukrainian Frontline," *The Guardian*, April 16, 2019, www.theguardian.com/film/2019/apr/16/donbass-true-lies-from-the-ukrainian-frontline; A.O. Scott, "'Donbass' Review: War in Ukraine, the Prequel," *New York Times*, April 7, 2022, www.nytimes.com/2022/04/07/movies/donbass-review.html.

5. See Henrik Gustafsson and Asbjørn Grønstad, eds., *Cinema and Agamben: Ethics, Biopolitics and the Moving Image* (Bloomsbury, 2014); and Alessandro Canade, ed., "Opening Horizons over What is Denied: A Conversation with Roberto Esposito," in *Conversations on Cinema* (Pellegrini Editore, 2013), n.p., Kindle edition. For the original Italian interview, see "Aprire un orizzonte su ciò che è negato: conversazione con Roberto Esposito," in "Bíos," ed. Roberto de Gaetano, Daniele Dottorini, and Bruno Roberti, special issue, Fata Morgana, no. 0 (2006): 7–23.

6. Maria Muhle, "Imitation of Life: Biopolitics and the Cinematographic Image," *Fillip*, no. 17 (Fall 2012), www.fillip.ca/content/imitation-of-life-biopolitics-and-the-cinematographic-image; Nitzan Lebovic, "The Biopolitical Film (A Nietzschean Paradigm)," *Postmodern Culture* 23, no. 1 (2012), www.pomoculture.org/2015/07/07/the-biopolitical-film-a-nietzschean-paradigm;

Elena del Río, "Biopolitical Violence and Affective Force: Michael Haneke's *Code Unknown*," in *Post-Cinema: Theorizing 21st-Century Film*, ed. Shane Denson and Julia Leyda (REFRAME Books, 2016), 538–668, reframe.sussex.ac.uk/post-cinema/4-5-del-rio/. See also del Río's book *The Grace of Destruction: A Vital Ethology of Extreme Cinemas* (Bloomsbury, 2016).

7. See Luca Barattoni, *Italian Post-Neorealist Cinema* (Edinburgh University Press, 2012). The fact that Italian theorists of biopolitics outnumber their counterparts elsewhere in the world is well acknowledged. Esposito offers a series of compelling and interlinked reasons for this: Italy is "a country on the frontier . . . between Europe and Mediterranean, and between North and South . . . Italy is traversed but also in a sense constituted by this fracture . . . perhaps the sensibility to a theme such as biopolitics may be linked to this liminal condition of the border." Esposito further links the Italian affinity for biopolitics to a more longstanding intellectual tradition that "has always been eminently concerned with the political . . . from Machiavelli to Vico, to Croce, and to Gramsci." It is necessary, however, to acknowledge, as Esposito does, that Italian thinkers do not constitute the whole of biopolitical theory, but form part of a much more transnational tradition of contemporary biopolitical thought that includes, or has cross-reference points with, the work of Donna Harraway, Agnes Heller, and Achille Mbembe, among others. Roberto Esposito, "Interview," interview by Timothy C. Campbell, trans. Anna Paparcone, *Diacritics* 36, no. 2 (Summer 2006): 49–50.

8. It must be noted that Foucault did not originate the term. For a more comprehensive history of the term, see Roberto Esposito, *Bíos: Biopolitics and Philosophy* (University of Minnesota Press, 2008), especially chapter 1. However, given that Foucault's work introduced biopolitics to a much wider scholarly audience and his work remains the foundation for discussions about biopolitics, for the purposes of this study, Foucault is named as the facilitator of this concept's introduction to philosophy and critical theory.

9. Indeed, as Thomas Lemke notes, Foucault is inconsistent in his use of the term, which "constantly shifts meaning in his texts." See Thomas Lemke, *Biopolitics: An Advanced Introduction*, trans. Eric Frederick Trump (New York University Press), 33. For Foucault's periodization of biopolitics, see Michel Foucault, *The Birth of Biopolitics: Lectures at the Collège de France 1978–79*, trans. Graham Burchell (Palgrave, 2008), 317.

10. Lemke, *Biopolitics*, 33.

11. Although Agamben discusses Jean-Martin Charcot, Gilles de la Tourette, and Salpêtrière in his essay on cinema, "Notes on Gesture," he does not explicitly discuss these photographs. See Georges Didi-Huberman, *Invention of Hysteria: Charcot and the Photographic Iconography of the Salpêtrière*, trans. Alisa Hartz (MIT Press, 2003).

12. "Wonderful Shell Shock Recovery," *British Pathé*, 1914–1918, video, 2:16, www.britishpathe.com/asset/77601. See also Ramsay Burt's excellent video essay on Agamben's *Means Without End*, "Agamben, Dance, Gesture," *Ramsay Burt*, January 5, 2017, video, 34:07, www.youtube.com/watch?v=NAesOjEKm9M.

13. Michel Foucault, *History of Sexuality: Volume 1: An Introduction*, trans. Robert Hurley (Pantheon, 1978), 143.

14. Timothy C. Campbell, *Improper Life: Technology and Biopolitics from Heidegger to Agamben* (University of Minnesota Press, 2011), 51. Foucault's closing question in this text is as follows: "How can one both make a biopower function and exercise the rights of war, the rights of murder and the function of death, without becoming racist? That was the problem and that, I think, is still the problem." See Michel Foucault, *"Society Must Be Defended": Lectures at the Collège de France, 1975–76*, trans. David Macey, ed. Mauro Bertani and Alessandro Fontana (Picador, 2003), 236.

15. Agamben, *Homo Sacer*, 4.

16. James Gordon Finlayson offers an excellent critique of Agamben's reading of Aristotle and the concept of bare life that it provokes. See Finlayson, "'Bare Life' and Politics in Agamben's Reading of Aristotle," *Review of Politics* 72, no. 1 (Winter 2010): 97–126.

17. Agamben, *Homo Sacer*, 1–2.

18. Thus contextualized, Aristotle's account of *bíos* and *zoē* invites crucial materialist and feminist perspectives on biopolitics, but Agamben unfortunately does not meaningfully develop his argument along these lines. For a thoughtful and relevant discussion of these elements, see Penelope Deutscher, *Foucault's Futures: A Critique of Reproductive Reason* (Columbia University Press, 2017).

19. Agamben, *Homo Sacer*, 6.

20. Agamben, *Homo Sacer*, 4.

21. Ewa Plonowska Ziarek, "Bare Life," in *Impasses of the Post Global: Theory in the Era of Climate Change*, vol. 2, ed. Henry Sussman (Open Humanities Press, 2012), 195. Italics mine.

22. Emrah Karakilic, "Acting Up with Hardt and Negri: Capitalism in the Biopolitical Context," *M@n@gement* 22, no. 3 (2019), 504.

23. Timothy Campbell, "'Enough of a Self': Esposito's Impersonal Biopolitics," *Law, Culture and the Humanities* 8, no. 1 (2012), 45.

24. Vappu Helmisaari, "Fear, the Sovereign, and Authority: Roberto Esposito and the Escape from the Hobbesian State," in *Debating Biopolitics: New Perspectives on the Government of Life*, ed. Marco Piasentier and Sara Raimondi (Edward Elgar, 2022), 46.

25. Chiara Bottici, "Rethinking the Biopolitical Turn: From the Thanatopolitical to the Geneapolitical Paradigm," *Graduate Faculty Philosophy Journal*

36, no. 1 (2015): 175–97; Laurette T. Liesen and Mary Barbara Walsh, "The Competing Meanings of 'Biopolitics' in Political Science: Biological and Postmodern Approaches to Politics," *Politics and the Life Sciences* 31, no. 1/2 (Spring/Fall 2012): 2–15; Google Books Ngram Viewer, "Biopolitics," books.google.com/ngrams/graph?content=biopolitics&year_start=1950&-year_end=2022&corpus=en&smoothing=3.

26. A schematic timeline of the biopolitical turn can be observed as follows: Giorgio Agamben's significant text *Homo Sacer* (1995) is translated into English in the late 1990s, followed by *State of Exception* in 2003, the same year Achille Mbembe publishes his influential article "Necropolitics," which becomes the basis for a full-length book, *Necropolitics*, published in 2016 and translated to English in 2019. See *Necropolitics*, trans. Steve Corcoran (Duke University Press, 2019). The early 2000s also saw the publication of some of Esposito's most crucial works, *Immunitas: Protezione e negazione della vita* (2002) and *Bíos: Biopolitica e filosofia* (2004), which reached the English-speaking academy in translation as *Immunitas: The Protection and Negation of Life* and *Bíos: Biopolitics and Philosophy* in 2011 and 2008, respectively. Michael Hardt and Antonio Negri have also explored biopolitics, presenting "postmodern biopolitics" in a number of publications throughout the early 2000s.

27. This figure comes from Stephanie Savell, "How Death Outlives War: The Reverberating Impact of the Post-9/11 Wars on Human Health" (Watson Institute for International and Public Affairs, Brown University, 2023), 39, watson.brown.edu/costsofwar/files/cow/imce/papers/2023/Indirect%20 Deaths.pdf. See also Giorgio Agamben, *The State of Exception* (University of Chicago Press, 2005).

28. Jasbir K. Puar, "Homonationalism as Assemblage: Viral Travels, Affective Sexualities," *Jindal Global Law Review* 4, no. 1 (November 2013), 37. See also Puar's *Terrorist Assemblages* (Duke University Press, 2007).

29. Timothy C. Campbell and Adam Sitze, "Introduction," in *Biopolitics: A Reader*, ed. Campbell and Sitze (Duke University Press, 2013), 9. My italics.

30. Benjamin, who was critically engaged with (and categorically opposed to) the ideas of Carl Schmitt, uses the phrase "mere life" in his famous essay "Critique of Violence," a formulation that has informed Agamben's own *nuda vita*, or "bare life." See Boštjan Nedoh, "Biopolitics Before Foucault: On Benjamin's Critique of Bare Life and Agamben's Theological Genealogy of the 'Apparatus,'" in *The Routledge Handbook of Biopolitics*, ed. Sergei Prozorov and Simona Rentea (Routledge, 2017), 66–78.

31. Catherine Mills, *Biopolitics* (Routledge, 2018), 81.

32. This capacity is similar to allegory—which literally "speaks otherwise"—but is more explicitly political and, in the Deleuzian sense, virtual. This distinction is made for two reasons: First, biopolitics is not transcendent,

it is not "sovereign," but rather it is a current governmentality that shapes experience; its becoming-otherwise would entail a reformation of the power relations that structure experience; second, biopolitics informs, but is not identical to, biopolitical allegories. It is striking to note that Dimitris Papanikolaou's 2021 study *Greek Weird Wave* is the most effective, if not the first, elaboration of the relationship between biopolitics, cinema, and allegory, suggesting a more intimate and compelling connection between the concerns and theoretical tropes of both cinema and biopolitics, which I will develop shortly. See Dimitris Papanikolaou, *Greek Weird Wave: A Cinema of Biopolitics* (Edinburgh University Press, 2021).

33. Adrian Ivakhiv, "The Art of Morphogenesis: Cinema In and Beyond the Capitalocene," in *Post-Cinema: Theorizing 21st-Century Film*, eds. Shane Denson and Julia Leyder (REFRAME Books, 2016), reframe.sussex.ac.uk/post-cinema/6-1-ivakhiv/.

34. Andre Bazin, "The Ontology of the Photographic Image," in *What Is Cinema?*, vol. 1, ed. and trans. Hugh Gray (University of California Press, 2005 [1965]), 9.

35. "If the history of the plastic arts is less a matter of their aesthetic than of their psychology then it will be seen to be essentially the story of resemblance, or, if you will, of realism." Bazin, 10.

36. Bazin, 9–10. My italics.

37. Tom Gunning, "Embarrassing Evidence: The Detective Camera and the Documentary Impulse," in *Collecting Visible Evidence*, ed. Jane Gaines and Michael Renov (University of Minnesota Press, 1999), 46–64.

38. Alessandro Canade, ed., "Opening Horizons Over What Is Denied: A Conversation with Roberto Esposito," in *Conversations on Cinema*. For the original Italian interview, see "Aprire un orizzonte su ciò che è negato: conversazione con Roberto Esposito," in "Bíos," ed. Roberto de Gaetano et al., special issue, *Fata Morgana*, no. 0 (2006): 7–23.

39. Edgar Morin, *The Cinema, or, The Imaginary Man*, trans. Lorraine Mortimer (University of Minnesota Press, 2005), 53.

40. Canade, "Opening Horizons Over What Is Denied."

41. Francesco Casetti, *L'occhio del Novecento: Cinema, esperienza, modernità* (Bompiani, 2005), 15–16.

42. Noël Burch, *Life to Those Shadows* (University of California Press, 1990), 40. Although Burch does not engage directly with the works of Foucault, both have a similar interest in the way Charles Baudelaire problematized the possibility of an authentic self-fashioning. For Foucault, Baudelaire finally establishes modernity as a particular stance toward history as differentiation and opts for a critique that does not define the transcendental, that is the conditions of possibility, but that investigates the conditions of reality, the

historical a priori leading to the microphysical events that have subjected us in a determined way; for Burch, the French poet is the counterpart of the "Frankensteinian" mode of representation, a metaphysical reconstruction of perceived lacks, thanks to his opposition to naturalist regimes of reproduction and his ironic elaboration of the self.

43. One may even go back to Jeremy Bentham and find in the search for maximum proximity and internalized contact via projected reciprocity, diffused sound, and the embryonic form of an audiovisual technology, as well as the prefiguration of individual segregations isolated in a multitude under a gaze that is always motivated.

44. Lorenzo Fabbri, *Cinema Is the Strongest Weapon: Race-Making and Resistance in Fascist Italy* (University of Minnesota Press, 2023), 110. Fabbri's book is an exceptional work study of Italian Fascist cinema and an important reassessment of neorealism. Fabbri writes of the normalizing, enforcing mode of realist cinema under the Fascist regime, which often used techniques normally associated with the politics of post-war Italian neorealism to reaffirm the status quo rather than critique power relations or take flight from restrictive roles and norms.

45. Fabbri, *Cinema Is the Strongest Weapon*, 233.

46. Roland Vegso and Marco Abel, "Biopolitical Education: *The Edukators* and the Politics of the Immanent Outside," *Studies in 20th & 21st Century Literature* 40, no. 2 (2016), 1.

47. Vegso and Abel, "Biopolitical Education," 3.

48. Carlos Natalio, "Cinema, Biopolitics and 'Cinematic Operative Model,'" *La Deleuziana—Online Journal of Philosophy*, vol. 1 (2015), 118.

49. Muhle, "Imitation of Life." In this essay Muhle also draws a historical excursus into the mechanical image, from Vertov (cinema as the only medium that can embrace life as totality) to Bazin (the photographic image that unembalms time and delivers duration) to Barthes (*punctum* as the out-of-field projection of a private, sudden interpellation.) The notion of *punctum* seems particularly appropriate to define the power of the mental image to transcend the suspension and control of subjectivity that cinema operates.

50. Hans Belting, *An Anthropology of Images: Picture, Medium, Body*, trans. Thomas Dunlap (Princeton University Press, 2011), 11.

51. William Max Nelson, *Enlightenment Biopolitics: A History of Race, Eugenics, and the Making of Citizens* (University of Chicago Press, 2024), 1.

52. Ewa Mazierska, "World Cinema, Third Cinema," *Studies in World Cinema* 1, no. 1 (2020), 16.

53. Stephanie Dennison and Song Hwee Lim, eds., "Introduction," in *Remapping World Cinema: Identity, Culture and Politics in Film* (Wallflower Press, 2006), 6.

54. Daniela Berghahn, "'The Past Is a Foreign Country': Exoticism and Nostalgia in Contemporary Transnational Cinema," *Transnational Screens* 10, no. 1 (2019): 35.

55. In their seminal *Unthinking Eurocentrism: Multiculturalism and the Media* (Routledge, 2014 [1994]).

56. Dennison and Lim, "Introduction," in *Remapping World Cinema*, 6.

57. Berghahn, "'The Past Is a Foreign Country,'" 35.

58. Shohat and Stam, *Unthinking Eurocentrism*, 396.

59. Lucía Nagib, "Towards a Positive Definition of World Cinema," in Dennison and Lim, *Remapping World Cinema*, 26.

60. Nagib, 26.

61. Nagib, 27–28.

62. Seung-hoon Jeong, "World Cinema in a Global Frame," *Studies in World Cinema* 1 (2020): 29. Jeong expands on this discussion in the introduction to his *Biopolitical Ethics in Global Cinema* (Oxford University Press, 2023).

63. Nagib, "Towards a Positive Definition of World Cinema," 31.

64. Nagib, 31.

65. Lucía Nagib, *Realist Cinema as World Cinema: Non-cinema, Intermedial Passages, Total Cinema* (Amsterdam University Press, 2020), 22.

66. See Sinnerbrink's *Cinematic Ethics: Exploring Ethical Experience Through Film* (Routledge, 2015).

67. See Ewa Mazierska and Lars Kristensen, *Third Cinema, World Cinema and Marxism* (Bloomsbury, 2020).

68. Mazierska and Kristensen, 11.

69. Roberto Alemanno, *Itinerari della violenza: Il film negli anni della restaurazione (1970–1980)* (Edizioni Dedalo, 1982), 135.

70. Katarzyna Marciniak and Bruce Bennett, eds., "Introduction: Teaching Transnational Cinema: Politics and Pedagogy," in *Transnational Cinema: Politics and Pedagogy* (Routledge, 2016), 1–35. Marciniak and Bennet's is also the study in world cinema in which a reflection on the "abject" first appears before Seong-hoon Jeong's use of the category.

71. Jeong, "World Cinema in a Global Frame," 29.

72. Dominique Moïsi, *The Geopolitics of Emotion: How Cultures of Fear, Humiliation, and Hope Are Reshaping the World* (Doubleday, 2009), 17.

73. Amber M. Buck and Theo Plothe, eds., "Introduction," in *Netflix at the Nexus: Content, Practice, and Production in the Age of Streaming Television*, ed. Buck and Plothe (Peter Lang, 2019), 3–4.

74. Quoted by Ester Corvi in *Nuovo cinema web—Netflix, Hulu, Amazon: La rivoluzione va in scena* (Hoepli, 2016), 6. My translation.

75. Sarah Atkinson, *Beyond the Screen: Emerging Cinema and Engaging Audiences* (Bloomsbury, 2014), 232.

76. Adam Nayman, "'Poor Things' Cancels Itself Out," *The Ringer,* December 7, 2023, www.theringer.com/movies/2023/12/7/23991965/poor-things-movie-review-emma-stone.

77. Manuela Lazic, "Does Yorgos Lanthimos Want to Be Liked?' *The Ringer*, December 11, 2023, www.theringer.com/movies/2023/12/11/23995888/poor-things-movie-director-yorgos-lanthimos.

78. Hans Belting, "Toward an Anthropology of the Image," in *Anthropologies of Art*, ed. Mariët Westermann (Yale University Press, 2005), 51.

79. Belting, "Toward an Anthropology of the Image," 47.

80. Paola Colonello, "L'Iran e le trappole neoliberiste in educazione. Conflitti e contagi," in *Educazione e neoliberismi: Idee, critiche e pratiche per una comune umanità*, ed. Emanuela Mancino and Marialisa Rizzo (Progedit, 2022), 141. My modified translation.

81. Paola Colonello, "L'Iran e le trappole neoliberiste in educazione," 141.

Chapter 1

1. Seung-hoon Jeong, *Biopolitical Ethics in Global Cinema* (Oxford University Press, 2023).

2. Pasi Väliaho, *Biopolitical Screens: Image, Power, and the Neoliberal Brain* (MIT Press, 2014).

3. Ivelise Perniola, "Cinema e biopolitica: Iconoclastia, eufemismo e falsa coscienza umanitaria," *Bianco e nero* 565 (2009), 76.

4. Rey Chow, *Sentimental Fabulations, Contemporary Chinese Films: Attachment in the Age of Global Visibility* (Columbia University Press, 2007), 21.

5. Chow, *Sentimental Fabulations*, 138.

6. Sheldon H. Lu, *Chinese Modernity and Global Biopolitics: Studies in Literal and Visual Culture* (University of Hawaiʻi Press, 2007), 4.

7. Lu, *Chinese Modernity*, 154.

8. Darren Byler, "'Disposable' Bodies on Screen in Xu Xin's *Karamay*: Biopolitics, Affect, and Ritual in Chinese Central Asia," in *Transnational Chinese Cinema: Corporeality, Desire, and the Ethics of Failure*, ed. Brian Bergen-Aurand, Mary Mazzilli, and Hee Wai-Siam (Bridge21, 2014), 159–80.

9. Byler, "'Disposable' Bodies,'" 177.

10. Michael J. Blouin, *Magical Thinking, Fantastic Film, and the Illusions of Neoliberalism* (Palgrave Macmillan, 2016), 173. See especially "Biopolitics and Movies About Magic," 170–204.

11. Blouin, 186.

12. Blouin, 181.

13. Blouin, 191.

14. Blouin, 196.

15. Roberto Esposito (with Antonio Negri and Salvatore Veca), "Dialogo su impero e democrazia," *Micromega* 5 (2001), 122–23. My translation.

16. Papanikolaou, *Greek Weird Wave: A Cinema of Biopolitics* (Edinburgh University Press, 2021), 46–47.

17. Papanikolaou, 227.

18. Papanikolaou, 162.

19. Papanikolaou, 166.

20. Garrett Stewart, "Counterfactual, Potential, Virtual," in *Cinema and Agamben*, ed. Henrik Gustafsson and Asbjørn Grønstadt (Bloomsbury, 2014), 176.

21. Stewart, 181.

22. Stewart, 186.

23. Kevin Wynter, "The Exorbitant Mirror: Violence, Disavowal, and the Logic of Terror in Michael Haneke's *Das weiße Band*," *JCMS: Journal of Cinema and Media Studies* 61, no. 1 (Fall 2021): 129–39.

24. Wynter, 135.

25. Seung-hoon Jeong, "Sovereign Agents of Mythical and (Pseudo-) Divine Violence: Walter Benjamin and Global Biopolitical Cinema," *Philosophical Journal of Conflict and Violence* 4 no. 2 (2020): 80–98.

26. Jeong, "Sovereign Agents," 85.

27. Jeong, "Sovereign Agents," 91.

28. Jeong, "Sovereign Agents," 94.

29. Jeong, "Sovereign Agents," 93.

30. Jeong, "Sovereign Agents," 97.

31. Jeong, "Sovereign Agents," 97.

32. Elena del Río, "Biopolitical Violence and Affective Force: Michael Haneke's *Code Unknown*," in *Post-Cinema: Theorizing 21st-Century Film*, ed. Shane Denson and Julia Leyder (REFRAME Books, 2016), reframe.sussex. ac.uk/post-cinema/4-5-del-rio/, 538–68; Elena del Río, "Bare Life," in *The Grace of Destruction: A Vital Ethology of Extreme Cinemas* (Bloomsbury, 2016), 77–116.

33. del Río, "Biopolitical Violence," 538–68; "Bare Life," 77–116. See also Steven Shaviro, *Post-Cinematic Affect* (Verso, 2010).

34. del Río, *Grace of Destruction*, 99.

35. del Río, *Grace of Destruction*, 103.

36. del Río, *Grace of Destruction*, 104.

37. del Río, *Grace of Destruction*, 107.

38. "Lungi dal rappresentare il braccio panoptico della società, che sorveglia e punisce, sovrintende e previene, l'insieme delle videocamere a circuito chiuso si offre come un'iconosfera dentro la quale l'istituzione assiste compiaciuta e imperturbabile al percorso di imbarbarimento." See Marco Dalla Gassa, "Bong Joon-ho, o dell'efferatezza inesorabile," in *Il cinema del*

nuovo millennio: Geografie, forme, autori, ed. Alessia Cervini (Carocci, 2020), 278. My translation.

39. Carla Marcantonio, "Biopolitical Embodiments: *Talk to Her* and *The Skin I Live In*," in *Global Melodrama: Nation, Body, and History in Contemporary Film* (Palgrave Macmillan, 2015), 25–52.

40. Marcantonio, 27.

41. Robert A. Rushing, *Descended from Hercules: Biopolitics and the Muscled Male Body on Screen* (Indiana University Press, 2016). See especially pp. 136–82.

42. Rushing, 157.

43. Rushing, 175.

44. Rushing, 165.

45. Rushing, 157, 164.

46. Hilary Neroni, *The Subject of Torture: Psychoanalysis and Biopolitics in Television and Film* (Columbia University Press, 2015).

47. Neroni, 24.

48. Neroni, 27.

49. Neroni, 33.

50. Neroni, 35.

51. Neroni, 35.

52. Neroni, 41.

53. Neroni, 41.

54. Neroni, 159.

55. Timothy C. Campbell, *The Techne of Giving: Cinema and the Generous Form of Life* (Fordham University Press, 2017), 164. For Campbell, the "grip" is a gesture that constitutes "an ethic of how we hold and how we let go," and that represents "forms of holding (and letting go) to potential forms of life that could offer a response to contemporary biopower," vii–viii.

56. According to Esposito, one of the most relevant qualities of the "Italian way" to philosophy is, due to the lack of a clearly established national identity, its constant investigation of the interconnectedness among life, history, and politics.

57. Campbell, *Techne of Giving*, 42.

58. Campbell, *Techne of Giving*, 71.

59. Campbell, *Techne of Giving*, 98.

60. Campbell, *Techne of Giving*, 117.

61. Campbell, *Techne of Giving*, 127.

62. Campbell, *Techne of Giving*, 157.

63. Muhle, "Imitation of Life."

64. A thorough recapitulation of the debate can be found in Lucía Nagib, "Towards a Positive Definition of World Cinema," in *Remapping World Cinema: Identity, Culture and Politics in Film*, ed. Stephanie Dennison and Song Hwee Lim (Wallflower Press, 2006), 30–37.

65. Andreas Gailus, *Forms of Life: Aesthetics and Biopolitics in German Culture* (Cornell University Press, 2020), 13. Gailus elects literature as the most potent medium for the revelation of forms of life and their interconnections, whereby "its own plenitude of expression constantly exceeds the forms of life it depicts," 14.

66. Robert Sinnerbrink, *Cinematic Ethics: Exploring Ethical Experience through Film* (Routledge, 2016).

67. Lucía Nagib, *Realist Cinema as World Cinema: Non-cinema, Intermedial Passages, Total Cinema* (Amsterdam University Press, 2020), 16.

68. Papanikolaou, *Greek Weird Wave*, 231. See especially "Introduction" (1–22) and "Epilogue" (227–33).

69. Papanikolaou, 113.

70. Papanikolaou, xii.

71. Nagib, *Realist Cinema as World Cinema*, 15.

72. "Patriotic films today are also uncontrollably taking up the form of aesthetic fascination with violence and death as such. The only thought that imposes on patriots today is that the best thing you can do for the country is to sacrifice your life for its sake." *UKRINFORM*, "Why Russian Cinema Can't Exist Without Propaganda and Manipulations," July 7, 2021, web.archive. org/web/20211108141635/https://www.ukrinform.net/rubric-society/3344917- why-russian-cinema-cant-exist-without-propaganda-and-manipulations.html. The Russian deployment of a productive thanatopolitics opens a new horizon that goes beyond the mere, as S.J. Murray puts it, "striking at the heart of neo-liberal capital and technologies"; "Thanatopolitics," in *Bloomsbury Handbook to Literary and Cultural Theory*, ed. J.R. Di Leo (Bloomsbury, 2018), 718. The many instances in which Kremlin mouthpieces such as Vladimir Solovyov affirmed that "life is vastly overrated" are also worth mentioning.

73. The appearance of a grotesquely subdued Stalin in Brius and Plyaskin's film points strategically to the relevance of the only one among former Soviet leaders whose symbolic radiance can by conveniently appropriated and repurposed by the Putin's regime, because of his managerial qualities in a strictly biopolitical sense and his putting an end to Lenin's lax position regarding the right to self-determination of Soviet satellite states, most notably Ukraine.

74. "Notably in *Stalingrad*, as in the other war films discussed here, virtually everyone dies, adding an element of martyrdom and quasi-religious reverence for the sacrifice." Justin Wilmes, "Empire Reloaded: Sacred Power in a Postmodern Era," in *Cinemasaurus: Russian Film in Contemporary Context*, ed. Nancy Condee, Alexander Prokhorov, and Elena Prokhorova (Academic Studies Press), 52.

75. As detailed by Jyotsna Kapur in "The Underdevelopment of Development: Neoliberalism and the Crisis of Bourgeois Individualism," in

Neoliberalism and Global Cinema: Capital, Culture, and Marxist Critique, edited by Kapur and Keith B. Wagner, 197–216 (Routledge, 2011).

76. Pablo Gómez-Muñoz touches on the biopolitical aspects of *Wall-E* in his book but focuses primarily on *2012* and *Snowpiercer*. See Gómez-Muñoz, *Science Fiction Cinema in the Twenty-First Century: Transnational Futures, Cosmopolitan Concerns* (Routledge, 2023), 78–79.

77. See for example the strike of teachers in West Virginia, with one of the points of contention being the substitution of healthcare insurance policies with Apple Watches monitoring physical exercise and lifestyle. Adam Gaffney, "The West Virginia Teachers' Strike Is Over. But the Fight for Healthcare Isn't," *The Guardian*, March 7, 2018 www.theguardian.com/commentisfree/2018/mar/07/west-virginia-teachers-strike-healthcare.

78. Stephen M. Hart, *A Companion to Latin American Film* (Tamesis, 2004), 65.

79. Giorgio Agamben, *The Use of Bodies*, trans. Adam Kotsko (Stanford University Press, 2016), 104.

80. Benjamin Morgan, "Undoing Legal Violence: Walter Benjamin's and Giorgio Agamben's Aesthetics of Pure Means," *Journal of Law and Society* 34, no. 1 (2007): 47.

81. John Lechte and Saul Newman, *Agamben and the Politics of Human Rights: Statelessness, Images, Violence* (Edinburgh University Press), 2013, vii.

82. Agamben, *The Use of Bodies*, 209.

83. I use "forms of life" to designate beings and ecologies other than the human. This is a more general term than Agamben's "form-of-life," which means "a life that can never be separated from its form, a life in which it is never possible to isolate something such as naked life." As is likely already evident, and as I suggest in the conclusion, the former, unhyphenated term is linked to Agamben's for specific connotation. See Agamben, *Means Without End: Notes on Politics*, trans. Vincenzo Binetti and Cesare Casarino (University of Minnesota Press, 2000), 3–4.

84. Mel Y. Chen, *Animacies: Biopolitics, Racial Mattering, and Queer Affect* (Duke University Press, 2012), 3.

85. Cornelius Borck, "Animism in the Sciences Then and Now," *e-flux*, no. 37 (July 2012), www.e-flux.com/journal/36/61266/animism-in-the-sciences-then-and-now. This essay appears in the journal's special issue on animism.

86. Tzu-I Chung, "Ecological Indigeneity in Global Indigenous Discourse," in *Aspects of Transnational and Indigenous Cultures*, ed. Clara Shu-Chun Chang and Hsinya Huang (Cambridge Scholars Publishing, 2014), 141.

87. Federico Luisetti, "Decolonizing the State of Nature: Notes on Political Animism," in *Critical Posthumanism and Planetary Futures*, ed. Debashish Banerji and Markarand R. Paranjape, 215–24 (Springer India, 2016), 218. Luisetti's full quote, which offers a more nuanced account of this approach, is as follows: "I will provide some . . . resonances between decolonial politics

of knowledge and approaches that, from within the boundaries of Western philosophical discourse, question the foundations of modernity's state of nature, mobilizing the unsettling energy of archaic relations to nonhumans. . . . In my opinion, it is exclusively by acknowledging the coexistence of archaisms and technological networks, colonial divides and technosciences, that we can avoid reifying the opposition between posthumanism and postcolonialism, thus deconstructing the attempts to purify posthuman approaches into a utopian and technophiliac transhumanism and reduce postcolonial perspectives to a denunciation of subalternity and marginalization."

88. Anselm Franke, "Animism: Notes on an Exhibition," *e-flux*, no. 36 (July 2012), www.e-flux.com/journal/36/61258/animism-notes-on-an-exhibition.

89. Louise Erdrich, qtd. in Kyle Whyte, "Settler Colonialism, Ecology, and Environmental Justice," *Environment and Society* 9 (2018), 127. See also Neera M. Singh, "The Nonhuman Turn or a Re-turn to Animism? Valuing Life Along and Beyond Capital," *Dialogues in Human Geography* 12, no. 1 (March 2022): 84–89. Singh also quotes Whyte's quotation of Erdrich (p. 127).

90. Singh, 84.

91. Singh, 85.

92. Singh, 85. For more on the nonhuman turn, see Richard A. Grusin, ed., *The Nonhuman Turn* (University of Minnesota Press, 2015).

93. Singh, 85.

94. Teresa Castro, "An Animistic History of the Camera: Filmic Forms and Machinic Subjectivity," in *A History of Cinema Without Names*, ed. Diego Cavalotti, Federico Giordano, and Leonardo Quaresima (Mimesis International, 2016), 248.

95. Epstein and Barry, qtd. in Castro, "An Animistic History," 249.

96. Castro, "An Animistic History," 250.

97. Walter Benjamin, "The Task of the Translator," in *Selected Writings Volume 1: 1913–1926*, ed. Marcus Bullock and Michael W. Jennings (Harvard University Press, 2002), 255.

98. Jean Epstein, qtd. in Teresa Castro, "The Mediated Plant," *e-flux*, no. 102 (September 2019), www.e-flux.com/journal/102/283819/the-mediated-plant.

99. André Parente and Victa de Carvalho, "Cinema as *dispositif:* Between Cinema and Contemporary Art," *Cinémas* 19, no. 1 (Autumn 2008), 46.

100. Fabio Vighi, "Pasolini and Exclusion: Žižek, Agamben and the Modern Sub-proletariat," *Theory, Culture & Society* 20, no. 5 (2003), 115.

101. Allan Sekula, *Fish Story* (Richter, 1995), 32.

102. Lindsay Turner, "In the Atmosphere: The Politics of Mati Diop's *Atlantics*," *Yale Review* 108, no. 2 (2020), 191.

103. A different conceptualization of cinematic persistence is that of Italian documentarist Giuseppe Taffarel. That which Taffarel's works may lose

in effectiveness because of explicit intervention—sentimental music, insisted voiceovers, didactic fictionalizations—they recover in the spatio-temporal expansion of a certain phenomenon or event through which reality ought to be apprehended. For example, in *Monte Grappa 1944* (1966) the Resistance to Nazi-Fascism is seen as the defining juncture in the history of a people, changing lives at several temporal trajectories—the destroyed lives of the young partisans, the forever changed lives of aging parents and siblings—and in the natural realm, with the trees from which the fighters were hanged existing as outposts for memory, more vivid than younger generations that at the time of the film were, to Taffarel's torment, starting to forget. Taffarel's sentient nature understood as authentic being contrasts with the indifference of the natural environment in Alain Resnais' *Night and Fog*. More recently, reconfigurations among the living realm, the animal, and inert matter are explored in the works of Michelangelo Frammartino, especially *The Four Times* (*Le quattro volte*, 2010) and *The Hole* (*Il buco*, 2021) and in the Mexican documentaries of Tatiana Huezo, especially *The Echo* (*El eco*, 2023) in which the cycle of life is intended as communal belonging among people, animals, and atmospheric events and every individual body emerges through its intensity made of movement and sound.

104. Besides individuating with necropolitical precision the bodies that can be turned into superfluous life, Mendonça Filho also looks at the intersection of colonialism and new segregating spaces that can graduate to the Foucauldian status of disciplinarian institutions, such as the gated community of *Neighboring Sounds*.

Chapter 2

1. Roberto Esposito, "Postdemocracy and Biopolitics," *European Journal of Social Theory* 22, no. 3 (2019), 318.

2. Nico Baumbach, "Shareable Cinema: The Politics of Abbas Kiarostami," in *The Global Auteur: The Politics of Authorship in 21st Century Cinema*, ed. Seung-hoon Jeong and Jeremi Szaniawski (Bloomsbury, 2016), 271. Baumbach's chapter in this volume offers a recontextualization of Kiarostami's cinema in political terms.

3. Mathew Abbott, *Abbas Kiarostami and Film-Philosophy* (Edinburgh University Press, 2017), 58, 63.

4. Hossein Khosrowjah, *Abbas Kiarostami and Iranian National Cinema* (Bloomsbury, 2025), 128.

5. Robin Wright, "The Challenge of Iran," in *The Iran Primer: Power, Politics, and U.S. Policy*, ed. Wright (United States Institute of Peace Press, 2010), 3.

6. Navid Fozi, "Governmentality and Crises of Representation, Knowledge, and Power in the Islamic Republic of Iran," *Asian Politics & Policy* 7, no. 1 (2015), 57.

7. Melinda Cooper, "The Law of the Household," in *The Government of Life: Foucault, Biopolitics, and Neoliberalism*, ed. Vanessa Lem and Miguel Vatter (Fordham University Press, 2014), 33.

8. "La biocrazia è definita come un ordine naturale e immanente agli animali disciplinabili." Antonella Cutro, "Introduzione: Che cosa significa biopolitica?" in *Biopolitica: Storia e attualità di un concetto*, ed. Cutro (Ombre Corte, 2005), 8.

9. Barry Hindess, *Discourses of Power: From Hobbes to Foucault* (Blackwell, 1996), 115.

10. Kenneth Katzman, *The Warriors of Islam: Iran's Revolutionary Guard* (Routledge, 2019) 180.

11. Abbas Kiarostami, interview by Paul Cronin, *The Guardian*, June 16, 2005, www.theguardian.com/film/2005/jun/17/1.

12. Norma Claire Moruzzi, "Through the Looking Glass: Reflexive Cinema and Society in Post-Revolution Iran," in *Iranian Cinema in a Global Context: Policy, Politics, and Form*, ed. Peter Decherney and Blake Atwood (Routledge, 2015), 128.

13. Alain Badiou, *Badiou and His Interlocutors: Lectures, Interviews, and Responses* (Bloomsbury, 2018), 20.

14. Jean-Luc Nancy, *Abbas Kiarostami: Evidence of Film*, trans. Christine Irizarry and Verena Andermatt Conley (Yves Gevaert Éditeur, 2001); Claire Moruzzi, "Through the Looking Glass," 120.

15. Agamben qtd. in Rahel Jaeggi, *On the Critique of Forms of Life*, trans. Ciaran Cronin (Harvard University Press, 2018), 339.

16. Xan Brooks, "Jafar Panahi: Public Enemy," *The Guardian*, September 2, 2003, www.theguardian.com/film/2003/sep/02/1. Brooks confirms the details about Hossein Emadeddin, who played the film's lead role.

17. Anne Démy-Geroe, *Iranian National Cinema: The Interaction of Policy, Genre, Funding, and Reception* (Routledge, 2020), 50.

18. Jeannette Catsoulis, "Truth as a Tinderbox That Must Disappear," *New York Times*, June 13, 2014, www.nytimes.com/2014/06/13/movies/manuscripts-dont-burn-about-repression-in-iran.html.

19. Esposito, *Bíos: Biopolitics and Philosophy* (University of Minnesota Press, 2008), 36.

20. For the pre-revolutionary formation of Iran's middle class see James Allan Bill, *The Politics of Iran: Groups, Classes and Modernization* (Merrill, 1972). See especially p. 61.

21. Nico Baumbach, *Cinema/Politics/Philosophy* (Columbia University Press, 2019), 91.

22. Wendy Brown, *Politics Out of History* (Princeton University Press, 2001), 118.

23. Esposito, *Terms of the Political: Community, Immunity, Biopolitics*, trans. Rhiannon Noel Welch (Fordham University Press, 2012), 67.

24. Mohammad Rasoulof, dir., *Manuscripts Don't Burn* (2013; Kino Lorber, 2014), 01:09:53.

25. Pejman Abdolmohammadi, "The Shiite Islamic Political Theology: The Debate between Ruhullah Khomeini (d. 1989) and Mehdi Bazargan (d. 1995)," in *Islamic Political Theology*, ed. Massimo Campanini and Marco Di Donato (Lexington Books, 2021), 87.

26. Sabeen Ahmed, "From Death Penalty to Thanatopolitics," *Philosophy Today* 63, no. 2 (Spring 2019), 308.

27. Hamid Dabashi, *Close Up: Iranian Cinema, Past, Present, and Future* (Verso, 2001), 4.

28. Dabashi, 4.

29. See Nader Hashemi, "Renegotiating Iran's Post-Revolutionary Social Contract: The Green Movement and the Struggle for Democracy in the Islamic Republic," in *Beyond the Arab Spring: The Evolving Ruling Bargain in the Middle East*, ed. Mehran Kamrava, 191–222 (Oxford University Press, 2014).

30. Foucault's critical enthusiasm for the revolution was roundly criticized at the time, and the philosopher himself refused to comment further on it in any substantial way. Patrick Gamez has written an excellent and nuanced account of Foucault's engagement with the Iranian revolution and the critical responses it has garnered. See "The Place of the Iranian Revolution in the History of Truth: Foucault on Neoliberalism, Spirituality and Enlightenment," *Philosophy and Social Criticism* 45, no. 1 (2019): 96–124.

31. Foucault, "Of Other Spaces," trans. Jay Miskowiec, *Diacritics* 16, no. 1 (Spring 1986): 23.

32. Shohini Chaudhuri and Howard Finn, "The Open Image: Poetic Realism and New Iranian Cinema," *Screen* 44, no. 1 (Spring 2003), 45.

33. Hamid Naficy, *A Social History of Iranian Cinema, Volume 4: The Globalizing Era, 1984–2010* (Duke University Press, 2012), 259.

34. This valence extends to Farhadi's own diplomatic Golden Globe acceptance speech in 2012, which included the following: "When I was coming up on stage, I was thinking what I should say here. I prefer to say something about my people. They are a truly peace-loving people." From Ali Chenar, "Comment: A Celebration for 'A Separation,' " *PBS*, January 17, 2012, www.pbs.org/wgbh/pages/frontline/tehranbureau/2012/01/dispatch-a-celebration-for-a-separation.html.

35. Naficy, 259.

36. Naficy dates this as 1988, but this appears to be a typo, as the IFM's own website consistently confirms this in fact occurred in 1998. With

respect to Naficy's otherwise brilliant book, I choose to date the IFM to 1998 as per the FIFF website. See www.fajriff.com/en/festival-2021/market.

37. Naficy, 259.

38. See Naficy, 256–57, for more on the US State Department's funding of international film festivals alongside harsh sanctions and embargos against Iran, as well as the strategic approval or denial of visas. Kiarostami has been refused entry to the US and Jafar Panahi, who is currently banned from film-making in Iran, was deported as soon as he landed at JFK Airport in 2001.

39. Asghar Farhadi, interview by Tina Hassannia, in *Asghar Farhadi: Life and Cinema* (The Critical Press, 2014), Kindle edition, n.p.

40. Farhadi, interview by Hassannia.

41. Foucault, "Confession of the Flesh" (1997), interview in *Power/ Knowledge Selected Interviews and Other Writings*, ed. and trans. Colin Gordon, 194–288 (Pantheon, 1980).

42. At a cursory glance, this may appear to be an imposition of Western philosophical values onto contemporary Iranian society; however, it must be noted that Iran not only welcomed Greek philosopher refugees after Byzantine Emperor Justinian closed the Athenian academy founded by Plato; by the time of the Crusades, the work of thinkers like Aristotle, which had been forgotten in Europe, was reintroduced to the West thanks to its preservation in Arabic translation. See John W. Limbert, *Negotiating with Iran: Wrestling the Ghosts of History* (US Institute of Peace Press, 2009), 20.

43. See Angeliki Coletsou, "Visual Representations of Iran in Western Media after 9/11," *9/11 Legacies*, 911legacies.com/Visual%20Representations%20of%20Iran.htm.

44. Michel Foucault, *History of Sexuality: Volume 1: An Introduction*, trans. Robert Hurley (Pantheon, 1978 [1976]), 106–7. Italics mine. In this text, Foucault uses *dispositif d'alliance*, which Michael Hurley translates to English as "the deployment of alliance"; however, *alliance* is often used to connote marriage, as Christopher Chitty explains: "*alliance* has the meaning of a harness or connecting strap in equestrian arts, and it is a metonym for the wedding ring." Christopher Chitty, "Reassessing Foucault: Modern Sexuality and the Transition to Capitalism," *Viewpoint Magazine*, April 20, 2017, www.viewpointmag.com/2017/04/20/reassessing-foucault-modern-sexuality-and-the-transition-to-capitalism. Though there are many English translations of *dispositif* (dispositive, apparatus, deployment, device, etc.), I use the French term throughout this book.

45. Jacques Rancière, "Politics, Identification, and Subjectivization," *October* 61 (1992), 59.

46. This motto was first introduced by the title of a 1969 essay by Carol Hanisch, a member of the New York Radical Women. See "The Personal is Political," www.carolhanisch.org/CHwritings/PIhtml. Originally published in

Notes from the Second Year: Women's Liberation, ed. Shulamith Firestone and Anne Koedt (Radical Feminism, 1970).

47. Gregg Lambert, *Who's Afraid of Deleuze and Guattari?* (Continuum, 2006), 141.

48. Robert Sinnerbrink, *Cinematic Ethics: Exploring Ethical Experience Through Film* (Routledge, 2016), 67.

49. Shampa Mazumdar and Sanjoy Mazumdar, "Rethinking Public and Private Space: Religion and Women in Muslim Society," *Journal of Architectural and Planning Research* 18, no. 4 (Winter 2001), 304.

50. Nikolas Rose and Peter Miller, "Political Power Beyond the State: Problematics of Government," *British Journal of Sociology* 43, no. 2, 192.

51. Mitchell Dean, *The Signature of Power: Sovereignty, Governmentality and Biopolitics* (Sage, 2013), 97.

52. Khomeini writes, "Islam . . . is concerned with the individual even if he is alone at home; that is, it tells him what he is supposed to do, how to behave and what ethics and intellectual perceptions he should adopt. It tells him . . . how families should behave among themselves or a family towards another. All of these have rules to follow in Islam, which takes everything into consideration." From *The Position of Women from the Viewpoint of Imam Khomeini*, trans. Juliana Shaw and Behrooz Arezoo (The Institute for Compilation and Publication of Imam Khomeini's Works, 2001), 101.

53. S. Sayyid, "Khomeini and the Decolonization of the Political," in *A Critical Introduction to Khomeini*, ed. Arshin Adib-Moghaddam (Cambridge University Press, 2014), 161.

54. Hammed Shahidian, *Women in Iran: Gender Politics in the Islamic Republic* (Greenwood, 2002), 200.

55. On the representation of middle-class families see especially William Brown, "*Cease Fire*: Rethinking Iranian Cinema Through Its Mainstream," *Third Text* 25, no. 3 (2011), 335–41. In an otherwise positive review, A.O. Scott has noted how "There are moments when the humanism of 'A Separation' feels a bit schematic, as if the characters were pulled from a box of available types rather than painted in the shades of life," whereas Peter Bradshaw noted how "a second viewing confirmed my feeling that this is a minor Farhadi film: forceful, steely, well-acted but a bit contrived and unsubtle." See Scott, "A House Divided by Exasperation," *New York Times*, December 29, 2011, www.nytimes.com/2011/12/30/movies/a-separation-directed-by-asghar-farhadi-review.html; and Bradshaw, "The Salesman Review—Asghar Farhadi's Potent, Disquieting Oscar-Winner," *The Guardian*, March 17, 2017, www.theguardian.com/film/2017/mar/17/the-salesman-review-asghar-farhadi-oscar-winner-iran.

56. On Sorrentino's film as a politico-theological essay see Daniele Fioretti, "Andreotti as *Katéchon*," *Italica* 96, no. 4 (2019), 625–46.

57. Maria Muhle, "A Genealogy of Biopolitics: The Notion of Life in Canguilhem and Foucault," in *The Government of Life: Foucault, Biopolitics, and Neoliberalism*, 87.

58. Lisa Downing and Libby Saxton, *Film and Ethics: Foreclosed Encounters* (Routledge, 2010), 92.

59. Michel Foucault, *"Society Must Be Defended": Lectures at the Collège de France, 1975–76*, trans. David Macey, ed. Mauro Bertani and Alessandro Fontana (Picador, 2003), 29.

60. Asghar Farhadi, dir., *Fireworks Wednesday* (2006; Grasshopper Film, 2013), 00:35:23.

61. Roberto Esposito, *Immunitas: The Protection and Negation of Life*, trans. Zakiya Hanafi (Polity, 2011), 26.

62. Andrey Makarychev and Alexandra Yatsyk, "Biopolitics and national identities: between liberalism and totalization," *Nationalities Papers*, vol. 45, no. 1 (2017), 2.

63. Farhadi, *Fireworks Wednesday*, 01:25:59.

64. Judith Butler, "Bodies and Power Revisited," in *Feminism and the Final Foucault*, ed. Dianna Taylor and Karen Vintges (University of Illinois Press, 2004), 190.

65. Hassannia, *Asghar Farhadi: Life and Cinema*, n.p.

66. Butler, "Bodies and Power Revisited," 190.

67. J.R. Cadwallader and D.W. Riggs, "The State of the Union: Toward a Biopolitics of Marriage." *M/C Journal* 15, no. 6 (2012), www.journal.media-culture.org.au/index.php/mcjournal/article/view/585.

68. Farhadi, *Fireworks Wednesday*, 01:32:02–01:32:04.

69. Bert Cardullo, *World Directors and Their Films: Essays on African, Asian, Latin American, and Middle Eastern Cinema* (Scarecrow, 2012), 188.

70. Michel Foucault, *Discipline and Punish: The Birth of the Prison*, trans. Alan Sheridan (Random House, 1995), 139.

71. Massimo Donà, "Immunity and Negation: On Possible Developments of the Theses Outlined in Roberto Esposito's 'Immunitas,'" trans. Loredana Comparone and Andrea Righi, *Diacritics* 36, no. 2 (Summer 2006), 63.

72. Michel Foucault, "The Ethics of the Concern for Self as a Practice of Freedom," interview by H. Becker et al., trans. P. Aranov and D. McGrath, in *Ethics: Subjectivity, and Truth*, vol. 1 of *The Essential Works of Foucault 1954–1984*, ed. Paul Rabinow (The New Press, 1997), 300.

73. Dean, *Signature of Power*, 216.

74. Jason Read, *The Politics of Transindividuality* (Brill, 2015), 6.

75. Janet Afary and Kevin B. Anderson, "Introduction," in *Foucault and the Iranian Revolution: Gender and the Seductions of Islamism*, ed. Afary and Anderson (University of Chicago Press, 2005), 2.

76. Beyzai's film *Death of Yazdgerd* (*Mard Yazdgerd*, 1982) hints at absolute mobility between social strata, age, and gender against institutionalized dogmatism. In the film, power is coextensive with fabulation and fluctuates across the fictive worlds created by the storytellers.

77. "Ogni individuo, anche il più stupido, può, se collocato in uno spazio precipuo, esercitare una forma di controllo sociale di normalizzazione e di omologazione." Stefano Berni, *Nietzsche e Foucault: Corporeità e potere in una critica radicale della modernità* (Giuffrè, 2005), 86. My translation.

78. "Law is interdependent with discipline, and the democratic characterization of law masks the control of the populace through disciplinary measures. Law in modernity does not recede, but becomes more involved in disciplinary control. Therefore the two interacted, overlapped and articulated one another, as well as being in a state of tension." Tom Frost, "Agamben's Sovereign Legalization of Foucault," *Oxford Journal of Legal Studies* 30, no. 3 (Autumn 2010), 550–51.

79. Godfrey Cheshire, review of *About Elly*, *Roger Ebert*, April 8, 2015, www.rogerebert.com/reviews/about-elly-2015.

80. Raz Zimmt, "Iran's Middle Class: An Agent of Political Change?" *Strategic Assessment* 20, no. 3 (October 2017), 64.

81. One finds this elsewhere in other films that depict frozen power systems preventing an upward expansion, as in Cristian Mungiu's *4 Months, 3 Weeks and 2 Days* (2007), where the young female protagonists seamlessly move from one disciplinarian institution to another—dorms and hotels as extensions of the prison, families in which they are produced as obsequious, mediocre, and lacking—before putting their lives on the line to challenge the regulation of their existence.

82. Dov Friedman, "The Turkish Model: The History of a Misleading Idea," *American Progress*, August 25, 2015, www.americanprogress.org/issues/security/reports/2015/08/25/119932/the-turkish-model/.

83. Foucault, "The Ethics of the Concern for Self," 293.

84. Farhadi, *About Elly*, 00:04:12.

85. William W. Young III, *Naming God and Friendship in Aquinas and Derrida* (Ashgate, 2007), 139.

86. Foucault, "The Ethics of the Concern for the Self," 283.

87. Michalinos Zembylas, "Derrida, Foucault and Critical Pedagogies of Friendship in Conflict-Troubled Societies," *Discourse: Studies in the Cultural Politics of Education* 36, no. 1 (2015), 9.

88. Michelle Langford, *Allegory in Iranian Cinema: The Aesthetics of Poetry and Resistance* (Bloomsbury, 2019), 231.

89. Daniel Garrett, "The Loss and Recovery of Identity: Appearance and Reality, Friendship and Betrayal in Asghar Farhadi's Film *About Elly*," *Off*

Screen 25, no. 2–3 (March 2021), offscreen.com/view/the-loss-and-recovery-of-identity-appearance-and-reality-friendship-and-betrayal-in-asghar-farhadis-film-about-elly.

90. Frost, "Agamben's Sovereign Legalization of Foucault," 548.

91. Cutro, "Introduzione," 8.

92. Materiali del Movimento Femminista, *Quaderni di lotta femminista*, no. 2, *Il personale è politico* (Musolini, 1973).

Chapter 3

1. See Michel Foucault, *"Society Must Be Defended": Lectures at the Collège de France, 1975–76*, trans. David Macey, ed. Mauro Bertani and Alessandro Fontana (Picador, 2003), 114–40.

2. Prosecutor: "I see, you don't understand how serious Nikolaev's case is. It concerns the state's interests. From the times of the Tartar invasion the main idea which unites us all, the idea which so many generations of our ancestors have served, is the idea of statehood. Powerful, great state is the ideal for which Russian is ready to suffer for, ready to take any hardship, to give his own life for. This is an irrational idea. This is not that pragmatic European desire to get the largest benefit for yourself. This is the idea of the Russian spirit, which dominates and dissolves yours and mine personally. But it gives back a hundred times more. This feeling of connection to a great organism gives the feeling of spirit, power and immortality. 'West' always wanted to compromise the idea of our statehood. But the biggest danger for our idea is not in the West—it is in ourselves. We ourselves grab these endless, fashionable little ideas from the West, being captivated by their clear practicality and rationality. Not even thinking that exactly in them is hidden the destructive force. It's all right. . . . Look for yourself—all of our revolutions in the end led not to the destruction but to the strengthening of the state. And it will be always this way. Not many people realize that this is one of the most critical moments of our history . . . Nikolaev's case, very simple at first glance, has incredibly deep meaning. So . . . Aleksey Mikhailovich, you can't leave the town."

Varakin: "What do I have to do?" Prosecutor: "Nothing. Just one thing . . . If somebody asks, don't deny you are the cook's son Makhmood." [Varakin nods in desperation]. Karen Shakhnazarov, *Gorod Zero*, 1:00:20–1:04:10. The name "Makhmood" is probably a nod to the Russian–Turkish wars between 1672 and 1914 and the tsarist expansion in parts of Southern Russia, the Caucasus, and Central Asia, and in a previous exchange with the little boy of the family temporarily hosting him, Varakin learns that he will in fact never leave the place and will have four daughters. Shakhnazarov correctly predicted that the idea of statehood would outlast Soviet Russia; given his powers of foresight, it is only appropriate that he was appointed Director of Mosfilm Studios in 1998. He then supported the seizing of Crimea in 2014 and the invasion of Ukraine in 2022, only to somewhat soften his position after the first difficulties encountered by the Russian Army. He also disapproved of the Best Director and the Critics' Award awarded to Loznitsa at the Kinotavr Film Festival in Sochi in 2010 for *My Joy*, calling it an anti-Russian film whose message was simply to "shoot all Russians." See Vladimir Lyashenko, "Schast'e moe, ya tvoy khaos," *Gazeta*, March 29, 2011, www.gazeta.ru/culture/2011/03/29/a_3568857.shtml.

3. Anton Weiss-Wendt, *Putin's Russia and the Falsification of History* (Bloomsbury, 2020), 373.

4. On the nature of historical films of the Soviet era see the work of David C. Gillespie.

5. See David C. Gillespie, *Russian Cinema* (Routledge, 2004). See also the work of Evgeny Dobrenko.

6. Elena Stishova, "Strakh I molchanie: Kak Andrej Zvyagintsev predskazal Putinskuyu Rossiyu, I ona emu otomstila," *Kino Art*, January 29, 2020. www.kinoart.ru/opinions/strah-i-molchanie-kak-andrey-zvyagintsev-predskazal-putinskuyu-rossiyu-i-ona-emu-otomstila.

7. See Peter Pomerantsev, "The Hidden Author of Putinism: How Vladislav Surkov Invented the New Russia," *The Atlantic*, November 7, 2014, www.theatlantic.com/international/archive/2014/11/hidden-author-putinism-russia-vladislav-surkov/382489/.

8. "Gross Box Office Revenue in Domestically Produced Films in Russia from 2018 to 2023," *Statista*, September 24, 2024, www.statista.com/statistics/1104169/russian-films-box-office-revenue-in-russia/.

9. Harry Bone, "Putin Backs WW2 Myth in New Russian Film," *BBC*, October 11, 2016, www.bbc.com/news/world-europe-37595972.

10. Boris Groys, "The Cold War Between the Medium and the Message: Western Modernism vs. Socialist Realism," *e-flux* 104, www.e-flux.com/journal/104/297103/the-cold-war-between-the-medium-and-the-message-western-modernism-vs-socialist-realism/.

11. Mariëlle Wijermars, *Memory Politics in Contemporary Russia: Television, Cinema and the State* (Routledge, 2019), 20.

12. Thomas Lemke, "Beyond Foucault: From Biopolitics to the Government of Life," in *Governmentality: Current Issues and Future Challenges*, ed. Ulrich Bröckling et al. (Routledge, 2011), 175.

13. See Peter Eltsov, *The Long Telegram 2.0: A Neo-Kennanite Approach to Russia* (Lexington Books, 2020). "Gumilev also introduced the notion of a parasite ethnos or state: such a state, according to Gumilev, lacks or loses its roots, surviving through the exploitation of someone else's resources—ter-

ritorial, natural, and intellectual. Both the French Republic and the United States of America, according to this theory, are parasite states linked to Jewish influence," n.p. (Kindle edition).

14. *Russiapedia*, "Prominent Russians: Lev Gumilev," accessed June 30, 2025, russiapedia.rt.com/prominent-russians/science-and-technology/lev-gumilev/.

15. Balabanov declares this explicitly in his interview in *Filmmaker Magazine*. See interview by Nick Dawson, *Filmmaker Magazine*, January 2, 2009, www.filmmakermagazine.com/1349-alexei-balabanov-cargo-200/#.YG-bV-d7lPY. The reference to "Russian Rambo" can be found in Andrey Plakhov, *Rezhissery nastoyashchego*, tom 2, *Radikaly i minimalisty* (Directors of nowadays, vol. 2, Radicals and minimalists) (Palmira, 2017).

16. Mark Bassin, *The Gumilev Mystique: Biopolitics, Eurasianism, and the Construction of Community in Modern Russia* (Cornell University Press, 2016), 126.

17. Bassin, 52–54.

18. Tekdeeps, "Putin Made Important Statements at a Meeting with Media Leaders," *Tekdeeps*, February 13, 2021, www.web.archive.org/web/20220225080621/https://tekdeeps.com/putin-made-important-statements-at-a-meeting-with-media-leaders-the-main-thing/.

19. Sergei Medvedev, *The Return of the Russian Leviathan*, trans. Stephen Dalziel (Polity, 2020), 26.

20. Farida Rustamova and Maxim Tovkaylo, "What Secret Russian State Polling Tells Us About the War," *Moscow Times*, June 12, 2022, www.themoscowtimes.com/2022/12/06/what-secret-russian-state-polling-tells-us-about-support-for-the-war-a79596.

21. Anastasya Manuilova, "Biopolitics of Authoritarianism: The Case of Russia," in *Debating Biopolitics*, ed. Marco Piasentier and Sarah Raimondi (Edward Elgar, 2022), 167.

22. James P. Scanlan, ed., "Interpretations and Uses of Slavophilism in Recent Russian Thought," in *Russian Thought After Communism: The Recovery of a Philosophical Heritage* (Routledge, 1994), 49.

23. Evgenii Troitskii, *Vozrozhdenie russkoi idei: Sotsial'no-filosofskie ocherki* (Filosofskoe obshchestvo SSSR, 1991), 55, qtd. in Scanlan, "Interpretations and Uses of Slavophilism in Recent Russian Thought," 47.

24. Lyashenko, "Schast'e moe, ya tvoy khaos."

25. Anastasiya Osipova, "Interview: Sergei Loznitsa on *Babi Yar. Context*," *Film Comment*, April 11, 2022, www.filmcomment.com/blog/interview-sergei-loznitsa-on-babi-yar-context. The film in question highlighted the Ukrainian involvement in the Babi Yar massacre.

26. Nolan Kelly has also remarked on Loznitsa's interest in crowds in his documentary work. See "The Returned Gaze: Ukraine in the Documentaries of Sergei

Loznitsa," *Film Quarterly*, October 7, 2022, www.filmquarterly.org/2022/10/07/the-returned-gaze-ukraine-in-the-documentaries-of-sergei-loznitsa.

27. Buñuel and his crew paid villagers to reenact scenes of poverty described in Legendre's book. For a fuller account, see Roman Gubern and Paul Hammon, *Luis Buñuel: The Red Years 1929–1939* (University of Wisconsin Press, 2009).

28. Sara Nadal-Melsió, "Buñuel's Eschatological Avant-Garde: *Las Hurdes* and Indexical Realism," *Revista Hispánica Moderna* 66, no. 2 (December 2013), 185.

29. Alison Smith, *Georges Didi-Huberman and Film: The Politics of the Image* (Bloomsbury, 2020), 12.

30. Georges Didi-Huberman, "People Exposed, People as Extras," *Radical Philosophy* 156 (July/August 2009), 16. This essay is extracted from an unfortunately as-yet untranslated French volume, *L'Œil de l'histoire*, vol. 4, *Peuples exposés, peuples figurants* (Minuit, 2012).

31. Didi-Huberman, "People Exposed, People as Extras," 16.

32. Didi-Huberman, "People Exposed, People as Extras," 19–20. In the original French volume, the author illustrates the significance of this by reproducing a photo of the dead insurgents of the Paris Commune: twelve bodies in narrow coffins stacked side by side, six at a time, with no space between them: they fit the frame of the camera exactly, which wholly encloses them in yet another square. See Smith, *Georges Didi-Huberman and Film*, 93.

33. Jacqueline Nacache, qtd. in Didi-Huberman, "People Exposed, People as Extras," 19. Italics mine.

34. Sergei Loznitsa, dir., *Landscape* (2003; New Wave Films, 2013), 00:31:20–00:32:48.

35. Nadal-Melsió, "Buñuel's Eschatological Avant-Garde," 186. The author uses these phrases to describe Buñuel's film.

36. It is easy to imagine that this film inspired the bus stop scene in *Donbass*, with which I first introduced this book.

37. Loznitsa, *Landscape*, 00:24:21–00:25:16.

38. Loznitsa, *Landscape*, 00:27:44–00:27:52.

39. Isaac Deutscher, *The Prophet Outcast: Trotsky 1929–1940* (Verso, 2003), 187.

40. Loznitsa, *Landscape*, 00:25:20–00:26:00.

41. Loznitsa, *Landscape*, 00:27:29–00:27:33.

42. Dennis Walder, *Postcolonial Nostalgias: Writing, Representation, and Memory* (Routledge, 2011), 113.

43. Luca Malavasi, "Il silenzio delle cose: Austerlitz," *Cineforum*, January 27, 2017, www.cineforum.it/recensione/Il-silenzio-delle-cose-Austerlitz.

44. Magdalena Zolkos, "Skulls, Tree Bark, Fossils: Memory and Materiality in Georges Didi-Huberman's Transvaluation of Surface," *Qui Parle* 30, no. 2 (December 2021), 274.

45. Jacques Rancière wrote of unconcerned landscapes whose only testimony is that of erasure, and characterized by "the simple inhumanity of soil and stones." See *Figures of History*, trans. Julie Rose (Polity, 2014), 49.

46. John Grant, "Marcuse Remade? Theory and Explanation in Hardt and Negri," *Science & Society* 74, no. 1 (Jan., 2010), 41.

47. Pasi Väliaho, "Biopolitics of Gesture: Cinema and the Neurological Body," in *Cinema and Agamben: Ethics, Biopolitics and the Moving Image*, ed. Henrik Gustafsson and Asbjørn Grønstadt (Bloomsbury, 2014), 111.

48. Giorgio Agamben, *The Coming Community*, trans. Michael Hardt (University of Minnesota Press, 1993), 43.

49. Adrienne de Ruiter, "The Political Character of Absolute Enmity: On Carl Schmitt's The Concept of the Political and Theory of the Partisan," *ARSP: Archiv für Rechts- und Sozialphilosophie/Archives for Philosophy of Law and Social Philosophy* 98, no. 1 (2012), 55.

50. Walter Benjamin, "On the Concept of History," in *Selected Writings Volume 4: 1938–1940*, ed. Howard Eiland and Michael W. Jennings, trans. Edmund Jephcott et al. (Harvard University Press, 2003), 390–91.

51. See Michael Hardt and Antonio Negri, *Assembly* (Oxford University Press, 2017), esp. pp. 166–70.

52. Fatimah Tobing Rony, *How Do We Look? Resisting Visual Biopolitics* (Duke University Press, 2022), 104.

53. See Loznitsa's comments on Sokurov's *The Evening Sacrifice* (*Zhertva vechernaya*, 1987) and its "metaphysical" insights into Elena Stishova's "Kakoy 'Portret,' kakoy 'Peizazh'! Leksikon Sergeya Loznitsy," *Kino Art*, no. 6 (2005), www.old.kinoart.ru/archive/2005/06/n6-article8.

54. Vlad Strukov, *Contemporary Russian Cinema: Symbols of a New Era* (Edinburgh University Press, 2016), 36.

55. Although in Russia the pervasiveness of a state-led economy has created a "minor" middle class wary of liberalizing and democratizing policies; see Evgeny Gontmakher and Cameron Ross, "The Middle Class and Democratisation in Russia," *Europe-Asia Studies* 67, no 2 (2015): 269–84.

56. "Les orthodoxes n'ont jamais eu de sympathie pour les 'sommes théologiques,' ni pour les systems scolastiques. Toute formulation ou définition excessive provoque une méfiance spontanée. L'Orthodoxie n'a pas besoin de formular, elle a besoin de ne pas formuler." See Paul Evdokimov, *Le Christ dans la pensée russe* (Les Editions du Cerf, 1986).

57. Ismail Xavier, *Allegories of Underdevelopment: Aesthetics and Politics in Modern Brazilian* Cinema (University of Minnesota, 1997), 14.

58. Xavier, *Allegories of Underdevelopment*, 15.

59. "Rather than modern states being a synthesis of sovereign and biopower, the heterogeneity of sovereignty and biopower means that the two instead exist, therefore, in irrevocable tension." Deana Heath, "The Tortured Body: The Irrevocable Tension between Sovereign and Biopower in Colonial

Indian Technologies of Rule," in *South Asian Governmentalities: Michel Foucault and the Question of Postcolonial Orderings*, ed. Stephen Legg and Deana Heath (Cambridge University Press, 2018), 230.

60. See, for example, Giovanni Codevilla, *La nuova Russia (1905–2015)* (Jaca Book, 2016), especially chapters 3–6.

61. Richard Sawka, *Putin: Russia's Choice* (Routledge, 2004), 32.

62. Timothy Frye, "Putin Touts Russia as a Great Power. But He's Made It a Weak One," *Washington Post*, June 6, 2019, www.washingtonpost.com/opinions/2019/06/06/putin-touts-russia-great-power-hes-made-it-weak-one.

63. Damian Tambini, *Nationalism in Italian Politics: The Stories of the Northern League, 1980–2000* (Routledge, 2012), n.p. (ebook).

64. See lecture given by former culture minister and chairman of the Russian Military Historical Society (RVIO) Vladimir Medinsky, "Mia Rossiya segodnya lektsiya Medinskogo V. R.," lecture at the Russian Military Historical Society, April 22, 2015, VPT "GRAFITSA," April 24, 2015, video, 1:44:45, www.youtube.com/watch?v=HE3QeZwfb5U.

65. Former speaker of the Duma Boris Gryslov was particularly vivacious in his stolid renditions of Putin's doctrine. Among the most exemplary are "We Russians want to live in friendship with others, and this trait is not inherent in other nationalities" and the immortal "Parliament is not a place for discussion." They are collected at www.kommersant.ru/doc/1838005.

66. Lena Johnson, "Russia: Culture, Cultural Policy, and the Swinging Pendulum of Politics," in *Cultural and Political Imaginaries in Putin's Russia*, ed. Niklas Bernsand and Barbara Törnquist-Plewa (Brill, 2019), 31.

67. Katharina Blum, "Russia's Conservative Counter-Movement: Genesis, Actors, and Core Concepts," in *New Conservatives in Russia and East Central Europe*, ed. Katharina Blum and Mihai Varga (Routledge, 2019), n.p. (ebook).

68. Giorgio Agamben, *Means Without End: Notes on Politics*, trans. Vincenzo Binetti and Cesare Casarino (University of Minnesota Press, 2000), 30.

69. Timothy C. Campbell, *Improper Life: Technology and Biopolitics from Heidegger to Agamben* (University of Minnesota Press, 2011), 33.

70. Majia Holmer Nadesan, *Governmentality, Biopower, and Everyday Life* (Routledge, 2008), 186.

71. Sergei Prozorov, *The Biopolitics of Stalinism: Ideology and Life in Soviet Socialism* (Edinburgh University Press, 2016) 102.

72. Nick Vaughan-Williams, "The Generalised Bio-Political Border? Re-Conceptualising the Limits of Sovereign Power," *Review of International Studies* 35 (2009), 738.

73. Also note Walter Benjamin: "The potentate is symbolized by the cold, unrestrained plotter, whose actions fill up the permanent state of exception stochastically, without meaning or morality. His counterpart is the masquerade of the allegory, which transforms reality into changing masks of continual metamorphosis. Benjamin criticizes authority as a masquerade of the

chaotic state of nature, the endless repetition of change without substance." Horst Bredekamp, "From Walter Benjamin to Carl Schmitt, via Thomas Hobbes," trans. Melissa Thorson Hause and Jackson Bond, *Critical Inquiry* 25, no. 2 (Winter, 1999), 260.

74. Thomas Lemke, *Biopolitics: An Advanced Introduction*, trans. by Eric Frederick Trump (New York University Press, 2011), 40.

75. "Na kostyakh muchenikov, kak na krepkom fundamente, budet vozdvignuta Rus' novaya." My translation. Ioann Kronshtasdky, *Ya predvizhu vosstanovlenie moshnoy Rossii* (Institut Russkoy Zivilisazii, 2012), 30.

76. See Medvedev, *The Return of the Russian Leviathan*, 167–69.

77. "In Putin's Russia, the sovereign uses the law and legal institutions to fulfill political goals, to communicate them to society, and to manage the authoritarian coalition that helps the president govern. As a result, the law is highly consequential, but its use tends to be arbitrary, expedient, and instrumental, rather than predictable and principled." Maria Popova, "Putin-Style 'Rule of Law' and the Prospects for Change," *Daedalus* 146, no. 2 (2017), 65.

78. Mona Lilja and Stellan Vinthagen, "Sovereign Power, Disciplinary Power and Biopower: Resisting What Power with What Resistance?," *Journal of Political Power* 7, no. 1 (2014), 114.

79. Popova, "Putin-Style 'Rule of Law' and the Prospects for Change," 71.

80. A type of resistance against sovereignty theorized by Jenny Edkins and Véronique Pin-Fat, "Through the Wire: Relations of Power and Relations of Violence," *Millennium—Journal of International Studies* 34, no. 1 (2005): 1–24.

81. Thomas Lemke, *Foucault's Analysis of Modern Governmentality: A Critique of Political Reason*, trans. Erik Butler (Verso, 2019), 84.

82. Robin Douglass and Johan Olsthoorn, "Introduction," *Hobbes's "On the Citizen": A Critical Guide*, ed. Douglass and Olsthoorn (Cambridge University Press, 2020), 8–9.

83. Fiona Hill and Clifford G. Gaddy, *Mr. Putin: Operative in the Kremlin* (Brookings Institution Press, 2013), 233.

84. "Non implica affatto la formazione e il mantenimento di quel 'supremo imperio' che è la sovranità statale." Paolo Virno, *E così via, all'infinito: Logia e antropologia* (Bollati Boringhieri, 2010), 173.

85. See M. K. Raghavendra, *Locating World Cinema: Interpretations of Film as Culture* (Bloomsbury, 2020).

Chapter 4

1. Emma Graham-Harrison, "Dying China Oil Town a Warning to Beijing," *Reuters*, April 17, 2008, www.reuters.com/article/us-energy-china-poverty-idUSPEK16604520080417.

2. Phillip Inman, "Chinese President Vows to 'Adjust Excessive Incomes' of the Super Rich," *The Guardian*, August 18, 2021, www.theguardian.com/world/2021/aug/18/chinese-president-xi-jinping-vows-to-adjust-excessive-incomes-of-super-rich.

3. Isabella Weber, "Origins of China's Contested Relation with Neoliberalism: Economics, the World Bank, and Milton Friedman at the Dawn of Reform," *Global Perspectives* 1, no. 1 (2020), 1.

4. Weber, 7.

5. Weber, 1.

6. "Some people say this was a covert scheme. We say it was an overt one." Mao Zedong, "Wen Hui Pao's Bourgeois Orientation Should Be Criticized." From *People's Daily*, July 1, 1957, in *Selected Works of Mao Tse-Tung*, www.marxists.org/reference/archive/mao/selected-works/volume-5/mswv5_64.htm.

7. Zhang helpfully problematizes the term "Sixth Generation" as follows: "It appears that the naming of this new generation has been problematic both in China and overseas. 'Newborn generation' and 'Sixth Generation' refer to the directors' ages and the period of their emergence in Chinese film history, but 'avante-garde' and 'personal' stress their artistic or stylistic character. For political reasons, most young directors refuse the term 'underground' and prefer 'independent.' In my view, 'independent' best describes the alternative modes of production and circulation of their works: if they are not entirely independent of state institutions . . . they are at least independent of official ideology." Yingjin Zhang, *Cinema, Space, and Polylocality in a Globalizing China* (University of Hawai'i Press, 2010), 106–7.

8. Xiaoping Lin, *Children of Marx and Coca Cola: Avant-garde Art and Independent Cinema* (University of Hawai'i Press, 2010), 94.

9. Angelos Koutsourakis, "Epic Cinema: Defining Our Terms," *JCMS: The Journal of Cinema and Media Studies* 61, no. 1 (2021), 57.

10. Luke Robinson, *Independent Chinese Documentary: From the Studio to the Street* (Palgrave Macmillan, 2013), 158.

11. Joe Mai, "Wang Bing's *'Til Madness Do Us Part*: An Apprenticeship in Seeing," *LOLA* 6 (2015), www.lolajournal.com/6/wang.html.

12. Bruno Lessard, *The Cinema of Wang Bing: Chinese Documentary between History and Labor* (Hong Kong University Press, 2025), 102.

13. Daniela Persico, ed., *Wang Bing: Il cinema della Cina che cambia* (Agenzia X, 2010). In the volume, published on the occasion of Wang Bing's retrospective during the thirtieth edition of the Filmmaker Film Festival in Milan, see especially Persico's and Goffredo Fofi's chapters.

14. Pierpaolo Antonello, "The (Political) Forms of Technology: Antonioni, Olmi, De Seta, and Post-World War II Industrial Cinema," *The Italianist* 2 (2019): 151–70.

15. Richard Letteri, "History, Silence and Homelessness in Contemporary Chinese Cinema: Wang Xiaoshuai's Shanghai Dreams," *Asian Studies Review* 34, no. 1 (March 2010): 8.

16. Letteri, "History, Silence and Homelessness," 8.

17. William Lakos, *Chinese Ancestor Worship: A Practice and Ritual Oriented Approach to Understanding Chinese Culture* (Cambridge Scholars, 2010), 6.

18. See Orna Ophir, *Schizophrenia: An Unfinished History* (Polity Press, 2022), n.p., ebook.

19. "L'inoperosità . . . Ma pure la tentazione dell'azzardo, o del buio, o del nocivo." Davide Tarizzo, "Dalla biopolitica all'etopolitica: Foucault e noi," *Noéma* 4–1 (2013): 51.

20. Wang Xiaoping, *Postsocialist Conditions: Ideas and History in China's "Independent Cinema," 1988–2008* (Brill, 2018), 247.

21. Wang Xiaoshuai, dir., *Frozen* (1996; Fox Lorber Home Video, 2001), 00:26:00–00:27:00.

22. Erik Bordeleau, "Surviving to Oneself after Tiananmen: Wang Xiaoshuai's *Frozen* (1996)," *Concentric: Literary and Cultural Studies* 40, no. 2 (September 2014), 119. Bordeleau's article is an excellent, explicitly Agambenian reading of the film.

23. Wang, *Frozen*, 00:39:50–00:40:00. Bordeleau expands on this scene in "Surviving to Oneself," 120.

24. Wang Xiaoshuai, interviewed by Michael Berry, *Speaking in Images: Interviews with Contemporary Chinese Filmmakers* (Columbia University Press, 2005), 168.

25. Silvia Fok, *Life & Death: Art and the Body in Contemporary China* (Intellect, 2013), 70.

26. Wang, *Frozen*, 00:50:00–00:51:45.

27. Wang, *Frozen*, 00:51:45–00:52:17.

28. Bordeleau, "Surviving to Oneself," 107.

29. Wang, *Frozen*, 00:33:53.

30. Jing Nie, "A City of Disappearance: Trauma, Displacement, and Spectral Cityscape in Contemporary Chinese Cinema," in *Chinese Ecocinema: In the Age of Environmental Challenge*, ed. Sheldon H. Lu and Jiayan Mi (Hong Kong University Press, 2009), 198.

31. Wang, *Frozen*, 00:01:00–00:04:33.

32. This, too, is a reference to a real-life event. However, it had a very different outcome: the artist had a parachute to break the fall and was later arrested and detained for fifteen days. See Fok, *Life and Death*, 73. *Frozen's* version of this performance ends in death. It is both an insider's reference to the world of young independent artists at the time and an ominous warning for those who knew about the performance.

33. Wang, *Frozen*, 1:33:00–1:33:31.

34. Wang, *Frozen*, 1:33:00–1:33:31. Ellipsis in original.

35. Juan David Cárdenas, "Cinema as Foucauldian dispositif: An Anachronistic and Materialistic Approach," *Palabra Clave* 20, no. 1 (2016), 77–78.

36. Giorgio Agamben, *Idea della prosa* (Feltrinelli, 1985), 84. My translation.

37. Susan Greenhalgh and Edwin A. Winckler, *Governing China's Population: From Leninist to Neoliberal Biopolitics* (Stanford University Press, 2005), 98.

38. Foucault, *Birth of Biopolitics*, 317.

39. For a full and nuanced account of Chinese family planning policy and its reforms, see Stuart Basten and Quanbao Jiang, "China's Family Planning Policies: Recent Reforms and Future Prospects," *Studies in Family Planning* 45, no. 4 (December 2014): 493–509. See also Stephen McDonnell, "China Allows Three Children in Major Policy Shift," *BBC News*, May 31, 2021, www.bbc.com/news/world-asia-china-57303592.

40. In this sense, the film is reminiscent of Fifth Generation epics, particularly Tian Zhuangzhuang's *The Blue Kite* (*Lan fengzheng*, 1993), substituting the one-child and relocation policies for the Hundred Flower campaign, the Great Leap Forward, and the Cultural Revolution.

41. Penelope Deutscher, "Reproductive Politics, Biopolitics and Autoimmunity: From Foucault to Esposito," *Bioethical Inquiry* 7 (2010), 217.

42. As Russell J.A. Kilbourn and others have written, this story is "likely apocryphal." See Kilbourn, *Cinema, Memory, Modernity: The Representation of Memory from the Art Film to Transnational Cinema* (Routledge, 2010), 120.

43. Barbara Mennel, *Cities and Cinema* (Routledge, 2008), 8.

44. Hongbing Zhang, "Ruins and Grassroots: Jia Zhangke's Cinematic Discontents in the Age of Globalization," in *Chinese Ecocinema*, ed. Lu and Mi, 129.

45. For an analysis of this subject from the perspective of Henri Lefebvre's *Production of Space* (1991), see Nie, "A City of Disappearance."

46. Wang Xiaoshuai, qtd. in Dave Crewe, "Scars of Time: Guilt and Forgiveness in Wang Xiaoshuai's *So Long, My Son*," *Metro Magazine*, October 28, 2019, www.metromagazine.com.au/scars-of-time.

47. Crewe, 73.

48. Hongbing Zhang, "Ruins and Grassroots," 130.

49. Wang Xiaoshuai, dir., *So Long, My Son* (2019; Curzon Artificial Eye, 2019), 02:08:52.

50. Wang, *So Long, My Son*, 02:34:15–02:34:40.

51. Wang, *So Long, My Son*, 02:28:00–02:29:00.

52. "The rise of a vital politics infused with a money ethic has led to the emergence of vast inequalities between reproductive haves and have nots. Today, the politics of reproduction is marked by growing gaps between city and village, coastal and interior regions, migrant and nonmigrant populations,

and Han and non-Han groups." Susan Greenhalgh, *Cultivating Global Citizens: Population in the Rise of China* (Harvard University Press, 2010), 67–68.

53. Ivan Franceschini and Christian Sorace, "The Proletariat Is Dead, Long Live the Proletariat!," in *Proletarian China: A Century of Chinese Labour*, ed. Franceschini and Sorace (Verso, 2022), 16.

54. I am expanding on David Leiwei Li's use of the term "neoliberal maternal subject" in *Economy, Emotion, and Ethics in Chinese Cinema: Globalization on Speed* (Routledge, 2016), 213.

55. Though it is not explicitly stated, it is suggested that Xiao Lu is not normally present in Hehe's life: The film establishes that Mei Zhu and Xiao Lu have been divorced for years, and Hehe calls Xiao Lu "Uncle" and Lao Zie "Daddy."

56. Xiaoping Wang, *Postsocialist Conditions*, 45.

57. Wang, *Postsocialist Conditions*, 45.

58. In *Red Amnesia*, as in Michelangelo Antonioni's *L'eclisse* (1962) and Michael Haneke's *Hidden*, capsules of ethical, historical, sexual virtuality are spontaneously generated by a reality in which life is compressed and thoroughly managed and reconciliation is impossible.

59. Shuqin Cui, "The Return of the Repressed: Masculinity and Sexuality Reconsidered," in *Companion to Chinese Cinema*, ed. Yingjin Zhang (Blackwell, 2012), 517.

60. Wang Xiaoshuai, dir., *In Love We Trust* (2008; Film Movement, 2011), 00:22:00–00:23:00).

61. Wang Xiaoping, *Postsocialist Conditions*, 354.

62. Wang, *In Love We Trust*, 00:31:00–00:32:00.

63. Wang, *In Love We Trust* 00:49:00–00:50:00.

64. As the earlier discussion of *So Long, My Son* demonstrates, the one-child policy was by no means as rigid as it is popularly understood in the West. In addition to paying fines for a second child, exceptions were also made for divorced people with a child who wished to conceive a child with a new, childless partner. However, having a third child would be incredibly rare and in any case expensive, even for professionals. See Immigration and Refugee Board of Canada, *China: One-Child Policies with Respect to Persons Who Remarry*, February 4, 2000, CHN33750.E, www.ecoi.net/en/document/1350406.html.

65. Wang, *In Love We Trust*, 01:17:00–01:18:06.

66. Wang, *In Love We Trust*, 01:18:00–01:18:30.

67. Wang, *In Love We Trust*, 1:22:01.

68. Wang Xiaoping, *Postsocialist Conditions*, 346.

69. Wang, *Postsocialist Conditions*, 346–47.

70. Cui, "The Return of the Repressed," 516.

71. Wang, *In Love We Trust*, 1:31:00–1:32:30.

72. Wang, *In Love We Trust*, 01:34:00–01:36:00.

73. Wang, *In Love We Trust*, 01:34:00–01:36:00.

74. Yingjin Zhang, *A Companion to Chinese Cinema* (Wiley-Blackwell, 2012), 516.

75. Miguel Vatter, "Natality and Biopolitics in Hannah Arendt," *Revista de ciencia política* 26, no. 2 (2006): 152.

76. Adriana Cavarero, *Surging Democracy: Notes on Hannah Arendt's Political Thought*, trans. Matthew Gervase (Stanford University Press, 2021), 3.

Chapter 5

1. Liviu Rebreaunu, *Forest of the Hanged*, trans. A.V. Wise (Casemate, 2017), 145.

2. Michel Foucault, *"Society Must Be Defended": Lectures at the Collège de France, 1975–76*, trans. David Macey, ed. Mauro Bertani and Alessandro Fontana (Picador, 2003), 47.

3. Vasidas Karalis, *Theo Angelopoulos: Filmmaker and Philosopher* (Bloomsbury, 2023), 15.

4. Lucian Pintilie, dir., *Reconstruction* (1968; Tf1 Video, DVD), 00:25:07. The original soundtrack says "ca în viață," or "as in life."

5. Monica Filimon, "Popular Cinema in 1960s Romania," in *Cinema, State Socialism and Society in the Soviet Union and Eastern Europe, 1917–1989*, ed. Sanja Bhun and John Haynes (Routledge, 2014), 110.

6. See Markus Bauer, "Mikrostruktur einer Tragödie: Zu *Reconstituirea* von Lucian Pintilie," *Cargo*, January 20, 2011 www.cargo-film.de/film/spielfilm/mikrosturktur-einer-tragodie/.

7. It should also be noted that Ceaușescu's Romania, in the framework of the Eastern Bloc, was the country with the most autonomous foreign and economic policies. Romania adhered to the General Agreement on Trade and Tariffs, or GATT, in 1971 and in the following year joined the International Monetary Fund and the World Bank. The country's commercial position was further reinforced when it acquired preferential trading status with the European Common Market in 1973, while remaining a member of the Comecon or CMEA (Council for Mutual Economic Assistance).

8. Lucian Boia, *History and Myth in Romanian Consciousness* (Central European University Press, 2001), 230.

9. The data for 2023 refer to a survey carried out by News.ro and is consistent with a similar study authored by the Center for Insight in Survey Research. See "Sondaj INSCOP pentru News.ro—Armata şi Biserica rămân instituţiile în care românii au cea mai mare încredere. Guvernul şi Parlamentul sunt pe ultimele poziţii, cu o cotă de încredere mai scăzută decât în urmă cu 10 ani," *News.ro*, November 14, 2023, www.news.ro/social/

sondaj-inscop-news-armata-biserica-raman-institutiile-romanii-au-cea-mare-incredere-guvernul-parlamentul-ultimele-pozitii-cota-incredere-scazuta-urma-10-ani-1922400014002023110821383603; and the Center for Insights in Survey Research, "Public Opinion in Romania," *IRI*, May–June 2018, www.iri.org/wp-content/uploads/2018/07/final_romania_poll_presentation.pdf.

10. Nicholas M. Nagi-Talavera, *The Green Shirts and the Others: A History of Fascism in Hungary and Romania* (The Center for Romanian Studies, 2001), 346.

11. My translation of "non immagina nessuna ribellione e neppure la desidera." See Francesco Saverio Marzaduri, *Noul Val: Il nuovo cinema romeno 1989–2009* (Archetipo, 2012), 125.

12. Doru Pop, *Romanian New Wave Cinema: An Introduction* (McFarland, 2014). See especially pp. 28–33.

13. Pop, *Romanian New Wave Cinema*, 32.

14. Lorenzo Borgotallo, "The Italian Neorealist Experience: The Orphan Child and New Ways of Looking at the World," in *A Companion to Italian Cinema*, ed. Frank Burke (Wiley, 2017), 123.

15. Elena Roxana Popan, "Recent Romanian Cinema: Is It a Real New Wave or Just a Splash in the Water?" *Communication Review* 17, no. 3 (2014), 221.

16. Conversation at the MOBRA company offices in Bucharest, June 2018.

17. Monica Filimon, *Cristi Puiu* (University of Illinois Press, 2017), 23.

18. Pop, *Romanian New Wave*, 22.

19. See László Strausz's concept of oscillation in his *Hesitant Histories on the Romanian Screen* (Palgrave Macmillan, 2017). See especially pp. 124–36. Agamben also speaks of Guy Debord's cinema as a "prolonged hesitation between image and meaning" via repetition and stoppage, a "zone of undecidability" where unique situations are constructed. Agamben, "Difference and Repetition: On Guy Debord's films," trans. Brian Holmes, in *Guy Debord and the Situationist International*, ed. Tom McDonough (MIT Press, 2002), 317.

20. Dominique Nasta, *Contemporary Romanian Cinema: The History of an Unexpected Miracle* (Wallflower, 2013), 5.

21. Andrei Gorzo and Veronica Lazar, "The New Romanian Cinema and Beyond: The Films of Radu Jude," *Transilvania*, April 2022, 4.

22. Gorzo and Lazar, "The New Romanian Cinema and Beyond," 1–2.

23. Roberto Esposito, *Institution*, trans. Zakiya Hanafi (Polity, 2022), 3.

24. Cristian Mungiu, private conversation with the author, June 26, 2018.

25. See the essay "Reverse Perspective" in Pavel Florensky, *Beyond Vision: Essays on the Perception of Art*, ed. Nicoletta Misler, trans. Wendy Salmond (Reaktion Books, 2002), 197–306.

26. Cristian Mungiu, private conversation with the author, June 26, 2018.

27. Anna Batori, *Space in Romanian and Hungarian Cinema* (Palgrave Macmillan, 2018), 137.

28. Alice Bardan, "Aftereffects of 1989: Corneliu Porumboiu's *12:08 East of Bucharest* (2006) and Romanian Cinema," in *A Companion to Eastern European Cinemas*, ed. Anikó Imre (Wiley, 2012), 128.

29. I expand on the interpretation given by Monica Filimon in *Cristi Puiu*, 39–50.

30. Katherine Verdery, *What Was Socialism, and What Comes Next?* (Princeton University Press, 1996), 57.

31. Jude, *The Happiest Girl in the World* (2009; HI Film Productions, Circe Films, 2009), 00:26:50.

32. Incidentally, it needs to be noted that Pietrangeli's article on Visconti's *Obsession* (*Ossessione*, 1942), "Analisi spettrale del film realistico," by insisting on the nervous tics and the involuntary twitching of the bodies, already captures the biopolitical charge of Visconti's operation—this is to say, the deployment of cinema as a medium capable of capturing the uncalculated potential for life to change and not to remain frozen in institutionally sanctioned forms such as regimented work both inside and outside of the domestic sphere. Pietrangeli spent some time as an assistant director on the set of *Obsession*. See Antonio Pietrangeli, "Analisi spettrale del film realistico," *Alla ricerca di Luchino Visconti*, April 3, 2009, alla-ricerca-di-luchino-visconti.com/2009/04/03/si-gira-ossessione-analisi-spettrale-del-film-realistico/.

33. Lorenzo Fabbri, *Cinema Is the Strongest Weapon: Race-Making and Resistance in Fascist Italy* (University of Minnesota Press, 2023), 73.

34. Konstanty Kuzma, "Radu Jude on *Aferim!*," interview, *East European Film Bulletin* 50 (February 2015), eefb.org/interviews/radu-jude-on-aferim/.

35. Giovanni Picker, *Racial Cities: Governance and the Segregation of Romani People in Urban Europe* (Routledge 2017), 15.

36. Ayten Gündoğdu, *Rightlessness in an Age of Rights: Hannah Arendt and the Contemporary Struggles of Migrants* (Oxford University Press, 2015), 126–27.

37. Mihai-Dan Cirjan, "Radu Jude's *Aferim!* and the Politics of Distance," *Brooklyn Rail*, April 2016, brooklynrail.org/2016/04/film/radu-judes-aferim-and-the-politics-of-distance.

38. Viorel Achim, *The Roma in Romanian History* (Central European University Press, 2004), 91.

39. Janet L. Meyer, *Sydney Pollack: A Critical Filmography* (McFarland, 1998), 44.

40. Judit Pieldner, "History, Cultural Memory and Intermediality in Radu Jude's *Aferim!*" *Acta Universitatis Sapientiae Film and Media Studies* 13 (2016), 94.

41. David Crowe, "The Gypsy Historical Experience in Romania," in *The Gypsies of Eastern Europe*, ed. David Crowe and John Kolsti (M.E. Sharpe, 1991), 61.

42. Radu Jude, dir., *Aferim!* (2015; Big World Pictures, 2015), 00:22:34–00:23:12.

43. Nicolae Roddy, "The Romanian Orthodox Church and the Roma," in *Religion, Race, and the Other*, ed. Ronald A. Simkins, *Journal of Religious & Society*, Supplement 24 (2023), 70.

44. See Andrei Gorzo and Veronica Lazăr, "An Updated Political Modernism: Radu Jude and 'I Do Not Care If We Go Down in History as Barbarians,'" *Close Up: Film and Media Studies* 3, no. 1–2 (2019): 7–19.

45. Diana Popa, "Hopeless Didacticism: Archival Sources and Spectatorial Address in 'I Do Not Care If We Go Down in History as Barbarians,'" *Law, Culture and the Humanities* 18, no. 3 (2019): 535–56.

46. Ludmila Martanovschi and Dana Mihăilescu, "Representations of the 'Aliens Within': Romanian Jews and Roma in Radu Jude's Cinema," in *The Aliens Within: Danger, Disease, and Displacement in Representations of the Racialized Poor*, ed. Geoffroy de Laforcade et al. (De Gruyter, 2022), 107.

47. Giorgio Agamben, *Remnants of Auschwitz: The Witness and the Archive* (Zone Books, 1999). The passages read in the film are from pages 70–71.

48. Martanovschi and Mihăilescu, "Representations of the 'Aliens Within,'" 107.

49. Pop, *Romanian New Wave Cinema*, 204.

50. Ágnes Pethő, *Caught In-Between: Intermediality in Contemporary Eastern European and Russian Cinema* (Edinburgh University Press, 2020), 121.

51. Strausz, *Hesitant Histories*, 218.

52. Christina Stojanova, "Historical Overview of Romanian Cinema," in *New Romanian Cinema*, ed. Stojanova (Edinburgh University Press, 2019), 333.

53. David Spaner, *Shoot It!: Hollywood Inc. and the Rising of Independent Film* (Arsenal Pulp, 2011), 230.

54. Andrei Gorzo and Veronica Lazăr, "A Slight Unease About Capitalism: Radu Jude's *The Happiest Girl in the World* and the New Romanian Cinema," *Revista Transilvania*, May 2022, 2.

55. Gorzo and Lazăr, "A Slight Unease About Capitalism," 9.

56. Bunyard, *Debord, Time and Spectacle*, 327.

57. Bunyard, 328n.

58. Chelcea, "Work-Discipline and Temporal Structures," 49.

59. Cătălin Augustin Stoica, "'Our Martyrs of 1989 Did Not Die for This!': Political Capitalism in Post-Communist Romania," *Historical Social Research/Historische Sozialforschung* 27, no. 2 (2012), 48.

Conclusion

1. Recall, for instance, Logan's reaction to the flash when Chris takes his picture. As Lenika Cruz astutely observes, "it triggers a bizarre

transformation: Logan's expression turns to fear . . . and he launches at Chris, screaming, 'Get out!' . . . It was hard not to watch that scene without thinking of how important camera phones and video recordings have been for many African Americans experiencing police violence." See Lenika Cruz, "In *Get Out*, the Eyes Have It," *The Atlantic*, March 3, 2017, www.theatlantic.com/entertainment/archive/2017/03/in-get-out-the-eyes-have-it/518370.

2. Nahum 3:6 (New King James Version).

3. Jordan Peele, dir., *Nope* (Monkey Paw Productions, 2022). Script available at *Indie Wire*, www.indiewire.com/wpcontent/uploads/2022/12/NOPE_Script_FINAL_2022.11.29.pdf.

4. Guy Debord, *Society of the Spectacle*, trans. Ron Adams (Unredacted Word, 2021), 37. By the end of the film, coins leak out of Jean Jacket like precipitation from a cloud, providing the means of its capture.

5. Peele, *Nope*, 00:10:30–00:11:41.

6. In fact, there were two jockeys and two horses. While the jockeys remain anonymous, the depicted horses were named (Occident and Sallie Gardner). See Jeff Scheible, "Throwing Punches: The Athletic Aesthetics of Kevin Jerome Everson's Filmmaking," *World Records Journal* 3 (2022), 31. In her study of race in early cinema, Alice Maurice cites Thomas Edison's 1896 film, a proof of concept and advertisement for the inventor's Kinematograph. *A Morning Bath*, which depicts a Black woman bathing her infant child, is described in Edison's catalogue as an example of "a clear and distinct picture in which the contrast between the complexion of the bather and the white soapsuds is strongly marked." As Maurice writes, this film "was one of many instances in which producers exploited the links between black and white and Black and White . . . the prowess of the [motion picture] apparatus is here made manifest by racializing the technical appeal of 'high contrast.' " Moreover, according to Maurice, this "was one of many instances in which producers exploited the links between black and white and Black and White . . . the prowess of the [motion picture] apparatus is here made manifest by racializing the technical appeal of 'high contrast.' " Alice Maurice, *The Cinema and its Shadow: Race and Technology in Early Cinema* (University of Minnesota Press, 2013), 3.

7. One might also recall Loznitsa's *Austerlitz* (chapter 2), the director's film on death camp tourism: There, he documents visitors looking at the remnants of one of Europe's most horrific crimes through their mobile phone screens.

8. Indeed, the police are active participants in the spectacle. Note, for instance, that Derek Chauvin, the murderer of George Floyd, made eye contact with the teenage bystander who recorded the killing. See Ethan Zuckerman, "Why Filming Police Violence Has Done Nothing to Stop It," *Technology Review*, June 3, 2020, www.technologyreview.com/2020/06/03/1002587/sousveillance-george-floyd-police-body-cams.

9. Amy Bridge, "What if It's Not a Ship: Reading the Monster Octopus in Jordan Peele's *Nope*," *Gothic Studies* 25, no. 2 (2023), 152.

10. Jordan Peele qtd. in Keith Book and Isra Daraiseh, "Jordan Peele's *Nope*: Saying No to the Society of the Spectacle," *Science Fiction Film and Television* 16, no. 1–2 (2023), 173.

11. Doing so is a Promethean act, one that indexes other mythic acts of looking, like the gorgon Medusa turning her beholders into stone, or Lot's wife, who, turning back to gaze upon the destruction of Sodom, is turned into a pillar of salt.

12. Neera M. Singh, "The Nonhuman Turn or a Re-turn to Animism? Valuing Life Along and Beyond Capital," *Dialogues in Human Geography* 12, no. 1 (March 2022): 85.

13. Kinitra Brooks, "The Coming of Age of Black Social Horror," interview with Bethany C. Morrow, *Electric Lit*, March 3, 2022, electricliterature.com/black-social-horror-bethany-c-morrow-cherish-farrah/.

14. Vlad Dima, *Meaninglessness: Time, Rhythm, and the Undead in Postcolonial Cinema* (Michigan State University Press, 2022), 63.

15. John Carlos Rowe, *Our Henry James in Fiction, Film, and Popular Culture* (Routledge, 2023), 193.

16. See Gregers Andersen and Esben Bjerggaard Nielsen, "Biopolitics in the Anthropocene: On the Invention of Future Biopolitics in *Snowpiercer*, *Elysium*, and *Interstellar*," *Journal of Popular Culture* 51, no. 3 (2018): 615–34.

17. Emiliano Morreale, "La vita nuda e la vita in mutande. Su Ciprì e Maresco," in "Bíos," ed. Roberto de Gaetano et al., special issue, *Fata Morgana*, no. 0 (2006), 197.

18. Albert Serra, dir., *Pacifiction* (2022; Grasshopper Film, 2022), 01:24:00–01:26:00.

19. Leonardo Goi, "Albert Serra on Pacifiction," *Reverse Shot*, February 16, 2023, www.reverseshot.org/interviews/entry/2990/serra_int.

20. James Slaymaker, "An Outcast of the Islands: Albert Serra's *Pacifiction* (2023)," *Film International*, July 26, 2023, www.filmint.nu/albert-serra-pacifiction-2023-review-james-slaymaker.

21. Adrian Cho, "France Grossly Underestimated Radioactive Fallout from Atom Bomb Tests, Study Finds," *Science*, March 11, 2021, www.science.org/content/article/france-grossly-underestimated-radioactive-fallout-atom-bomb-tests-study-finds.

22. Jon Henley, "France Has Underestimated Impact of Nuclear Tests in French Polynesia, Research Finds," *The Guardian*, March 9, 2021, www.theguardian.com/world/2021/mar/09/france-has-underestimated-impact-of-nuclear-tests-in-french-polynesia-research-finds. Notice the biopolitical bureaucracy at play in this situation, where a government that has dropped multiple nuclear bombs on a territory requires the local inhabitants to *apply* for a compensation that would be decided by a French court.

23. Slaymaker, "An Outcast of the Islands."

24. Serra, *Pacifiction*, 00:42:00–00:43:24.

25. Serra, *Pacifiction*, 01:01:00–01:01:07.

26. Serra, *Pacifiction*, 01:58:00–02:01:32.

27. Joseph Masco, *The Nuclear Borderlands: The Manhattan Project in Post-Cold War New Mexico* (Princeton University Press, 2006), 30. Masco calls this "the nuclear uncanny."

28. Serra, *Pacifiction*, 02:06:00–02:12:00.

29. Emmanuel Alloa, "Phasmid Thinking: On George Didi-Huberman's Method," trans. Christopher Woodall, *Angelaki* 23, no. 4 (2018), 105.

30. Chris Salter, "The Long Horizon: Temporal Imaginaries in the More-than-Human Arts," in *The Routledge International Handbook of More-than-Human Studies*, ed. Adrian Franklin (Routledge, 2024), 341.

31. For a biopolitical interpretation of the expanded role of policing and the mercantile vocation of post-Westphalian Germany, see Serena Marcenó, *Biopolitica e sovranità: Concetti e pratiche di governo alla soglia della modernità* (Mimesis, 2011), especially pp. 127–92.

32. "Superficie d'iscrizione di processi, dinamiche e tensioni che attraversano il corpo sociale." Giacamo Tagliani, "Biografie italiane. Cinema e immagini della vita," in *Pensiero in immagine. Forme, metodi, oggetti teorici per un Italian Visual Thought*, ed. Angela Mengoni and Francesco Zucconi (Mimesis, 2022), 287.

33. "Arbitrio, controllo, dominio. Oppure come macchinazione, come segreto, come congiura." See Gianni Canova, "Potere," in *Lessico del cinema italiano: Forme di rappresentazione e forme di vita*, ed. Roberto de Gaetano, vol. 2 (Mimesis, 2015), 432.

34. "Like Foucault, Rosi believes that *truth* is circularly linked to systems of power who produce it and support it, and to the effects of power that it induces and that reproduce it." Roberto Andò, "La bellezza della verità: Da 'Salvatore Giuliano' a 'Dimenticare Palermo,'" in *Francesco Rosi*, ed. Sebastiano Gesù (Incontri con il cinema, 1991), 161. "Foucaultianamente, Rosi crede che la *verità* sia legata circolarmente a sistemi di potere che la producono e la sostengono, e ad effetti di potere che essa induce e che la riproducono."

35. "Il refuse de croire." Alain Carbonnier, "Bianca," *Cinéma* 350, April 16, 1986, 3. My translation.

36. Sam Rohdie, *The Passion of Pier Paolo Pasolini* (British Film Institute, 2019), n.p. (e-book).

37. "Una nostalgia bruciante per il mondo premoderno." My translation. Bruno Pischedda, "*Petrolio*, una significativa illeggibilità," *Studi Novecenteschi* 27, no. 59 (2000), 165.

38. Chiara Frugoni, *San Francesco e il lupo*, illustrated by Felice Feltracco (Feltrinelli, 2013).

39. Alice Rohrwacher, *Happy as Lazzaro* (2018; 01 Distribution, 2018), 01:31:20.

40. Federico Luisetti, "Pier Paolo Pasolini's Political Animism," in *Pier Paolo Pasolini, Frames and Unframed: A Thinker for the Twenty-First Century*, ed. Luca Peretti and Karen T. Raizen (Bloomsbury, 2019), 217.

41. See Luc Boltanski and Ève Chiapello, *The New Spirit of Capitalism*, trans. Gregory Elliott (Verso, 2018), especially pp. 118–33.

42. Violetta Bellocchio, "Funeralopolis, tutto quello che non volevi vedere," *Esquire*, December 20, 2018, www.esquire.com/it/cultura/film/a25627638/funeralopolis-film-recensione/.

43. Anselm Franke, "Animism: Notes on an Exhibition," *e-flux*, no. 36, www.e-flux.com/journal/36/61258/animism-notes-on-an-exhibition.

44. Eduardo Viveiros de Castro, "Exchanging Perspectives: The Transformation of Objects into Subjects in Amerindian Ontologies," *Common Knowledge* 10, no. 3 (2004), 466.

45. Marta Segarra, "New Animism and Shamanic Cinema: Human–Animal–Machine Interactions," in *Cinema of/for the Anthropocene: Affect, Ecology, and More-Than-Human Kinship*, ed. Katarzyna Paszkiewicz and Andrea Ruthven (Routledge, 2025), 131.

46. Giorgio Agamben, *Means Without End: Notes on Politics*, trans. Vincenzo Binetti and Cesare Casarino (University of Minnesota Press, 2000), 21.

47. Roberto Esposito, *Terms of the Politics: Community, Immunity, Biopolitics*, trans. Rhiannon Noel Welch (Fordham University Press, 2013), 84.

48. Esposito, *Terms of Politics*, 124.

49. T.J. Demos, *The Migrant Image: The Art and Politics of Documentary During Global Crisis* (Duke University Press, 2013), 4.

50. Giovanni Cioni (filmmaker) in discussion with author, March 13, 2024.

51. See Michelle Smiley, "The Mechanical Against Objectivity: Industrialism and Inoperativity in Eadweard Muybridge's *Animal Locomotion* (1887)," *History of Photography* 47, no. 3 (2023), 203–33.

52. Massimo D'Anolfi and Martina Parenti, dirs., *Bestiari, erbari, lapidari* (Montmorency Film, 2024), 00:02:27.

53. Sylvain George, dir., *May They Rest in Revolt* (Noir Production, 2010), 00:49:53–00:50:08.

54. Federico Luisetti, "From Biopolitics to Political Animism: Roberto Esposito's Things," in *Roberto Esposito: Biopolitics and Philosophy*, ed. Inna Viriasova and Antonio Calcagno, 161–78 (State University of New York Press, 2018), 164.

55. Timothy C. Campbell, "'Enough of a Self': Esposito's Impersonal Biopolitics," *Law, Culture and the Humanities* 8, no. 1 (2012), 46. This is one of the clearest essays on Esposito's rather enigmatic concept of the impersonal.

56. Timothy C. Campbell, "'Foucault Was Not a Person': Idolatry and the Impersonal in Roberto Esposito's 'Third Person,'" *CR: The New Centennial Review* 10, no. 2 (Fall 2010), 141.

57. George, *May They Rest in Revolt*, 00:37:44–00:37:52.

58. Debarati Sanyal, "Calais's 'Jungle': Refugees, Biopolitics, and the Arts of Resistance," *Representations*, no. 139 (Summer 2017), 16. Sanyal also discusses Esposito's immunitary *dispositif* in her article.

59. Sanyal, "Calais's 'Jungle,'" 19.

60. George, *May They Rest in Revolt*, 00:41:00–00:42:30.

61. Sanyal, "Calais's 'Jungle,'" 20.

62. Harriet Grant and John Domokos, "Dublin Regulation Leaves Asylum Seekers with Their Fingers Burnt," *The Guardian*, October 7, 2011, www.theguardian.com/world/2011/oct/07/dublin-regulation-european-asylum-seekers. Awet, one of the asylum seekers interviewed in this article, also compares the Dublin regulation to a virus, "like Aids [sic]."

63. Roberto Esposito, "For a Philosophy of the Impersonal," trans. Timothy Campbell, *CR: The New Centennial Review* 10, no. 2 (Fall 2010), 124.

64. Roberto Esposito, "The *Dispositif* of the Person," *Law, Culture and the Humanities* 8, no. 1 (2012), 24.

Bibliography

Abbott, Mathew. *Abbas Kiarostami and Film-Philosophy*. University of Edinburgh Press, 2018.

Abdolmohammadi, Pejman. "The Shiite Islamic Political Theology: The Debate between Ruhullah Khomeini (d. 1989) and Mehdi Bazargan (d. 1995)." In *Islamic Political Theology*, edited by Massimo Campanini and Marco Di Donato, 83–96. Lexington Books, 2021.

Achim, Viorel. *The Roma in Romanian History*. Central European University Press, 2004.

Afary, Janet, and Kevin B. Anderson, eds. *Foucault and the Iranian Revolution: Gender and the Seductions of Islamism*. University of Chicago Press, 2005.

Agamben, Giorgio. *The Coming Community*. Translated by Michael Hardt. University of Minnesota Press, 1993.

Agamben, Giorgio. "Difference and Repetition: On Guy Debord's Films." Translated by Brian Holmes. In *Guy Debord and the Situationist International*, edited by Tom McDonough, 313–19. MIT Press, 2002.

Agamben, Giorgio. *Homo Sacer: Sovereign Power and Bare Life*. Translated by Daniel Heller-Roazen. Stanford University Press, 1998.

Agamben, Giorgio. *Idea della prosa*. Feltrinelli, 1985.

Agamben, Giorgio. *Means Without End: Notes on Politics*. Translated by Vincenzo Binetti and Cesare Casarino. University of Minnesota Press, 2000.

Agamben, Giorgio. *Remnants of Auschwitz: The Witness and the Archive*. Zone Books, 1999. *The State of Exception*. University of Chicago Press, 2005.

Agamben, Giorgio. *The Use of Bodies*. Translated by Adam Kotsko. Stanford University Press, 2016.

Ahmed, Sabeen. "From Death Penalty to Thanatopolitics." *Philosophy Today* 63, no. 2 (Spring 2019): 293–314.

Alemanno, Roberto. *Itinerari della violenza: Il film negli anni della restaurazione (1970–1980)*. Edizioni Dedalo, 1982.

Alloa, Emmanuel. "Phasmid Thinking: On George Didi-Huberman's Method." Translated by Christopher Woodall. *Angelaki* 23, no. 4 (2018): 103–12.

Anderson, Gregers, and Esben Bjerggaard Nielsen. "Biopolitics in the Anthropocene: On the Invention of Future Biopolitics in *Snowpiercer*, *Elysium*, and *Interstellar*." *Journal of Popular Culture* 51, no. 3 (2018): 615–34.

Andò, Roberto. "La bellezza della verità: Da 'Salvatore Giuliano' a 'Dimenticare Palermo.'" In *Francesco Rosi*, edited by Sebastiano Gesù, 161–67. Incontri con il cinema, 1991.

Antonello, Pierpaolo. "The (Political) Forms of Technology: Antonioni, Olmi, De Seta, and Post-World War II Industrial Cinema." *The Italianist* 39, no. 3 (2019): 151–70.

Atkinson, Sarah. *Beyond the Screen: Emerging Cinema and Engaging Audiences*. Bloomsbury, 2014.

Badiou, Alain. *Badiou and His Interlocuters: Lectures, Interviews, and Responses*. Bloomsbury, 2018.

Balabanov, Alexei. Interview by Nick Dawson. *Filmmaker Magazine*. January 2, 2009. www.filmmakermagazine.com/1349-alexei-balabanov-cargo-200/#. YG-bV-d7lPY.

Barattoni, Luca. *Italian Post-Neorealist Cinema*. Edinburgh University Press, 2012.

Bardan, Alice. "Aftereffects of 1989: Corneliu Porumboiu's *12:08 East of Bucharest* (2006) and Romanian Cinema." In *A Companion to Eastern European Cinema*, edited by Anikó Imre, 125–47. Wiley, 2012.

Bassin, Mark. *The Gumilev Mystique: Biopolitics, Eurasianism, and the Construction of Community in Modern Russia*. Cornell University Press, 2016.

Basten, Stuart, and Quanbao Jiang. "China's Family Planning Policies: Recent Reforms and Future Prospects." *Studies in Family Planning* 45, no. 4 (December 2014): 493–509.

Batori, Anna. *Space in Romanian and Hungarian Cinema*. Palgrave Macmillan, 2018.

Bauer, Markus. "Mikrostruktur einer Tragödie: Zu *Reconstituirea* von Lucian Pintilie." *Cargo*, January 20, 2011. www.cargo-film.de/film/spielfilm/ mikrosturktur-einer-tragodie/.

Baumbach, Nico. *Cinema/Politics/Philosophy*. Columbia University Press, 2019.

Baumbach, Nico. "Shareable Cinema: The Politics of Abbas Kiarostami." In *The Global Auteur: The Politics of Authorship in 21st Century Cinema*, edited by Seung-hoon Jeong and Jeremi Szaniawski, 271–86. Bloomsbury, 2016.

Bazin, André. *What Is Cinema?* Edited and translated by Hugh Gray. University of California Press, 2005 [1965].

Bellocchio, Violetta. "Funeralopolis, tutto quello che non volevi vedere." *Esquire*, December 20, 2018. www.esquire.com/it/cultura/film/a25627638/ funeralopolis-film-recensione/.

Belting, Hans. *An Anthropology of Images: Picture, Medium, Body*. Translated by Thomas Dunlap. Princeton University Press, 2011.

Belting, Hans. "Toward an Anthropology of the Image." In *Anthropologies of Art*, edited by Mariët Westermann, 41–57. Yale University Press, 2005.

Benjamin, Walter. "On the Concept of History." In *Selected Writings Volume 4: 1938–1940*, edited by Howard Eiland and Michael W. Jennings, translated by Edmund Jephcott et al., 389–400. Harvard University Press, 2003.

Benjamin, Walter. "The Task of the Translator." In *Selected Writings Volume 1: 1913–1926*, edited by Marcus Bullock and Michael W. Jennings, 253–63. Harvard University Press, 2002.

Berghahn, Daniela. "'The Past Is a Foreign Country': Exoticism and Nostalgia in Contemporary Transnational Cinema." *Transnational Screens* 10, no. 1 (2019): 34–52.

Bernauer, James, and David Rasmussen, eds. *The Final Foucault*. MIT Press, 1994.

Berni, Stefano. *Nietzsche e Foucault: Corporeità e potere in una critica radicale della modernità*. Giuffrè, 2005.

Berry, Michael. *Speaking in Images: Interviews with Contemporary Chinese Filmmakers*. Columbia University Press, 2005.

Bill, James Allan. *The Politics of Iran: Groups, Classes and Modernization*. Merrill, 1972.

Bird, Greg, and Heather Lynch. "Introduction to the Politics of Life: A Biopolitical Mess." *European Journal of Social Theory* 22, no. 3 (2019): 301–3.

Blouin, Michael J. *Magical Thinking, Fantastic Film, and the Illusions of Neoliberalism*. Palgrave MacMillan, 2016.

Blum, Katharina, "Russia's Conservative Counter-Movement: Genesis, Actors, and Core Concepts." In *New Conservatives in Russia and East Central Europe*, edited by Katharina Blum and Mihai Varga. Routledge, 2019.

Boia, Lucian. *History and Myth in Romanian Consciousness*. Central European University Press, 2001.

Boltanski, Luc, and Ève Chiapello. *The New Spirit of Capitalism*. Translated by Gregory Elliott. Verso, 2018.

Bone, Harry. "Putin Backs WW2 Myth in New Russian Film." *BBC*, October 11, 2016, www.bbc.com/news/world-europe-37595972.

Book, Keith, and Isra Daraiseh. "Jordan Peele's *Nope*: Saying No to the Society of the Spectacle." *Science Fiction Film and Television* 16, no. 1–2 (2023): 165–82.

Borck, Cornelius. "Animism in the Sciences Then and Now." *e-flux*, no. 37 (July 2012), www.e-flux.com/journal/36/61266/animism-in-the-sciences-then-and-now.

Bordeleau, Erik. "Surviving to Oneself after Tiananmen: Wang Xiaoshuai's *Frozen* (1996)." *Concentric: Literary and Cultural Studies* 40, no. 2 (September 2014): 105–24.

Borgotallo, Lorenzo. "The Italian Neorealist Experience: The Orphan Child and New Ways of Looking at the World." In *A Companion to Italian Cinema*, edited by Franke Burke, 121–38. Wiley, 2017.

Bottici, Chiara. "Rethinking the Biopolitical Turn: From the Thanatopolitical to the Geneapolitical Paradigm." *Graduate Faculty Philosophy Journal* 36, no. 1 (2015): 175–97.

Bradshaw, Peter. "The Salesman Review—Asghar Farhadi's Potent, Disquieting Oscar-Winner." *The Guardian*, March 17, 2017. www.theguardian.com/film/2017/mar/17/the-salesman-review-asghar-farhadi-oscar-winner-iran.

Bredekamp, Horst. "From Walter Benjamin to Carl Schmitt, via Thomas Hobbes." *Critical Inquiry* 25, no. 2 (Winter 1999): 247–66.

Bridge, Amy. "What if It's Not a Ship: Reading the Monster Octopus in Jordan Peele's *Nope*." *Gothic Studies* 25, no. 2 (2023): 137–59.

Brooks, Kinitra. "The Coming of Age of Black Social Horror." Interview with Bethany C. Morrow. *Electric Lit*, March 3, 2022. electricliterature.com/black-social-horror-bethany-c-morrow-cherish-farrah/.

Brooks, Xan. "Jafar Panahi: Public Enemy." *The Guardian*. September 2, 2003. www.theguardian.com/film/2003/sep/02/1.

Brown, Wendy. *Politics Out of History*. Princeton University Press, 2001.

Brown, William. "*Cease Fire*: Rethinking Iranian Cinema Through Its Mainstream." *Third Text* 25, no. 3 (2011): 335–41.

Buck, Amber A., and Theo Plothe, eds. "Introduction." In *Netflix at the Nexus: Content, Practice, and Production in the Age of Streaming Television*, 1–10. Peter Lang, 2019.

Bunyard, Tom. *Debord, Time and Spectacle: Hegelian Marxism and Situationist Theory*. Brill, 2019.

Burch, Noël. *Life to Those Shadows*. University of California Press, 1990.

Burt, Ramsay. "Agamben, Dance, Gesture." *Ramsay Burt*, January 5, 2017. Video, 34:07. www.youtube.com/watch?v=NAesOjEKm9M.

Butler, Judith. "Bodies and Power Revisited." In *Feminism and the Final Foucault*, edited by Dianna Taylor and Karen Vintges, 183–94. University of Illinois Press, 2004.

Byler, Darren. "'Disposable' Bodies on Screen in Xu Xin's *Karamay*: Biopolitics, Affect, and Ritual in Chinese Central Asia." In *Transnational Chinese Cinema: Corporeality, Desire, and the Ethics of Failure*, edited by Brian Bergen-Aurand, Marry Mazzilli, and Hee Wai-Siam, 159–80. Bridge21, 2014.

Cadwallader, J.R., and D.W. Riggs. "The State of the Union: Toward a Biopolitics of Marriage." *M/C Journal* 15, no. 6 (2012).

Calcagno, Antonio, and Inna Viriasova, eds. *Roberto Esposito: Biopolitics and Philosophy*. State University of New York Press, 2018.

Campbell, Timothy C. "'Enough of a Self': Esposito's Impersonal Biopolitics." *Law, Culture and the Humanities* 8, no. 1 (2012): 31–46.

Campbell, Timothy C. "'Foucault Was Not a Person': Idolatry and the Impersonal in Roberto Esposito's 'Third Person.'" *CR: The New Centennial Review* 10, no. 2 (Fall 2010): 135–50.

Campbell, Timothy C. *Improper Life: Technology and Biopolitics from Heidegger to Agamben*. University of Minnesota Press, 2011.

Campbell, Timothy C. *The Techne of Giving: Cinema and the Generous Form of Life*. Fordham University Press, 2017.

Campbell, Timothy, and Adam Sitze, eds. "Introduction." In *Biopolitics: A Reader*, 1–40. Duke University Press, 2013.

Canade, Alessandro. *Conversations on Cinema*. Pellegrini Editore, 2013.

Canova, Gianni. "Potere." In *Lessico del cinema Italiano: Forme di rappresentazione e forme di vita*, edited by Roberto de Gaetano, vol. 2, 429–506. Mimesis, 2022.

Carbonnier, Alain. "Bianca." *Cinéma* 350, April 16, 1986.

Cárdenas, Juan David. "Cinema as a Foucauldian Dispositif: An Anachronistic and Materialistic Approach." *Palabra Clave* 20, no. 1 (2016): 69–95.

Cardullo, Bert. *World Directors and Their Films: Essays on African, Asian, Latin American, and Middle Eastern Cinema*. Scarecrow, 2012.

Casetti, Francesco. *L'occhio del Novecento: Cinema, esperienza, modernità*. Bompiani, 2005.

Castro, Teresa. "An Animistic History of the Camera: Filmic Forms and Machinic Subjectivity." In *A History of Cinema Without Names*, edited by Diego Cavalotti, Federico Giordano, and Leonardo Quaresima, 247–55. Mimesis International, 2016.

Castro, Teresa. "The Mediated Plant." *e-flux*, no. 102 (September 2019). www.e-flux.com/journal/102/283819/the-mediated-plant.

Catsoulis, Jeannette. "Truth as a Tinderbox That Must Disappear." *New York Times*, June 13, 2014. www.nytimes.com/2014/06/13/movies/manuscripts-dont-burn-about-repression-in-iran.html.

Cavarero, Adriana. *Surging Democracy: Notes on Hannah Arendt's Political Thought*. Translated by Matthew Gervase. Stanford University Press, 2021.

Center for Insights in Survey Research. "Public Opinion in Romania." *IRI*, May–June 2018. www.iri.org/wp-content/uploads/2018/07/final_romania_poll_presentation.pdf.

Chaudhuri, Shohini, and Howard Finn. "The Open Image: Poetic Realism and New Iranian Cinema." *Screen* 44, no. 1 (Spring 2003): 38–57.

Chayka, Kyle. "Watching the World's 'First TikTok War.'" *New Yorker*, March 3, 2022. www.newyorker.com/culture/infinite-scroll/watching-the-worlds-first-tiktok-war.

Chelcea, Liviu. "Work-Discipline and Temporal Structures in a Multinational Bank in Romania." In *Neoliberalism, Personhood, and Postsocialism: Enterprising Selves in Changing Economies*, edited by Nicolette Makovicky, 37–52. Ashgate, 2014.

Chen, Mel Y. *Animacies: Biopolitics, Racial Mattering, and Queer Affect*. Duke University Press, 2012.

Chenar, Ali. "Comment: A Celebration for 'A Separation.'" *PBS*, January 17, 2012, www.pbs.org/wgbh/pages/frontline/tehranbureau/2012/01/dispatch-a-celebration-for-a-separation.html.

Cheshire, Godfrey. Review of *About Elly*. *Roger Ebert*, April 8, 2015. www.rogerebert.com/reviews/about-elly-2015.

Chitty, Christopher. "Reassessing Foucault: Modern Sexuality and the Transition to Capitalism." *Viewpoint Magazine*, April 20, 2017.

Cho, Adrian. "France Grossly Underestimated Radioactive Fallout from Atom Bomb Tests, Study Finds." *Science*, March 11, 2021. www.science.org/content/article/france-grossly-underestimated-radioactive-fallout-atom-bomb-tests-study-finds.

Chow, Rey. *Sentimental Fabulations, Contemporary Chinese Films: Attachment in the Age of Global Visibility*. Columbia University Press, 2007.

Chung, Tzu-I. "Ecological Indigeneity in Global Indigenous Discourse." In *Aspects of Transnational and Indigenous Cultures*, edited by Clara Shu-Chun Chang and Hsinya Huang, 141–64. Cambridge Scholars Publishing, 2014.

Cirjan, Mihai-Dan. "Radu Jude's *Aferim!* and the Politics of Distance." *Brooklyn Rail*, April 2016, brooklynrail.org/2016/04/film/radu-judes-aferim-and-the-politics-of-distance.

Codevilla, Giovanni. *La nuova Russia (1905–2015)*. Jaca Book, 2016.

Coletsou, Angeliki. "Visual Representations of Iran in Western Media after 9/11." *9/11 Legacies*, 911legacies.com/Visual%20Representations%20of%20Iran.htm.

Cooper, Melinda. "The Law of the Household." In *The Government of Life: Foucault, Biopolitics, and Neoliberalism*, edited by Vanessa Lem and Miguel Vatter, 29–58. Fordham University Press, 2014.

Colonello, Paola. "L'Iran e le trappole neoliberiste in educazione conflitti e contagi." In *Educazione e neoliberismi: Idee, critiche e pratiche per una comune umanità*, edited by Emanuela Mancino and Marialisa Rizzo, 141–51. Progedit, 2022.

Corvi, Ester. *Nuovo cinema web—Netflix, Hulu, Amazon: La rivoluzione va in scena*. Hoepli, 2016.

Crewe, Dave. "Scars of Time: Guilt and Forgiveness in Wang Xiaoshuai's *So Long, My Son*." *Metro Magazine*, October 28, 2019. www.metromagazine.com.au/scars-of-time/.

Crowe, David. "The Gypsy Historical Experience in Romania." In *The Gypsies of Eastern Europe*, edited by David Crowe and John Kolsti, 61–79. M.E. Sharpe, 1991.

Cruz, Lenika. "In *Get Out*, the Eyes Have It." *The Atlantic*, March 3, 2017. www.theatlantic.com/entertainment/archive/2017/03/in-get-out-the-eyes-have-it/518370.

Cui, Shuqin. "The Return of the Repressed: Masculinity and Sexuality Reconsidered." In *Companion to Chinese Cinema*, edited by Yingjin Zhang, 499–517. Blackwell, 2012.

Cutro, Antonella. "Introduzione: Che cosa significa biopolitica?" In *Biopolitica: Storia e attualità di un concetto*, ed. Cutro. Ombre Corte, 2005.

Dabashi, Hamid. *Close Up: Iranian Cinema, Past, Present, and Future*. Verso, 2001.

Dalla Gassa, Marco. "Bong Joon-ho, o dell'efferatezza inesorabile." In *Il cinema del nuovo millennio: Geografie, forme, autori*, edited by Alessia Cervini, 277–84. Carocci, 2020.

De Gaetano, Roberto, et al., eds. "Bíos." Special issue, *Fata Morgana*, no. 0 (2006): 7–27.

de Ruiter, Adrienne. "The Political Character of Absolute Enmity: On Carl Schmitt's The Concept of the Political and Theory of the Partisan." *ARSP: Archiv für Rechts- und Sozialphilosophie/Archives for Philosophy of Law and Social Philosophy* 98, no. 1 (2012): 52–66.

Dean, Mitchell. *The Signature of Power: Sovereignty, Governmentality and Biopolitics*. Sage, 2013.

Debord, Guy. *Society of the Spectacle*. Translated by Ron Adams. Unredacted Word, 2021.

del Río, Elena. "Biopolitical Violence and Affective Force: Michael Haneke's *Code Unknown*." In *Post-Cinema: Theorizing 21st-Century Film*, edited by Shane Denson and Julia Leyda, 538–668. REFRAME Books, 2016. reframe.sussex.ac.uk/post-cinema/4-5-del-rio/.

del Río, Elena. *The Grace of Destruction: A Vital Ethology of Extreme Cinemas*. Bloomsbury, 2016.

Demos, T.J. *The Migrant Image: The Art and Politics of Documentary During Global Crisis*. Duke University Press, 2013.

Démy-Geroe, Anne. *Iranian National Cinema: The Interaction of Policy, Genre, Funding, and Reception*. Routledge, 2020.

Dennison, Stephanie, and Song Hwee Lim, eds. "Introduction." In *Remapping World Cinema: Identity, Culture, and Politics in Film*, 1–18. Wallflower Press, 2006.

Deutscher, Isaac. *The Prophet Outcast: Trotsky 1929–1940*. Verso, 2003.

Deutscher, Penelope. *Foucault's Futures: A Critique of Reproductive Reason*. Columbia University Press, 2017.

Deutscher, Penelope. "Reproductive Politics, Biopolitics and Auto-immunity: From Foucault to Esposito." *Bioethical Inquiry* 7 (2010): 217–26.

Didi-Huberman, Georges. *Invention of Hysteria: Charcot and the Photographic Iconography of the Salpêtrière*. Translated by Alisa Hartz. MIT Press, 2003.

Didi-Huberman, Georges. *L'Œil de l'histoire*, vol. 4, *Peuples exposés, peuples figurants*. Minuit, 2012.

Didi-Huberman, Georges. "People Exposed, People as Extras." *Radical Philosophy* 156 (July/August 2009): 16–22.

Dietrich, René, and Kerstin Knope, eds. *Biopolitics, Geopolitics, Life: Settler States and Indigenous Presence*. Duke University Press, 2023.

Dima, Vlad. *Meaninglessness: Time, Rhythm, and the Undead in Postcolonial Cinema*. Michigan State University Press, 2022.

Donà, Massimo. "Immunity and Negation: On Possible Developments of the Theses Outlined in Roberto Esposito's 'Immunitas.'" Translated by Loredana Comparone and Andrea Righi. *Diacritics* 36, no. 2 (Summer 2006): 57–69.

Douglass, Robin, and Johan Olsthoorn. "Introduction." In *Hobbes's "On the Citizen": A Critical Guide*, 1–11. Cambridge University Press, 2020.

Downing, Lisa, and Libby Saxton. *Film and Ethics: Foreclosed Encounters*. Routledge, 2010.

Edkins, Jenny, and Veronique Pin-Fat. "Through the Wire: Relations of Power and Relations of Violence." *Millennium—Journal of International Studies* 34, no. 1 (2005): 1–24.

Esposito, Roberto. *Bíos: Biopolitics and Philosophy*. University of Minnesota Press, 2008.

Esposito, Roberto. "The Dispositif of the Person." *Law, Culture and the Humanities* 8, no. 1 (2012): 17–30.

Esposito, Roberto. "For a Philosophy of the Impersonal." Translated by Timothy Campbell. *CR: The New Centennial Review* 10, no. 2 (Fall 2010): 124–34.

Esposito, Roberto. *Immunitas: The Protection and Negation of Life*. Translated by Zakiya Hanafi. Polity, 2011.

Esposito, Roberto. *Institution*. Translated by Zakiya Hanafi. Polity, 2022.

Esposito, Roberto. "Interview." Interview by Timothy C. Campbell. Translated by Anna Paparcone. *Diacritics* 36, no. 2 (Summer 2006): 49–50.

Esposito, Roberto. "Postdemocracy and Biopolitics." *European Journal of Social Theory* 22, no. 3 (2019): 317–24.

Esposito, Roberto. *Terms of the Political: Community, Immunity, Biopolitics*. Translated by Rhiannon Noel Welch. Fordham University Press, 2012.

Esposito, Roberto, Antonio Negri, and Salvatore Veca. "Dialogo su impero e democrazia." *Micromega* 5 (2001): 115–35.

Evdokimov, Paul. *Le Christ dans la pensée russe*. Les Editions du Cerf, 1986.

Fabbri, Lorenzo. *Cinema Is the Strongest Weapon: Race-Making and Resistance in Fascist Italy.* University of Minnesota Press, 2023.

Filimon, Monica. *Cristi Puiu.* University of Illinois Press, 2017.

Filimon, Monica. "Popular Cinema in 1960s Romania." In *Cinema, State Socialism and Society in the Soviet Union and Eastern Europe, 1917–1989,* edited by Sanja Bhun and John Haynes, 94–114. Routledge, 2014.

Finlayson, James Gordon. "'Bare Life' and Politics in Agamben's Reading of Aristotle." *Review of Politics* 72, no. 1 (Winter 2010): 97–126.

Fioretti, Daniele. "Andreotti as *Katéchon.*" *Italica* 96, no. 4 (2019): 625–46.

Florensky, Pavel. *Beyond Vision: Essays on the Perception of Art.* Edited by Nicoletta Misler, translated by Wendy Salmond. Reaktion Books, 2002.

Fok, Silvia. *Life & Death: Art and the Body in Contemporary China.* Intellect, 2013.

Foucault, Michel. *The Birth of Biopolitics: Lectures at the Collège de France 1978–79.* Translated by Graham Burchell. Palgrave, 2008.

Foucault, Michel. "Confession of the Flesh." In *Power/Knowledge: Selected Interviews and Other Writings,* edited and translated by Colin Gordon, 194–288. Pantheon, 1980.

Foucault, Michel. *Discipline and Punish: The Birth of the Prison.* Translated by Alan Sheridan. Random House, 1995.

Foucault, Michel. "The Ethics of the Concern for the Self as a Practice of Freedom." Interview by H. Becker, R. Fornet-Betancourt, and A. Gomez-Muller, translated by P. Aranov and D. McGrath. In *Ethics: Subjectivity and Truth,* 281–302. Vol. 1 of *The Essential Works of Foucault 1954–1984,* edited by Paul Rabinow. The New Press, 1997.

Foucault, Michel. *History of Sexuality: Volume 1: An Introduction.* Translated by Robert Hurley. Pantheon, 1978.

Foucault, Michel. "Of Other Spaces." Translated by Jay Miskowiec. *Diacritics* 16, no. 1 (Spring 1986): 22–27.

Foucault, Michel. *"Society Must Be Defended": Lectures at the Collège de France, 1975–76.* Translated by David Macey, edited by Mauro Bertani and Alessandro Fontana. Picador, 2003.

Fozi, Navid. "Governmentality and Crises of Representation, Knowledge, and Power in the Islamic Republic of Iran." *Asian Politics & Policy* 7, no. 1 (2015): 57–78.

Franceschini, Ivan, and Christian Sorace, eds. *Proletarian China: A Century of Chinese Labour.* Verso, 2022.

Franke, Anselm. "Animism: Notes on an Exhibition." *e-flux,* no. 36 (July 2012). www.e-flux.com/journal/36/61258/animism-notes-on-an-exhibition.

Friedman, Dov. "The Turkish Model: the History of a Misleading Idea." *American Progress,* August 25, 2015. www.americanprogress.org/issues/security/reports/2015/08/25/119932/the-turkish-model.

Frost, Tom. "Agamben's Sovereign Legalization of Foucault." *Oxford Journal of Legal Studies* 30, no. 3 (Autumn 2010): 545–77.

Frugoni, Chiara. *San Francesco e il lupo.* Illustrated by Felice Feltracco. Feltrinelli, 2013.

Frye, Timothy. "Putin Touts Russia as a Great Power. But He's Made It a Weak One." *Washington Post*, June 6, 2019. www.washingtonpost.com/opinions/2019/06/06/putin-touts-russia-great-power-hes-made-it-weak-one.

Gaffney, Adam. "The West Virginia Teachers' Strike Is Over. But the Fight for Healthcare Isn't." *The Guardian*, March 7, 2018, www.theguardian.com/commentisfree/2018/mar/07/west-virginia-teachers-strike-healthcare.

Gailus, Andreas. *Forms of Life: Aesthetics and Biopolitics in German Culture.* Cornell University Press, 2020.

Gamez, Patrick. "The Place of the Iranian Revolution in the History of Truth: Foucault on Neoliberalism, Spirituality and Enlightenment." *Philosophy and Social Criticism* 45, no. 1 (2019): 96–124.

Garrett, Daniel. "The Loss and Recovery of Identity: Appearance and Reality, Friendship and Betrayal in Asghar Farhadi's Film *About Elly*." *Off Screen* 25, no. 2–3 (March 2021). offscreen.com/view/the-loss-and-recovery-of-identity-appearance-and-reality-friendship-and-betrayal-in-asghar-farhadis-film-about-elly.

Gillespie, David C. *Russian Cinema.* Routledge, 2004.

Goi, Leonardo. "Albert Serra on Pacifiction." *Reverse Shot*, February 16, 2023. www.reverseshot.org/interviews/entry/2990/serra_int.

Gómez-Muñoz, Pablo. *Science Fiction Cinema in the Twenty-First Century: Transnational Futures, Cosmopolitan Concerns.* Routledge, 2023.

Gontmakher, Evgeny, and Cameron Ross. "The Middle Class and Democratisation in Russia." *Europe-Asia Studies* 67, no. 2 (2015): 269–84.

Gorzo, Andrei, and Veronica Lazăr. "The New Romanian Cinema and Beyond: The Films of Radu Jude." *Transilvania*, April 2022, 1–9.

Gorzo, Andrei, and Veronica Lazăr. "A Slight Unease About Capitalism: Radu Jude's *The Happiest Girl in the World* and the New Romanian Cinema." *Revisista Transilvania*, May 2022, 1–15.

Gorzo, Andrei, and Veronica Lazăr. "An Updated Political Modernism: Radu Jude and 'I Do Not Care If We Go Down in History as Barbarians.'" *Close Up: Film and Media Studies* 3, no. 1–2 (2019): 7–19.

Graham-Harrison, Emma. "Dying China Oil Town a Warning to Beijing." *Reuters*, April 17, 2008. www.reuters.com/article/us-energy-china-poverty-idUSPEK16604520080417.

Grant, Harriet, and John Domokos. "Dublin Regulation Leaves Asylum Seekers with Their Fingers Burnt." *The Guardian*, October 7, 2011. www.theguardian.com/world/2011/oct/07/dublin-regulation-european-asylum-seekers.

Grant, John. "Marcuse Remade? Theory and Explanation in Hardt and Negri." *Science & Society* 74, no. 1 (January 2010): 37–62.

Greenhalgh, Susan, and Edwin A. Winckler. *Cultivating Global Citizens: Population in the Rise of China*. Harvard University Press, 2010.

Greenhalgh, Susan, and Edwin A. Winckler. *Governing China's Population: From Leninist to Neoliberal Biopolitics*. Stanford University Press, 2005.

Groys, Boris. "The Cold War Between the Medium and the Message: Western Modernism vs. Socialist Realism." *e-flux* 104, www.e-flux.com/journal/104/297103/the-cold-war-between-the-medium-and-the-message-western-modernism-vs-socialist-realism/.

Grusin, Richard A., ed. *The Nonhuman Turn*. University of Minnesota Press, 2015.

Gubern, Roman, and Paul Hammon, *Luis Buñuel: The Red Years 1929–1939*. University of Wisconsin Press, 2009.

Gündoğdu, Ayten. *Rightlessness in an Age of Rights: Hannah Arendt and the Contemporary Struggles of Migrants*. Oxford University Press, 2015.

Gunning, Tom. "Embarrassing Evidence: The Detective Camera and the Documentary Impulse." In *Collecting Visible Evidence*, edited by Jane Gaines and Michael Renov, 46–64. University of Minnesota Press, 1999.

Gustafsson, Henrik, and Asbjørn Grønstadt, eds. *Cinema and Agamben: Ethics, Biopolitics and the Moving Image*. Bloomsbury, 2014.

Hanisch, Carol. "The Personal is Political." In *Notes from the Second Year: Women's Liberation*, edited by Shulamith Firestone and Anne Koedt. Radical Feminism, 1970.

Hardt, Michael, and Antonio Negri. *Assembly*. Oxford University Press, 2017.

Hart, Stephen M. *A Companion to Latin American Film*. Tamesis, 2004.

Hashemi, Nader. "Renegotiating Iran's Post-Revolutionary Social Contract: The Green Movement and the Struggle for Democracy in the Islamic Republic." In *Beyond the Arab Spring: The Evolving Ruling Bargain in the Middle East*, edited by Mehran Kamrava, 191–222. Oxford University Press, 2014.

Hassannia, Tina. *Asghar Farhadi: Life and Cinema*. The Critical Press, 2014.

Heath, Deana. "The Tortured Body: The Irrevocable Tension between Sovereign and Biopower in Colonial Indian Technologies of Rule." In *South Asian Governmentalities: Michel Foucault and the Question of Postcolonial Orderings*, edited by Stephen Legg and Deana Heath, 221–44. Cambridge University Press, 2018.

Helmisaari, Vappu. "Fear, the Sovereign, and Authority: Roberto Esposito and the Escape from the Hobbesian State." In *Debating Biopolitics: New Perspectives on the Government of Life*, edited by Marco Piasentier and Sara Raimondi, 30–48. Edward Elgar, 2022.

Henley, Jon. "France Has Underestimated Impact of Nuclear Tests in French Polynesia, Research Finds." *The Guardian*, March 9, 2021, www.

theguardian.com/world/2021/mar/09/france-has-underestimated-impact-of-nuclear-tests-in-french-polynesia-research-finds.

Hill, Fiona, and Clifford G. Gaddy. *Mr Putin: Operative in the Kremlin.* Brookings Institution Press, 2013.

Hindess, Barry. *Discourses of Power: From Hobbes to Foucault.* Blackwell, 1996.

Hobbes, Thomas. *De Cive: The English Version.* Vol. 3 of *The Clarendon Edition of the Philosophical Works of Thomas Hobbes*, edited by Howard Warrender. Clarendon Press, 1987.

Immigration and Refugee Board of Canada. *China: One-Child Policies with Respect to Persons Who Remarry.* February 4, 2000. www.ecoi.net/en/document/1350406.html.

Hynes, Eric. "Interview: Sergei Loznitsa." *Film Comment*, May 16, 2018. www.filmcomment.com/blog/cannes-interview-sergei-loznitsa-donbass.

Inman, Phillip. "Chinese President Vows to 'Adjust Excessive Incomes' of the Super Rich." *The Guardian*, August 18, 2021. www.theguardian.com/world/2021/aug/18/chinese-president-xi-jinping-vows-to-adjust-excessive-incomes-of-super-rich.

Ivakhiv, Adrian. "The Art of Morphogenesis: Cinema In and Beyond the Capitalocene." In *Post-Cinema: Theorizing 21st-Century Film*, edited by Shane Denson and Julia Leyder. REFRAME Books, 2016. reframe.sussex.ac.uk/post-cinema/6-1-ivakhiv/.

Jaeggi, Rahel. *On the Critique of Forms of Life.* Translated by Ciaran Cronin. Harvard University Press, 2018.

James, Caryn. "Donbass: The Ukrainian Satire That's Too Real." *BBC*, April 7, 2022. www.bbc.com/culture/article/20220401-donbass-the-ukrainian-satire-thats-too-real.

Jeong, Seung-hoon. *Biopolitical Ethics in Global Cinema.* Oxford University Press, 2023.

Jeong, Seung-hoon. "Sovereign Agents of Mythical and (Pseudo-)Divine Violence: Walter Benjamin and Global Biopolitical Cinema." *Philosophical Journal of Conflict and Violence* 4, no. 2 (2020): 80–98.

Jeong, Seung-hoon. "World Cinema in a Global Frame." *Studies in World Cinema*, no. 1 (2020): 29–38.

Johnson, Lena. "Russia: Culture, Cultural Policy, and the Swinging Pendulum of Politics." In *Cultural and Political Imaginaries in Putin's Russia*, edited by Niklas Bernsand and Barbar Tornquist-Plewa, 13–36. Brill, 2019.

Justin Wilmes. "Empire Reloaded: Sacred Power in a Postmodern Era." In *Cinemasaurus: Russian Film in Contemporary Context*, edited by Nancy Condee, Alexander Prokhorov, and Elena Prokhorova, 48–64. Academic Studies Press, 2020.

Kapur, Jyotsna, and Keith B. Wagner, ed. *Neoliberalism and Global Cinema: Capital, Culture, and Marxist Critique.* Routledge, 2011.

Karakilic, Emrah. "Acting Up with Hardt and Negri: Capitalism in the Biopolitical Context." *M@N@GEMENT* 22, no. 3 (2019): 496–506.

Karalis, Vasidas. *Theo Angelopoulos: Filmmaker and Philosopher.* Bloomsbury, 2023.

Khosrowjah, Hossein. *Abbas Kiarostami and Iranian National Cinema.* Bloomsbury, 2025.

Marciniak, Katarzyna, and Bruce Bennett, eds. "Introduction: Teaching Transnational Cinema: Politics and Pedagogy." In *Teaching Transnational Cinema: Politics and Pedagogy,* 1–35. Routledge, 2016.

Katzman, Kenneth. *The Warriors of Islam: Iran's Revolutionary Guard.* Routledge, 2019.

Kelly, Nolan. "The Returned Gaze: Ukraine in the Documentaries of Sergei Loznitsa." *Film Quarterly,* October 7, 2022, www.filmquarterly.org/2022/10/07/the-returned-gaze-ukraine-in-the-documentaries-of-sergei-loznitsa.

Khomeini, Ruhollah. *The Position of Women from the Viewpoint of Imam Khomeini.* Translated by Juliana Shaw and Behrooz Arezoo. The Institute for Compilation and Publication of Imam Khomeini's Works, 2001.

Kiarostami, Abbas. Interview by Paul Cronin. *The Guardian,* June 16, 2005. www.theguardian.com/film/2005/jun/17/1.

Kilbourn, Russell J.A. *Cinema, Memory, Modernity: The Representation of Memory from the Art Film to Transnational Cinema.* Routledge, 2010.

Koutsourakis, Angelos. "Epic Cinema: Defining Our Terms." *JCMS: The Journal of Cinema and Media Studies* 61, no. 1 (2021): 51–74.

Kronshtasdky, Ioann. *Ya predvizhu vosstanovlenie moshnoy Rossii.* Institut Russkoy Zivilisazii, 2012.

Kuzma, Konstanty. ""Radu Jude on *Aferim!*" Interview. *East European Film Bulletin* 50 (February 2015). eefb.org/interviews/radu-jude-on-aferim/.

Lakos, William. *Chinese Ancestor Worship: A Practice and Ritual Oriented Approach to Understanding Chinese Culture.* Cambridge Scholars, 2010.

Lambert, Gregg. *Who's Afraid of Deleuze and Guattari?* Continuum, 2006.

Langford, Michelle. *Allegory in Iranian Cinema: The Aesthetics of Poetry and Resistance.* Bloomsbury, 2019.

Lazic, Manuela. "Does Yorgos Lanthimos Want to Be Liked?" Review of *Poor Things* by Yorgos Lanthimos. *The Ringer,* December 11, 2023. www.theringer.com/movies/2023/12/11/23995888/poor-things-movie-director-yorgos-lanthimos.

Lebovic, Nitzan. "The Biopolitical Film (A Nietzschean Paradigm)," *Postmodern Culture* 23, no. 1 (2012), www.pomoculture.org/2015/07/07/the-biopolitical-film-a-nietzschean-paradigm.

Lechte, John, and Saul Newman. *Agamben and the Politics of Human Rights: Statelessness, Images, Violence.* University of Edinburgh Press, 2013.

Lemke, Thomas. "Beyond Foucault: From Biopolitics to the Government of Life." In *Governmentality: Current Issues and Future Challenges*, edited by Ulrich Brockling et al., 165–84. Routledge, 2011.

Lemke, Thomas. *Biopolitics: An Advanced Introduction*. Translated by Eric Frederick Trump. New York University Press, 2011.

Lemke, Thomas. *Foucault's Analysis of Modern Governmentality: A Critique of Political Reason*. Translated by Erik Butler. Verso, 2019.

Lessard, Bruno. *The Cinema of Wang Bing: Chinese Documentary between History and Labor*. Hong Kong University Press, 2025.

Letteri, Richard. "History, Silence and Homelessness in Contemporary Chinese Cinema: Wang Xiaoshuai's *Shanghai Dreams*." *Asian Studies Review* 34, no. 1 (March 2010): 3–18.

Li, David Leiwei. *Economy, Emotion, and Ethics in Chinese Cinema: Globalization on Speed*. Routledge, 2016.

Liesen, Laurette T., and Mary Barbara Walsh. "The Competing Meanings of 'Biopolitics' in Political Science: Biological and Postmodern Approaches to Politics." *Politics and the Life Sciences* 31, no. 1/2 (Spring/Fall 2012): 2–15.

Lilja, Mona, and Stellan Vinthagen. "Sovereign Power, Disciplinary Power and Biopower: Resisting What Power with What Resistance?" *Journal of Political Power* 7, no. 1 (2014): 107–26.

Limbert, John W. *Negotiating with Iran: Wrestling the Ghosts of History*. US Institute of Peace Press, 2009.

Lin, Xiaoping. *Children of Marx and Coca-Cola: Avant-Garde Art and Independent Cinema*. University of Hawai'i Press, 2010.

Loznitsa, Sergei. "Kakoj 'Portret,' kakoj 'Peizazh'! Leksikon Sergeya Loznitsy." *Kino Art*, no. 6 (2005), www.old.kinoart.ru/archive/2005/06/n6-article8.

Lu, Sheldon H. *Chinese Modernity and Global Biopolitics: Studies in Literature and Visual Culture*. University of Hawai'i Press, 2007.

Luisetti, Federico. "Decolonizing the State of Nature: Notes on Political Animism." In *Critical Posthumanism and Planetary Futures*, edited by Debashish Banerji and Markarand R. Paranjape, 215–24. Springer India, 2016.

Luisetti, Federico. "From Biopolitics to Political Animism: Roberto Esposito's *Things*." In *Roberto Esposito: Biopolitics and Philosophy*, edited by Inna Viriasova and Antonio Calcagno, 161–78. State University of New York Press, 2018.

Luisetti, Federico. "Pier Paolo Pasolini's Political Animism." In *Pier Paolo Pasolini, Framed and Unframed: A Thinker for the Twenty-First Century*, edited by Luca Peretti and Karen T. Raizen, 211–22. Bloomsbury, 2019.

Lyashenko, Vladimir. "Schast'e moe, ya tvoy khaos." *Gazeta*, March 29, 2011, www.gazeta.ru/culture/2011/03/29/a_3568857.shtml.

Mai, Joe. "Wang Bing's *'Til Madness Do Us Part:* An Apprenticeship in Seeing." *LOLA* 6 (2015). www.lolajournal.com/6/wang.html.

Makarychev, Andrey, and Alexandra Yatsyk. "Biopolitics and National Identities: Between Liberalism and Totalization." *Nationalities Papers* 45, no. 1 (2017): 1–7.

Malavasi, Luca. "Il silenzio delle cose: Austerlitz." *Cineforum*, January 27, 2017. www.cineforum.it/recensione/Il-silenzio-delle-cose-Austerlitz.

Manuilova, Anastasya. "Biopolitics of Authoritarianism: The Case of Russia." In *Debating Biopolitics*, edited by Marco Piasentier and Sara Raimondi, 151–70. Edward Elgar, 2022.

Marcantonio, Carla. "Biopolitical Embodiments: *Talk to Her* and *The Skin I Live In*." In *Global Melodrama: Nation, Body and History in Contemporary Film*. Palgrave MacMillan, 2015.

Marcenó, Serena. *Biopolitica e sovranitá: Concetti e pratiche di governo alla soglia della modernitá*. Mimesis, 2011.

Martanovschi, Ludmila, and Dana Mihăilescu. "Representations of the 'Aliens Within': Romanian Jews and Roma in Radu Jude's Cinema." In *The Aliens Within: Danger, Disease, and Displacement in Representations of the Racialized Poor*, edited by Geoffroy de Laforcade et al., 85–113. De Gruyter, 2022.

Marzaduri, Saverio. *Noul Val: Il nuovo cinema romeno 1989–2009*. Archetipo, 2012.

Masco, Joseph. *The Nuclear Borderlands: The Manhattan Project in Post-Cold War New Mexico*. Princeton University Press, 2006.

Materiali del Movimento Femminista. *Quaderni di lotta femminista*, no. 2, *Il personale è politico*. Musolini, 1973.

Maurice, Alice. *The Cinema and its Shadow: Race and Technology in Early Cinema*. University of Minnesota Press, 2013.

Mazierska, Ewa. "World Cinema, Third Cinema." *Studies in World Cinema* 1, no. 1 (2020): 14–21.

Mazierska, Ewa, and Lars Kristensen. *Third Cinema, World Cinema and Marxism*. Bloomsbury 2020.

Mazumdar, Shampa, and Sanjoy Mazumdar. "Rethinking Public and Private Space: Religion and Women in Muslim Society." *Journal of Architectural and Planning Research* 18, no. 4 (Winter 2001): 302–24.

Mbembe, Achille. *Necropolitics*. Translated by Steve Corcoran. Duke University Press, 2019.

McDonnell, Stephen. "China Allows Three Children in Major Policy Shift." *BBC News*, May 31, 2021. www.bbc.com/news/world-asia-china-57303592.

Medinsky, Vladimir. "Mia Rossiya segodnya lektsiya Medinskogo V. R. Istoricheskaya znachimost' 70-letya Pobedy v Velikoy Otechestvennosoy Voine." Lecture at Russian Military Historical Society, April 22, 2015.

VPT "Grafitsa," April 24, 2015. Video, 1:44:45. www.youtube.com/watch?v=HE3QeZwfb5U.

Medvedev, Sergei. *The Return of the Russian Leviathan*. Translated by Stephen Dalziel. Polity Press, 2020.

Mennel, Barbara. *Cities and Cinema*. Routledge, 2008.

Meyer, Janet L. *Sydney Pollack: A Critical Filmography*. McFarland, 1998.

Mills, Catherine. *Biopolitics*. Routledge, 2018.

Moïsi, Dominique. *The Geopolitics of Emotion: How Cultures of Fear, Humiliation, and Hope Are Reshaping the World*. Doubleday, 2009.

Morgan, Benjamin. "Undoing Legal Violence: Walter Benjamin's and Giorgio Agamben's Aesthetics of Pure Means." *Journal of Law and Society* 34, no. 1 (2007): 46–64.

Morin, Edgar. *The Cinema, or, the Imaginary Man*. Translated by Lorraine Mortimer. University of Minnesota Press, 2005.

Morreale, Emiliano. "La vita nuda e la vita in mutande. Su Ciprì e Maresco." In "Bíos," edited by Roberto de Gaetanoet al., special issue, *Fata Morgana*, no. 0 (2006), 195–98.

Moruzzi, Norma Claire. "Reflexive Cinema." In *Iranian Cinema in a Global Context: Policy, Politics and Form*, edited by Peter Decherney and Blake Atwood. Routledge, 2015.

Moruzzi, Norma Claire. "Through the Looking Glass: Reflexive Cinema and Society in Post-Revolution Iran." In *Iranian Cinema in a Global Context: Policy, Politics, and Form*, edited by Peter Decherney and Blake Atwood, 112–42. Routledge, 2015.

Muhle, Maria. "A Genealogy of Biopolitics: The Notion of Life in Canguilhem and Foucault." In *The Government of Life: Foucault, Biopolitics, and Neoliberalism*, edited by Vanessa Lemm and Miguel Vatter, 77–97. Fordham University Press, 2014.

Muhle, Maria. "Imitation of Life: Biopolitics and the Cinematographic Image." *Fillip*, no. 17, www.fillip.ca/content/imitation-of-life-biopolitics-and-the-cinematographic-image.

Murray, S.J. "Thanatopolitics." In *Bloomsbury Handbook to Literary and Cultural Theory*, edited by J.R. Di Leo, 718–19. Bloomsbury, 2018.

Nadal-Melsió, Sara. "Buñuel's Eschatological Avant-Garde: *Las Hurdes* and Indexical Realism." *Revista Hispánica Moderna* 66, no. 2 (2018): 183–203.

Nadesan, Majia Holmer. *Governmentality, Biopower, and Everyday Life*. Routledge, 2008.

Naficy, Hamid. *A Social History of Iranian Cinema, Volume 4: The Globalizing Era, 1984–2010*. Duke University Press, 2012.

Nagib, Lucía. *Realist Cinema as World Cinema: Non-cinema, Intermedial Passages, Total Cinema*. Amsterdam University Press, 2020.

Nagib, Lucía. "Towards a Positive Definition of World Cinema." In *Remapping World Cinema: Identity, Culture and Politics in Film*, edited by Stephanie Dennison and Song Hwee Lim, 30–37. Wallflower Press, 2006.

Nagi-Talavera, Nicholas M. *The Green Shirts and the Others: A History of Fascism in Hungary and Romania.* The Center for Romanian Studies, 2001.

Nancy, Jean-Luc. *Abbas Kiarostami: The Evidence of Film.* Translated by Christine Irizarry and Verena Andermatt Conley. Yves Gevaert Éditeur, 2001.

Nasta, Dominique. *Contemporary Romanian Cinema: The History of an Unexpected Miracle.* Wallflower, 2013.

Natalio, Carlos, "Cinema, Biopolitics and 'Cinematic Operative Model.'" *La Deleuziana—Online Journal of Philosophy*, no. 1 (2015): 107–20.

Nayman, Adam. "'Poor Things' Cancels Itself Out." *The Ringer*, December 7, 2023. www.theringer.com/movies/2023/12/7/23991965/poor-things-movie-review-emma-stone.

Nedoh, Boštjan. "Biopolitics Before Foucault: On Benjamin's Critique of Bare Life and Agamben's Theological Genealogy of the 'Apparatus.'" In *The Routledge Handbook of Biopolitics*, edited by Sergei Prozorov and Simona Rentea, 66–78. Routledge, 2017.

Nelson, William Max. *Enlightenment Biopolitics: A History of Race, Eugenics, and the Making of Citizens.* University of Chicago Press, 2024.

Neroni, Hilary. *The Subject of Torture: Psychoanalysis and Biopolitics in Television and Film.* Columbia University Press, 2015.

News.ro. "Sondaj INSCOP pentru News.ro—Armata şi Biserica rămân instituţiile în care românii au cea mai mare încredere. Guvernul şi Parlamentul sunt pe ultimele poziţii, cu o cotă de încredere mai scăzută decât în urmă cu 10 ani." *News.ro*, November 14, 2023. www.news.ro/social/sondaj-inscop-news-armata-biserica-raman-institutiile-romanii-au-cea-mare-incredere-guvernul-parlamentul-ultimele-pozitii-cota-incredere-scazuta-urma-10-ani-1922400014002023110821383603.

Nie, Jing. "A City of Disappearance: Trauma, Displacement, and Spectral Cityscape in Contemporary Chinese Cinema." In *Chinese Ecocinema: In the Age of Environmental Challenge*, edited by Sheldon H. Lu and Jiayan Mi, 195–214. Hong Kong University Press, 2009.

Ophir, Orna. *Schizophrenia: An Unfinished History.* Polity Press, 2022.

Osipova, Anastasiya. "Interview: Sergei Loznitsa on *Babi Yar. Context*." *Film Comment*, April 11, 2022. www.filmcomment.com/blog/interview-sergei-loznitsa-on-babi-yar-context.

Papanikolaou, Dimitris. *Greek Weird Wave: A Cinema of Biopolitics.* Edinburgh University Press, 2021.

Parente, André, and Victa de Carvalho. "Cinema as *Dispositif*: Between Cinema and Contemporary Art." *Cinémas* 19, no. 1 (Autumn 2008): 37–55.

Peele, Jordan. *Nope*. Los Angeles: Monkey Paw Productions, 2022. Script available at *Indie Wire*, www.indiewire.com/wpcontent/uploads/2022/12/NOPE_Script_FINAL_2022.11.29.pdf.

Perniola, Ivelise. "Cinema e biopolitica: Iconoclastia, eufemismo e falsa coscienza umanitaria." *Bianco e nero* 565 (2009): 75–77.

Persico, Daniela, *Wang Bing: Il cinema della Cina che cambia*. Agenzia X, 2010.

Peter Eltsov. *The Long Telegram 2.0: A Neo-Kennanite Approach to Russia*. Lexington Books, 2020.

Pethő, Ágnes. *Caught In-Between: Intermediality in Contemporary Eastern European and Russian Cinema*. Edinburgh University Press, 2020.

Picker, Giovanni. *Racial Cities: Governance and the Segregation of Romani People in Urban Europe*. Routledge, 2017.

Pieldner, Judit. "History, Cultural Memory and Intermediality in Radu Jude's *Aferim!*" *Acta Universitatis Sapientiae Film and Media Studies* 13 (2016): 89–105.

Pietrangeli, Antonio. "Analisi spettrale del film realistico." *Alla ricerca di Luchino Visconti*, April 3, 2009. alla-ricerca-di-luchino-visconti.com/2009/04/03/si-gira-ossessione-analisi-spettrale-del-film-realistico/.

Pischedda, Bruno. "*Petrolio*, una significativa illeggibilità." *Studi Novocenteschi* 27, no. 59 (2000): 161–95.

Plakhov, Andrei. *Rezhissery nastoyashchego*, tom 2, *Radikaly i minimalisty* (Directors of nowadays, vol. 2, Radicals and minimalists). Palmira, 2017.

Pomerantsev, Peter. "The Hidden Author of Putinism: How Vladislav Surkov Invented the New Russia." *The Atlantic*, November 7, 2014. www.theatlantic.com/international/archive/2014/11/hidden-author-putinism-russia-vladislav-surkov/382489/.

Pop, Doru. *Romanian New Wave Cinema: An Introduction*. McFarland, 2014.

Popa, Diana. "Hopeless Didacticism: Archival Sources and Spectatorial Addresses in '*I Do Not Care If We Go Down in History as Barbarians*.'" *Law, Culture and the Humanities* 18, no. 3 (2019): 535–56.

Popan, Elena Roxana. "Recent Romanian Cinema: Is It a Real New Wave or Just a Splash in the Water?" *Communication Review* 17, no. 3 (2014): 217–32.

Popova, Maria. "Putin-Style 'Rule of Law' and the Prospects for Change." *Daedalus* 146, no. 2 (Spring 2017): 64–75.

Povinelli, Elizabeth. *Geontologies: A Requiem to Later Liberalism*. Duke University Press, 2016.

Prozorov, Sergei. *The Biopolitics of Stalinism: Ideology and Life in Soviet Socialism*. University of Edinburgh Press, 2016.

Puar, Jasbir K. "Homonationalism as Assemblage: Viral Travels, Affective Sexualities." *Jindal Global Law Review* 4, no. 1 (November 2013): 23–43.

Puar, Jasbir K. *The Right to Maim: Debility, Capacity, Disability*. Duke University Press, 2017.

Puar, Jasbir K. *Terrorist Assemblages*. Duke University Press, 2007.

Raghavendra, M.K. *Locating World Cinema: Interpretations of Film as Culture*. Bloomsbury, 2020.

Rancière, Jacques. *Figures of History*. Translated by Julie Rose. Polity Press, 2014.

Rancière, Jacques. "Politics, Identification, and Subjectivization." *October* 61 (1992): 58–64.

Read, Jason. *The Politics of Transindividuality*. Brill, 2015.

Rebreaunu, Liviu. *Forest of the Hanged*. Translated by A.V. Wise. Casemate, 2017.

Robinson, Luke. *Independent Chinese Documentary: From the Studio to the Street*. Palgrave Macmillan, 2013.

Roddy, Nicolae. "The Romanian Orthodox Church and the Roma." In *Religion, Race, and the Other*, edited by Ronald A. Simkins, *Journal of Religious & Society*, Supplement 24 (2023): 53–74.

Rohdie, Sam. *The Passion of Pier Paolo Pasolini*. British Film Institute, 2019.

Rony, Fatimah Tobing. *How Do We Look? Resisting Visual Biopolitics*. Duke University Press, 2022.

Rose, Nikolas, and Peter Miller. "Political Power Beyond the State: Problematics of Government." *British Journal of Sociology* 43, no. 2 (June 1992): 173–205.

Rowe, John Carlos. *Our Henry James in Fiction, Film, and Popular Culture*. Routledge, 2023.

Rushing, Robert A. *Descended from Hercules: Biopolitics and the Muscled Male Body on Screen*. Indiana University Press, 2016.

Rustamova, Farida, and Maxim Tovkaylo. "What Secret Russian State Polling Tells Us About Support for the War." *Moscow Times*, December 9, 2022. www.themoscowtimes.com/2022/12/06/what-secret-russian-state-polling-tells-us-about-support-for-the-war-a79596.

Salter, Chris. "The Long Horizon: Temporal Imaginaries in the More-than-Human Arts." In *The Routledge International Handbook of More-than-Human Studies*, edited by Adrian Franklin, 334–47. Routledge, 2024.

Sanyal, Debarati. "Calais's 'Jungle: Refugees, Biopolitics, and the Arts of Resistance.'" *Representations*, no. 139 (Summer 2017): 1–33.

Savell, Stephanie. "How Death Outlives War: The Reverberating Impact of the Post-9/11 Wars on Human Health." Watson Institute for International and Public Affairs, Brown University, 2023. watson.brown.edu/costsofwar/files/cow/imce/papers/2023/Indirect%20Deaths.pdf.

Sawka, Richard. *Putin: Russia's Choice*. Routledge, 2004.

Sayyid, S. "Khomeini and the Decolonization of the Political." In *A Critical Introduction to Khomeini*, edited by Arshin Adib-Moghaddam, 161–67. Cambridge University Press, 2014.

Scanlan, James P., ed. *Russian Thought After Communism: The Recovery of a Philosophical Heritage*. Routledge, 1994.

Scheible, Jeff. "Throwing Punches: The Athletic Aesthetics of Kevin Jerome Everson's Filmmaking." *World Records Journal* 3 (2020): 26–37. worldrecordsjournal.org/throwing-punches-the-athletic-aesthetics-of-kevin-jerome-eversons-filmmaking/.

Scott, A.O. "'Donbass' Review: War in the Ukraine, the Prequel." *New York Times*, April 7, 2022. www.nytimes.com/2022/04/07/movies/donbass-review.html.

Scott, A.O. "A House Divided by Exasperation." Review of *A Separation* by Asghar Farhadi. *New York Times*, December 29, 2011. www.nytimes.com/2011/12/30/movies/a-separation-directed-by-asghar-farhadi-review.html.

Segarra, Marta. "New Animism and Shamanic Cinema: Human–Animal–Machine Interactions." In *Cinema of/for the Anthropocene: Affect, Ecology, and More-Than-Human Kinship*, edited by Katarzyna Paszkiewicz and Andrea Ruthven, 131–43. Routledge, 2025.

Sekula, Allan. *Fish Story*. Richter, 1995.

Shahidian, Hammed. *Women in Iran: Gender Politics in the Islamic Republic*. Greenwood, 2002.

Shaviro, Steven. *Post-Cinematic Affect*. Verso, 2010.

Shohat, Ella, and Robert Stam. *Unthinking Eurocentrism: Multiculturalism and the Media*. Routledge, 2014 [1994].

Singh, Neera M. "The Nonhuman Turn or a Re-turn to Animism? Valuing Life Along and Beyond Capital." *Dialogues in Human Geography* 12, no. 1 (March 2022): 84–89.

Sinnerbrink, Robert. *Cinematic Ethics: Exploring Ethical Experience Through Film*. Routledge, 2016.

Slaymaker, James. "An Outcast of the Islands: Albert Serra's *Pacifiction* (2023)." *Film International*, July 26, 2023. www.filmint.nu/albert-serra-pacifiction-2023-review-james-slaymaker.

Smiley, Michelle. "The Mechanical Against Objectivity: Industrialism and Inoperativity in Eadweard Muybridge's *Animal Locomotion* (1887)." *History of Photography* 47, no. 3 (2023): 203–33.

Smith, Alison. *Georges Didi-Huberman and Film: The Politics of the Image*. Bloomsbury, 2020.

Spaner, David. *Shoot It!: Hollywood Inc. and the Rising of Independent Film*. Arsenal Pulp, 2011.

Statista. "Gross Box Office Revenue in Domestically Produced Films in Russia from 2018 to 2023." *Statista*, September 24, 2024, www.statista.com/statistics/1104169/russian-films-box-office-revenue-in-russia.

Stewart, Garrett. "Counterfactual, Potential, Virtual." In *Cinema and Agamben*, edited by Henrik Gustafsson and Asbjørn Grønstadt, 161–90. Bloomsbury, 2014.

Stishova, Elena. "Kakoy 'Portret,' kakoy 'Peizazh'! Leksikon Sergeya Loznitsy." *Kino Art*, no. 6 (2005). www.old.kinoart.ru/archive/2005/06/n6-article8.

Stishova, Elena. "Strakh I molchanie: Kak Andrej Zvyagintsev predskazal Putinskuyu Rossiyu, I ona emu otomstila." *Kino Art*, January 29, 2020. www.kinoart.ru/opinions/strah-i-molchanie-kak-andrey-zvyagintsev-predskazal-putinskuyu-rossiyu-i-ona-emu-otomstila.

Stoica, Cătălin Augustin. "'Our Martyrs of 1989 Did Not Die for This!': Political Capitalism in Post-Communist Romania." *Historical Social Research/Historische Sozialforschung* 27, no. 2 (2012): 26–52.

Stojanova, Christina. "Historical Overview of Romanian Cinema." In *New Romanian Cinema*, ed. Stojanova, 297–347. Edinburgh University Press, 2019.

Strausz, László. *Hesitant Histories on the Romanian Screen*. Palgrave Macmillan, 2017.

Strukov, Vlad. *Contemporary Russian Cinema: Symbols of a New Era*. Edinburgh University Press, 2016.

Tagliani, Giacomo. "Biografie italiane. Cinema e immagini della vita." In *Pensiero in immagine: Forme, metodi, oggetti teorici per un Italian Visual Thought*, edited by Angela Mengoni and Francesco Zucconi, 272–89. Mimesis, 2022.

Tambini, Damian. *Nationalism in Italian Politics: The Stories of the Northern League, 1980–2000*. Routledge, 2012.

Tarizzo, Davide. "Dalla biopolitica all'etopolitica: Foucault e noi." *Noéma* 4–1 (2013): 43–51.

Tekdeeps. "Putin Made Important Statements at a Meeting with Media Leaders." *Tekdeeps*, February 13, 2021, www.web.archive.org/web/20220225080621/https://tekdeeps.com/putin-made-important-statements-at-a-meeting-with-media-leaders-the-main-thing/.

Troitskii, Evgenii. *Vozrozhdenie russkoi idei: Sotsial'no-filosofskie ocherki*. Filosofskoe obshchestvo SSSR, 1991.

Turner, Lindsay. "In the Atmosphere: The Politics of Mati Diop's *Atlantics*." *Yale Review* 108, no. 2 (2020): 186–91.

UKRINFORM. "Why Russian Cinema Can't Exist Without Propaganda and Manipulations." *UKRINFORM*, July 7, 2021, web.archive.org/web/20211108141635/https://www.ukrinform.net/rubric-society/3344917-why-russian-cinema-cant-exist-without-propaganda-and-manipulations.html.

Väliaho, Pasi. *Biopolitical Screens: Image, Power, and the Neoliberal Brain*. MIT Press, 2014.

Väliaho, Pasi. "Biopolitics of Gesture: Cinema and the Neurological Body." In *Cinema and Agamben: Ethics, Biopolitics and the Moving Image*, ed. Henrik Gustafsson and Asbjørn Grønstadt, 103–20. Bloomsbury, 2014.

Vatter, Miguel. "Natality and Biopolitics in Hannah Arendt." *Revista de ciencia política* 26, no. 2 (2006): 137–59.

Vaughan-Williams, Nick. "The Generalized Bio-Political border? Re-conceptualising the Limits of Sovereign Power." *Review of International Studies* 35 (2009): 729–949.

Vegso, Roland, and Marco Abel. "Biopolitical Education: *The Edukators* and the Politics of the Immanent Outside." *Studies in 20th & 21st Century Literature* 40, no. 2 (2016): 1–28.

Verdery, Katherine. *What Was Socialism, and What Comes Next?* Princeton University Press, 1996.

Vighi, Fabio. "Pasolini and Exclusion: Žižek, Agamben and the Modern Sub-proletariat." *Theory, Culture & Society* 20, no. 5 (2003): 99–121.

Virno, Paolo. *E così via, all'infinito: Logia e antropologia.* Bollati Boringhieri, 2010.

Viveiros de Castro, Eduardo. "Exchanging Perspectives: The Transformation of Objects into Subjects in Amerindian Ontologies." *Common Knowledge* 10, no. 3 (2004): 463–84.

Walder, Dennis. *Postcolonial Nostalgias: Writing, Representation, and Memory.* Routledge, 2011.

Walker, Shaun. "Donbass: True Lies from the Ukrainian Frontline." *The Guardian*, April 16, 2019. www.theguardian.com/film/2019/apr/16/donbass-true-lies-from-the-ukrainian-frontline.

Wang Xiaoping. *Postsocialist Conditions: Ideas and History in China's "Independent Cinema," 1988–2008.* Brill, 2018.

Wang, Xiaoshuai. Interview by Michael Berry. In *Speaking in Images: Interviews with Contemporary Chinese Filmmakers*, 162–81. Columbia University Press, 2005.

Weber, Isabella. "Origins of China's Contested Relation with Neoliberalism: Economics, the World Bank, and Milton Friedman at the Dawn of Reform." *Politics, Governance, and the Law* 1, no. 1 (2020): 1–14.

Weheliye, Alexander G. *Habeas Viscus: Racializing Assemblages, Biopolitics and Black Feminist Theories of the Human.* Duke University Press, 2014.

Weiss-Wendt, Anton. *Putin's Russia and the Falsification of History.* Bloomsbury, 2020.

Whyte, Kyle. "Settler Colonialism, Ecology, and Environmental Justice." *Environment and Society* 9 (2018): 125–44.

Wijermars, Mariëlle. *Memory Politics in Contemporary Russia: Television, Cinema and the State.* Routledge, 2019.

"Wonderful Shell Shock Recovery." *British Pathé*, 1914–1918. Video, 2:16. www.britishpathe.com/asset/77601.

Wright, Robin, ed. *The Iran Primer: Power, Politics, and U.S. Policy.* United States Institute of Peace Press, 2010.

Wynter, Kevin. "The Exorbitant Mirror: Violence, Disavowal, and the Logic of Terror in Michael Haneke's *Das weiße Band*." *JCMS: Journal of Cinema and Media Studies* 61, no. 1 (Fall 2021): 123–39.

Xavier, Ismail. *Allegories of Underdevelopment: Aesthetics and Politics in Modern Brazilian Cinema*. University of Minnesota Press, 1997.

Young, William W. III. *Naming God and Friendship in Aquinas and Derrida*. Ashgate, 2007.

Zedong, Mao. "Wen Hui Pao's Bourgeois Orientation Should Be Criticized." From *People's Daily*, July 1, 1957, in *Selected Works of Mao Tse-Tung*. www.marxists.org/reference/archive/mao/selected-works/volume-5/mswv5_64.htm.

Zavattini, Cesare. "Che cos'è il film lampo" (1953). In *Opere: Cinema: Diario cinematografico: Neorealismo, ecc.*, edited by Valentina Fortichiari and Mino Argentieri, 708–10. Bompiani, 2002.

Zavattini, Cesare. "Film-lampo: Sviluppo del neorealismo" (1952). In *Opere: Cinema: Diario cinematografico: Neorealismo, ecc.*, edited by Valentina Fortichiari and Mino Argentieri, 711–13. Bompiani, 2002.

Zembylas, Michalinos. "Derrida, Foucault and Critical Pedagogies of Friendship in Conflict-Troubled Societies." *Discourse: Studies in the Cultural Politics of Education* 36, no. 1 (2015): 1–14.

Zhang, Hongbing. "Ruins and Grassroots: Jia Zhangke's Cinematic Discontents in the Age of Globalization." In *Chinese Ecocinema: In the Age of Environmental Challenge*, edited by Sheldon Lu and Jiayan Mi, 129–54. Hong Kong University Press, 2009.

Zhang, Yingjin. *Cinema, Space, and Polylocality in a Globalizing China*. University of Hawai'i Press, 2010.

Zhang, Yingjin. *A Companion to Chinese Cinema*. Wiley-Blackwell, 2012.

Ziarek, Ewa Plonowska. "Bare Life." In *Impasses of the Post Global: Theory in the Era of Climate Change*, vol. 2, edited by Henry Sussman, 194–211. Open Humanities Press, 2012.

Zimmt, Raz. "Iran's Middle Class: An Agent of Political Change?" *Strategic Assessment* 20, no. 3 (October 2017): 59–69.

Zolkos, Magdalena. "Skulls, Tree Bark, Fossils: Memory and Materiality in George Didi-Huberman's Transvaluation of Surface." *Qui Parle* 30, no. 2 (December 2021): 249–91.

Zuckerman, Ethan. "Why Filming Police Violence Has Done Nothing to Stop It." *Technology Review*, June 3, 2020. www.technologyreview.com/2020/06/03/1002587/sousveillance-george-floyd-police-body-cams.

Index

Blue (1993), 30
Bogatyrev, Andrey, 104
Boia, Lucian, 175
Bondarchuk, Fedor, 46
Bonello, Bertrand, 201–3
Bong, Joon Ho, 37
Bork, Cornelius, 54
Brass, Tinto, 144
Brat (1997). See *Brother* (1997)
Bratu, Lucian, 193
Brius, Maksim, and Plyaskin, Leonid, 46
Brother (1997), 106
Buñuel, Luis, 113
Burger, Neil, 32

Caché (2005). See *Hidden* (2005)
Calais, 228, 232
Calamity (1982), 182
Caligari, Claudio, 223
Campbell, Timothy, 7, 13, 40–41, 232
Captive Wild Woman (1943), 227
Cárdenas, Juan David, 152–53
Cardino, Dan, 32
Casetti, Francesco, 16
Cassavetes, John, 76
Castro, Tessa, 55
Cavarero, Adriana, 170
Cea mai fericită fată din lume (2009). See *Happiest Girl in the World* (2009)
Ceaușescu, Nicolae, 26, 175–76
Chaharshanbe-soori (2006). See *Fireworks Wednesday* (2006)
Chelchea, Liviu, 192
Chen, Mel Y., 54
Chernobyl disaster, 117
Cheshire, Godfrey, 96
Chi lavora è perduto (1963), 144
China, post-Mao development, 139–40

Chinese Portrait (2018), 146
Chow, Rey, 30–31
Chrysostom, Saint John, 130
Chuangru zhe (2014). See *Red Amnesia* (2014)
Chytilová, Věra, 182
cinéma vérité, 182, 187
Cinico TV (television series), 204
Cioni, Giovanni, 27, 225, 227–28
Ciprì, Daniele, and Maresco, Franco, 204
Citti, Sergio, 216–17
Ciulei, Liviu, 171, 177, 220
Code l'inconnu: Récit incomplete de divers voyages (2000). See *Code Unknown* (2000)
Code Unknown (2000), 36
Colonialism, 6, 124, 202–3, 210, 232
Comodin, Alessandro, 27, 210–12
concentration and death camps, 7–8, 118, 120, 187
Condee, Nancy, 106
Conversation, The (1974), 61
Coppola, Francis Ford, 61
Corpo celeste (2011). See *Heavenly Body* (2011)
Cremonini, Alessio, 214
Crimson Gold (2005), 66, 114–16, 119, 212
Crowe, David, 185
Cui, Shuqin, 165, 169
Cultural Revolution, 141–42, 155

D'Anolfi, Massimo, and Parenti, Martina, 27, 225, 227–28
Dabashi, Hamid, 74
Dal pianeta degli umani (2021). See *From the Planet of the Humans* (2021)
Dalla Gassa, Marco, 38
Dan-Cirjan, Mihai, 185